Concise Reader in
Sociological Theory

Concise Reader in Sociological Theory

Theorists, Concepts, and Current Applications

EDITED BY

Michele Dillon

WILEY Blackwell

Registered Offices
John Wiley & Sons, Inc., 111 River Street, Hoboken, NJ 07030, USA
John Wiley & Sons Ltd, The Atrium, Southern Gate, Chichester, West Sussex, PO19 8SQ, UK

Editorial Office
9600 Garsington Road, Oxford, OX4 2DQ, UK

For details of our global editorial offices, customer services, and more information about Wiley products visit us at www.wiley.com.

Wiley also publishes its books in a variety of electronic formats and by print-on-demand. Some content that appears in standard print versions of this book may not be available in other formats.

Library of Congress Cataloging-in-Publication Data
Names: Dillon, Michele, 1960– editor.
Title: Concise reader in sociological theory : theorists, concepts, and
    current applications / edited by Michele Dillon.
Description: First Edition. | Hoboken : Wiley, 2020. | Includes index.
Identifiers: LCCN 2020029242 (print) | LCCN 2020029243 (ebook) | ISBN
    9781119536185 (paperback) | ISBN 9781119536192 (adobe pdf) | ISBN
    9781119536178 (epub)
Subjects: LCSH: Sociology. | Social scientists.
Classification: LCC HM585 .C65397 2020 (print) | LCC HM585 (ebook) | DDC
    301–dc23
LC record available at https://lccn.loc.gov/2020029242
LC ebook record available at https://lccn.loc.gov/2020029243

Cover Design: Wiley
Cover Image: Courtesy of Michele Dillon

Set in 10/13pt Minion Pro by SPi Global, Pondicherry, India

CONTENTS

INTRODUCTION

Sociological theory offers a rich conceptual tool-kit with which to think about and analyze our contemporary society. As we reflect upon what it means to live and to understand others in today's complex world, the insights of sociological theorists provide us with concepts that greatly illuminate the array of social and institutional processes, group dynamics, and cultural motivations that drive the patterns of persistence and change variously evident across local, national, and global contexts. Sociology is a comparatively young discipline. It owes its origins to the principles and values established by eighteenth-century Enlightenment philosophers, namely the core assumptions that human reason is the source of knowledge, and though of different orders, the source of moral truth and of scientific truth; and that, by virtue of being endowed with human reason, all people are created equal and thus should be free to govern themselves in all matters, including political governance – thus motivating the democratic revolutions of the eighteenth century in America (1776) and in France (1789) and leading to the decline of monarchies and the establishment instead of democratic societies.

It was the French philosopher Auguste Comte (1798–1857) who coined the term sociology in 1839. He was influenced by the Enlightenment emphasis on scientific principles and believed that a science of the social world was necessary to discover and illuminate based on rigorous empirical observation how society works, that is to identify, as he saw it, a "social physics" parallel to the laws of physics and other natural sciences, and to advance social progress as a result of the data yielded from the scientific study of society. In his view, because sociology could and should study all aspects of social life, he argued that sociology would be *the* science of humanity, *the* science of society, and would outline "the most systematic theory of the human order"

Concise Reader in Sociological Theory: Theorists, Concepts, and Current Applications,
First Edition. Edited by Michele Dillon. Editorial material and organization
© 2021 John Wiley & Sons Ltd. Published 2021 by John Wiley & Sons Ltd.

(Comte 1891/1973: 1). Harriet Martineau (1802–76), the English feminist and writer, commonly regarded as the first woman sociologist, translated Comte's writings into English in 1855 (Hoecker-Drysdale 1992). Additionally, in her own influential writing she emphasized both the breadth of topics that sociologists can/should study as well as the importance of studying them with rigor and objectivity. In her well-known book *How to Observe Morals and Manners* (1838), morals and manners referencing the substantive, wide-ranging content of sociology (and its encompassing of social class, religion, health, suicide, pop culture, crime, and the arts, among other topics), Martineau also argued that because social life is human-centered it is different to the natural world. Unlike atoms, for example, humans have emotions. Hence, Martineau pointed to the need for sociologists as scientists to develop the empathy necessary to the observation and understanding of the human condition and to how it manifests in the course of their inquiry. She wrote:

> The observer must have sympathy; and his sympathy must be untrammeled and unreserved. If a traveler be a geological inquirer he may have a heart as hard as the rocks he shivers, and yet succeed in his immediate objects . . . if he be a statistical investigator he may be as abstract as a column of figures, and yet learn what he wants to know: but an observer of morals and manners will be liable to deception at every turn, if he does not find his way to hearts and minds. (Martineau 1838: 52)

As sociology became further established in the mid-to-late nineteenth century it did so amid major societal changes, propelled by industrial capitalism, factory production, the expansion of manufacturing and of railroads, increased urbanization, mass immigration of Irish, Italian, Swedish, German, Polish, and other European individuals and families to the US, the bolstering of democratic institutions and procedures (e.g. voting rights), nation-building, and mass-circulating newspapers. Living in a time swirling with change, sociology's founders were thus well situated to observe and to recognize how large-scale, macro societal forces take hold, interpenetrate, and structure institutional processes, community, and the organization of everyday life, as well as to ponder the relationship of the individual to society.

This *Reader* presents a selection of key excerpts from major writings in sociological theory, the classics from the foundations of the discipline to contemporary approaches. As with all disciplines, the classics are so defined not merely because they originated in a different time, but precisely because they contain the essential points or concepts that have endured through a long swath of time and have proven resilient in their explanatory relevance of the dynamic complexity of society even, or especially, amid its many ongoing patterns of change. Sociology, as a social science, is an empirical discipline; this means that sociologists are interested in and committed to knowing the truth about reality – how things actually are and why they are as they are, rather than how ideally they ought to be. Consequently, sociologists embrace scientific method as a way of studying the social world and accept the objective facticity of (properly gathered) data. Sociologists use both qualitative (e.g. ethnographic description, interview and blog transcripts, historical documents) and quantitative (e.g. surveys, census data)

data-gathering methods, and in using data they tend to lean either toward investigating the relationship between a number of macro-level variables (e.g. education, crime, income inequality, gender) or focusing on how individuals in a particular micro-context and small groups or communities carve meaning into and make sense of their lives. Regardless of the research method(s) chosen (a decision made based on the specific research question motivating the sociologist's empirical study), sociologists do not and cannot let the resulting data stand on their own. Data always need to be interpreted. And this is why sociological theory is so important. Theory provides the ideas or concepts that sensitize sociologists about what to think about – what questions to ask about the social world and how it is structured and with what consequences – and theory is equally fundamental in helping sociologists make sense of what they find in their actual research, both of what they might have (empirically or theoretically) expected to find but also of the unexpected. As such, sociological theory is the vocabulary sociologists use to anchor and interpret empirical data about any aspect of society, and to drive the ongoing, back-and-forth conversation between theory and data. This, necessarily, given the dynamic nature of social life, is always an energetic and dynamic dialogue. Sociological theory does not exist for the sake of theory, but for the sake of sociological understanding and explanation of the multilayered empirical reality in any given sociohistorical context.

This *Reader* is organized into five sections. Each section includes excerpts from a core set of theorists, and I provide a short commentary or introduction prior to each specific theorist or to a cluster of theorists in the given section. The *Reader* begins with a lengthy first section with excerpts from sociology's classical theorists: **Karl Marx** (chapter 1), **Emile Durkheim** (chapter 2), and **Max Weber** (chapter 3). These three dominant theorists largely comprise the foundational canon of sociology; their respective conceptual contributions have well withstood the test of time despite, from the hindsight of our contemporary experience, some notable silences in their writings with respect to, for example, sexuality and a limited discussion of the significance of gender and race.

The classical tradition was largely introduced to English-speaking audiences by the towering American social theorist, Talcott Parsons. The excerpts in section II comprise an amalgam representing Parsons's theorizing, generally referred to as *structural functionalism*, and different theoretical perspectives that it, in turn, gave rise to based on specific critiques of some of Parsons's emphases. I briefly introduce Parsons's ideas (in chapter 4) but because much of his writing is quite dense I do not include an excerpt from him but instead an excerpt from his student and renowned fellow-theorist **Robert K. Merton**, exemplifying the structural functionalist perspective. Parsons was famously concerned with how values consensus translated into the social roles and social institutions functional to maintain social order. Countering this focus, conflict theory, exemplified by **Ralf Dahrendorf**, highlighted the normalcy and functionality of conflict (as opposed to consensus) in society. From a different context, critiquing Parsons's focus on American society as the paradigm of modernization, neo-Marxist dependency theorists including **Fernando Henrique Cardoso** and **Enzo Faletto** highlighted the conflicting power interests between the West and Latin

America, and within Latin American countries dependent on the US (chapter 5). Still other theorists pushed back against Parsons's main focus on macro structures and what they saw as his diminishment of the individual (even though Parsons affirmed the relevance of the individual as a motivated social actor). With a micro focus on individuals and small groups (chapter 6), this line of critique was spearheaded by another student of Parsons, George Homans. Contrary to Parsons, he emphasized the core centrality of the individual and of individual interpersonal interaction or exchange as the foundational basis of all institutional and societal life. Homans's student, **Peter M. Blau**, took a broader, more sociological view than Homans and elaborated on how power and status in particular interpersonal contexts are conveyed through, and result from, social exchange relations. Another theorist, **James S. Coleman**, adopted Parsons's focus on shared societal values to focus on the functionality of trust to the accumulation of human and social capital in interpersonal and small group settings. Decades later, writing with a focus on a different set of questions – sexuality and gender in contemporary American society – **Paula England** elaborates on the relation between personal characteristics (skills/human capital, values) and social identity or social position to show the dynamic interaction between individuals' personal characteristics and social position in accounting for variation in individual decision-making outcomes.

Section III includes what are generally seen as the three most prominent micro-level perspectives in sociological theory: (1) symbolic interactionism which, building on **George H. Mead**'s theorizing on the self and elaborated by **Erving Goffman**, focuses on the micro-dynamics of face-to-face or interpersonal interaction (chapter 7); (2) phenomenology which establishes credibility for the relevance of the individual's subjective experiences of the social world and for the individual's intra-subjective reality, a perspective outlined by Alfred Schutz and elaborated by **Peter L. Berger** and **Thomas Luckmann** in their widely influential book, *The Social Construction of Reality* (chapter 8); and (3) ethnomethodology which focuses on how individuals actually do the work of being members of a society in particular localized settings; its framing is indebted to **Harold Garfinkel** and subsequently further applied to gender issues by **Sarah Fenstermaker** and **Candace West** (chapter 9). It is important to note here, however, that though largely micro in their focus, each of these theories (and especially phenomenology) also variously point to the significance of macro structures, the dynamic interrelation of macro and micro social processes, and to the fact that the self is always necessarily in conversation with society, and is so at once both at a micro- and macro-level.

Section IV returns us to the influence of European theorists on the development of sociology, especially as the discipline both emerged from the influence of Parsons in the late 1970s, and also attempted to take stock of the social changes of the post-World War II era, an era that for all of its progress – increased affluence, the expansion of university education, the growth of the middle classes, and the expansion of mass media – did not eliminate social inequality. This section includes excerpts from theorists associated with the Frankfurt School (chapter 10), most notably **Max Horkheimer** and **Theodor W. Adorno** who wrote extensively and in a withering manner critiquing the strategic manipulation and manipulating effects of politics and consumer culture by economic interests. The Frankfurt School's second generation, and undoubtedly the most renowned social theorist alive today, **Jürgen Habermas**, outlines a way forward from the contemporary debasement of reason, one that returns attention to the possibility of using reason to discuss societal problems and to craft solutions that serve the common good. This section also includes excerpts from the extensive work of **Pierre Bourdieu** (chapter 11) who has been highly impactful in getting sociologists to think differently and to conduct innovative research (e.g. Lareau 1987) about how social inequality is reproduced, especially through the informal cultures of school and in the ordinary everyday habits and tastes prevalent in family life. **Michel Foucault** is perhaps the most intellectually radical of all social theorists (chapter 12). His originality is especially seen in his construal of biopower and how he frames and analyzes the birth of sexuality and of other body-controlling structures (clinics, prisons). Widely read beyond sociology, his analysis of the fluidity of sexuality and power underpins much of queer theory, elaborated for sociologists by **Steven Seidman** (chapter 12).

The fifth and final section continues the emancipatory spirit of the post-1970s critique. This vibrant body of work includes (in chapter 13) selections from the early feminist theorist **Charlotte Perkins Gilman,** the ground-breaking focus by **Arlie Hochschild** on emotion work and its gendered structure, and leading contemporary feminist theorist **Dorothy E. Smith** articulating the necessity of standpoints that seek to understand from within the experiences of outsiders (e.g. women, members of minority racial and ethnic groups, LGBTQ+). Additionally, **Patricia Hill Collins** gives sustained attention to a Black women's standpoint as well as the complex intersectionality of individuals' identities and experiences, and to what this requires of scholars who seek to study intersectionality. Important here also is the construal and reassessment of hegemonic and nonhegemonic masculinities by **R.W. Connell** and **James W. Messerschmidt**.

In a parallel vein, postcolonial theories (chapter 14) draw attention to the structured dehumanization of racial and ethnic outsiders, and to the enduring legacies of slavery and colonial domination on the delegitimation of postcolonial identities and cultures. The pioneering Black sociologist **W.E. Burghardt Du Bois** was the first to forcefully articulate the bifurcating effect of slavery on the consciousness and identity of enslaved people and its legacy on postslavery generations of Black people. **Edward W. Said** focuses on the West's construal of the (inferior) Otherness of the Orient, while **Frantz Fanon** evocatively conveys the everyday reality and experience of being a Black man in a racist society. **Stuart Hall** underscores the plurality and diversity of postcolonial histories, cultures, and identities and offers an emancipatory vision of cultural identity as an ongoing project that can dynamically integrate past and present into a new authentic synthesis. Contemporary scholars also increasingly point to the colonial and Northern/Western biases in what is regarded as legitimate knowledge, including biases in sociological knowledge, as elaborated by **Raewyn Connell** and colleagues. Others, such as **Alondra Nelson**, draw out the somewhat unexpected progressive social consequences of DNA testing and the use of genetic data by universities engaged in initiatives to make reparations to the descendants of freed slaves.

The final chapter (chapter 15) features excerpts highlighting what is distinctive about global society, our contemporary moment of late modernity, characterized by an array of transnational actors and processes. **Zygmunt Bauman** highlights what he sees as the diminishing role of the nation state and of its protective function toward its citizens and their well-being. **Anthony Giddens** discusses the disembeddedness of time and space and its consequences for individual selves and social processes. **Ulrich Beck** elaborates on the globalization of risk society and highlights its encompassing nature. Additionally, he and **Edgar Grande** highlight the variations in modernity and suggest the need for a cosmopolitanism that would more fully recognize the mutuality of all peoples and societies across the world. Focusing primarily on the post-secular West, and the political and cultural divisions between moderate religious and secular impulses, **Jürgen Habermas** articulates how we might go about crafting more respectful and enriching discourses with those whose beliefs, ideas and experiences are different to ours.

REFERENCES

Comte, Auguste. 1891/1973. *The Catechism of Positive Religion*. 3rd ed. Trans. Richard Congreve. Clifton, NJ: Augustus M. Kelley.

Hoecker-Drysdale, Susan. 1992. *Harriet Martineau: First Woman Sociologist*. Oxford: Berg.

Lareau, Annette, 1987. "Social Class Differences in Family–School Relationships: The Importance of Cultural Capital." *Sociology of Education* 60: 73–85.

Martineau, Harriet. 1838. *How to Observe Morals and Manners*. London: Charles Knight.

PART I
CLASSICAL THEORISTS

CHAPTER ONE

KARL MARX

CHAPTER MENU

Karl Marx who was born in Germany in 1818 and died in London, England, in 1883, remains the foremost theorist in explaining the deep structural inequalities within capitalism. Despite the rapid pace of ongoing social change today – just think of the use and impact of the iPhone alone – and the many transformative changes in society since Marx's lifetime, which was the epoch of expanding industrialization, factory production, and urbanization – his understanding of how capitalism works, and why it expands and endures, exposes the economic, political, and cultural logics that enable capitalism to thrive despite the many personal and societal ills it simultaneously causes. In the popular imagination – among those who have not studied Marx – Marx is frequently thought of as someone who is opposed to work and for this reason postulated *The Communist Manifesto* (not included) as a vision of a world in which work would not be necessary. This, however, is a gross mischaracterization and misunderstanding of Marx and his theorizing. Yes, Marx envisioned the revolutionary downfall of capitalism as part of a long historical process and its replacement with a society built

Concise Reader in Sociological Theory: Theorists, Concepts, and Current Applications,
First Edition. Edited by Michele Dillon. Editorial material and organization
© 2021 John Wiley & Sons Ltd. Published 2021 by John Wiley & Sons Ltd.

on a utopian equality in which, with each person working or contributing based on their particular skills and talents, the individual and collective needs of the community would be satisfied. Clearly this vision has not been realized, and in fact capitalism has grown exponentially such that today we live in a truly global capitalist society, with capitalist processes and consequences apparent in every country in the world (including those that are nominally communist, such as Cuba and North Korea). However, the explanatory power of much of Marx's theorizing (notwithstanding its frequent polemical tone and some erroneous assumptions and predictions) is such that it sharply illuminates why and how capitalism has so successfully endured.

It's not that Marx was opposed to work or to labor. Rather, what he critiqued was the empirical fact that across history – from slavery through feudal times and in capitalist society – work and inequality were two sides of the same coin. He emphasizes a materialist conception of history wherein the way in which wealth is produced and distributed is based on a system of unequal social classes (Engels1878/1978: 700–1). Workers – the producers or makers of things or of ideas – do not get to fully own or fully enjoy the fruits of their labor. Rather, their creative work and its products are extracted from them by others for their own advancement. The ancient slave-master, the feudal lord, and the capitalist, though occupying quite distinct positions in historical formation, share in common the fact that their material and social well-being relies on the labor of others. Focusing on capitalism in particular, Marx, along with his frequent coauthor Friedrich Engels (1820–95), drew attention to and analyzed the inherent inequality structured into the relation between capitalists or the bourgeois class and wage-workers or the proletariat, and how such inequality is structured into and is sustained within capitalism. Moreover, in Marx's analysis, the economic logic of capitalism (anchored in the capitalist motive to make profit and accumulate economic capital), extends beyond the purely economic sector and economic relationships to underlie and motivate all social, political, and cultural activity. The excerpts I include here illuminate the lived material processes involved in the production and maintenance of capitalist inequalities, and also convey a far more searing analysis of capitalism – and of how it is talked about and understood – than is typically found in the discourse of economists or indeed in the everyday conversations of ordinary people. Thus Marx compels us to critique the principles, processes, and vocabulary of our everyday existence in what is today a global capitalist society.

For example, wages for Marx (see excerpt *1a Wage Labour and Capital*) are not merely a worker's take-home pay or salary determined by a formula that pays attention to a worker's skills and education, the cost of living, and the scarcity of particular kinds of workers. Rather, as he elaborates, wages are a function of the exploitation of workers by the owners of capital (whether corporations or landowners) and result from the system of commodity production that is distinctive to capitalism and which in essence requires that workers, too, be considered as, and used and exploited, in ways similar to other commodities. As Marx also elaborates, profit, that motivating engine of capital accumulation (and of capitalist greed) cannot be seen simply as the reward to capitalists for their entrepreneurialism and hard work. To the contrary, profit for Marx is only possible because the capital and investments required to maintain the capitalist production system are inherently tied to the work produced by workers on a daily basis and whose wages (whether they are relatively low or impressively high) are always going to be less than the actual amount of products or value they produce for their employers (whether factory owners or the owners of a sports team franchise or a hospital). The difference between the cost of maintaining a worker (the costs of wages, raw materials, infrastructure, etc.) and the value the worker produces is the surplus the employer receives and takes as profit. And this profit is assured by the structured organization of the production process (which includes the specialized division of labor) and the fact that profit can never be sacrificed for the betterment of workers. Moreover, it is the whole class of workers which is exploited and alienated within capitalism; a worker is free to leave any given employer and go work for another; but is never free to not work – because in capitalism, workers are reliant on the class of employers for the wages (the livelihood) that allows them to live. In capitalist society, if a worker can't earn a wage (a wage that is invariably less than capitalist profit), they can't have much of a life; hence for Marx, the relationship between workers and capitalists/employers is inherently antagonistic and this is necessarily and objectively the case owing to the structural inequality built into the organization and workings of capitalism, no matter how benign the employer and how subjectively happy or fulfilled the worker.

Marx elaborates on the objective alienation or estrangement of the worker (see excerpt *1b Economic and Philosophical Manuscripts of 1844*) and shows how this alienation inheres in the capitalist production process. Importantly, too, alienation results in private property being appropriated by the capitalists as rightfully theirs (though it is the product of alienated labor) and used by them as an object (such as money) in furthering their own ends. Therefore, while humans have, as Marx notes, a higher consciousness than animals and a great capacity for much creativity (see excerpt *1c The German Ideology*), the capitalist production process diminishes them of their creativity and reduces them (as commodities) to cogs in the profit–production process.

Marx's insights about the labor process – what's entailed in the actual production and commodification of work – extend beyond work/labor to the whole lifeworld of the worker (and of the capitalist). A critical and enduring insight of Marx is that people's being, their everyday material existence, determines what they think about and how they think about or evaluate the things they think about (see excerpt *1c The German Ideology*). For Marx, ideas do not come from nowhere or from a mind abstracted from material existence. Ideas, rather, emerge from individuals' lived everyday experiences. The economic or material activity of individuals and the actual circumstances (of structured inequality and objective alienation) in which they do these activities determine and circumscribe their whole consciousness and, by extension, their personal relationships, social lives, and political ideas. Marx notes that people have a certain freedom to make or to remake their lives but they must necessarily do so in circumstances which are not of their own choosing. As he states: "Men make their own history, but they do not make it just as they please; they do not make it under circumstances chosen by themselves, but under circumstances…transmitted from the past"; *Eighteenth Brumaire*, p. 103; excerpt not included). As Marx conveys, individuals and social and political protest movements must always operate within the actual material circumstances they have inherited, and in a capitalist society, these circumstances are always inherently unequal and determined by the ruling capitalist class. Hence, for Marx, ideology, i.e. the dominating or ruling ideas in society – everyday ideas about the nature of capitalism, hard work, money, consumerism, the law, politics, relationships, etc. – is derived from and controlled by the dominance of the standpoint of the capitalist class, a standpoint which marginalizes the objective human and social interests of the workers (who are invariably exploited by capitalism) even as the ruling class (capitalists) insists that capitalism advances not only the interest of capital (e.g. profit) but simultaneously the interests of workers.

REFERENCES

Engels, Friedrich. 1878/1978. "Socialism: Utopian and Scientific," pp. 683–717 in Robert Tucker, ed. *The Marx–Engels Reader*. 2nd ed. New York: Norton.

Marx, Karl and Friedrich Engels. 1848/1967. *The Communist Manifesto*. Introduction by A.J.P. Taylor. London: Penguin.

Marx, Karl. 1852/ 1978. "The Eighteenth Brumaire of Louis Bonaparte," pp. 594–617 in Robert Tucker, ed. *The Marx–Engels Reader*. 2nd ed. New York: Norton.

1A Karl Marx from *Wage Labour and Capital*

Original publication details: Karl Marx, from *Wage Labour and Capital* (1891/1978). Lawrence & Wishart, 2010, pp. 17–18, 19–21, 27–29, 29–30, 41. Reproduced with permission of Lawrence & Wishart via PLS Clear.

What are wages? How are they determined?

If workers were asked: "What are your wages?" one would reply: "I get a franc[1] a day from my bourgeois"; another, "I get two francs," and so on. According to the different trades to which they belong, they would mention different sums of money which they receive from their respective bourgeios for a particular labour time[2] or for the performance of a particular piece of work, for example, weaving a yard of linen or type-setting a printed sheet. In spite of the variety of their statements, they would all agree on one point: wages are the sum of money paid by the bourgeois[3] for a particular labour time or for a particular output of labour.

The bourgeois,[4] therefore, *buys* their labour with money. They *sell* him their labour for money.[5] For the same sum with which the bourgeois has bought their labour,[6] for example, two francs, he could have bought two pounds of sugar or a definite amount of any other commodity. The two francs, with which he bought two pounds of sugar, are the *price* of the two pounds of sugar. The two francs, with which he bought twelve hours' labour,[7] are the price of twelve hours' labour. Labour,[8] therefore, is a commodity, neither more nor less than sugar. The former is measured by the clock, the latter by the scales.

[…]

Wages are, therefore, not the worker's share in the commodity produced by him. Wages are the part of already existing commodities with which the capitalist buys a definite amount of productive labour as such.[9]

Labour[10] is, therefore, a commodity which its possessor, the wage-worker, sells to capital. Why does he sell it? In order to live.

But,[11] labour is the worker's own life-activity, the manifestation of his own life. And this *life-activity* he sells to another person in order to secure the necessary *means of subsistence.* Thus his life-activity is for him only a means to enable him to exist. He works in order to live. He does not even reckon labour as part of his life, it is rather a sacrifice of his life. It is a commodity which he has made over to another. Hence, also, the product of his activity is not the object of his activity. What he produces for himself is not the silk that he weaves, not the gold that he draws from the mine, not the palace that he builds. What he produces for himself is *wages,* and silk, gold, palace resolve themselves for him into a definite quantity of the means of subsistence, perhaps into a cotton jacket, some copper coins and a lodging in a cellar. And the worker, who for twelve hours weaves, spins, drills, turns, builds, shovels, breaks stones, carries loads, etc. – does he consider this twelve hours' weaving, spinning, drilling, turning, building, shovelling, stone-breaking as a manifestation of his life, as life? On the contrary, life begins for him where this activity ceases, at table, in the public house, in bed. The twelve hours' labour, on the other hand, has no meaning for him as weaving, spinning, drilling, etc., but as *earnings,* which bring him to the table, to the public house, into bed. If the silkworm were to spin in order to continue its existence as a caterpillar, it would be a complete wage-worker.

Labour[12] was not always a *commodity.* Labour was not always wage labour, that is, *free* labour. The *slave* did not sell his labour[13] to the slave owner, any more than the ox sells its services to the peasant. The slave, together with his labour,[14] is sold once and for all to his owner. He is a commodity which can pass from the hand of one owner to that of another. He *is himself* a commodity, but the labour[15] is not *his* commodity. The *serf* sells only a part of his labour.[16] He does not receive a wage from the owner of the land; rather the owner of the land receives a tribute from him. The serf belongs to the land and turns over to the owner of the land the fruits thereof. The *free labourer,* on the other hand, sells himself and, indeed, sells himself piecemeal. He auctions off eight, ten, twelve, fifteen hours of his life, day after day, to the highest bidder, to the owner of the raw materials, instruments of labour and means of subsistence, that is, to the capitalist. The worker belongs neither to an owner nor to the land, but eight, ten, twelve, fifteen hours of his daily life belong to him who buys them. The worker leaves the capitalist to whom he hires himself whenever he likes, and the capitalist discharges him whenever he thinks fit, as soon as he no longer gets any profit out of him, or not the anticipated profit. But the worker, whose sole source of livelihood is the sale of his labour,[17] cannot leave the *whole class of purchasers, that is, the capitalist class,* without renouncing his existence. *He belongs not to this or that capitalist but to the capitalist class,*[18] and, moreover, it is his business to dispose of himself, that is, to find a purchaser within this bourgeois class.[19]

[...]

II

Now, the same general laws that regulate the price of commodities in general of course also regulate *wages,* the *price of labour.*

Wages will rise and fall according to the relation of demand and supply, according to the turn taken by the competition between the buyers of labour, the capitalists, and the sellers of labour,[20] the workers. The fluctuations in wages correspond in general to the fluctuations in prices and commodities. *Within the fluctuations, however, the price of labour will be determined by the cost of production, by the labour time necessary to produce this commodity – labour.*[21]

What, then, is the cost of production of labour?[22]

It is the cost required for maintaining the worker as a worker and for developing him into a worker.

The less the period of training, therefore, that any work requires, the smaller is the cost of production of the worker and the lower is the price of his labour, his wages. In those branches of industry in which hardly any period of apprenticeship is required and where the mere bodily existence of the worker suffices, the cost necessary for his production is almost confined to the commodities necessary for keeping him alive.[23] The *price of his labour* will, therefore, be determined by the *price of the necessary means of subsistence*.

Another consideration, however, also comes in.

The manufacturer in calculating his cost of production and, accordingly, the price of the products takes into account the wear and tear of the instruments of labour. If, for example, a machine costs him 1,000 francs and wears out in ten years, he adds 100 francs annually to the price of the commodities so as to be able to replace the worn-out machine by a new one at the end of ten years. In the same way, in calculating the cost of production of simple labour,[24] there must be included the cost of reproduction, whereby the race of workers is enabled to multiply and to replace worn-out workers by new ones. Thus the depreciation of the worker is taken into account in the same way as the depreciation of the machine.

The cost of production of simple labour, therefore, amounts to the *cost of existence and reproduction of the worker*. The price of this cost of existence and reproduction constitutes wages. Wages so determined are called the *wage minimum*. This wage minimum, like the determination of the price of commodities by the cost of production in general, does not hold good for the *single individual* but for the *species*. Individual workers, millions of workers, do not get enough to be able to exist and reproduce themselves; *but the wages of the whole working class* level down, within their fluctuations, to this minimum.

[...]

In production, men enter into relation not only with nature.[25] They produce only by co-operating in a certain way and mutually exchanging their activities. In order to produce, they enter into definite connections and relations with one another and only within these social connections and relations does their relation with nature,[26] does production, take place.

These social relations into which the producers enter with one another, the conditions under which they exchange their activities and participate in the whole act of production, will naturally vary according to the character of the means of production. With the invention of a new instrument of warfare, firearms, the whole internal organization of the army necessarily changed; the relationships within which individuals can constitute an army and act as an army were transformed and the relations of different armies to one another also changed.

Thus the social relations within which individuals produce, the social relations of production, change, are transformed, with the change and development of the material means of production, the productive forces. The relations of production in their totality constitute what are called the social relations, society, and, specifically, a society at a definite stage of historical development, a society with a peculiar, distinctive character. Ancient society, feudal society, bourgeois society are such totalities of production relations, each of which at the same time denotes a special stage of development in the history of mankind.

Capital, also, is a social relation of production. *It is a bourgeois production relation, a production relation of bourgeois society.* Are not the means of subsistence, the instruments of labour, the raw materials of which capital consists, produced and accumulated under given social conditions, in definite social relations? Are they not utilized for new production under given social conditions, in definite social relations? And is it not just this definite social character which turns the products serving for new production into *capital?*

Capital consists not only of means of subsistence, instruments of labour and raw materials, not only of material products; it consists just as much of *exchange values.* All the products of which it consists are *commodities.* Capital is, therefore, not only a sum of material products; it is a sum of commodities, of exchange values, of *social magnitudes.*

[…]

The interests of the capitalist and those of the worker are, therefore, one and the same, assert the bourgeois and their economists. Indeed! The worker perishes if capital does not employ him. Capital perishes if it does not exploit labour,[27] and in order to exploit it, it must buy it. The faster capital intended for production, productive capital, increases, the more, therefore, industry prospers, the more the bourgeoisie enriches itself and the better business is, the more workers does the capitalist need, the more dearly does the worker sell himself.

The indispensable condition for a tolerable situation of the worker is, therefore, the *fastest possible growth of productive capital.*

But what is the growth of productive capital? Growth of the power of accumulated labour over living labour. Growth of the domination of the bourgeoisie over the working class. If wage labour produces the wealth of others that rules over it, the power that is hostile to it, capital, then the means of employment [*Beschäftigungsmittel*], that is, the means of subsistence, flow back to it from this hostile power, on condition that it makes itself afresh into a part of capital, into the lever which hurls capital anew into an accelerated movement of growth.

To say that the interests of capital and those of labour[28] are one and the same is only to say that capital and wage labour are two sides of one and the same relation. The one conditions the other, just as usurer and squanderer condition each other.

As long as the wage-worker is a wage-worker his lot depends upon capital. That is the much-vaunted community of interests between worker and capitalist.

Even the *most favourable situation* for the working class, the *most rapid possible growth of capital*, however much it may improve the material existence of the worker, does not remove the antagonism between his interests and the interests of the bourgeoisie, the interests of the capitalist. *Profit and wages* remain as before in *inverse proportion.*

If capital is growing rapidly, wages may rise; the profit of capital rises incomparably more rapidly. The material position of the worker has improved, but at the cost of his social position. The social gulf that divides him from the capitalist has widened.

Finally:

To say that the most favourable condition for wage labour is the most rapid possible growth of productive capital is only to say that the more rapidly the working class increases and enlarges the power that is hostile to it, the wealth that does not belong to it and that rules over it, the more favourable will be the conditions under which it is allowed to labour anew at increasing bourgeois wealth, at enlarging the power of capital, content with forging for itself the golden chains by which the bourgeoisie drags it in its train.

NOTES

1 1 franc equals 8 Prussian silver groschen. (In the 1891 edition the word "mark" is used everywhere instead of "franc". – *Ed.*

2 The words "for a particular labour time" are omitted in the 1891 edition. – *Ed.*

3 The 1891 edition has "capitalist" here instead of "bourgeois". – *Ed.*

4 The 1891 edition has "capitalist" here and the words "it seems" are added. – *Ed.*

5 In the 1891 edition here follows the passage: "But this is merely the appearance. In reality what they sell to the capitalist for money is their labour *power*. The capitalist buys this labour power for a day, a week, a month, etc. And after he has bought it, he uses it by having the workers work for the stipulated time." – *Ed.*

6 The 1891 edition has "the capitalist has bought their labour power" instead of "the bourgeois has bought their labour power". – *Ed.*

7 The 1891 edition has "use of labour power" instead of "labour". – *Ed.*

8 The 1891 edition has "labour power" instead of "labour". – *Ed.*

9 The 1891 edition has "labour power" instead of "labour". – *Ed.*

10 The 1891 edition has "labour power" instead of "labour". – *Ed.*

11 The 1891 edition has after this: "the exercise of labour power". – *Ed.*

12 The 1891 edition has "labour power" instead of "labour". – *Ed.*

13 The 1891 edition has "labour power" instead of "labour". – *Ed.*

14 The 1891 edition has "labour power" instead of "labour". – *Ed.*

15 The 1891 edition has "labour power" instead of "labour". – *Ed.*

16 The 1891 edition has "labour power" instead of "labour". – *Ed.*

17 The 1891 edition has "labour power" instead of "labour". – *Ed.*

18 The 1891 edition has *"not to this or that capitalist but to the capitalist class"* instead of *"not to this or that bourgeois but to the bourgeois class"*. – *Ed.*

19 The 1891 edition has *"capitalist class"* instead of *"bourgeois class"*. – *Ed.*

20 The 1891 edition has "the buyers of labour power" and "the sellers of labour power" instead of "the buyers of labour" and "the sellers of labour". – *Ed.*

21 The 1891 edition has "labour power" instead of "labour". – *Ed.*

22 The 1891 edition has "labour power" instead of "labour". – *Ed.*

23 In the 1891 edition the words "and capable of working" are added here. – *Ed.*

24 The 1891 edition has here and in the next paragraph "simple labour power" instead of "simple labour". – *Ed.*

25 The 1891 edition has "not only act on nature but also on one another" instead of "enter into relation not only with nature". – *Ed.*

26 The 1891 edition has "action on nature" instead of "relation with nature". – *Ed.*

27 The 1891 edition has "labour power" instead of "labour". – *Ed.*

28 The 1891 edition has *"workers"* instead of *"labour"*. – *Ed.*

1B Karl Marx and Frederick Engels from *Economic and Philosophical Manuscripts of 1844*

Original publication details: Karl Marx, from "Economic and Philosophical Manuscripts of 1844" in *Karl Marx and Frederick Engels: Volume 3, Marx and Engels 1843–44*. International Publishers, 1975, pp. 235–239, 246–248, 271–277, 322–323, 324. Reproduced with permission of International Publishers.

||I, 1| *Wages* are determined through the antagonistic struggle between capitalist and worker. Victory goes necessarily to the capitalist. The capitalist can live longer without the worker than can the worker without the capitalist. Combination among the capitalists is customary and effective; workers' combination is prohibited and painful in its consequences for them. Besides, the landowner and the capitalist can make use of industrial advantages to augment their revenues; the worker has neither rent nor interest on capital to supplement his industrial income. Hence the intensity of the competition among the workers. Thus only for the workers is the separation of capital, landed property, and labour an inevitable, essential and detrimental separation. Capital and landed property need not remain fixed in this abstraction, as must the labour of the workers.

The separation of capital, rent, and labour is thus fatal for the worker.

The lowest and the only necessary wage rate is that providing for the subsistence of the worker for the duration of his work and as much more as is necessary for him to support a family and for the race of labourers not to die out. The ordinary wage, according to Smith, is the lowest compatible with common humanity, that is, with cattle-like existence.

The demand for men necessarily governs the production of men, as of every other commodity. Should supply greatly exceed demand, a section of the workers sinks into beggary or starvation. The worker's existence is thus brought under the same condition as the existence of every other commodity. The worker has become a commodity, and it is a bit of luck for him if he can find a buyer. And the demand on which the life of the worker depends, depends on the whim of the rich and the capitalists. Should supply ex[ceed][1] demand, then one of the consti[tuent] parts of the price – profit, rent or wages – is paid below its *rate*, [a part of these] factors is therefore withdrawn from this application, and thus the market price gravitates [towards the] natural price as the centre-point. But (1) where there is considerable division of labour it is most difficult for the worker to direct his labour into other channels; (2) because of his subordinate relation to the capitalist, he is the first to suffer.

Thus in the gravitation of market price to natural price it is the worker who loses most of all and necessarily. And it is just the capacity of the capitalist to direct his capital into another channel which either renders the worker,[2] who is restricted to some particular branch of labour, destitute, or forces him to submit to every demand of this capitalist.

||II, 1| The accidental and sudden fluctuations in market price hit rent less than they do that part of the price which is resolved into profit and wages; but they hit profit less than they do wages. In most cases, for every wage that rises, one remains *stationary* and one *falls*.

The worker need not necessarily gain when the capitalist does, but he necessarily loses when the latter loses. Thus, the worker does not gain if the capitalist keeps the market price above the natural price by virtue of some manufacturing or trading secret, or by virtue of monopoly or the favourable situation of his land.

Furthermore, *the prices of labour are much more constant than the prices of provisions.* Often they stand in inverse proportion. In a dear year wages fall on account of the decrease in demand, but rise on account of the increase in the prices of provisions – and thus balance. In any case, a number of workers are left without bread. In cheap years wages rise on account of the rise in demand, but decrease on account of the fall in the prices of provisions – and thus balance.

Another respect in which the worker is at a disadvantage:

The labour prices of the various kinds of workers show much wider differences than the profits in the various branches in which capital is applied. In labour all the natural, spiritual, and social variety of individual activity is manifested and is variously rewarded, whilst dead capital always keeps the same pace and is indifferent to *real* individual activity.

In general we should observe that in those cases where worker and capitalist equally suffer, the worker suffers in his very existence, the capitalist in the profit on his dead mammon.

The worker has to struggle not only for his physical means of subsistence; he has to struggle to get work, i. e., the possibility, the means, to perform his activity.

Let us take the three chief conditions in which society can find itself and consider the situation of the worker in them:

(1) If the wealth of society declines the worker suffers most of all, and for the following reason: although the working class cannot gain so much as can the class of property owners in a prosperous state of society, *no one suffers so cruelly from its decline as the working class.*[3]

||III, 1| (2) Let us now take a society in which wealth is increasing. This condition is the only one favourable to the worker. Here competition between the capitalists sets in. The demand for workers exceeds their supply. But:

In the first place, the raising of wages gives rise to *overwork* among the workers. The more they wish to earn, the more must they sacrifice their time and carry out slave-labour, completely losing all their freedom, in the service of greed. Thereby they shorten their lives. This shortening of their life-span is a favourable circumstance for the working class as a whole, for as a result of it an ever-fresh supply of labour becomes necessary. This class has always to sacrifice a part of itself in order not to be wholly destroyed.

Furthermore: When does a society find itself in a condition of advancing wealth? When the capitals and the revenues of a country are growing. But this is only possible:

(*α*) As the result of the accumulation of much labour, capital being accumulated labour; as the result, therefore, of the fact that more and more of his products are being taken away from the worker, that to an increasing extent his own labour confronts him as another man's property and that the means of his existence and his activity are increasingly concentrated in the hands of the capitalist.

(*β*) The accumulation of capital increases the division of labour, and the division of labour increases the number of workers. Conversely, the number of workers increases the division of labour, just as the division of labour increases the accumulation of capital. With this division of labour on the one hand and the accumulation of capital on the other, the worker becomes ever more exclusively dependent on labour, and on a particular, very one-sided, machine-like labour at that. Just as he is thus depressed spiritually and physically to the condition of a machine and from being a man becomes an abstract activity and a belly, so he also becomes ever more dependent on every fluctuation in market price, on the application of capital, and on the whim of the rich. Equally, the increase in the ||IV, 1| class of people wholly dependent on work intensifies competition among the workers, thus lowering their price. In the factory system this situation of the worker reaches its climax.

(γ) In an increasingly prosperous society only the richest of the rich can continue to live on money interest. Everyone else has to carry on a business with his capital, or venture it in trade. As a result, the competition between the capitalists becomes more intense. The concentration of capital increases, the big capitalists ruin the small, and a section of the erstwhile capitalists sinks into the working class, which as a result of this supply again suffers to some extent a depression of wages and passes into a still greater dependence on the few big capitalists. The number of capitalists having been diminished, their competition with respect to the workers scarcely exists any longer; and the number of workers having been increased, their competition among themselves has become all the more intense, unnatural, and violent. Consequently, a section of the working class falls into beggary or starvation just as necessarily as a section of the middle capitalists falls into the working class.

Hence even in the condition of society most favourable to the worker, the inevitable result for the worker is overwork and premature death, decline to a mere machine, a bond servant of capital, which piles up dangerously over and against him, more competition, and starvation or beggary for a section of the workers.

||V, 1| The raising of wages excites in the worker the capitalist's mania to get rich, which he, however, can only satisfy by the sacrifice of his mind and body. The raising of wages presupposes and entails the accumulation of capital, and thus sets the product of labour against the worker as something ever more alien to him. Similarly, the division of labour renders him ever more one-sided and dependent, bringing with it the competition not only of men but also of machines. Since the worker has sunk to the level of a machine, he can be confronted by the machine as a competitor. Finally, as the amassing of capital increases the amount of industry and therefore the number of workers, it causes the same amount of industry to manufacture a *larger amount of products*, which leads to over-production and thus either ends by throwing a large section of workers out of work or by reducing their wages to the most miserable minimum.

[...]

Profit of Capital

Capital

||I, 2|What is the basis of *capital*, that is, of private property in the products of other men's labour?

"Even if capital itself does not merely amount to theft or fraud, it still requires the co-operation of legislation to sanctify inheritance." (Say, [*Traité d'économie politique,*] t. I, p. 136, note.)[4]

How does one become a proprietor of productive stock? How does one become owner of the products created by means of this stock?

By virtue of *positive law*. (Say, t. II, p. 4.)

What does one acquire with capital, with the inheritance of a large fortune, for instance?

"The person who [either acquires, or] succeeds to a great fortune, does not necessarily [acquire or] succeed to any political power [....] The power which that possession immediately and directly conveys to him, is the *power of purchasing*; a certain command over all the labour, or over all the produce of labour, which is then in the market." (*Wealth of Nations*, by Adam Smith, Vol. I, pp. 26–27 [Garnier, t. I, p. 61].)[5]

Capital is thus the *governing power* over labour and its products. The capitalist possesses this power, not on account of his personal or human qualities, but inasmuch as he is an *owner* of capital. His power is the *purchasing* power of his capital, which nothing can withstand.

Later we shall see first how the capitalist, by means of capital, exercises his governing power over labour, then, however, we shall see the governing power of capital over the capitalist himself.

What is capital?

"A certain quantity of *labour stocked* and stored up to be employed." (Adam Smith, op. cit., Vol. I, p. 295 [Garnier, t. II, p. 312].)

Capital is *stored-up labour*.

(2) *Fonds*, or stock,[6] is any accumulation of products of the soil or of manufacture. Stock is called *capital* only when it yields to its owner a revenue or profit. (Adam Smith, op. cit., p. 243 [Garnier, t. II, p. 191].

The Profit of Capital

The *profit* or *gain of capital* is altogether different from the *wages of labour*. This difference is manifested in two ways: in the first place, the profits of capital are regulated altogether by the value of the capital employed, although the labour of inspection and direction associated with different capitals may be the same. Moreover in large works the whole of this labour is committed to some principal clerk, whose salary bears no regular proportion to the ||II,2| capital of which he oversees the management. And although the labour of the proprietor is here reduced almost to nothing, he still demands profits in proportion to his capital. (Adam Smith, op. cit., Vol. I, p. 43 [Garnier, t. I, pp. 97–99].)[7]

Why does the capitalist demand this proportion between profit and capital?

> He would have no *interest* in employing the workers, unless he expected from the sale of
> their work something more than is necessary to replace the stock advanced by him as
> wages and he would have no *interest* to employ a great stock rather than a small one,
> unless his profits were to bear some proportion to the extent of his stock. (Adam Smith,
> op. cit., Vol. I, p. 42 [Garnier, t. I, pp. 96–97].)

The capitalist thus makes a profit, first, on the wages, and secondly on the raw
materials advanced by him.

[...]

We proceed from an *actual* economic fact.

The worker becomes all the poorer the more wealth he produces, the more his
production increases in power and size. The worker becomes an ever cheaper commodity the more commodities he creates. The *devaluation* of the world of men is in
direct proportion to the *increasing value* of the world of things. Labour produces not
only commodities: it produces itself and the worker as a *commodity* – and this at the
same rate at which it produces commodities in general.

This fact expresses merely that the object which labour produces – labour's product – confronts it as *something alien*, as a *power independent* of the producer. The
product of labour is labour which has been embodied in an object, which has become
material: it is the *objectification* of labour. Labour's realisation is its objectification.
Under these economic conditions this realisation of labour appears as *loss of realisation* for the workers; objectification as *loss of the object and bondage to it*; appropriation as *estrangement, as alienation*.

So much does labour's realisation appear as loss of realisation that the worker loses
realisation to the point of starving to death. So much does objectification appear as loss
of the object that the worker is robbed of the objects most necessary not only for his life
but for his work. Indeed, labour itself becomes an object which he can obtain only with
the greatest effort and with the most irregular interruptions. So much does the appropriation of the object appear as estrangement that the more objects the worker produces
the less he can possess and the more he falls under the sway of his product, capital.

All these consequences are implied in the statement that the worker is related to the
product of his labour as to an *alien* object. For on this premise it is clear that the more
the worker spends himself, the more powerful becomes the alien world of objects
which he creates over and against himself, the poorer he himself – his inner
world – becomes, the less belongs to him as his own. It is the same in religion. The
more man puts into God, the less he retains in himself. The worker puts his life into the
object; but now his life no longer belongs to him but to the object. Hence, the greater
this activity, the more the worker lacks objects. Whatever the product of his labour is,
he is not. Therefore the greater this product, the less is he himself. The *alienation* of the
worker in his product means not only that his labour becomes an object, an *external*
existence, but that it exists *outside him*, independently, as something alien to him, and

that it becomes a power on its own confronting him. It means that the life which he has conferred on the object confronts him as something hostile and alien.

||XXIII/ Let us now look more closely at the *objectification*, at the production of the worker; and in it at the *estrangement*, the *loss* of the object, of his product.

The worker can create nothing without *nature*, without the *sensuous external world*. It is the material on which his labour is realised, in which it is active, from which and by means of which it produces.

But just as nature provides labour with [the] *means of life* in the sense that labour cannot *live* without objects on which to operate, on the other hand, it also provides the *means of life* in the more restricted sense, i.e., the means for the physical subsistence of the *worker* himself.

Thus the more the worker by his labour *appropriates* the external world, sensuous nature, the more he deprives himself of *means of life* in two respects: first, in that the sensuous external world more and more ceases to be an object belonging to his labour – to be his labour's *means of life*; and secondly, in that it more and more ceases to be *means of life* in the immediate sense, means for the physical subsistence of the worker.

In both respects, therefore, the worker becomes a servant of his object, first, in that he receives an *object of labour*, i.e., in that he receives *work*; and secondly, in that he receives *means of subsistence*. This enables him to exist, first, as a *worker*, and, second, as a *physical subject*. The height of this servitude is that it is only as a *worker* that he can maintain himself as a *physical subject*, and that it is only as a *physical subject* that he is a worker.

(According to the economic laws the estrangement of the worker in his object is expressed thus: the more the worker produces, the less he has to consume; the more values he creates, the more valueless, the more unworthy he becomes; the better formed his product, the more deformed becomes the worker; the more civilised his object, the more barbarous becomes the worker; the more powerful labour becomes, the more powerless becomes the worker; the more ingenious labour becomes, the less ingenious becomes the worker and the more he becomes nature's servant.)

Political economy conceals the estrangement inherent in the nature of labour by not considering the direct *relationship between the* worker (labour) *and production.* It is true that labour produces wonderful things for the rich – but for the worker it produces privation. It produces palaces – but for the worker, hovels. It produces beauty – but for the worker, deformity. It replaces labour by machines, but it throws one section of the workers back to a barbarous type of labour, and it turns the other section into a machine. It produces intelligence – but for the worker, stupidity, cretinism.

The direct relationship of labour to its products is the relationship of the worker to the objects of his production. The relationship of the man of means to the objects of production and to production itself is only a *consequence* of this first relationship – and confirms it. We shall consider this other aspect later. When we ask, then, what is the essential relationship of labour we are asking about the relationship of the *worker* to production.

Till now we have been considering the estrangement; the alienation of the worker only in one of its aspects, i.e., the worker's *relationship to the products of his labour*. But the estrangement is manifested not only in the result but in the *act of production*, within the *producing activity* itself. How could the worker come to face the product of his activity as a stranger, were it not that in the very act of production he was estranging himself from himself? The product is after all but the summary of the activity, of production. If then the product of labour is alienation, production itself must be active alienation, the alienation of activity, the activity of alienation. In the estrangement of the object of labour is merely summarised the estrangement, the alienation, in the activity of labour itself.

What, then, constitutes the alienation of labour?

First, the fact that labour is *external* to the worker, i.e., it does not belong to his intrinsic nature; that in his work, therefore, he does not affirm himself but denies himself, does not feel content but unhappy, does not develop freely his physical and mental energy but mortifies his body and ruins his mind. The worker therefore only feels himself outside his work, and in his work feels outside himself. He feels at home when he is not working, and when he is working he does not feel at home. His labour is therefore not voluntary, but coerced; it is *forced labour*. It is therefore not the satisfaction of a need; it is merely a *means* to satisfy needs external to it. Its alien character emerges clearly in the fact that as soon as no physical or other compulsion exists, labour is shunned like the plague. External labour, labour in which man alienates himself, is a labour of self-sacrifice, of mortification. Lastly, the external character of labour for the worker appears in the fact that it is not his own, but someone else's, that it does not belong to him, that in it he belongs, not to himself, but to another. Just as in religion the spontaneous activity of the human imagination, of the human brain and the human heart, operates on the individual independently of him – that is, operates as an alien, divine or diabolical activity – so is the worker's activity not his spontaneous activity. It belongs to another; it is the loss of his self.

As a result, therefore, man (the worker) only feels himself freely active in his animal functions – eating, drinking, procreating, or at most in his dwelling and in dressing-up, etc.; and in his human functions he no longer feels himself to be anything but an animal. What is animal becomes human and what is human becomes animal.

Certainly eating, drinking, procreating, etc., are also genuinely human functions. But taken abstractly, separated from the sphere of all other human activity and turned into sole and ultimate ends, they are animal functions.

We have considered the act of estranging practical human activity, labour, in two of its aspects. (1) The relation of the worker to the *product of labour* as an alien object exercising power over him. This relation is at the same time the relation to the sensuous external world, to the objects of nature, as an alien world inimically opposed to him. (2) The relation of labour to the *act of production* within the *labour* process. This relation is the relation of the worker to his own activity as an alien activity not belonging to him; it is activity as suffering, strength as weakness, begetting as emasculating, the worker's *own* physical and mental energy, his personal life – for what is life but activity? – as an activity which is turned against him, independent of him and not belonging to him. Here we have *self-estrangement*, as previously we had the estrangement of the *thing*.

||XXIV| We have still a third aspect of *estranged labour* to deduce from the two already considered.

Man is a species-being, not only because in practice and in theory he adopts the species (his own as well as those of other things) as his object, but – and this is only another way of expressing it – also because he treats himself as the actual, living species; because he treats himself as a *universal* and therefore a free being.

The life of the species, both in man and in animals, consists physically in the fact that man (like the animal) lives on inorganic nature; and the more universal man (or the animal) is, the more universal is the sphere of inorganic nature on which he lives. Just as plants, animals, stones, air, light, etc., constitute theoretically a part of human consciousness, partly as objects of natural science, partly as objects of art – his spiritual inorganic nature, spiritual nourishment which he must first prepare to make palatable and digestible – so also in the realm of practice they constitute a part of human life and human activity. Physically man lives only on these products of nature, whether they appear in the form of food, heating, clothes, a dwelling, etc. The universality of man appears in practice precisely in the universality which makes all nature his *inorganic* body – both inasmuch as nature is (1) his direct means of life, and (2) the material, the object, and the instrument of his life activity. Nature is man's *inorganic body* – nature, that is, insofar as it is not itself human body. Man *lives* on nature – means that nature is his *body*, with which he must remain in continuous interchange if he is not to die. That man's physical and spiritual life is linked to nature means simply that nature is linked to itself, for man is a part of nature.

In estranging from man (1) nature, and (2) himself, his own active functions, his life activity, estranged labour estranges the *species* from man. It changes for him the *life of the species* into a means of individual life. First it estranges the life of the species and individual life, and secondly it makes individual life in its abstract form the purpose of the life of the species, likewise in its abstract and estranged form.

For labour, *life activity, productive life* itself, appears to man in the first place merely as a *means* of satisfying a need – the need to maintain physical existence. Yet the productive life is the life of the species. It is life-engendering life. The whole character of a species – its species-character – is contained in the character of its life activity; and free, conscious activity is man's species-character. Life itself appears only as a *means to life*.

The animal is immediately one with its life activity. It does not distinguish itself from it. It is *its life activity.* Man makes his life activity itself the object of his will and of his consciousness. He has conscious life activity. It is not a determination with which he directly merges. Conscious life activity distinguishes man immediately from animal life activity. It is just because of this that he is a species-being. Or it is only because he is a species-being that he is a conscious being, i.e., that his own life is an object for him. Only because of that is his activity free activity. Estranged labour reverses this relationship, so that it is just because man is a conscious being that he makes his life activity, his *essential being*, a mere means to his *existence*.

In creating a *world of objects* by his practical activity, in his *work upon* inorganic nature, man proves himself a conscious species-being, i.e., as a being that treats the species as its own essential being, or that treats itself as a species-being. Admittedly animals also produce. They build themselves nests, dwellings, like the bees, beavers, ants, etc. But an animal only produces what it immediately needs for itself or its young. It produces one-sidedly, whilst man produces universally. It produces only under the dominion of immediate physical need, whilst man produces even when he is free from physical need and only truly produces in freedom therefrom. An animal produces only itself, whilst man reproduces the whole of nature. An animal's product belongs immediately to its physical body, whilst man freely confronts his product. An animal forms objects only in accordance with the standard and the need of the species to which it belongs, whilst man knows how to produce in accordance with the standard of every species, and knows how to apply everywhere the inherent standard to the object. Man therefore also forms objects in accordance with the laws of beauty.

It is just in his work upon the objective world, therefore, that man really proves himself to be a *species-being*. This production is his active species-life. Through this production, nature appears as *his* work and his reality. The object of labour is, therefore, the *objectification of man's species-life*: for he duplicates himself not only, as in consciousness, intellectually, but also actively, in reality, and therefore he sees himself in a world that he has created. In tearing away from man the object of his production, therefore, estranged labour tears from him his *species-life*, his real objectivity as a member of the species, and transforms his advantage over animals into the disadvantage that his inorganic body, nature, is taken away from him.

Similarly, in degrading spontaneous, free activity to a means, estranged labour makes man's species-life a means to his physical existence.

The consciousness which man has of his species is thus transformed by estrangement in such a way that species[-life] becomes for him a means.

Estranged labour turns thus:

(3) *Man's species-being*, both nature and his spiritual species-property, into a being *alien* to him, into a *means* for his *individual existence*. It estranges from man his own body, as well as external nature and his spiritual aspect, his *human* aspect.

(4) An immediate consequence of the fact that man is estranged from the product of his labour, from his life activity, from his species-being is the *estrangement of man* from *man*. When man confronts himself, he confronts the *other* man. What applies to a man's relation to his work, to the product of his labour and to himself, also holds of a man's relation to the other man, and to the other man's labour and object of labour.

[…]

Private property thus results by analysis from the concept of *alienated labour*, i.e., of *alienated man*, of estranged labour, of estranged life, of *estranged* man.

[…]

(5) The meaning of private property – apart from its estrangement – is the *existence of essential objects* for man, both as objects of enjoyment and as objects of activity.

By possessing the *property* of buying everything, by possessing the property of appropriating all objects, *money* is thus the *object* of eminent possession. The universality of its *property* is the omnipotence of its being. It is therefore regarded as omnipotent…. Money is the *procurer* between man's need and the object, between his life and his means of life. But *that which* mediates *my* life for me, also *mediates* the existence of other people for me. For me it is the *other* person.

[…]

That which is for me through the medium of *money* – that for which I can pay (i.e., which money can buy) – that am *I myself*, the possessor of the money. The extent of the power of money is the extent of my power. Money's properties are my – the possessor's – properties and essential powers. Thus, what I *am* and *am capable of* is by no means determined by my individuality. I *am* ugly, but I can buy for myself the *most beautiful* of women. Therefore I am not *ugly*, for the effect of *ugliness* – its deterrent power – is nullified by money. I, according to my individual characteristics, am *lame*, but money furnishes me with twenty-four feet. Therefore I am not lame. I am bad, dishonest, unscrupulous, stupid; but money is honoured, and hence its possessor. Money is the supreme good, therefore its possessor is good. Money, besides, saves me the trouble of being dishonest: I am therefore presumed honest. I am *brainless*, but money is the *real brain* of all things and how then should its possessor be brainless? Besides, he can buy clever people for himself, and is he who has[8] power over the clever not more clever than the clever? Do not I, who thanks to money am capable of *all* that the human heart longs for, possess all human capacities? Does not my money, therefore, transform all my incapacities into their contrary?

If *money* is the bond binding me to *human* life, binding society to me, connecting me with nature and man, is not money the bond of all *bonds*? Can it not dissolve and bind all ties? Is it not, therefore, also the universal *agent of separation*? It is the *coin* that really *separates* as well as the real *binding agent* – the […][9] *chemical* power of society.

NOTES

1 The letters and words enclosed in square brackets in this sentence are indecipherable as they are covered by an inkspot.– *Ed.*

2 Here and occasionally later Marx uses the French word *ouvrier*. – *Ed.*

3 Cf. Adam Smith, *Wealth of Nations*, Vol. I, p. 230 (Garnier, t. II, p. 162). – *Ed.*

4 Unlike the quotations from a number of other French writers such as Constantin Pecqueur and Eugène Buret, which Marx gives in French in this work, the excerpts from J.B. Say's book are given in his German translation.

5 From this page of the manuscript quotations from Adam Smith's book (in the French translation), which Marx cited so far sometimes in French and sometimes in German, are, as a rule, given in German. … The corresponding pages of the English edition are substituted for the French by the editor and Marx's references are given in square brackets.

6 Marx uses the English word "stock". – *Ed.*

7 The text published in small type here and below is not an exact quotation from Smith but a summary of the corresponding passages from his work. Such passages are subsequently given in small type but without quotation marks.

8 In the manuscript: "is".– *Ed.*

9 In the manuscript one word cannot be deciphered. – *Ed.*

1C Karl Marx and Friedrich Engels from *The German Ideology*

Original publication details: Karl Marx, from *The German Ideology Parts I & III*, edited by R. Pascal. International Publishers, 1947, pp. 6–9, 13–15, 38–41. Reproduced with permission of International Publishers.

The premises from which we begin are not arbitrary ones, not dogmas, but real premises from which abstraction can only be made in the imagination. They are the real individuals, their activity and the material conditions under which they live, both those which they find already existing and those produced by their activity. These premises can thus be verified in a purely empirical way.

The first premise of all human history is, of course, the existence of living human individuals. Thus the first fact to be established is the physical organization of these individuals and their consequent relation to the rest of nature. Of course, we cannot here go either into the actual physical nature of man, or into the natural conditions in which man finds himself – geological, orohydrographical, climatic and so on. The writing of history must always set out from these natural bases and their modification in the course of history through the action of man.

Men can be distinguished from animals by consciousness, by religion or anything else you like. They themselves begin to distinguish themselves from animals as soon as they begin to *produce* their means of subsistence, a step which is conditioned by their physical organization. By producing their means of subsistence men are indirectly producing their actual material life.

The way in which men produce their means of subsistence depends first of all on the nature of the actual means they find in existence and have to reproduce. This mode of production must not be considered simply as being the reproduction of the physical existence of the individuals. Rather it is a definite form of activity of these individuals, a definite form of expressing their life, a definite *mode of life* on their part. As individuals express their life, so they are. What they are, therefore, coincides with their production, both with *what* they produce and with *how* they produce. The nature of individuals thus depends on the material conditions determining their production.

This production only makes its appearance with the increase of population. In its turn this presupposes the intercourse of individuals with one another. The form of this intercourse is again determined by production.

The relations of different nations among themselves depend upon the extent to which each has developed its productive forces, the division of labour and internal intercourse. This statement is generally recognized. But not only the relation of one nation to others, but also the whole internal structure of the nation itself depends on the stage of development reached by its production and its internal and external intercourse. How far the productive forces of a nation are developed is shown most manifestly by the degree to which the division of labour has been carried. Each new productive force, in so far as it is not merely a quantitative extension of productive forces already known, (for instance the bringing into cultivation of fresh land), brings about a further development of the division of labour.

The division of labour inside a nation leads at first to the separation of industrial and commercial from agricultural labour, and hence to the separation of town and country and a clash of interests between them. Its further development leads to the separation of commercial from industrial labour. At the same time through the division of labour there develop further, inside these various branches, various divisions among the individuals co-operating in definite kinds of labour. The relative position of these individual groups is determined by the methods employed in agriculture, industry and commerce (patriarchalism, slavery, estates, classes). These same conditions are to be seen (given a more developed intercourse) in the relations of different nations to one another.

The various stages of development in the division of labour are just so many different forms of ownership; i.e. the existing stage in the division of labour determines also the relations of individuals to one another with reference to the material, instrument, and product of labour.

[...]

The production of ideas, of conceptions, of consciousness, is at first directly interwoven with the material activity and the material intercourse of men, the language of real life. Conceiving, thinking, the mental intercourse of men, appear at this stage as the direct efflux of their material behaviour. The same applies to mental production as expressed in the language of the politics, laws, morality, religion, metaphysics of a people. Men are the producers of their conceptions, ideas, etc. – real, active men, as they are conditioned by a definite development of their productive forces and of the intercourse corresponding to these, up to its furthest forms. Consciousness can never be anything else than conscious existence, and the existence of men is their actual life-process. If in all ideology men and their circumstances appear upside down as in a *camera obscura,* this phenomenon arises just as much from their historical life-process as the inversion of objects on the retina does from their physical life-process.

In direct contrast to German philosophy which descends from heaven to earth, here we ascend from earth to heaven. That is to say, we do not set out from what men say, imagine, conceive, nor from men as narrated, thought of, imagined, conceived, in order to arrive at men in the flesh. We set out from real, active men, and on the basis of their real life-process we demonstrate the development of the ideological reflexes and echoes of this life-process. The phantoms formed in the human brain are also, necessarily, sublimates of their material life-process, which is empirically verifiable and bound to material premises. Morality, religion, metaphysics, all the rest of ideology and their corresponding forms of consciousness, thus no longer retain the semblance of independence. They have no history, no development; but men, developing their material production and their material intercourse, alter, along with this their real existence, their thinking and the products of their thinking. Life is not determined by consciousness but consciousness by life. In the first method of approach the starting-point is consciousness taken as the living individual; in the second it is the real living individuals themselves, as they are in actual life, and consciousness is considered solely as *their* consciousness.

This method of approach is not devoid of premises. It starts out from the real premises and does not abandon them for a moment. Its premises are men, not in any fantastic isolation or abstract definition, but in their actual, empirically perceptible process of development under definite conditions. As soon as this active life-process is described, history ceases to be a collection of dead facts as it is with the empiricists (themselves still abstract), or an imagined activity of imagined subjects, as with the idealists.

Where speculation ends – in real life – there real, positive science begins: the representation of the practical activity, of the practical process of development of men. Empty talk about consciousness ceases, and real knowledge has to take its place.

[…]

History is nothing but the succession of the separate generations, each of which exploits the materials, the forms of capital, the productive forces handed down to it by all preceding ones, and thus on the one hand continues the traditional activity in completely changed circumstances and, on the other, modifies the old circumstances with a completely changed activity. This can be speculatively distorted so that later history is made the goal of earlier history, e.g. the goal ascribed to the discovery of America is to further the eruption of the French Revolution. Thereby history receives its own special aims and becomes "a person ranking with other persons" (to wit: "self-consciousness, criticism, the Unique," etc.), while what is designated with the words "destiny," "goal," "germ," or "idea" of earlier history is nothing more than an abstraction formed from later history, from the active influence which earlier history exercises on later history. The further the separate spheres, which interact on one another, extend in the course of this development, the more the original isolation of the separate nationalities is destroyed by the developed mode of production and intercourse and the division of labour naturally brought forth by these, the more history becomes world-history. Thus, for instance, if in England a machine is invented, which in India or China deprives countless workers of bread, and overturns the whole form of existence of these empires, this invention becomes a world-historical fact. Or again, take the case of sugar and coffee which have proved their world-historical importance in the nineteenth century by the fact that the lack of these products, occasioned by the Napoleonic Continental system, caused the Germans to rise against Napoleon, and thus became the real basis of the glorious Wars of Liberation of 1813. From this it follows that this transformation of history into world-history is not indeed a mere abstract act on the part of the "self-consciousness," the world-spirit, or of any other metaphysical spectre, but a quite material, empirically verifiable act, an act the proof of which every individual furnishes as he comes and goes, eats, drinks and clothes himself.

The ideas of the ruling class are in every epoch the ruling ideas: i.e. the class, which is the ruling material force of society, is at the same time its ruling intellectual force. The class which has the means of material production at its disposal, has control at the same time over the means of mental production, so that thereby, generally speaking, the ideas of those who lack the means of mental production are subject to it. The ruling ideas are nothing more than the ideal expression of the dominant material relationships, the dominant material relationships grasped as ideas; hence of the relationships which make the one class the ruling one, therefore the ideas of its dominance. The individuals composing the ruling class possess among other things consciousness, and therefore think. In so far, therefore, as they rule as a class and determine the extent and compass of an epoch, it is self-evident that they do this in their whole range, hence among other things rule also as thinkers, as producers of ideas, and regulate the production and distribution of the ideas of their age: thus their ideas are the ruling ideas of the epoch. For instance, in an age and in a country where royal power, aristocracy and bourgeoisie are contending for mastery and where, therefore, mastery is shared, the doctrine of the separation of powers proves to be the dominant idea and is expressed as an "eternal law." The division of labour, which we saw above as one of the chief forces of history up till now, manifests itself also in the ruling class as the division of mental and material labour, so that inside this class one part appears as the thinkers of the class (its active, conceptive ideologists, who make the perfecting of the illusion of the class about itself their chief source of livelihood), while the others' attitude to these ideas and illusions is more passive and receptive, because they are in reality the active members of this class and have less time to make up illusions and ideas about themselves. Within this class this cleavage can even develop into a certain opposition and hostility between the two parts, which, however, in the case of a practical collision, in which the class itself is endangered, automatically comes to nothing, in which case there also vanishes the semblance that the ruling ideas were not the ideas of the ruling class and had a power distinct from the power of this class. The existence of revolutionary ideas in a particular period presupposes the existence of a revolutionary class; about the premises for the latter sufficient has already been said above.

If now in considering the course of history we detach the ideas of the ruling class from the ruling class itself and attribute to them an independent existence, if we confine ourselves to saying that these or those ideas were dominant, without bothering ourselves about the conditions of production and the producers of these ideas, if we then ignore the individuals and world conditions which are the source of the ideas, we can say, for instance, that during the time that the aristocracy was dominant, the concepts honour, loyalty, etc., were dominant, during the dominance of the bourgeoisie the concepts freedom, equality, etc. The ruling class itself on the whole imagines this to be so. This conception of history, which is common to all historians, particularly since the eighteenth century, will necessarily come up against the phenomenon that increasingly abstract ideas hold sway, i.e. ideas which increasingly take on the form of universality. For each new class which puts itself in the place of one ruling before it, is compelled, merely in order to carry through its aim, to represent its interest as the common interest of all the members of society, put in an ideal form; it will give its ideas the form of universality, and represent them as the only rational, universally valid ones.

CHAPTER TWO

EMILE DURKHEIM

CHAPTER MENU

Emile Durkheim, who was born in France in 1858 and died in 1917, provides sociologists with a clear blueprint of how to conduct systematic sociological analysis. If inequality and alienation are the concepts at the core of Karl Marx's theory of modern capitalism/industrial society, their approximate opposites – interdependence and integration – are the core concepts in Durkheim's analysis of modern society. A preoccupying question for Durkheim is: What holds society together – especially modern society which, unlike traditional society that is characterized largely by homogeneity or sameness (sameness of social backgrounds, experiences, values), is instead characterized by multiple points of fracture based on the differences among and between individuals, groups and institutions? Like Mark, Durkheim focused on the transformation wrought by modern industrialization and, in particular, on the specialized occupational division of labor that emerged with factory production, and the transition from a mostly rural, agricultural-based social structure to the density and impersonality of urban life (in *Division of Labour*, not included). Unlike Marx, however, Durkheim saw the structuring of the division of labor (whether of occupations; between rural and urban communities; or among various institutions such as the family, school, church, work) as functional to the organization of social relationships

Concise Reader in Sociological Theory: Theorists, Concepts, and Current Applications,
First Edition. Edited by Michele Dillon. Editorial material and organization
© 2021 John Wiley & Sons Ltd. Published 2021 by John Wiley & Sons Ltd.

and the crafting and maintenance of social cohesion. The interdependence that such specialization of function requires means that individuals (and diverse groups and institutions) have to engage in social interaction with others (not like them) and are necessarily reliant on and tied to these (specialized) others for their effective functioning and well-being. A plumber needs to work with a carpenter and a roofer if a house is to be built properly and not leak, that is, to be functional. Similarly, parliament makes laws but another specialized branch of government, the judiciary, oversees them to ensure that they are aligned with the constitution, and enforced. Each occupational specialization and each branch of government has its own function and it is only through working together (regardless of how they feel about this) – acting on their functional interdependence – can the value of the whole be realized. For Durkheim, these structures are functional to the everyday workings of society and, additionally, are functional to social integration or cohesion. This is especially significant in modern urban society, characterized as it is by an enormous amount of occupational, political, cultural, and ethnic diversity. What knits people together – integrates them into society – is not some shared family or social background (as would be typical in more traditional, largely rural communities) but the structure of interdependent relations and the organic ties they necessarily require and produce.

This cohesion is the social solidarity that, for Durkheim, is the outcome variable to be explained by sociological analysis; solidarity is dependent on several interrelated structural factors that variously impact the level of social integration in any given community at any given time. The first excerpt included here, *The Rules of Sociological Method*, encapsulates Durkheim's understanding of the constraining and thus the cohesion-imposing force of society on the individual. His opening sentences, about family roles, for example, or the kind of currency used for transactions cogently capture how society imposes itself as an objective and external reality to which we must adhere. The ways of acting, thinking, and feeling in a given community/society are social phenomena, or social facts, structured into society and external to and constraining of any and all individuals. These ways of being may seem natural and spontaneous to a given individual but they are inscribed into the collective conscience, and their socially constraining or controlling force is keenly felt especially when we step out of line. The job of the sociologist is to describe these ways of being – these externally imposing social facts or social phenomena – and, impartially, without assumptions, analyze and explain their consequences on other social facts/social phenomena. And if we follow Durkheim's rules as outlined in this excerpt, we will be doing precisely what all quantitative sociologists do today in their research studies, especially those who gather and use survey data – they define or operationalize a concept (e.g., social belonging), empirically assess or measure its prevalence in a given society/community/university campus, and examine its relation to other sociological variables (e.g., whether one is a member of an organized social group on campus, whether one is a first generation student, whether one seeks psychological or behavioral health counseling). This is what it means, as Durkheim advises, to treat social facts as things.

Durkheim himself modeled what is entailed in sociological analysis in his own quantitative study of *Suicide* (the second excerpt included here). Typical of the sociological paradigm, Durkheim defined suicide as a social or collective societal fact – not merely an outcome associated with an individual – and he examined how other social variables impact suicide rates. The variables informing his analysis – fully in line with his theoretical understanding of society as being external to the individual – focus on social structures and forms of social organization that mediate between the individual and the larger society and, as such, constrain or attach the individual to something beyond the self; in other words, the circumstances and factors that tie the individual to others and oblige consideration of their needs. As a sociological variable, suicide varies by social and organizational context. Settings and circumstances that foster a healthy amount of integration decrease the tendency toward suicide, while circumstances with little or indeed too much group integration increase its likelihood. As Durkheim documents, married people and those with children – because of the obligations, expectations and constraints imposed in such relationships – tend to have lower rates of suicide. And Catholics have a lower incidence of suicide than Protestants. This is not because of differences in religious beliefs about the afterlife, but due to the structural organization of Catholicism which is more hierarchical and communal and thus more constraining of individuals than is Protestantism. Any time a community is disrupted, and its norms and ways of acting, thinking and feeling are undermined as, for example, when there is economic upheaval, a tragedy, or a natural disaster, the resulting anomie unmoors individuals, and tendencies toward social disintegration loom more intensely, thus increasing suicide rates (or other indicators of stress/social disintegration). Yet, as the same time, social upheaval – a major tragedy, for example, or war, may have the effect of bringing people, including strangers, closer. This is because, as Durkheim argues, individuals are inherently social beings and in modern society, which not only is highly individualistic but which in fact requires and rewards individualism and a certain egoism, individuals still need to be connected with others, integrated with others into a community of solidarity.

Accordingly, any community or society needs to (and does) come together, to publicly assemble in ritualistic ways on a regular basis (see *The Elementary Forms of Religious Life*, not included). Collectively shared rituals function to reinforce and to regenerate the bonds that necessarily tie individuals into something larger than themselves. This is the thoroughly social function of funerals: the individuals present – the community - mourn the loss of a beloved family member or friend but also unify around and find comfort in their shared ties (however weakly they might overlap) to the deceased person and to the community at large; and this is what similarly happens at public memorials whether they emerge spontaneously in response to unexpected tragedies or they are elaborately planned for deceased presidents and other celebrities. Indeed, for Durkheim, ritual is at the core of social life; it's the basis of society, of collective life. And the core function of all rituals, including holiday celebrations such as Thanksgiving, Christmas, or Rosh Hashanah, and of sports events, is to bring people together, and in the collective assembling to reaffirm the interdependent ties that bind individuals, including strangers, to each other. Robert Bellah (1967), a Durkheimian sociologist, coined the term civil religion to capture the functional necessity of routine civic rituals and social assemblies as a way to unify individuals in a culturally pluralistic and diverse society. As he succinctly notes, in the "process of ritual interaction the members of the group, through their shared experience, feel a sense of membership, however fleeting, with a sense of boundary between those sharing the experience and all those outside it; they feel some sense of moral obligation to each other...", itself further charged by the moral force of the collective emotion propelling and derived from the interaction (Bellah 2003:32).

REFERENCES

Bellah, Robert. 1967. "Civil Religion in America." *Daedalus* 96: 1–21.

Bellah, Robert. 2003. "The Ritual Roots of Society and Culture," pp. 31–44 in Michele Dillon, ed. *Handbook of the Sociology of Religion*. New York: Cambridge University Press.

Durkheim, Emile. 1893/1984. *The Division of Labour in Society*. Introduction by Lewis Coser. Trans. W.D. Halls. New York: Free Press.

Durkheim, Emile. 1912/2001. *The Elementary Forms of Religious Life*. Trans. Carol Cosman. Oxford: Oxford University Press.

2A Emile Durkheim from *The Rules of Sociological Method*

Original publication details: Emile Durkheim, *The Rules of Sociological Method*, edited by Steven Lukes, translated by W.D. Halls, pp. 50–53, 59, 69–70, 72–76. Free Press, 1982. Reproduced with permission of Simon & Schuster.

What is a Social Fact?

When I perform my duties as a brother, a husband or a citizen and carry out the commitments l have entered into, I fulfil obligations which are defined in law and custom and which are external to myself and my actions. Even when they conform to my own sentiments and when I feel their reality within me, that reality does not cease to be objective, for it is not I who have prescribed these duties; I have received them through education. Moreover, how often does it happen that we are ignorant of the details of the obligations that we must assume, and that, to know them, we must consult the legal code and its authorised interpreters! Similarly the believer has discovered from birth, ready fashioned, the beliefs and practices of his religious life; if they existed before he did, it follows that they exist outside him. The system of signs that I employ to express my thoughts, the monetary system I use to pay my debts, the credit instruments I utilise in my commercial relationships, the practices I follow in my profession, etc., all function independently of the use I make of them. Considering in turn each member of society, the foregoing remarks can be repeated for each single one of them. Thus there are ways of acting, thinking and feeling which possess the remarkable property of existing outside the consciousness of the individual.

Not only are these types of behaviour and thinking external to the individual, but they are endued with a compelling and coercive power by virtue of which, whether he wishes it or not, they impose themselves upon him. Undoubtedly when I conform to them of my own free will, this coercion is not felt or felt hardly at all, since it is unnecessary. None the less it is intrinsically a characteristic of these facts; the proof of this is that it asserts itself as soon as I try to resist. If I attempt to violate the rules of law they react against me so as to forestall my action, if there is still time. Alternatively, they annul it or make my action conform to the norm if it is already accomplished but capable of being reversed; or they cause me to pay the penalty for it if it is irreparable. If purely moral rules are at stake, the public conscience restricts any act which infringes them by the surveillance it exercises over the conduct of citizens and by the special punishments it has at its disposal. In other cases the constraint is less violent; nevertheless, it does not cease to exist. If I do not conform to ordinary conventions, if in my mode of dress I pay no heed to what is customary in my country and in my social class, the laughter I provoke, the social distance at which I am kept, produce, although in a more mitigated form, the same results as any real penalty. In other cases, although it may be indirect, constraint is no less effective. I am not forced to speak French with my compatriots, nor to use the legal currency, but it is impossible for me to do otherwise. If I tried to escape the necessity, my attempt would fail miserably. As an industrialist nothing prevents me from working with the processes and methods of the previous century, but if I do I will most certainly ruin myself. Even when in fact I can struggle free from these rules and successfully break them, it is never without being forced to fight against them. Even if in the end they are overcome, they make their constraining power sufficiently felt in the resistance that they afford. There is no innovator, even a fortunate one, whose ventures do not encounter opposition of this kind.

Here, then, is a category of facts which present very special characteristics: they consist of manners of acting, thinking and feeling external to the individual, which are invested with a coercive power by virtue of which they exercise control over him. Consequently, since they consist of representations and actions, they cannot be confused with organic phenomena, nor with psychical phenomena, which have no existence save in and through the individual consciousness. Thus they constitute a new species and to them must be exclusively assigned the term *social*. It is appropriate, since it is clear that, not having the individual as their substratum, they can have none other than society, either political society in its entirety or one of the partial groups that it includes – religious denominations, political and literary schools, occupational corporations, etc. Moreover, it is for such as these alone that the term is fitting, for the word 'social' has the sole meaning of designating those phenomena which fall into none of the categories of facts already constituted and labelled. They are consequently the proper field of sociology. It is true that this word 'constraint', in terms of which we define them, is in danger of infuriating those who zealously uphold out-and-out individualism. Since they maintain that the individual is completely autonomous, it seems to them that he is diminished every time he is made aware that he is not dependent on himself alone. Yet since it is indisputable today that most of our ideas and tendencies are not developed by ourselves, but come to us from outside, they can only penetrate us by imposing themselves upon us. This is all that our definition implies. Moreover, we know that all social constraints do not necessarily exclude the individual personality.[1]

Yet since the examples just cited (legal and moral rules, religious dogmas, financial systems, etc.) consist wholly of beliefs and practices already well established, in view of what has been said it might be maintained that no social fact can exist except where there is a well defined social organisation. But there are other facts which do not present themselves in this already crystallised form but which also possess the same objectivity and ascendancy over the individual. These are what are called social 'currents'. Thus in a public gathering the great waves of enthusiasm, indignation and pity that are produced have their seat in no one individual consciousness. They come to each one of us from outside and can sweep us along in spite of ourselves. If perhaps I abandon myself to them I may not be conscious of the pressure that they are exerting upon me, but that pressure makes its presence felt immediately I attempt to struggle against them. If an individual tries to pit himself against one of these collective manifestations, the sentiments that he is rejecting will be turned against him. Now if this external coercive power asserts itself so acutely in cases of resistance, it must be because it exists in the other instances cited above without our being conscious of it. Hence we are the victims of an illusion which leads us to believe we have ourselves produced what has been imposed upon us externally. But if the willingness with which we let ourselves be carried along disguises the pressure we have undergone, it does not eradicate it. Thus air does not cease to have weight, although we no longer feel that weight. Even when we have individually and spontaneously shared in the common emotion, the impression we have experienced is utterly different from what we would have felt if we had been alone. Once the assembly has broken up and these social influences have ceased to act upon us, and we are once more on our own, the emotions we have felt seem an alien phenomenon, one in which we no longer recognise ourselves. It is then we perceive that we have undergone the emotions much more than generated them.

[. . .]

Our definition will therefore subsume all that has to be defined it if states:

A social fact is any way of acting, whether fixed or not, capable of exerting over the individual an external constraint;

or:

which is general over the whole of a given society whilst having an existence of its own, independent of its individual manifestations.[2]

[. . .]

Yet social phenomena are things and should be treated as such. To demonstrate this proposition one does not need to philosophise about their nature or to discuss the analogies they present with phenomena of a lower order of existence. Suffice to say that they are the sole *datum* afforded the sociologist. A thing is in effect all that is given, all that is offered, or rather forces itself upon our observation. To treat phenomena as things is to treat them as *data*, and this constitutes the starting point for science. Social phenomena unquestionably display this characteristic. What is given is not the idea that men conceive of value, because that is unattainable; rather is it the values actually exchanged in economic transactions. It is also not some conception or other of the moral ideal; it is the sum total of rules that in effect determine behaviour. It is not the idea of utility or wealth; it is all the details of economic organisation. Social life may possibly be merely the development of certain notions, but even if this is assumed to be the case, these notions are not revealed to us immediately. They cannot therefore be attained directly, but only through the real phenomena that express them. We do not know a *priori* what ideas give rise to the various currents into which social life divides, nor whether they exist. It is only after we have traced the currents back to their source that we will know from where they spring.

Social phenomena must therefore be considered in themselves, detached from the conscious beings who form their own mental representations of them. They must be studied from the outside, as external things, because it is in this guise that they present themselves to us. If this quality of externality proves to be only apparent, the illusion will be dissipated as the science progresses and we will see, so to speak, the external merge with the internal. But the outcome cannot be anticipated, and even if in the end social phenomena may not have all the features intrinsic to things, they must at first be dealt with as if they had. This rule is therefore applicable to the whole of social reality and there is no reason for any exceptions to be made. Even those phenomena which give the greatest appearance of being artificial in their arrangement should be considered from this viewpoint. *The conventional character of a practice or an institution should never be assumed in advance.* If, moreover, we are allowed to invoke personal experience, we believe we can state with confidence that by following this procedure one will often have the satisfaction of seeing the apparently most arbitrary facts, after more attentive observation, display features of constancy and regularity symptomatic of their objectivity.

II

But our predecessors' experience has shown us that, in order to realise in practice the truth just established, it is not enough to demonstrate it theoretically or even to absorb it oneself. The mind has such a natural disposition to fail to recognise it that inevitably we will relapse into past errors unless we submit ourselves to a rigorous discipline. We shall formulate the principal rules for this discipline, all of which are corollaries of the previous rule.

(1) The first of these corollaries is: *One must systematically discard all preconceptions*. Special proof of this rule is unnecessary: it follows from all that we have stated above. Moreover, it is the basis of all scientific method. Descartes' method of doubt is in essence only an application of it. If at the very moment of the foundation of science Descartes prescribed a rule for himself to question all the ideas he had previously accepted, it is because he wished to use only concepts which had been scientifically worked out, that is, constructed according to the method that he devised. All those of another origin had therefore to be rejected, at least for the time being. We have seen that Bacon's theory of the idols has the same significance. The two great doctrines, so often placed in contradiction to each other, agree on this essential point. Thus the sociologist, either when he decides upon the object of his research or in the course of his investigations, must resolutely deny himself the use of those concepts formed outside science and for needs entirely unscientific. He must free himself from those fallacious notions which hold sway over the mind of the ordinary person, shaking off,

once and for all, the yoke of those empirical categories that long habit often makes tyrannical. If necessity sometimes forces him to resort to them, let him at least do so in full cognisance of the little value they possess, so as not to assign to them in the investigation a role which they are unfit to play.

What makes emancipation from such notions peculiarly difficult in sociology is that sentiment so often intervenes. We enthuse over our political and religious beliefs and moral practices very differently from the way we do over the objects of the physical world. Consequently this emotional quality is transmitted to the way in which we conceive and explain our beliefs. The ideas that we form about them are deeply felt, just as are their purposes, thereby taking on such authority that they brook no contradiction. Any opinion which is embarrassing is treated as hostile. For example, a proposition may not accord with our view of patriotism or personal dignity. If is therefore denied, whatever may be the proofs advanced. We cannot allow it to be true. It is rejected, and our strong emotions, seeking a justification for so doing, have no difficulty in suggesting reasons which we find readily conclusive. These notions may even be so prestigious that they will not tolerate scientific examination. The mere fact of subjecting them, as well as the phenomena they express, to cold, dry analysis is repugnant to certain minds. The sociologist who undertakes to study morality objectively as an external reality seems to such sensitive souls bereft of moral sense, just as the vivisectionist seems to the ordinary person devoid of normal feelings. Far from admitting that these sentiments are subject to science, it is believed that it is to them one should address on[e]self in order to construct the science of things to which they relate. 'Woe', writes an eloquent historian of religions, 'Woe to the scientist who approaches the things of God without having in the depths of his consciousness, in the innermost indestructible parts of his being, in which sleep the souls of his ancestors, an unknown sanctuary from which at times there arises the fragrance of incense, a verse of a psalm, a cry of sorrow or triumph that as a child, following his brothers' example, he raised to heaven, and which suddenly joins him once again in communion with the prophets of yore!'[3]

One cannot protest too strongly against this mystical doctrine which – like all mysticism, moreover – is in essence only a disguised empiricism, the negation of all science. Feelings relating to social things enjoy no pride of place over other sentiments, for they have no different origin. They too have been shaped through history. They are a product of human experience, albeit one confused and unorganised. They are not due to some transcendental precognition of reality, but are the result of all kinds of disordered impressions and emotions accumulated through chance circumstance, lacking systematic interpretation. Far from bringing enlightenment of a higher order than the rational, they are composed exclusively of states of mind which, it is true, are strong but also confused. To grant them such a predominant role is to ascribe to the lower faculties of the intelligence supremacy over superior ones and to condemn oneself more or less to a rhetorical logomachy. A science constituted in this way can only satisfy those minds who prefer to think with their sensibility rather than their understanding, who prefer the immediate and confused syntheses of sensation to the patient, illuminating analyses of the reason. Feeling is an object for scientific study, not the criterion of scientific truth. But there is no science which at its beginnings has not encountered similar resistances. There was a time when those feelings relating to the things of the physical world, since they also possessed a religious or moral character, opposed no less violently the establishment of the physical sciences. Thus one can believe that, rooted out from one science after another, this prejudice will finally disappear from sociology as well, its last refuge, and leave the field clear for the scientist.

(2) But the above rule is entirely negative. It teaches the sociologist to escape from the dominance of commonly held notions and to direct his attention to the facts, but does not state how he is to grasp the facts in order to study them objectively.

Every scientific investigation concerns a specific group of phenomena which are subsumed under the same definition. The sociologist's first step must therefore be to define the things he treats, so that we may know – he as well – exactly what his subject matter is. This is the prime and absolutely indispensable condition of any proof or verification. A theory can only be checked if we know how to recognise the facts for which it must account. Moreover, since this initial definition determines the subject matter itself of the science, that subject matter will either consist of a thing or not, according to how this definition is formulated.

To be objective the definition clearly must express the phenomena as a function, not of an idea of the mind, but of their inherent properties. It must characterise them according to some integrating element in their nature and not according to whether they conform to some more or less ideal notion. When research is only just beginning and the facts have not yet been submitted to any analysis, their sole ascertainable characteristics are those sufficiently external to be immediately apparent. Those less apparent are doubtless more essential. Their explanatory value is greater, but they remain unknown at this stage of scientific knowledge and cannot be visualised save by substituting for reality some conception of the mind. Thus it is among the first group of visible characteristics that must be sought the elements for this basic definition. Yet it is clear that the definition will have to include, without exception or distinction, all the phenomena which equally manifest these same characteristics, for we have no reason nor the means to discriminate between them. These properties, then, are all that we know of reality. Consequently they must determine absolutely how the facts should be classified. We possess no other criterion which can even partially invalidate the effect of this rule. Hence the following rule: *The subject matter of research must only include a group of phenomena defined beforehand by certain common external characteristics and all phenomena which correspond to this definition must be so included.* For example, we observe that certain actions exist which all possess the one external characteristic that, once they have taken place, they provoke on the part of society that special reaction known as punishment. We constitute them as a group *sui generis* and classify them under a single heading: any action that is punished is termed a crime and we make crime, so defined, the subject matter of a special science of criminology. Likewise we observe within all known societies the existence of a smaller society outwardly recognisable because it is formed for the most part of individuals linked by a blood relationship and joined to each other by legal ties. From the relevant facts we constitute a special group to which we assign a distinctive name: phenomena of domestic life. We term every aggregate of this kind a family and make the family, so defined, the subject matter of a specific investigation which has not yet received a special designation in sociological terminology. When we later pass on from the family in general to the different types of family, the same rule should be applied. For example, embarking upon a study of the clan, or the maternal or patriarchal family, we should begin by defining them according to the same method. The subject matter of each topic, whether general or specialised, should be constituted according to the same principle.

By proceeding in this way from the outset the sociologist is immediately grounded firmly in reality. Indeed, how the facts are classified does not depend on him, or on his own particular cast of mind, but on the nature of things. The criterion which determines whether they are to be grouped in a particular category can be demonstrated and generally accepted by everybody, and the observer's statements can be verified by others. It is true that a notion built up in this way does not always chime – or does not generally even chime at all – with the notion commonly held. For example, it is evident that acts relating to freedom of thought or lapses in etiquette which are so regularly and severely punished in many societies, from the viewpoint of common sense are not regarded as crimes when people consider those societies. In the same way a clan is not a family in the usual sense of the word. But this is of no consequence, for it is not simply a question of how we can discover with a fair degree of accuracy the facts to which the words of common parlance refer and the ideas that they convey. What has to be done is to form fresh concepts *de novo*, ones appropriate to the needs of science and expressed by the use of a special terminology. It is certainly not true that the commonly held concept is useless to the scientist. It serves as a benchmark, indicating to him that somewhere there exists a cluster of phenomena bearing the same name and which consequently are likely to possess common characteristics. Moreover, since the common concept is never without some relationship to the phenomena, it occasionally points to the approximate direction in which they are to be discovered. But as the concept is only crudely formulated, it is quite natural for it not to coincide exactly with the scientific concept which it has been instrumental in instituting.[4]

NOTES

1   Moreover, this is not to say that all constraint is normal. . . .
2   This close affinity of life and structure, organ and function, can be readily established in sociology because there exists between these two extremes a whole series of intermediate stages, immediately observable, which reveal the link between them. Biology lacks this methodological resource. But one may believe legitimately that sociological inductions on this subject are applicable to biology and that, in organisms as in societies, between these two categories of facts only differences in degree exist.
3   J. Darmester, *Les Prophètes d'Israël* (Paris, 1982). p9.
4   It is in practice always the common concept and the common term which are the point of departure. Among the things that in a confused fashion this term denotes, we seek to discover whether any exist which present common external characteristics. If there are any, and if the concept formed by grouping the facts brought together in this way coincides, if not entirely (which is rare) but at least for the most part, with the common concept, it will be possible to continue to designate the former by the same common term, retaining in the science the expression used in everyday parlance. But if the difference is too considerable, if the common notion mixes up a number of different notions, the creation of new and special terms become a necessity.

2B Emile Durkheim from *Suicide: A Study in Sociology*

Original publication details: Emile Durkheim, *Suicide: A Study in Sociology*, translated by John A. Spaulding and George Simpson, pp. 208–213, 252–254. New York: Free Press, 1951. Reproduced with permission of Simon & Schuster.

We have thus successively set up the three following propositions:

> *Suicide varies inversely with the degree of integration of religious society.*
> *Suicide varies inversely with the degree of integration of domestic society.*
> *Suicide varies inversely with the degree of integration of political society.*

This grouping shows that whereas these different societies have a moderating influence upon suicide, this is due not to special characteristics of each but to a characteristic common to all. Religion does not owe its efficacy to the special nature of religious sentiments, since domestic and political societies both produce the same effects when strongly integrated. This, moreover, we have already proved when studying directly the manner of action of different religions upon suicide. Inversely, it is not the specific nature of the domestic or political tie which can explain the immunity they confer, since religious society has the same advantage. The cause can only be found in a single quality possessed by all these social groups, though perhaps to varying degrees. The only quality satisfying this condition is that they are all strongly integrated social groups. So we reach the general conclusion: suicide varies inversely with the degree of integration of the social groups of which the individual forms a part.

But society cannot disintegrate without the individual simultaneously detaching himself from social life, without his own goals becoming preponderant over those of the community, in a word without his personality tending to surmount the collective personality. The more weakened the groups to which he belongs, the less he depends on them, the more he consequently depends only on himself and recognizes no other rules of conduct than what are founded on his private interests. If we agree to call this state egoism, in which the individual ego asserts itself to excess in the face of the social ego and at its expense, we may call egoistic the special type of suicide springing from excessive individualism.

But how can suicide have such an origin?

First of all, it can be said that, as collective force is one of the obstacles best calculated to restrain suicide, its weakening involves a development of suicide. When society is strongly integrated, it holds individuals under its control, considers them at its service and thus forbids them to dispose wilfully of themselves. Accordingly it opposes their evading their duties to it through death. But how could society impose its supremacy upon them when they refuse to accept this subordination as legitimate? It no longer then possesses the requisite authority to retain them in their duty if they wish to desert; and conscious of its own weakness, it even recognizes their right to do freely what it can no longer prevent. So far as they are the admitted masters of their destinies, it is their privilege to end their lives. They, on their part, have no reason to endure life's sufferings patiently. For they cling to life more resolutely when belonging to a group they love, so as not to betray interests they put before their own. The bond that unites them with the common cause attaches them to life and the lofty goal they envisage prevents their feeling personal troubles so deeply. There is, in short, in a cohesive and animated society a constant interchange of ideas and feelings from all to each and each to all, something like a mutual moral support, which instead of throwing the individual on his own resources, leads him to share in the collective energy and supports his own when exhausted.

But these reasons are purely secondary. Excessive individualism not only results in favoring the action of suicidogenic causes, but it is itself such a cause. It not only frees man's inclination to do away with himself from a protective obstacle, but creates this inclination out of whole cloth and thus gives birth to a special suicide which bears its mark. This must be clearly understood for this is what constitutes the special character of the type of suicide just distinguished and justifies the name we have given it. What is there then in individualism that explains this result?

It has been sometimes said that because of his psychological constitution, man cannot live without attachment to some object which transcends and survives him, and that the reason for this necessity is a need we must have not to perish entirely. Life is said to be intolerable unless some reason for existing is involved, some purpose justifying life's trials. The individual alone is not a sufficient end for his activity. He is too little. He is not only hemmed in spatially; he is also strictly limited temporally. When, therefore, we have no other object than ourselves we cannot avoid the thought that our efforts will finally end in nothingness, since we ourselves disappear. But annihilation terrifies us. Under these conditions one would lose courage to live, that is, to act and struggle, since nothing will remain of our exertions. The state of egoism, in other words, is supposed to be contradictory to human nature and, consequently, too uncertain to have chances of permanence.

In this absolute formulation the proposition is vulnerable. If the thought of the end of our personality were really so hateful, we could consent to live only by blinding ourselves voluntarily as to life's value. For if we may in a measure avoid the prospect of annihilation we cannot extirpate it; it is inevitable, whatever we do. We may push back the frontier for some generations, force our name to endure for some years or centuries longer than our body; a moment, too soon for most men, always comes when it will be nothing. For the groups we join in order to prolong our existence by their means are themselves mortal; they too must dissolve, carrying with them all our deposit of ourselves. Those are few whose memories are closely enough bound to the very history of humanity to be assured of living until its death. So, if we really thus thirsted after immortality, no such brief perspectives could ever appease us. Besides, what of us is it that lives? A word, a sound, an imperceptible trace, most often anonymous,[1] therefore nothing comparable to the violence of our efforts or able to justify them to us. In actuality, though a child is naturally an egoist who feels not the slightest craving to survive himself, and the old man is very often a child in this and so many other respects, neither ceases to cling to life as much or more than the adult; indeed we have seen that suicide is very rare for the first fifteen years and tends to decrease at the other extreme of life. Such too is the case with animals, whose psychological constitution differs from that of men only in degree. It is therefore untrue that life is only possible by its possessing its rationale outside of itself.

Indeed, a whole range of functions concern only the individual; these are the ones indispensable for physical life. Since they are made for this purpose only, they are perfected by its attainment. In everything concerning them, therefore, man can act reasonably without thought of transcendental purposes. These functions serve by merely serving him. In so far as he has no other needs, he is therefore self-sufficient and can live happily with no other objective than living. This is not the case, however, with the civilized adult. He has many ideas, feelings and practices unrelated to organic needs. The roles of art, morality, religion, political faith, science itself are not to repair organic exhaustion nor to provide sound functioning of the organs. All this supra-physical life is built and expanded not because of the demands of the cosmic environment but because of the demands of the social environment. The influence of society is what has aroused in us the sentiments of sympathy and solidarity drawing us toward others; it is society which, fashioning us in its image, fills us with religious, political and moral beliefs that control our actions. To play our social role we have striven to extend our intelligence and it is still society that has supplied us with tools for this development by transmitting to us its trust fund of knowledge.

Through the very fact that these superior forms of human activity have a collective origin, they have a collective purpose. As they derive from society they have reference to it; rather they are society itself incarnated and individualized in each one of us. But for them to have a raison d'etre in our eyes, the purpose they envisage must be one not indifferent to us. We can cling to these forms of human activity only to the degree that we cling to society itself. Contrariwise, in the same measure as we feel detached from society we become detached from that life whose source and aim is society. For what purpose do these rules of morality, these precepts of law binding us to all sorts of sacrifices, these restrictive dogmas exist, if there is no being outside us whom they serve and in whom we participate? What is the purpose of science itself? If its only use is to increase our chances for survival, it does not deserve the trouble it entails. Instinct acquits itself better of this role; animals prove this. Why substitute for it a more hesitant and uncertain reflection? What is the end of suffering, above all? If the value of things can only be estimated by their relation to this positive evil for the individual, it is without reward and incomprehensible. This problem does not exist for the believer firm in his faith or the man strongly bound by ties of domestic or political society. Instinctively and unreflectively they ascribe all that they are and do, the one to his Church or his God, the living symbol of the Church, the other to his family, the third to his country or party. Even in their sufferings they see only a means of glorifying the group to which they belong and thus do homage to it. So, the Christian ultimately desires and seeks suffering to testify more fully to his contempt for the flesh and more fully resemble his divine model. But the more the believer doubts, that is, the less he feels himself a real participant in the religious faith to which he belongs, and from which he is freeing himself; the more the family and community become foreign to the individual, so much the more does he become a mystery to himself, unable to escape the exasperating and agonizing question: to what purpose?

If, in other words, as has often been said, man is double, that is because social man superimposes himself upon physical man. Social man necessarily presupposes a society which he expresses and serves. If this dissolves, if we no longer feel it in existence and action about and above us, whatever is social in us is deprived of all objective foundation. All that remains is an artificial combination of illusory images, a phantasmagoria vanishing at the least reflection; that is, nothing which can be a goal for our action.

[...]

In normal conditions the collective order is regarded as just by the great majority of persons. Therefore, when we say that an authority is necessary to impose this order on individuals, we certainly do not mean that violence is the only means of establishing it. Since this regulation is meant to restrain individual passions, it must come from a power which dominates individuals; but this power must also be obeyed through respect, not fear.

It is not true, then, that human activity can be released from all restraint. Nothing in the world can enjoy such a privilege. All existence being a part of the universe is relative to the remainder; its nature and method of manifestation accordingly depend not only on itself but on other beings, who consequently restrain and regulate it. Here there are only differences of degree and form between the mineral realm and the thinking person. Man's characteristic privilege is that the bond he accepts is not physical but moral; that is, social. He is governed not by a material environment brutally imposed on him, but by a conscience superior to his own, the superiority of which he feels. Because the greater, better part of his existence transcends the body, he escapes the body's yoke, but is subject to that of society.

But when society is disturbed by some painful crisis or by beneficent but abrupt transitions, it is momentarily incapable of exercising this influence; thence come the sudden rises in the curve of suicides which we have pointed out above.

In the case of economic disasters, indeed, something like a declassification occurs which suddenly casts certain individuals into a lower state than their previous one. Then they must reduce their requirements, restrain their needs, learn greater self-control. All the advantages of social influence are lost so far as they are concerned; their moral education has to be recommenced. But society cannot adjust them instantaneously to this new life and teach them to practice the increased self-repression to which they are unaccustomed. So they are not adjusted to the condition forced on them, and its very prospect is intolerable; hence the suffering which detaches them from a reduced existence even before they have made trial of it.

It is the same if the source of the crisis is an abrupt growth of power and wealth. Then, truly, as the conditions of life are changed, the standard according to which needs were regulated can no longer remain the same; for it varies with social resources, since it largely determines the share of each class of producers. The scale is upset; but a new scale cannot be immediately improvised. Time is required for the public conscience to reclassify men and things. So long as the social forces thus freed have not regained equilibrium, their respective values are unknown and so all regulation is lacking for a time. The limits are unknown between the possible and the impossible, what is just and what is unjust, legitimate claims and hopes and those which are immoderate. Consequently, there is no restraint upon aspirations. If the disturbance is profound, it affects even the principles controlling the distribution of men among various occupations. Since the relations between various parts of society are necessarily modified, the ideas expressing these relations must change. Some particular class especially favored by the crisis is no longer resigned to its former lot, and, on the other hand, the example of its greater good fortune arouses all sorts of jealousy below and about it. Appetites, not being controlled by a public opinion become disoriented, no longer recognize the limits proper to them. Besides, they are at the same time seized by a sort of natural erethism simply by the greater intensity of public life. With increased prosperity desires increase. At the very moment when traditional rules have lost their authority, the richer prize offered these appetites stimulates them and makes them more exigent and impatient of control. The state of de-regulation or anomy is thus further heightened by passions being less disciplined, precisely when they need more disciplining.

But then their very demands make fulfillment impossible. Over-weening ambition always exceeds the results obtained, great as they may be, since there is no warning to pause here. Nothing gives satisfaction and all this agitation is uninterruptedly maintained without appeasement. Above all, since this race for an unattainable goal can give no other pleasure but that of the race itself, if it is one, once it is interrupted the participants are left empty-handed. At the same time the struggle grows more violent and painful, both from being less controlled and because competition is greater. All classes contend among themselves because no established classification any longer exists. Effort grows, just when it becomes less productive. How could the desire to live not be weakened under such conditions?

This explanation is confirmed by the remarkable immunity of poor countries. Poverty protects against suicide because it is a restraint in itself. No matter how one acts, desires have to depend upon resources to some extent; actual possessions are partly the criterion of those aspired to. So the less one has the less he is tempted to extend the range of his needs indefinitely. Lack of power, compelling moderation, accustoms men to it, while nothing excites envy if no one has superfluity. Wealth, on the other hand, by the power it bestows, deceives us into believing that we depend on ourselves only. Reducing the resistance we encounter from objects, it suggests the possibility of unlimited success against them. The less limited one feels, the more intolerable all limitation appears. Not without reason, therefore, have so many religions dwelt on the advantages and moral value of poverty. It is actually the best school for teaching self-restraint. Forcing us to constant self-discipline, it prepares us to accept collective discipline with equanimity, while wealth, exalting the individual, may always arouse the spirit of rebellion which is the very source of immorality. This, of course, is no reason why humanity should not improve its material condition. But though the moral danger involved in every growth of prosperity is not irremediable, it should not be forgotten.

NOTE

1 We say nothing of the ideal protraction of life involved in the belief in immortality of the soul, for (1) this cannot explain why the family or attachment to political society preserves us from suicide; and (2) it is not even this belief which forms religion's prophylactic influence, as we have shown above.

CHAPTER THREE

MAX WEBER

CHAPTER MENU

While one can consider Karl Marx as among the most the impactful public thinkers of the modern era, and of Emilie Durkheim as the founding father of quantitative sociology, it is **Max Weber** who is perhaps the most influential in informing *what* sociologists study, even as *how* they study various questions and topics may draw equally on either (or both) Durkheim's and Weber's methodology. A German, Weber lived from 1864 to 1920 and thus, like Marx and Durkheim, grappled with the economic, social and political transformation of the western world during the era of progressive industrialization and its associated impact on all aspects of everyday life and on all institutional sectors.

Concise Reader in Sociological Theory: Theorists, Concepts, and Current Applications,
First Edition. Edited by Michele Dillon. Editorial material and organization
© 2021 John Wiley & Sons Ltd. Published 2021 by John Wiley & Sons Ltd.

Weber's most famous work, *The Protestant Ethic and the Spirit of Capitalism* (published in 1904/05; excerpt *3a*) is a highly innovative cultural and historical analysis of modernity and its hallmark ethos: individualism. Unlike Marx who saw economic (capitalist, profit-accumulation) logic at the root of and driving force of all things in society (including non-economic relationships and decisions), Weber examined how non-economic ideas, specifically Calvinist religious beliefs, unintentionally fostered an ethos that accelerated the expansion of capitalism and more generally, the individualism and the cold rationality that informs economic life and increasingly with modernity, all aspects of society (see excerpt *3a*). Weber illuminates how ideas and assumptions (not just, as for Marx, material circumstances) are engines of behavior or social action. He elaborates how the Calvinist belief in predestination, and the belief that the individual stands alone in their relation to an almighty and powerful God (and thus unlike Catholics are devoid of mediating institutions intervening on their behalf before God), led Calvinists to adopt certain everyday habits and practices such as a highly disciplined work-ethic, self-control, and the avoidance of emotion and pleasure, whose consequences led to results (productivity, monetary investment, savings) that contributed significantly to the acceleration of capitalist development.

Exemplified by Weber's own investigation of the relation between Calvinist belief and economic growth, the role of the sociologist is to uncover, trace, and explain the motivating forces driving individual, institutional, and societal action, and the consequences of those actions. Following Weber's definition of sociology (see excerpt *3b Economy and Society*), by paying close attention to understanding the subjective meanings in and behind why social actors behave as they do, the sociologist is equipped to shed light on all behavior, including behavior that may on the surface seem rather puzzling. All behavior, for Weber, has meanings and contextual motivations that can be identified and understood through systematic, empathic investigation. It is important here to note that while Weber takes an interpretive approach to understanding subjective meaning, and interpretive analysis is invariably more contextual and nuanced than the quantitative or statistical approach advocated by Durkheim (as in "Treat social facts as things…as things external to the individual"; see excerpt *2a The Rules of Sociological Method*), he was also emphatic that the sociologist – as any scientist – must adhere to principles of objectivity (see *Science as a vocation* in excerpt *3c*). Thus the Weberian sociologist studies all manner of social action and all social behavior that is culturally salient and, in doing so as an objective scientific analyst, does not necessarily agree or disagree with, or advocate for or against, the behavior they are studying and seeking to understand and explain. Similarly in line with Weber's understanding of analytical objectivity, he elaborated that "politics is out of place in the lecture-room" (see *Science as a vocation* in excerpt *3c*). In short, the sociologist's task is to add clarity to the analytical understanding of society and how and why its various structures, institutions and groups behave as they do and with what consequences.

The sociologist is greatly helped in their task of understanding the complexity of social life by Weber's use of typologies or categorizations of social action. As a conceptual-methodological tool, Weber draws on what he calls ideal types – categorical schemas that help anchor the sociologist's description of the empirical social behavior observed even as those named types or categories may not be as pure (or as idealistic) as the actual empirical reality they help to capture. A great deal of Weber's theoretical analysis uses typologies to help illuminate the differentiated, multistranded and multidimensional nature of the many social phenomena he analyzes. Most basically, his typology of social action (see excerpt *3b Economy and Society*) cogently encompasses the wide-ranging breadth of social behavior, differentiated by the critically important distinction between rational and non-rational motivating forces; and within the former, an equally important distinction between instrumental rational and value rational action. Similarly, the category of non-rational behavior encompasses further differentiation – that between the driving force of emotion, and the hold of tradition on decisions and actions.

Rationality is a key concept for Weber because as his analysis of the *Protestant Ethic* revealed, rationality is the principle par excellence of Enlightenment and modernity. The rationality of the intellect – scientific or empirical reasoning, for example, and its assumed, evidence-based superiority over the hold of non-rational customs and empirically unverifiable beliefs (e.g. religious beliefs, superstitions, political dogmas), is the hallmark of humanity and of human-societal progress. Similarly, principles of rationality are institutionalized in modern forms of social and political organization, most notably bureaucracy. Weber's essay on bureaucracy (see *Bureaucracy* in excerpt *3c*) is a clear explication of the operationalization of rational principles in structuring organizational practices; and how such practices are based on the differentiation of roles and authority and qualifications, and whose rational hierarchical organization is expected to lead to efficient and methodical social interaction and resolutions/outcomes. In modern society, the authority of rationality is such that it is formal educational credentials (merit/meritocracy) rather than age-seniority or family connections or ethnic tribalism that has greater sway in determining social action and social outcomes. In an analytical or ideal typical sense, and empirically too, this is largely true even as we frequently may witness the triumph of family connections or ethnic loyalties over individual qualifications/merit in who is rewarded with a coveted job.

While rational principles underlie much of the authority structure of modern society, we should not be surprised – given Weber's emphasis on differentiation, such as is evident in his typology of social action (see excerpt *3b Economy and Society*) – that authority itself – who has it, what forms it takes, and how and why power or control is exercised – is also highly differentiated. Indeed, notwithstanding the fact that rational principles inform the hierarchical organizational structure of a great deal of small and large organizations in contemporary society (universities, the military, local and national government, symphonies, sports teams, banks, media corporations, etc.), authority in organizations and in society at large can also be derived from non-rational sources such as tradition (e.g. the authority of the monarchy in the U.K.). Moreover, as Weber's essay on charisma illustrates (see *The sociology of charismatic authority* in excerpt *3c*) (non-rational) emotional authority also matters as demonstrated by the highly effective impact of a charismatic leader in persuading individuals, groups and organizations to follow a certain path (whether political, economic, cultural, or religious).

More generally, the structure of power in society is highly stratified. All political structures, including the nation and its multiple governing bureaucratic organizational parts, are highly differentiated entities. As Weber elaborates (see excerpt *3c Structures of power*), a nation's prestige and its attitude toward other nations, and how any given nation uses its differentiated military, economic and cultural power varies depending on a host of geo-political factors. And within the nation, who has power and to what extent different groups and political parties use power also varies, as do the sources of national solidarity. Weber's analysis of stratification within a given society or community is also built on attentiveness to the multiple or differentiated sources of status that have authority (see *Class, Status, Party* in excerpt *3c*). Again, unlike Marx's one-dimensional focus on the overarching or determining power of economic capital (wealth), Weber sees economic power or a person's class or market situation as but one source of authority. It co-exists alongside but is also analytically separate from social status or prestige – sources of authority derived from family background and lifestyle that, while frequently dependent on or interrelated to economic assets, can also be independent of wealth. And similarly, political power is a distinct source of authority that exists independent of economic and status authority (even as all three can be and frequently are empirically intertwined). Further, Weber's construal of the economic class structure also points to its differentiated or multilayered nature, unlike Marx's dichotomization between the capitalist/bourgeois class versus the working class/proletariat. Weber, while fully recognizing the significance of property ownership in determining individuals' life-chances, also recognized that there are different class positions in relation to property, and that the propertyless, too, do not constitute a single class; the owners of services (e.g. the various professions) also have their own hierarchical positioning relative to economic power as well as of course to status/prestige. Given Weber's extensive writings on the hierarchical structuring of authority, it is no surprise that his theorizing underpins a significant amount of important research conducted by sociologists interested in organizational behavior (bureaucracy), political sociology (the nation; political parties), and on inequality and social class dynamics.

3A Max Weber from *The Protestant Ethic and the Spirit of Capitalism*

Original publication details: Max Weber, 1905/1958, from *The Protestant Ethic and the Spirit of Capitalism*, translated by Talcott Parsons, pp. 35–37, 48–54, 108–112, 115, 124–125, 180–182. Charles Scribner & Sons.

Religious Affiliation and Social Stratification[1]

A GLANCE at the occupational statistics of any country of mixed religious composition brings to light with remarkable frequency[2] a situation which has several times provoked discussion in the Catholic press and literature,[3] and in Catholic congresses in Germany, namely, the fact that business leaders and owners of capital, as well as the higher grades of skilled labour, and even more the higher technically and commercially trained personnel of modern enterprises, are overwhelmingly Protestant.[4] This is true not only in cases where the difference in religion coincides with one of nationality, and thus of cultural development, as in Eastern Germany between Germans and Poles. The same thing is shown in the figures of religious affiliation almost wherever capitalism, at the time of its great expansion, has had a free hand to alter the social distribution of the population in accordance with its needs, and to determine its occupational structure. The more freedom it has had, the more clearly is the effect shown. It is true that the greater relative participation of Protestants in the ownership of capital,[5] in management, and the upper ranks of labour in great modern industrial and commercial enterprises,[6] may in part be explained in terms of historical circumstances[7] which extend far back into the past, and in which religious affiliation is not a cause of the economic conditions, but to a certain extent appears to be a result of them. Participation in the above economic functions usually involves some previous ownership of capital, and generally an expensive education; often both. These are to-day largely dependent on the possession of inherited wealth, or at least on a certain degree of material well-being. A number of those sections of the old Empire which were most highly developed economically and most favoured by natural resources and situation, in particular a majority of the wealthy towns, went over to Protestantism in the sixteenth century. The results of that circumstance favour the Protestants even to-day in their struggle for economic existence. There arises thus the historical question: why were the districts of highest economic development at the same time particularly favourable to a revolution in the Church? The answer is by no means so simple as one might think.

The emancipation from economic traditionalism appears, no doubt, to be a factor which would greatly strengthen the tendency to doubt the sanctity of the religious tradition, as of all traditional authorities. But it is necessary to note, what has often been forgotten, that the Reformation meant not the elimination of the Church's control over everyday life, but rather the substitution of a new form of control for the previous one. It meant the repudiation of a control which was very lax, at that time scarcely perceptible in practice, and hardly more than formal, in favour of a regulation of the whole of conduct which, penetrating to all departments of private and public life, was infinitely burdensome and earnestly enforced. The rule of the Catholic Church, "punishing the heretic, but indulgent to the sinner", as it was in the past even more than to-day, is now tolerated by peoples of thoroughly modern economic character, and was borne by the richest and economically most advanced peoples on earth at about the turn of the fifteenth century. The rule of Calvinism, on the other hand, as it was enforced in the sixteenth century in Geneva and in Scotland, at the turn of the sixteenth and seventeenth centuries in large parts of the Netherlands, in the seventeenth in New England, and for a time in England itself, would be for us the most absolutely unbearable form of ecclesiastical control of the individual which could possibly exist. That was exactly what large numbers of the old commercial aristocracy of those times, in Geneva as well as in Holland and England, felt about it. And what the reformers complained of in those areas of high economic development was not too much supervision of life on the part of the Church, but too little. Now how does it happen that at that time those countries which were most advanced economically, and within them the rising bourgeois middle classes, not only failed to resist this unexampled tyranny of

Puritanism, but even developed a heroism in its defence? For bourgeois classes as such have seldom before and never since displayed heroism.

[…]

Thus, if we try to determine the object, the analysis and historical explanation of which we are attempting, it cannot be in the form of a conceptual definition, but at least in the beginning only a provisional description of what is here meant by the spirit of capitalism. Such a description is, however, indispensable in order clearly to understand the object of the investigation. For this purpose we turn to a document of that spirit which contains what we are looking for in almost classical purity, and at the same time has the advantage of being free from all direct relationship to religion, being thus, for our purposes, free of preconceptions.

"Remember, that *time* is money. He that can earn ten shillings a day by his labour, and goes abroad, or sits idle, one half of that day, though he spends but sixpence during his diversion or idleness, ought not to reckon *that* the only expense; he has really spent, or rather thrown away, five shillings besides.

"Remember, that *credit* is money. If a man lets his money lie in my hands after it is due, he gives me the interest, or so much as I can make of it during that time. This amounts to a considerable sum where a man has good and large credit, and makes good use of it.

"Remember, that money is of the prolific, generating nature. Money can beget money, and its offspring can beget more, and so on. Five shillings turned is six, turned again it is seven and threepence, and so on, till it becomes a hundred pounds. The more there is of it, the more it produces every turning, so that the profits rise quicker and quicker. He that kills a breeding-sow, destroys all her offspring to the thousandth generation. He that murders a crown, destroys all that it might have produced, even scores of pounds."

"Remember this saying, *The good paymaster is lord of another man's purse*. He that is known to pay punctually and exactly to the time he promises, may at any time, and on any occasion, raise all the money his friends can spare. This is sometimes of great use. After industry and frugality, nothing contributes more to the raising of a young man in the world than punctuality and justice in all his dealings; therefore never keep borrowed money an hour beyond the time you promised, lest a disappointment shut up your friend's purse for ever.

"The most trifling actions that affect a man's credit are to be regarded. The sound of your hammer at five in the morning, or eight at night, heard by a creditor, makes him easy six months longer; but if he sees you at a billiard-table, or hears your voice at a tavern, when you should be at work, he sends for his money the next day; demands it, before he can receive it, in a lump.

"It shows, besides, that you are mindful of what you owe; it makes you appear a careful as well as an honest man, and that still increases your credit.

"Beware of thinking all your own that you possess, and of living accordingly. It is a mistake that many people who have credit fall into. To prevent this, keep an exact account for some time both of your expenses and your income. If you take the pains at first to mention particulars, it will have this good effect: you will discover how wonderfully small, trifling expenses mount up to large sums, and will discern what might have been, and may for the future be saved, without occasioning any great inconvenience."

"For six pounds a year you may have the use of one hundred pounds, provided you are a man of known prudence and honesty.

"He that spends a groat a day idly, spends idly above six pounds a year, which is the price for the use of one hundred pounds.

"He that wastes idly a groat's worth of his time per day, one day with another, wastes the privilege of using one hundred pounds each day.

"He that idly loses five shillings' worth of time, loses five shillings, and might as prudently throw five shillings into the sea.

"He that loses five shillings, not only loses that sum, but all the advantage that might be made by turning it in dealing, which by the time that a young man becomes old, will amount to a considerable sum of money."[8]

It is Benjamin Franklin who preaches to us in these sentences, the same which Ferdinand Kürnberger satirizes in his clever and malicious *Picture of American Culture*[9] as the supposed confession of faith of the Yankee. That it is the spirit of capitalism which here speaks in characteristic fashion, no one will doubt, however little we may wish to claim that everything which could be understood as pertaining to that spirit is contained in it. Let us pause a moment to consider this passage, the philosophy of which Kürnberger sums up in the words, "They make tallow out of cattle and money out of men". The peculiarity of this philosophy of avarice appears to be the ideal of the honest man of recognized credit, and above all the idea of a duty of the individual toward the increase of his capital, which is assumed as an end in itself. Truly what is here preached is not simply a means of making one's way in the world, but a peculiar ethic. The infraction of its rules is treated not as foolishness but as forgetfulness of duty. That is the essence of the matter. It is not mere business astuteness, that sort of thing is common enough, it is an ethos. *This* is the quality which interests us.

When Jacob Fugger, in speaking to a business associate who had retired and who wanted to persuade him to do the same, since he had made enough money and should let others have a chance, rejected that as pusillanimity and answered that "he (Fugger) thought otherwise, he wanted to make money as long as he could",[10] the spirit of his statement is evidently quite different from that of Franklin. What in the former case was an expression of commercial daring and a personal inclination morally neutral,[11] in the latter takes on the character of an ethically coloured maxim for the conduct of life. The concept spirit of capitalism is here used in this specific sense,[12] it is the spirit of modern capitalism. For that we are here dealing only with Western European and American capitalism is obvious from the way in which the problem was stated. Capitalism existed in China, India, Babylon, in the classic world, and in the Middle Ages. But in all these cases, as we shall see, this particular ethos was lacking.

Now, all Franklin's moral attitudes are coloured with utilitarianism. Honesty is useful, because it assures credit; so are punctuality, industry, frugality, and that is the reason they are virtues. A logical deduction from this would be that where, for instance, the appearance of honesty serves the same purpose, that would suffice, and an unnecessary surplus of this virtue would evidently appear to Franklin's eyes as unproductive waste. And as a matter of fact, the story in his autobiography of his conversion to those virtues,[13] or the discussion of the value of a strict maintenance of the appearance of modesty, the assiduous belittlement of one's own deserts in order to gain general recognition later[14] confirms this impression. According to Franklin, those virtues, like all others, are only in so far virtues as they are actually useful to the individual, and the surrogate of mere appearance is always sufficient when it accomplishes the end in view. It is a conclusion which is inevitable for strict utilitarianism. The impression of many Germans that the virtues professed by Americanism are pure hypocrisy seems to have been confirmed by this striking case. But in fact the matter is not by any means so simple. Benjamin Franklin's own character, as it appears in the really unusual candidness of his autobiography, belies that suspicion. The circumstance that he ascribes his recognition of the utility of virtue to a divine revelation which was intended to lead him in the path of righteousness, shows that something more than mere garnishing for purely egocentric motives is involved.

In fact, the *summum bonum* of this ethic, the earning of more and more money, combined with the strict avoidance of all spontaneous enjoyment of life, is above all completely devoid of any eudæmonistic, not to say hedonistic, admixture. It is thought of so purely as an end in itself, that from the point of view of the happiness of, or utility to, the single individual, it appears entirely transcendental and absolutely irrational.[15] Man is dominated by the making of money, by acquisition as the ultimate purpose of his life. Economic acquisition is no longer subordinated to man as the means for the satisfaction of his material needs. This reversal of what we should call the natural relationship, so irrational from a naïve point of view, is evidently as definitely a leading principle of capitalism as it is foreign to all peoples not under capitalistic influence. At the same time it expresses a type of feeling which is closely connected with certain religious ideas. If we thus ask, *why* should "money be made out of men", Benjamin Franklin himself, although he was a colourless deist, answers in his autobiography with a quotation from the Bible, which his strict Calvinistic father drummed into him again and again in his youth: "Seest thou a man diligent in his business? He shall stand before kings" (Prov. xxii. 29). The earning of money within the modern economic order is, so long as it is done legally, the result and the expression of virtue and proficiency in a calling; and this virtue and proficiency are, as it is now not difficult to see, the real Alpha and Omega of Franklin's ethic, as expressed in the passages we have quoted, as well as in all his works without exception.[16]

And in truth this peculiar idea, so familiar to us to-day, but in reality so little a matter of course, of one's duty in a calling, is what is most characteristic of the social ethic of capitalistic culture, and is in a sense the fundamental basis of it. It is an obligation which the individual is supposed to feel and does feel towards the content of his professional[17] activity, no matter in what it consists, in particular no matter whether it appears on the surface as a utilization of his personal powers, or only of his material possessions (as capital).

[...]

However strange it may seem, it follows from the peculiar form which the Christian brotherly love was forced to take under the pressure of the inner isolation of the individual through the Calvinistic faith. In the first place it follows dogmatically.[18] The world exists to serve the glorification of God and for that purpose alone. The elected Christian is in the world only to increase this glory of God by fulfilling His commandments to the best of his ability. But God requires social achievement of the Christian because He wills that social life shall be organized according to His commandments, in accordance with that purpose. The social[19] activity of the Christian in the world is solely activity *in majorem gloriam Dei*. This character is hence shared by labour in a calling which serves the mundane life of the community. Even in Luther we found specialized labour in callings justified in terms of brotherly love. But what for him remained an uncertain, purely intellectual suggestion became for the Calvinists a characteristic element in their ethical system. Brotherly love, since it may only be practised for the glory of God[20] and not in the service of the flesh,[21] is expressed in the first place in the fulfilment of the daily tasks given by the *lex naturæ*; and in the process this fulfilment assumes a peculiarly objective and impersonal character, that of service in the interest of the rational organization of our social environment. For the wonderfully purposeful organization and arrangement of this cosmos is, according both to the revelation of the Bible and to natural intuition, evidently designed by God to serve the utility of the human race. This makes labour in the service of impersonal social usefulness appear to promote the glory of God and hence to be willed by Him. The complete elimination of the theodicy problem and of all those questions about the meaning of the world and of life, which have tortured others, was as self-evident to the Puritan as, for quite different reasons, to the Jew, and even in a certain sense to all the non-mystical types of Christian religion.

To this economy of forces Calvinism added another tendency which worked in the same direction. The conflict between the individual and the ethic (in Sören Kierkegaard's sense) did not exist for Calvinism, although it placed the individual entirely on his own responsibility in religious matters. This is not the place to analyse the reasons for this fact, or its significance for the political and economic rationalism of Calvinism. The source of the utilitarian character of Calvinistic ethics lies here, and important peculiarities of the Calvinistic idea of the calling were derived from the same source as well.[22] But for the moment we must return to the special consideration of the doctrine of predestination.

For us the decisive problem is: How was this doctrine borne[23] in an age to which the after-life was not only more important, but in many ways also more certain, than all the interests of life in this world?[24] The question, Am I one of the elect? must sooner or later have arisen for every believer and have forced all other interests into the background. And how can I be sure of this state of grace?[25] For Calvin himself this was not a problem. He felt himself to be a chosen agent of the Lord, and was certain of his own salvation. Accordingly, to the question of how the individual can be certain of his own election, he has at bottom only the answer that we should be content with the knowledge that God has chosen and depend further only on that implicit trust in Christ which is the result of true faith. He rejects in principle the assumption that one can learn from the conduct of others whether they are chosen or damned. It is an unjustifiable attempt to force God's secrets. The elect differ externally in this life in no way from the damned[26]; and even all the subjective experiences of the chosen are, as *ludibria spiritus sancti*, possible for the damned with the single exception of that *finaliter* expectant, trusting faith. The elect thus are and remain God's invisible Church.

Quite naturally this attitude was impossible for his followers as early as Beza, and, above all, for the broad mass of ordinary men. For them the *certitudo salutis* in the sense of the recognizability of the state of grace necessarily became of absolutely dominant importance.[27] So, wherever the doctrine of predestination was held, the question could not be suppressed whether there were any infallible criteria by which membership in the *electi* could be known. Not only has this question continually had a central importance in the development of the Pietism which first arose on the basis of the Reformed Church; it has in fact in a certain sense at times been fundamental to it. But when we consider the great political and social importance of the Reformed doctrine and practice of the Communion, we shall see how great a part was played during the whole seventeenth century outside of Pietism by the possibility of ascertaining the state of grace of the individual. On it depended, for instance, his admission to Communion, i.e. to the central religious ceremony which determined the social standing of the participants.

It was impossible, at least so far as the question of a man's own state of grace arose, to be satisfied[28] with Calvin's trust in the testimony of the expectant faith resulting from grace, even though the orthodox doctrine had never formally abandoned that criterion.[29] Above all, practical pastoral work, which had immediately to deal with all the suffering caused by the doctrine, could not be satisfied. It met these difficulties in various ways.[30] So far as predestination was not reinterpreted, toned down, or fundamentally abandoned,[31] two principal, mutually connected, types of pastoral advice appear. On the one hand it is held to be an absolute duty to consider oneself chosen, and to combat all doubts as temptations of the devil,[32] since lack of self-confidence is the result of insufficient faith, hence of imperfect grace. The exhortation of the apostle to make fast one's own call is here interpreted as a duty to attain certainty of one's own election and justification in the daily struggle of life. In the place of the humble sinners to whom Luther promises grace if they trust themselves to God in penitent faith are bred those self-confident saints[33] whom we can rediscover in the hard Puritan merchants of the heroic age of capitalism and in isolated instances down to the present. On the other hand, in order to attain that self-confidence intense worldly activity is recommended as the most suitable means.[34] It and it alone disperses religious doubts and gives the certainty of grace.

That worldly activity should be considered capable of this achievement, that it could, so to speak, be considered the most suitable means of counteracting feelings of religious anxiety, finds its explanation in the fundamental peculiarities of religious feeling in the Reformed Church, which come most clearly to light in its differences from Lutheranism in the doctrine of justification by faith.

[...]

In practice this means that God helps those who help themselves.[35] Thus the Calvinist, as it is sometimes put, himself creates[36] his own salvation, or, as would be more correct, the conviction of it. But this creation cannot, as in Catholicism, consist in a gradual accumulation of individual good works to one's credit, but rather in a systematic self-control which at every moment stands before the inexorable alternative, chosen or damned.

[...]

As he observed his own conduct, the later Puritan also observed that of God and saw His finger in all the details of life. And, contrary to the strict doctrine of Calvin, he always knew why God took this or that measure. The process of sanctifying life could thus almost take on the character of a business enterprise.[37] A thoroughgoing Christianization of the whole of life was the consequence of this methodical quality of ethical conduct into which Calvinism as distinct from Lutheranism forced men. That this rationality was decisive in its influence on practical life must always be borne in mind in order rightly to understand the influence of Calvinism. On the one hand we can see that it took this element to exercise such an influence at all. But other faiths as well necessarily had a similar influence when their ethical motives were the same in this decisive point, the doctrine of proof.

[...]

One of the fundamental elements of the spirit of modern capitalism, and not only of that but of all modern culture: rational conduct on the basis of the idea of the calling, was born – that is what this discussion has sought to demonstrate – from the spirit of Christian asceticism. One has only to re-read the passage from Franklin, quoted at the beginning of this essay, in order to see that the essential elements of the attitude which was there called the spirit of capitalism are the same as what we have just shown to be the content of the Puritan worldly asceticism,[38] only without the religious basis, which by Franklin's time had died away. The idea that modern labour has an ascetic character is of course not new. Limitation to specialized work, with a renunciation of the Faustian universality of man which it involves, is a condition of any valuable work in the modern world; hence deeds and renunciation inevitably condition each other today. This fundamentally ascetic trait of middle-class life, if it attempts to be a way of life at all, and not simply the absence of any, was what Goethe wanted to teach, at the height of his wisdom, in the *Wanderjahren*, and in the end which he gave to the life of his *Faust*.[39] For him the realization meant a renunciation, a departure from an age of full and beautiful humanity, which can no more be repeated in the course of our cultural development than can the flower of the Athenian culture of antiquity.

The Puritan wanted to work in a calling; we are forced to do so. For when asceticism was carried out of monastic cells into everyday life, and began to dominate worldly morality, it did its part in building the tremendous cosmos of the modern economic order. This order is now bound to the technical and economic conditions of machine production which to-day determine the lives of all the individuals who are born into this mechanism, not only those directly concerned with economic acquisition, with irresistible force. Perhaps it will so determine them until the last ton of fossilized coal is burnt. In Baxter's view the care for external goods should only lie on the shoulders of the "saint like a light cloak, which can be thrown aside at any moment".[40] But fate decreed that the cloak should become an iron cage.

Since asceticism undertook to remodel the world and to work out its ideals in the world, material goods have gained an increasing and finally an inexorable power over the lives of men as at no previous period in history. To-day the spirit of religious asceticism – whether finally, who knows? – has escaped from the cage. But victorious capitalism, since it rests on mechanical foundations, needs its support no longer. The rosy blush of its laughing heir, the Enlightenment, seems also to be irretrievably fading, and the idea of duty in one's calling prowls about in our lives like the ghost of dead religious beliefs. Where the fulfilment of the calling cannot directly be related to the highest spiritual and cultural values, or when, on the other hand, it need not be felt simply as economic compulsion, the individual generally abandons the attempt to justify it at all. In the field of its highest development, in the United States, the pursuit of wealth, stripped of its religious and ethical meaning, tends to become associated with purely mundane passions, which often actually give it the character of sport.[41]

No one knows who will live in this cage in the future, or whether at the end of this tremendous development entirely new prophets will arise, or there will be a great rebirth of old ideas and ideals, or, if neither, mechanized petrification, embellished with a sort of convulsive self-importance. For of the last stage of this cultural development, it might well be truly said: "Specialists without spirit, sensualists without heart; this nullity imagines that it has attained a level of civilization never before achieved."

But this brings us to the world of judgments of value and of faith, with which this purely historical discussion need not be burdened. The next task would be rather to show the significance of ascetic rationalism, which has only been touched in the foregoing sketch, for the content of practical social ethics, thus for the types of organization and the functions of social groups from the conventicle to the State.

NOTES

1   From the voluminous literature which has grown up around this essay I cite only the most comprehensive criticisms. (1) F. Rachfahl, "Kalvinismus und Kapitalismus", *Internationale Wochenschrift für Wissenschaft, Kunst und Technik* (1909), Nos. 39–43. In reply, my article: "Antikritisches zum Geist des Kapitalismus," *Archiv für Sozialwissenschaft und Sozialpolitik* (Tübingen), XX, 1910. Then Rachfahl's reply to that: "Nochmals Kalvinismus und Kapitalismus", 1910, Nos. 22–25, of the *Internationale Wochenschrift*. Finally my "Antikritisches Schlusswort", *Archiv,* XXXI. (Brentano, in the criticism presently to be referred to, evidently did not know of this last phase of the discussion, as he does not refer to it.) I have not incorporated anything in this edition from the somewhat unfruitful polemics against Rachfahl. He is an author whom I otherwise admire, but who has in this instance ventured into a field which he has not thoroughly mastered. I have only added a few supplementary references from my anti-critique, and have attempted, in new passages and footnotes, to make impossible any future misunderstanding. (2) W. Sombart, in his book *Der Bourgeois* (Munich and Leipzig, 1913,

also translated into English under the title *The Quintessence of Capitalism,* London, 1915), to which I shall return in footnotes below. Finally (3) Lujo Brentano in Part II of the Appendix to his Munich address (in the Academy of Sciences, 1913) on *Die Anfänge des modernen Kapitalismus,* which was published in 1916. (Since Weber's death Brentano has somewhat expanded these essays and incorporated them into his recent book *Der wirtschaftende Mensch in der Geschichte.* – TRANSLATOR'S NOTE.) I shall also refer to this criticism in special footnotes in the proper places. I invite anyone who may be interested to convince himself by comparison that I have not in revision left out, changed the meaning of, weakened, or added materially different statements to, a single sentence of my essay which contained any essential point. There was no occasion to do so, and the development of my exposition will convince anyone who still doubts. The two latter writers engaged in a more bitter quarrel with each other than with me. Brentano's criticism of Sombart's book, *Die Juden und das Wirtschaftsleben,* I consider in many points well founded, but often very unjust, even apart from the fact that Brentano does not himself seem to understand the real essence of the problem of the Jews (which is entirely omitted from this essay, but will be dealt with later [in a later section of the *Religionssoziologie.* – TRANSLATOR'S NOTE]).

From theologians I have received numerous valuable suggestions in connection with this study. Its reception on their part has been in general friendly and impersonal, in spite of wide differences of opinion on particular points. This is the more welcome to me since I should not have wondered at a certain antipathy to the manner in which these matters must necessarily be treated here. What to a theologian is valuable in his religion cannot play a very large part in this study. We are concerned with what, from a religious point of view, are often quite superficial and unrefined aspects of relligious life, but which, and precisely because they were superficial and unrefined, have often influenced outward behaviour most profoundly.

Another book which, besides containing many other things, is a very welcome confirmation of and supplement to this essay in so far as it deals with our problem, is the important work of E. Troeltsch, *Die Soziallehren der christlichen Kirchen und Gruppen* (Tübingen, 1912). It deals with the history of the ethics of Western Christianity from a very comprehensive point of view of its own. I here refer the reader to it for general comparison instead of making repeated references to special points. The author is principally concerned with the doctrines of religion, while I am interested rather in their practical results.

2 The exceptions are explained, not always, but frequently, by the fact that the religious leanings of the labouring force of an industry are naturally, in the first instance, determined by those of the locality in which the industry is situated, or from which its labour is drawn. This circumstance often alters the impression given at first glance by some statistics of religious adherence, for instance in the Rhine provinces. Furthermore, figures can naturally only be conclusive if individual specialized occupations are carefully distinguished in them. Otherwise very large employers may sometimes be grouped together with master craftsmen who work alone, under the category of "proprietors of enterprises". Above all, the fully developed capitalism of the present day, especially so far as the great unskilled lower strata of labour are concerned, has become independent of any influence which religion may have had in the past. I shall return to this point.

3 Compare, for instance, Schell, *Der Katholizismus als Prinzip des Fortschrittes* (Würzburg, 1897), p. 31, and V. Herding, *Das Prinzip des Katholizismus und die Wissenschaft* (Freiburg, 1899), p. 58.

4 One of my pupils has gone through what is at this time the most complete statistical material we possess on this subject: the religious statistics of Baden. See Martin Offenbacher, "Konfession und soziale Schichtung", *Eine Studie über die wirtschaftliche Lage der Katholiken und Protestanten in Baden* (Tübingen und Leipzig, 1901), Vol. IV, part v, of the *Volkswirtschaftliche Abhandlungen der badischen Hochschulen.* The

facts and figures which are used for illustration below are all drawn from this study.

5   For instance, in 1895 in Baden there was taxable capital available for the tax on returns from capital:

Per 1,000 Protestants .. .. .. 954,000 marks
Per 1,000 Catholics .. .. .. 589,000 marks

It is true that the Jews, with over four millions per 1,000, were far ahead of the rest. (For details see Offenbacher, *op. cit.*, p. 21.)

6   On this point compare the whole discussion in Offenbacher's study.

7   On this point also Offenbacher brings forward more detailed evidence for Baden in his first two chapters.

8   The final passage is from *Necessary Hints to Those That Would Be Rich* (written 1736, Works, Sparks edition, II, p. 80), the rest from *Advice to a Young Tradesman* (written 1748, Sparks edition, II, pp. 87 ff.). The italics in the text are Franklin's.

9   *Der Amerikamüde* (Frankfurt, 1855), well known to be an imaginative paraphrase of Lenau's impressions of America. As a work of art the book would to-day be somewhat difficult to enjoy, but it is incomparable as a document of the (now long since blurred-over) differences between the German and the American out-look, one may even say of the type of spiritual life which, in spite of everything, has remained common to all Germans, Catholic and Protestant alike, since the German mysticism of the Middle Ages, as against the Puritan capital-istic valuation of action.

10   Sombart has used this quotation as a motto for his section dealing with the genesis of capitalism (*Der moderne Kapitalismus*, first edition, I, p. 193. See also p. 390).

11   Which quite obviously does not mean either that Jacob Fugger was a morally indifferent or an irreligious man, or that Benjamin Franklin's ethic is completely covered by the above quota-tions. It scarcely required Brentano's quotations (*Die Anfänge des modernen Kapitalismus*, pp. 150 ff.) to protect this well-known philanthro-pist from the misunderstanding which Brentano seems to attribute to me. The problem is just the reverse: how could such a philanthropist come to write these particular sentences (the espe-cially characteristic form of which Brentano has neglected to reproduce) in the manner of a moralist?

12   This is the basis of our difference from Sombart in stating the problem. Its very considerable practical significance will become clear later. In anticipation, however, let it be remarked that Sombart has by no means neglected this ethical aspect of the capitalistic entrepreneur. But in his view of the problem it appears as a result of capi-talism, whereas for our purposes we must assume the opposite as an hypothesis. A final position can only be taken up at the end of the investigation. For Sombart's view see *op. cit.*, pp. 357. 380, etc. His reasoning here connects with the brilliant analysis given in Simmel's *Philosophie des Geldes* (final chapter). Of the polemics which he has brought forward against me in his *Bourgeois* I shall come to speak later. At this point any thorough discussion must be postponed.

13   "I grew convinced that truth, sincerity, and integ-rity in dealings between man and man were of the utmost importance to the felicity of life; and I formed written resolutions, which still remain in my journal book to practise them ever while I lived. Revelation had indeed no weight with me as such; but I entertained an opinion that, though certain actions might not be bad because they were forbidden by it, or good because it com-manded them, yet probably these actions might be forbidden because they were bad for us, or commanded because they were beneficial to us in their own nature, all the circumstances of things considered." *Autobiography* (ed. F. W. Pine, Henry Holt, New York, 1916), p. 112.

14   "I therefore put myself as much as I could out of sight and started it" – that is the project of a library which he had initiated – "as a scheme of a *number of friends*, who had requested me to go about and propose it to such as they thought lov-ers of reading. In this way my affair went on smoothly, and I ever after practised it on such occasions; and from my frequent successes, can heartily recommend it. The present little sacrifice of your vanity will afterwards be amply repaid. If it remains awhile uncertain to whom the merit belongs, someone more vain than yourself will be

encouraged to claim it, and then even envy will be disposed to do you justice by plucking those assumed feathers and restoring them to their right owner." *Autobiography*, p. 140.

15 Brentano (*op. cit.*, pp. 125, 127, note 1) takes this remark as an occasion to criticize the later discussion of "that rationalization and discipline" to which worldly asceticism has subjected men. That, he says, is a rationalization toward an irrational mode of life. He is, in fact, quite correct. A thing is never irrational in itself, but only from a particular rational point of view. For the unbeliever every religious way of life is irrational, for the hedonist every ascetic standard, no matter whether, measured with respect to its particular basic values, that opposing asceticism is a rationalization. If this essay makes any contribution at all, may it be to bring out the complexity of the only superficially simple concept of the rational.

16 In reply to Brentano's (*Die Anfänge des modernen Kapitalismus*, pp. 150 ff.) long and somewhat inaccurate apologia for Franklin, whose ethical qualities I am supposed to have misunderstood, I refer only to this statement, which should, in my opinion, have been sufficient to make that apologia superfluous.

17 The two terms profession and calling I have used in translation of the German *Beruf*, whichever seemed best to fit the particular context. Vocation does not carry the ethical connotation in which Weber is interested. It is especially to be remembered that profession in this sense is not contrasted with business, but it refers to a particular attitude toward one's occupation, no matter what that occupation may be. This should become abundantly clear from the whole of Weber's argument. – Translator's Note.

18 Of the relation between dogmatic and practical psychological consequence we shall often have to speak. That the two are not identical it is hardly necessary to remark.

19 Social, used of course without any of the implications attached to the modern sense of the word, meaning simply activity within the Church, politics, or any other social organization.

20 "Good works performed for any other purpose than the glory of God are sinful" (*Hanserd Knolly's Confession*, chap. xvi).

21 What such an impersonality of brotherly love, resulting from the orientation of life solely to God's will, means in the field of religious group life itself may be well illustrated by the attitude of the China Inland Mission and the International Missionaries Alliance (see Warneck, *Gesch. d. prot. Missionaren*, pp. 99, 111). At tremendous expense an army of missionaries was fitted out, for instance one thousand for China alone, in order by itinerant preaching to offer the Gospel to all the heathen in a strictly literal sense, since Christ had commanded it and made His second coming dependent on it. Whether these heathen should be converted to Christianity and thus attain salvation, even whether they could understand the language in which the missionary preached, was a matter of small importance and could be left to God, Who alone could control such things. According to Hudson Taylor (see Warneck, *op. cit*), China has about fifty million families; one thousand missionaries could each reach fifty families per day (!) or the Gospel could be presented to all the Chinese in less than three years. It is precisely the same manner in which, for instance, Calvinism carried out its Church discipline. The end was not the salvation of those subject to it, which was the affair of God alone (in practice their own) and could not be in any way influenced by the means at the disposal of the Church, but simply the increase of God's glory. Calvinism as such is not responsible for those feats of missionary zeal, since they rest on an interdenominational basis. Calvin himself denied the duty of sending missions to the heathen since a further expansion of the Church is *unius Dei opus*. Nevertheless, they obviously originate in the ideas, running through the whole Puritan ethic, according to which the duty to love one's neighbour is satisfied by fulfilling God's commandments to increase His glory. The neighbour thereby receives all that is due him, and anything further is God's affair. Humanity in relation to one's neighbour has, so to speak, died out. That is indicated by the most various circumstances.

Thus, to mention a remnant of that atmosphere, in the field of charity of the Reformed

Church, which in certain respects is justly famous, the Amsterdam orphans, with (in the twentieth century!) their coats and trousers divided vertically into a black and a red, or a red and a green half, a sort of fool's costume, and brought in parade formation to church, formed, for the feelings of the past, a highly uplifting spectacle. It served the glory of God precisely to the extent that all personal and human feelings were necessarily insulted by it. And so, as we shall see later, even in all the details of private life. Naturally all that signified only a tendency and we shall later ourselves have to make certain qualifications. But as one very important tendency of this ascetic faith, it was necessary to point it out here.

22   In all these respects the ethic of Port Royal, although predestinationist, takes quite a different standpoint on account of its mystical and otherworldly orientation, which is in so far Catholic (see Honigsheim, *op. cit.*).

23   Hundeshagen (*Beitr. z. Kirchenverfassungsgesch. u. Kirchenpolitik*, 1864, I, p. 37) takes the view, since often repeated, that predestination was a dogma of the theologians, not a popular doctrine. But that is only true if the people is identified with the mass of the uneducated lower classes. Even then it has only limited validity. Köhler ... found that in the forties of the nineteenth century just those masses (meaning the *petite bourgeoisie* of Holland) were thoroughly imbued with predestination. Anyone who denied the double decree was to them a heretic and a condemned soul. He himself was asked about the time of his rebirth (in the sense of predestination). Da Costa and the separation of de Kock were greatly influenced by it. Not only Cromwell, in whose case Zeller (*Das Theologische System Zwinglis*, p. 17) has already shown the effects of the dogma most effectively, but also his army knew very well what it was about. Moreover, the canons of the synods of Dordrecht and Westminster were national questions of the first importance. Cromwell's tryers and ejectors admitted only believers in predestination, and Baxter (*Life*, I, p. 72), although he was otherwise its opponent, considers its effect on the quality of the clergy to be important.

That the Reformed Pietists, the members of the English and Dutch conventicles, should not have understood the doctrine is quite impossible. It was precisely what drove them together to seek the *certitudo salutis*.

What significance the doctrine of predestination does or does not have when it remains a dogma of the theologians is shown by perfectly orthodox Catholicism, to which it was by no means strange as an esoteric doctrine under various forms. What is important is that the idea of the individual's obligation to consider himself of the elect and prove it to himself was always denied. Compare for the Catholic doctrine, for instance, A. Van Wyck, *Tract. de prædestinatione* (Cologne, 1708). To what extent Pascal's doctrine of predestination was correct, we cannot inquire here.

Hundeshagen, who dislikes the doctrine, evidently gets his impressions primarily from German sources. His antipathy is based on the purely deductive opinion that it necessarily leads to moral fatalism and antinomianism. This opinion has already been refuted by Zeller, *op. cit.* That such a result was possible cannot, of course, be denied. Both Melanchthon and Wesley speak of it. But it is characteristic that in both cases it is combined with an emotional religion of faith. For them, lacking the rational idea of proof, this consequence was in fact not unnatural.

The same consequences appeared in Islam. But why? Because the Mohammedan idea was that of predetermination, not predestination, and was applied to fate in this world, not in the next. In consequence the most important thing, the proof of the believer in predestination, played no part in Islam. Thus only the fearlessness of the warrior (as in the case of *moira*) could result, but there were no consequences for rationalization of life; there was no religious sanction for them. See the (Heidelberg) theological dissertation of F. Ullrich, *Die Vorherbestimmungslehre im Islam u. Christenheit*, 1900. The modifications of the doctrine which came in practice, for instance Baxter, did not disturb it in essence so long as the idea that the election of God, and its proof, fell upon the concrete individual, was not shaken. Finally, and above all, all the great men of Puritanism (in the broadest sense) took their departure from this doctrine, whose terrible seriousness deeply influenced their youthful development. Milton like, in declining order it is true, Baxter, and, still later, the free-thinker Franklin. Their later emancipation from its strict interpretation is directly parallel to the development which the religious movement as a whole underwent in the same direction. And all the great religious revivals, at least in Holland, and most of those in England, took it up again.

24   As is true in such a striking way of the basic atmosphere of Bunyan's *Pilgrim's Progress*.

25   This question meant less to the later Lutheran, even apart from the doctrine of predestination, than to the Calvinist. Not because he was less interested in the salvation of his soul, but because, in the form which the Lutheran Church had taken, its character as an institution for salvation (*Heilsanstalt*) came to the fore. The individual thus felt himself to be an object of its care and dependent on it. The problem was first raised within Lutheranism characteristically enough through the Pietist movement. The question of *certitudo salutis itself* has, however, for every non-sacramental religion of salvation, whether Buddhism, Jainism, or anything else, been absolutely fundamental; that must not be forgotten. It has been the origin of all psychological drives of a purely religious character.

26   Thus expressly in the letter to Bucer, *Corp. Ref.* 29, p. 883 f. Compare with that again Scheibe, ... p. 30.

27   The *Westminster Confession* (XVIII, p. 2) also assures the elect of indubitable certainty of grace, although with all our activity we remain useless servants and the struggle against evil lasts one's whole life long. But even the chosen one often has to struggle long and hard to attain the *certitudo* which the consciousness of having done his duty gives him and of which a true believer will never entirely be deprived.

28   The orthodox Calvinistic doctrine referred to faith and the consciousness of community with God in the sacraments, and mentioned the "other fruits of the Spirit" only incidentally. See the passages in Heppe, *op. cit.*, p. 425. Calvin

himself most emphatically denied that works were indications of favour before God, although he, like the Lutherans, considered them the fruits of belief (*Instit. Christ*, III, 2, 37, 38). The actual evolution to the proof of faith through works, which is characteristic of asceticism, is parallel to a gradual modification of the doctrines of Calvin. As with Luther, the true Church was first marked off primarily by purity of doctrine and sacraments, but later the *disciplina* came to be placed on an equal footing with the other two. This evolution may be followed in the passages given by Heppe, *op. cit.*, pp. 194–5, as well as in the manner in which Church members were acquired in the Netherlands by the end of the sixteenth century (express subjection by agreement to Church discipline as the principal prerequisite).

29   For example, Olevian, *De substantia fœderis gratuiti inter Deum et electos* (1585), p. 257; Heidegger, *Corpus Theologiæ*, XXIV, p. 87; and other passages in Heppe, *Dogmatik der ev. ref. Kirche* (1861), p. 425.

30   On this point see the remarks of Schneckenburger ... p. 48.

31   Thus, for example, in Baxter the distinction between mortal and venial sin reappears in a truly Catholic sense. The former is a sign of the lack of grace which can only be attained by the conversion of one's whole life. The latter is not incompatible with grace.

32   As held in many different shades by Baxter, Bailey, Sedgwick, Hoornbeek. Further see examples given by Schneckenburger ... p. 262.

33   The conception of the state of grace as a sort of social estate (somewhat like that of the ascetics of the early Church) is very common. See for instance Schortinghuis, *Het innige Christendom* (1740 proscribed by the States-General)!

34   Thus, as we shall see later, in countless passages, especially the conclusion, of Baxter's *Christian Directory*. This recommendation of worldly activity as a means of overcoming one's own feeling of moral inferiority is reminiscent of Pascal's psychological interpretation of the impulse of acquisition and ascetic activity as means to deceive oneself about one's own moral worthlessness. For him the belief in predestination

and the conviction of the original sinfulness of everything pertaining to the flesh resulted only in renunciation of the world and the recommendation of contemplation as the sole means of lightening the burden of sin and attaining certainty of salvation. Of the orthodox Catholic and the Jansenist versions of the idea of calling an acute analysis has been made by Dr. Paul Honigsheim in the dissertation cited above (part of a larger study, which it is hoped will be continued). The Jansenists lacked every trace of a connection between certainty of salvation and worldly activity. Their concept of calling has, even more strongly than the Lutheran or even the orthodox Catholic, the sense of acceptance of the situation in life in which one finds oneself, sanctioned not only, as in Catholicism by the social order, but also by the voice of one's own conscience (Honigsheim, *op. cit.*, pp. 139 ff.).

35   Augustine is supposed to have said "si non es prædestinatus, fac ut prædestineris".

36   One is reminded of a saying of Goethe with essentially the same meaning: "How can a man know himself? Never by observation, but through action. Try to do your duty and you will know what is in you. And what is your duty? Your daily task."

37   Baxter (*Saints' Everlasting Rest*, chap, xii) explains God's invisibility with the remark that just as one can carry on profitable trade with an invisible foreigner through correspondence, so is it possible by means of holy commerce with an invisible God to get possession of the one priceless pearl. These commercial similes rather than the forensic ones customary with the older moralists and the Lutherans are thoroughly characteristic of Puritanism, which in effect makes man buy his own salvation. Compare further the following passage from a sermon: "We reckon the value of a thing by that which a wise man will give for it, who is not ignorant of it nor under necessity. Christ, the Wisdom of God, gave Himself, His own precious blood, to redeem souls, and He knew what they were and had no need of them" (Matthew Henry, *The Worth of the Soul, Works of the Puritan Divines*, p. 313).

38   That those other elements, which have here not yet been traced to their religious roots, especially the idea that honesty is the best policy (Franklin's discussion of credit), are also of Puritan origin, must be proved in a somewhat different connection. ... Here I shall limit myself to repeating the following remark of J. A. Rowntree (*Quakerism, Past and Present*, pp. 95–6), to which E. Bernstein has called my attention: "Is it merely a coincidence, or is it a consequence, that the lofty profession of spirituality made by the Friends has gone hand in hand with shrewdness and tact in the transaction of mundane affairs? Real piety favours the success of a trader by insuring his integrity and fostering habits of prudence and forethought, important items in obtaining that standing and credit in the commercial world, which are requisites for the steady accumulation of wealth" ... "Honest as a Huguenot" was as proverbial in the seventeenth century as the respect for law of the Dutch which Sir W. Temple admired, and, a century later, that of the English as compared with those Continental peoples that had not been through this ethical schooling.

39   Well analysed in Bielschowsky's *Goethe*, II, chap, xviii. For the development of the scientific cosmos Windelband, at the end of his *Blütezeit der deutschen Philosophie* (Vol. II of the *Gesch. d. Neueren Philosophie*), has expressed a similar idea.

40   *Saints' Everlasting Rest*, chap. xii.

41   "Couldn't the old man be satisfied with his $75,000 a year and rest? No! The frontage of the store must be widened to 400 feet. Why? That beats everything, he says. In the evening when his wife and daughter read together, he wants to go to bed. Sundays he looks at the clock every five minutes to see when the day will be over – what a futile life!" In these terms the son-in-law (who had emigrated from Germany) of the leading dry-goods man of an Ohio city expressed his judgment of the latter, a judgment which would undoubtedly have seemed simply incomprehensible to the old man. A symptom of German lack of energy.

3B Max Weber from *Economy and Society*

Original publication details: Max Weber, from *Economy and Society, Vol. 1*. Edited by Guenther Roth and Claus Wittich (1968/1978), pp. 3–9, 21–26. University of California Press. Reproduced with permission of University of California Press.

The Definition of Sociology and of Social Action

Sociology (in the sense in which this highly ambiguous word is used here) is a science concerning itself with the interpretive understanding of social action and thereby with a causal explanation of its course and consequences. We shall speak of "action" insofar as the acting individual attaches a subjective meaning to his behavior – be it overt or covert, omission or acquiescence. Action is "social" insofar as its subjective meaning takes account of the behavior of others and is thereby oriented in its course.[1]

Methodological Foundations[2]

1. "Meaning" may be of two kinds. The term may refer first to the actual existing meaning in the given concrete case of a particular actor, or to the average or approximate meaning attributable to a given plurality of actors; or secondly to the theoretically conceived *pure type*[3] of subjective meaning attributed to the hypothetical actor or actors in a given type of action. In no case does it refer to an objectively "correct" meaning or one which is "true" in some metaphysical sense. It is this which distinguishes the empirical sciences of action, such as sociology and history, from the dogmatic disciplines in that area, such as jurisprudence, logic, ethics, and esthetics, which seek to ascertain the "true" and "valid" meanings associated with the objects of their investigation.

2. The line between meaningful action and merely reactive behavior to which no subjective meaning is attached, cannot be sharply drawn empirically. A very considerable part of all sociologically relevant behavior, especially purely traditional behavior, is marginal between the two. In the case of some psychophysical processes, meaningful, i.e., subjectively understandable, action is not to be found at all; in others it is discernible only by the psychologist. Many mystical experiences which cannot be adequately communicated in words are, for a person who is not susceptible to such experiences, not fully understandable. At the same time the ability to perform a similar action is not a necessary prerequisite to understanding; "one need not have been Caesar in order to understand Caesar." "Recapturing an experience" is important for accurate understanding, but not an absolute precondition for its interpretation. Understandable and non-understandable components of a process are often intermingled and bound up together.

3. All interpretation of meaning, like all scientific observations, strives for clarity and verifiable accuracy of insight and comprehension (*Evidenz*).[4] The basis for certainty in understanding can be either rational, which can be further subdivided into logical and mathematical, or it can be of an emotionally empathic or artistically

appreciative quality. Action is rationally evident chiefly when we attain a completely clear intellectual grasp of the action-elements in their intended context of meaning. Empathic or appreciative accuracy is attained when, through sympathetic participation, we can adequately grasp the emotional context in which the action took place. The highest degree of rational understanding is attained in cases involving the meanings of logically or mathematically related propositions; their meaning may be immediately and unambiguously intelligible. We have a perfectly clear understanding of what it means when somebody employs the proposition $2 \times 2 = 4$ or the Pythagorean theorem in reasoning or argument, or when someone correctly carries out a logical train of reasoning according to our accepted modes of thinking. In the same way we also understand what a person is doing when he tries to achieve certain ends by choosing appropriate means on the basis of the facts of the situation, as experience has accustomed us to interpret them. The interpretation of such rationally purposeful action possesses, for the understanding of the choice of means, the highest degree of verifiable certainty. With a lower degree of certainty, which is, however, adequate for most purposes of explanation, we are able to understand errors, including confusion of problems of the sort that we ourselves are liable to, or the origin of which we can detect by sympathetic self-analysis.

On the other hand, many ultimate ends or values toward which experience shows that human action may be oriented, often cannot be understood completely, though sometimes we are able to grasp them intellectually. The more radically they differ from our own ultimate values, however, the more difficult it is for us to understand them empathically. Depending upon the circumstances of the particular case we must be content either with a purely intellectual understanding of such values or when even that fails, sometimes we must simply accept them as given data. Then we can try to understand the action motivated by them on the basis of whatever opportunities for approximate emotional and intellectual interpretation seem to be available at different points in its course. These difficulties confront, for instance, people not susceptible to unusual acts of religious and charitable zeal, or persons who abhor extreme rationalist fanaticism (such as the fanatic advocacy of the "rights of man").

The more we ourselves are susceptible to such emotional reactions as anxiety, anger, ambition, envy, jealousy, love, enthusiasm, pride, vengefulness, loyalty, devotion, and appetites of all sorts, and to the "irrational" conduct which grows out of them, the more readily can we empathize with them. Even when such emotions are found in a degree of intensity of which the observer himself is completely incapable, he can still have a significant degree of emotional understanding of their meaning and can interpret intellectually their influence on the course of action and the selection of means.

For the purposes of a typological scientific analysis it is convenient to treat all irrational, affectually determined elements of behavior as factors of deviation from a conceptually pure type of rational action. For example a panic on the stock exchange can be most conveniently analysed by attempting to determine first what the course of action would have been if it had not been influenced by irrational affects; it is then possible to introduce the irrational components as accounting for the observed deviations from this hypothetical course. Similarly, in analysing a political or military campaign it is convenient to determine in the first place what would have been a rational course, given the ends of the participants and adequate knowledge of all the circumstances. Only in this way is it possible to assess the causal significance of irrational factors as accounting for the deviations from this type. The construction of a purely rational course of action in such cases serves the sociologist as a type (ideal type) which has the merit of clear understandability and lack of ambiguity. By comparison with this it is possible to understand the ways in which actual action is influenced by irrational factors of all sorts, such as affects and errors, in that they account for the deviation from the line of conduct which would be expected on the hypothesis that the action were purely rational.

Only in this respect and for these reasons of methodological convenience is the method of sociology "rationalistic." It is naturally not legitimate to interpret this procedure as involving a rationalistic bias of sociology, but only as a methodological device. It certainly does not involve a belief in the actual predominance of rational elements in human life, for on the question of how far this predominance does or does not exist, nothing whatever has been said. That there is, however, a danger of rationalistic interpretations where they are out of place cannot be denied. All experience unfortunately confirms the existence of this danger.

4. In all the sciences of human action, account must be taken of processes and phenomena which are devoid of subjective meaning, in the role of stimuli, results, favoring or hindering circumstances. To be devoid of meaning is not identical with being lifeless or non-human; every artifact, such as for example a machine, can be understood only in terms of the meaning which its production and use have had or were intended to have; a meaning which may derive from a relation to exceedingly various purposes. Without reference to this meaning such an object remains wholly unintelligible. That which is intelligible or understandable about it is thus its relation to human action in the role either of means or of end; a relation of which the actor or actors can be said to have been aware and to which their action has been oriented. Only in terms of such categories is it possible to "understand" objects of this kind. On the other hand processes or conditions, whether they are animate or inanimate, human or non-human, are in the present sense devoid of meaning in so far as they cannot be related to an intended purpose. That is to say they are devoid of meaning if they cannot be related to action in the role of means or ends but constitute only the stimulus, the favoring or hindering circumstances. It may be that the flooding of the Dollart [at the mouth of the Ems river near the Dutch-German border] in 1277 had historical significance as a stimulus to the beginning of certain migrations of considerable importance. Human mortality, indeed the organic life cycle from the helplessness of infancy to that of old age, is naturally of the very greatest sociological importance through the various ways in which human action has been oriented to these facts. To still another category of facts devoid of meaning belong certain psychic or psychophysical phenomena such as fatigue, habituation, memory, etc.; also certain typical states of euphoria under some conditions of ascetic mortification; finally, typical variations in the reactions of individuals according to reaction-time, precision, and other modes. But in the last analysis the same principle applies to these as to other phenomena which are devoid of meaning. Both the actor and the sociologist must accept them as data to be taken into account.

It is possible that future research may be able to discover non-interpretable uniformities underlying what has appeared to be specifically meaningful action, though little has been accomplished in this direction thus far. Thus, for example, differences in hereditary biological constitution, as of "races," would have to be treated by sociology as given data in the same way as the physiological facts of the need of nutrition or the effect of senescence on action. This would be the case if, and insofar as, we had statistically conclusive proof of their influence on sociologically relevant behavior. The recognition of the causal significance of such factors would not in the least alter the specific task of sociological analysis or of that of the other sciences of action, which is the interpretation of action in terms of its subjective meaning. The effect would be only to introduce certain non-interpretable data of the same order as others which are already present, into the complex of subjectively understandable motivation at certain points. (Thus it may come to be known that there are typical relations between the frequency of certain types of teleological orientation of action or of the degree of certain kinds of rationality and the cephalic index or skin color or any other biologically inherited characteristic.)

5. Understanding may be of two kinds: the first is the direct observational understanding[5] of the subjective meaning of a given act as such, including verbal utterances. We thus understand by direct observation, in this case, the meaning of the proposition $2 \times 2 = 4$ when we hear or read it. This is a case of the direct rational understanding of ideas. We also understand an outbreak of anger as manifested by facial expression, exclamations or irrational movements. This is direct observational understanding of irrational emotional reactions. We can understand in a similar observational way the action of a woodcutter or of somebody who reaches for the knob to shut a door or who aims a gun at an animal. This is rational observational understanding of actions.

Understanding may, however, be of another sort, namely explanatory understanding. Thus we understand in terms of *motive* the meaning an actor attaches to the proposition twice two equals four, when he states it or writes it down, in that we understand what makes him do this at precisely this moment and in these circumstances. Understanding in this sense is attained if we know that he is engaged in balancing a ledger or in making a scientific demonstration, or is engaged in some other task of which this particular act would be an appropriate part. This is rational understanding of motivation, which consists in placing the act in an intelligible and more inclusive context of meaning.[6] Thus we understand the chopping of wood or aiming of a gun in terms of motive in addition to direct observation if we know that the woodchopper is working for a wage or is chopping a supply of firewood for his own use or possibly is doing it for recreation. But he might also be working off a fit of rage, an irrational case. Similarly we understand the motive of a person aiming a gun if we know that he has been commanded to shoot as a member of a firing squad, that he is fighting against an enemy, or that he is doing it for revenge. The last is affectually determined and thus in a certain sense irrational. Finally we have a motivational understanding of the outburst of anger if we know that it has been provoked by jealousy, injured pride, or an insult. The last examples are all affectually determined and hence derived from irrational motives. In all the above cases the particular act has been placed in an understandable sequence of motivation, the understanding of which can be treated as an explanation of the actual course of behavior. Thus for a science which is concerned with the subjective meaning of action, explanation requires a grasp of the complex of meaning in which an actual course of understandable action thus interpreted belongs. In all such cases, even where the processes are largely affectual, the subjective meaning of the action, including that also of the relevant meaning complexes, will be called the intended meaning.[7] (This involves a departure from ordinary usage, which speaks of intention in this sense only in the case of rationally purposive action.)

[...]

The theoretical concepts of sociology are ideal types not only from the objective point of view, but also in their application to subjective processes. In the great majority of cases actual action goes on in a state of inarticulate half-consciousness or actual unconsciousness of its subjective meaning. The actor is more likely to "be aware" of it in a vague sense than he is to "know" what he is doing or be explicitly self-conscious about it. In most cases his action is governed by impulse or habit. Only occasionally and, in the uniform action of large numbers, often only in the case of a few individuals, is the subjective meaning of the action, whether rational or irrational, brought clearly into consciousness. The ideal type of meaningful action where the meaning is fully conscious and explicit is a marginal case. Every sociological or historical investigation, in applying its analysis to the empirical facts, must take this fact into account. But the difficulty need not prevent the sociologist from systematizing his concepts by the classification of possible types of subjective meaning. That is, he may reason as if action actually proceeded on the basis of clearly self-conscious meaning. The resulting deviation from the concrete facts must continually be kept in mind whenever it is a question of this level of concreteness, and must be carefully studied with reference both to degree and kind. It is often necessary to choose between terms which are either clear or unclear. Those which are clear will, to be sure, have the abstractness of ideal types, but they are none the less preferable for scientific purposes. ...

Social Action

1. Social action, which includes both failure to act and passive acquiescence, may be oriented to the past, present, or expected future behavior of others. Thus it may be motivated by revenge for a past attack, defence against present, or measures of defence against future aggression. The "others" may be individual persons, and may be known to the actor as such, or may constitute an indefinite plurality and may be entirely unknown as individuals. (Thus, money is a means of exchange which the actor accepts in payment because he orients his action to the expectation that a large but unknown number of individuals he is personally unacquainted with will be ready to accept it in exchange on some future occasion.)

2. Not every kind of action, even of overt action, is "social" in the sense of the present discussion. Overt action is non-social if it is oriented solely to the behavior of inanimate objects. Subjective attitudes constitute social action only so far as they are oriented to the behavior of others. For example, religious behavior is not social if it is

simply a matter of contemplation or of solitary prayer. The economic activity of an individual is social only if it takes account of the behavior of someone else. Thus very generally it becomes social insofar as the actor assumes that others will respect his actual control over economic goods. Concretely it is social, for instance, if in relation to the actor's own consumption the future wants of others are taken into account and this becomes one consideration affecting the actor's own saving. Or, in another connexion, production may be oriented to the future wants of other people.

3. Not every type of contact of human beings has a social character; this is rather confined to cases where the actor's behavior is meaningfully oriented to that of others. For example, a mere collision of two cyclists may be compared to a natural event. On the other hand, their attempt to avoid hitting each other, or whatever insults, blows, or friendly discussion might follow the collision, would constitute "social action."

4. Social action is not identical either with the similar actions of many persons or with every action influenced by other persons. Thus, if at the beginning of a shower a number of people on the street put up their umbrellas at the same time, this would not ordinarily be a case of action mutually oriented to that of each other, but rather of all reacting in the same way to the like need of protection from the rain. It is well known that the actions of the individual are strongly influenced by the mere fact that he is a member of a crowd confined within a limited space. Thus, the subject matter of studies of "crowd psychology," such as those of Le Bon, will be called "action conditioned by crowds." It is also possible for large numbers, though dispersed, to be influenced simultaneously or successively by a source of influence operating similarly on all the individuals, as by means of the press. Here also the behavior of an individual is influenced by his membership in a "mass" and by the fact that he is aware of being a member. Some types of reaction are only made possible by the mere fact that the individual acts as part of a crowd. Others become more difficult under these conditions. Hence it is possible that a particular event or mode of human behavior can give rise to the most diverse kinds of feeling – gaiety, anger, enthusiasm, despair, and passions of all sorts – in a crowd situation which would not occur at all or not nearly so readily if the individual were alone. But for this to happen there need not, at least in many cases, be any meaningful relation between the behavior of the individual and the fact that he is a member of a crowd. It is not proposed in the present sense to call action "social" when it is merely a result of the effect on the individual of the existence of a crowd as such and the action is not oriented to that fact on the level of meaning. At the same time the borderline is naturally highly indefinite. In such cases as that of the influence of the demagogue, there may be a wide variation in the extent to which his mass clientele is affected by a meaningful reaction to the fact of its large numbers; and whatever this relation may be, it is open to varying interpretations.

But furthermore, mere "imitation" of the action of others, such as that on which Tarde has rightly laid emphasis, will not be considered a case of specifically social action if it is purely reactive so that there is no meaningful orientation to the actor imitated. The borderline is, however, so indefinite that it is often hardly possible to discriminate. The mere fact that a person is found to employ some apparently useful procedure which he learned from someone else does not, however, constitute, in the present sense, social action. Action such as this is not oriented to the action of the other person, but the actor has, through observing the other, become acquainted with certain objective facts; and it is these to which his action is oriented. His action is then *causally* determined by the action of others, but not meaningfully. On the other hand, if the action of others is imitated because it is fashionable or traditional or exemplary, or lends social distinction, or on similar grounds, it is meaningfully oriented either to the behavior of the source of imitation or of third persons or of both. There are of course all manner of transitional cases between the two types of imitation. Both the phenomena discussed above, the behavior of crowds and imitation, stand on the indefinite borderline of social action. The same is true, as will often appear, of traditionalism and charisma. The reason for the indefiniteness of the line in these and other cases lies in the fact that both the orientation to the behavior of others and the meaning which can be imputed by the actor himself, are by no means always capable of clear determination and are often altogether unconscious and seldom fully self-conscious. Mere "influence" and meaningful orientation cannot therefore always be clearly differentiated on the empirical level. But conceptually it is essential to distinguish them, even though merely reactive imitation may well have a degree of sociological importance at least equal to that of the type which can be called social action in the strict sense. Sociology, it goes without saying, is by no means confined to the study of social action; this is only, at least for the kind of sociology being developed here, its central subject matter, that which may be said to be decisive for its status as a science. But this does not imply any judgment on the comparative importance of this and other factors.

Types of Social Action

Social action, like all action, may be oriented in four ways. It may be:

(1) *instrumentally rational (zweckrational)*, that is, determined by expectations as to the behavior of objects in the environment and of other human beings; these expectations are used as "conditions" or "means" for the attainment of the actor's own rationally pursued and calculated ends;
(2) *value-rational (wertrational)*, that is, determined by a conscious belief in the value for its own sake of some ethical, aesthetic, religious, or other form of behavior, independently of its prospects of success;
(3) *affectual* (especially emotional), that is, determined by the actor's specific affects and feeling states;
(4) *traditional*, that is, determined by ingrained habituation.

1. Strictly traditional behavior, like the reactive type of imitation discussed above, lies very close to the borderline of what can justifiably be called meaningfully oriented action, and indeed often on the other side. For it is very often a matter of almost automatic reaction to habitual stimuli which guide behavior in a course which has been repeatedly followed. The great bulk of all everyday action to which people have become habitually accustomed approaches this type. Hence, its place in a systematic

classification is not merely that of a limiting case because … attachment to habitual forms can be upheld with varying degrees of self-consciousness and in a variety of senses. In this case the type may shade over into value rationality (*Wertrationalität*).

2. Purely affectual behavior also stands on the borderline of what can be considered "meaningfully" oriented, and often it, too, goes over the line. It may, for instance, consist in an uncontrolled reaction to some exceptional stimulus. It is a case of sublimation when affectually determined action occurs in the form of conscious release of emotional tension. When this happens it is usually well on the road to rationalization in one or the other or both of the above senses.

3. The orientation of value-rational action is distinguished from the affectual type by its clearly self-conscious formulation of the ultimate values governing the action and the consistently planned orientation of its detailed course to these values. At the same time the two types have a common element, namely that the meaning of the action does not lie in the achievement of a result ulterior to it, but in carrying out the specific type of action for its own sake. Action is affectual if it satisfies a need for revenge, sensual gratification, devotion, contemplative bliss, or for working off emotional tensions (irrespective of the level of sublimation).

Examples of pure value-rational orientation would be the actions of persons who, regardless of possible cost to themselves, act to put into practice their convictions of what seems to them to be required by duty, honor, the pursuit of beauty, a religious call, personal loyalty, or the importance of some "cause" no matter in what it consists. In our terminology, value-rational action always involves "commands" or "demands" which, in the actor's opinion, are binding on him. It is only in cases where human action is motivated by the fulfillment of such unconditional demands that it will be called value-rational. This is the case in widely varying degrees, but for the most part only to a relatively slight extent. Nevertheless, it will be shown that the occurrence of this mode of action is important enough to justify its formulation as a distinct type; though it may be remarked that there is no intention here of attempting to formulate in any sense an exhaustive classification of types of action.

4. Action is instrumentally rational (*zweckrational*) when the end, the means, and the secondary results are all rationally taken into account and weighed. This involves rational consideration of alternative means to the end, of the relations of the end to the secondary consequences, and finally of the relative importance of different possible ends. Determination of action either in affectual or in traditional terms is thus incompatible with this type. Choice between alternative and conflicting ends and results may well be determined in a value-rational manner. In that case, action is instrumentally rational only in respect to the choice of means. On the other hand, the actor may, instead of deciding between alternative and conflicting ends in terms of a rational orientation to a system of values, simply take them as given subjective wants and arrange them in a scale of consciously assessed relative urgency. He may then orient his action to this scale in such a way that they are satisfied as far as possible in order of urgency, as formulated in the principle of "marginal utility." Value-rational action may thus have various different relations to the instrumentally rational action. From the latter point of view, however, value-rationality is always irrational. Indeed, the more the value to which action is oriented is elevated to the status of an absolute

value, the more "irrational" in this sense the corresponding action is. For, the more unconditionally the actor devotes himself to this value for its own sake, to pure sentiment or beauty, to absolute goodness or devotion to duty, the less is he influenced by considerations of the consequences of his action. The orientation of action wholly to the rational achievement of ends without relation to fundamental values is, to be sure, essentially only a limiting case.

5. It would be very unusual to find concrete cases of action, especially of social action, which were oriented *only* in one or another of these ways. Furthermore, this classification of the modes of orientation of action is in no sense meant to exhaust the possibilities of the field, but only to formulate in conceptually pure form certain sociologically important types to which actual action is more or less closely approximated or, in much the more common case, which constitute its elements. The usefulness of the classification for the purposes of this investigation can only be judged in terms of its results.

NOTES

1   In this series of definitions Weber employs several important terms which need discussion. In addition to *Verstehen*, ... there are four important ones: *Deuten, Sinn, Handeln*, and *Verhalten*. *Deuten* has generally been translated as "interpret." As used by Weber in this context it refers to the interpretation of subjective states of mind and the meanings which can be imputed as intended by an actor. Any other meaning of the word "interpretation" is irrelevant to Weber's discussion. The term *Sinn* has generally been translated as "meaning"; and its variations, particularly the corresponding adjectives, *sinnhaft, sinnvoll, sinnfremd*, have been dealt with by appropriately modifying the term *meaning*. The reference here again is always to features of the content of subjective states of mind or of symbolic systems which are ultimately referable to such states of mind.

The terms *Handeln* and *Verhalten* are directly related. *Verhalten* is the broader term referring to any mode of behavior of human individuals, regardless of the frame of reference in terms of which it is analysed. "Behavior" has seemed to be the most appropriate English equivalent. *Handeln*, on the other hand, refers to the concrete phenomenon of human behavior only insofar as it is capable of "understanding," in Weber's technical sense, in terms of subjective categories. The most appropriate English equivalent has seemed to be "action." This corresponds to [Parsons'] usage in *The Structure of Social Action* and would seem to be fairly well established. "Conduct" is also similar and has sometimes been used. *Deuten, Verstehen*, and *Sinn* are thus applicable to human behavior only insofar as it constitutes action or conduct in this specific sense.

2   Weber's text in Part One is organized in a manner frequently found in the German academic literature of his day, in that he first lays down certain fundamental definitions and then proceeds to comment on them. These comments, which apparently were not intended to be "read" in the ordinary sense, but rather serve as reference material for the clarification and systematization of the theoretical concepts and their implications, are in the German edition printed in a smaller type, a convention which we have followed in the rest of Part One. However, while in most cases the comments are relatively brief, under the definitions of "sociology" and "social action" Weber wrote what are essentially methodological essays (sec. 1: A–B), which because of their length we have printed in the ordinary type. (R)

3   Weber means by "pure type" what he himself generally called and what has come to be known in the literature about his methodology as the "ideal type." The reader may be referred for

general orientation to Weber's own essay (to which he himself refers below), "Die 'Objektivität' sozialwissenschaftlicher Erkenntnis" ("'Objectivity' in Social Science and Social Policy," in *Max Weber: The Methodology of the Social Sciences*. Edward Shils and Henry Finch, trans. and eds. (Glencoe: The Free Press, 1949). 50–113; originally published in *AfS*, vol. 19, 1904, reprinted in *GAzW*, 146–214); to two works of Alexander von Schelting, "Die logische Theorie der historischen Kulturwissenschaften von Max Weber," *AfS*, vol. 49, 1922, 623ff and *Max Webers Wissenschaftslehre*, 1934; Talcott Parsons, *The Structure of Social Action* (New York: McGraw-Hill, 1937), ch. 16; Theodore Abel, *Systematic Sociology in Germany*, (New York: Columbia University Press, 1929). [See now also Raymond Aron, *German Sociology*, trans. by M. and T. Bottomore (New York: The Free Press of Glencoe, 1964), based on 2nd French ed. of 1950.]

4   This is an imperfect rendering of the German term *Evidenz*, for which, unfortunately, there is no good English equivalent. It has hence been rendered in a number of different ways, varying with the particular context in which it occurs. The primary meaning refers to the basis on which a scientist or thinker becomes satisfied of the certainty or acceptability of a proposition. As Weber himself points out, there are two primary aspects of this. On the one hand a conclusion can be "seen" to follow from given premises by virtue of logical, mathematical, or possibly other modes of meaningful relation. In this sense one "sees" the solution of an arithmetical problem or the correctness of the proof of a geometrical theorem. The other aspect is concerned with empirical observation. If an act of observation is competently performed, in a similar sense one "sees" the truth of the relevant descriptive proposition. The term *Evidenz* does not refer to the process of observing, but to the quality of its result, by virtue of which the observer feels justified in affirming a given statement. Hence "certainty" has seemed a suitable translation in some contexts, "clarity" in others, "accuracy" in still others. The term "intuition" is not usable because it refers to the process rather than to he result.

5   Weber here uses the term *aktuelles Verstehen*, which he contrasts with *erklärendes Verstehen*. The latter he also refers to as *motivationsmässig*. "*Aktuell*" in this context has been translated as "observational." It is clear from Weber's discussion that the primary criterion is the possibility of deriving the meaning of an act or symbolic expression from immediate observation without reference to any broader context. In *erklärendes Verstehen*, on the other hand, the particular act must be placed in a broader context of meaning involving facts which cannot be derived from immediate observation of a particular act or expression.

6   The German term is *Sinnzusammenhang*. It refers to a plurality of elements which form a coherent whole on the level of meaning. There are several possible modes of meaningful relation between such elements, such as logical consistency, the esthetic harmony of a style, or the appropriateness of means to an end. In any case, however, a *Sinnzusammenhang* must be distinguished from a system of elements which are causally interdependent. There seems to be no single English term or phrase which is always adequate. According to variations in context, "context of meaning," "complex of meaning," and sometimes "meaningful system" have been employed.

7   The German is *gemeinter Sinn*. Weber departs from ordinary usage not only in broadening the meaning of this conception. As he states at the end of the present methodological discussion, he does not restrict the use of this concept to cases where a clear self-conscious awareness of such meaning can be reasonably attributed to every individual actor. Essentially, what Weber is doing is to formulate an operational concept. The question is not whether in a sense obvious to the ordinary person such an intended meaning "really exists," but whether the concept is capable of providing a logical framework within which scientifically important observations can be made. The test of validity of the observations is not whether their object is immediately clear to common sense, but whether the results of these technical observations can be satisfactorily organized and related to those of others in a systematic body of knowledge.

3C Max Weber from *Essays in Sociology*

Original publication details: Max Weber, from *Essays in Sociology*, translated and edited by H.H. Gerth and C. Wright Mills (1946), pp. 196–198 ("Bureaucracy"); 159, 172–174 ("Structures of Power"); 180–182, 186–188, 193–195 ("Class, Status, Party"); 245–248 ("The Sociology of Charismatic Authority); 145–147, 151–153 ("Science as a Vocation"). Reproduced with permission of Oxford University Press via PLS Clear.

Bureaucracy

CHARACTERISTICS OF BUREAUCRACY[1]

MODERN officialdom functions in the following specific manner:

I. There is the principle of fixed and official jurisdictional areas, which are generally ordered by rules, that is, by laws or administrative regulations.

1 The regular activities required for the purposes of the bureaucratically governed structure are distributed in a fixed way as official duties.
2 The authority to give the commands required for the discharge of these duties is distributed in a stable way and is strictly delimited by rules concerning the coercive means, physical, sacerdotal, or otherwise, which may be placed at the disposal of officials.
3 Methodical provision is made for the regular and continuous fulfilment of these duties and for the execution of the corresponding rights; only persons who have the generally regulated qualifications to serve are employed.

In public and lawful government these three elements constitute 'bureaucratic authority.' In private economic domination, they constitute bureaucratic 'management.' Bureaucracy, thus understood, is fully developed in political and ecclesiastical communities only in the modern state, and, in the private economy, only in the most advanced institutions of capitalism. Permanent and public office authority, with fixed jurisdiction, is not the historical rule but rather the exception. This is so even in large political structures such as those of the ancient Orient, the Germanic and Mongolian empires of conquest, or of many feudal structures of state. In all these cases, the ruler executes the most important measures through personal trustees, table-companions, or court-servants. Their commissions and authority are not precisely delimited and are temporarily called into being for each case.

II. The principles of office hierarchy and of levels of graded authority mean a firmly ordered system of super- and subordination in which there is a supervision of the lower offices by the higher ones. Such a system offers the governed the possibility of appealing the decision of a lower office to its higher authority, in a definitely regulated manner. With the full development of the bureaucratic type, the office hierarchy is monocratically organized. The principle of hierarchical office authority is found in all bureaucratic structures: in state and ecclesiastical structures as well as in large party organizations and private enterprises. It does not matter for the character of bureaucracy whether its authority is called 'private' or 'public.'

When the principle of jurisdictional 'competency' is fully carried through, hierarchical subordination – at least in public office – does not mean that the 'higher' authority is simply authorized to take over the business of the 'lower.' Indeed, the opposite is the rule. Once established and having fulfilled its task, an office tends to continue in existence and be held by another incumbent.

III. The management of the modern office is based upon written documents ('the files'), which are preserved in their original or draught form. There is, therefore, a staff of subaltern officials and scribes of all sorts. The body of officials actively engaged in a 'public' office, along with the respective apparatus of material implements and the files, make up a 'bureau.' In private enterprise, 'the bureau' is often called 'the office.'

In principle, the modern organization of the civil service separates the bureau from the private domicile of the official, and, in general, bureaucracy segregates official activity as something distinct from the sphere of private life. Public monies and equipment are divorced from the private property of the official. This condition is everywhere the product of a long development. Nowadays, it is found in public as well as in private enterprises; in the latter, the principle extends even to the leading entrepreneur. In principle, the executive office is separated from the household, business from private correspondence, and business assets from private fortunes. The more consistently the modern type of business management has been carried through the more are these separations the case. The beginnings of this process are to be found as early as the Middle Ages.

It is the peculiarity of the modern entrepreneur that he conducts himself as the 'first official' of his enterprise, in the very same way in which the ruler of a specifically modern bureaucratic state [may speak of being] … 'the first servant' of the state. The idea that the bureau activities of the state are intrinsically different in character from the management of private economic offices is a continental European notion and, by way of contrast, is totally foreign to the American way.

IV. Office management, at least all specialized office management – and such management is distinctly modern – usually presupposes thorough and expert training. This increasingly holds for the modern executive and employee of private enterprises, in the same manner as it holds for the state official.

V. When the office is fully developed, official activity demands the full working capacity of the official, irrespective of the fact that his obligatory time in the bureau may be firmly delimited. In the normal case, this is only the product of a long development, in the public as well as in the private office. Formerly, in all cases, the normal state of affairs was reversed: official business was discharged as a secondary activity.

VI. The management of the office follows general rules, which are more or less stable, more or less exhaustive, and which can be learned. Knowledge of these rules represents a special technical learning which the officials possess. It involves jurisprudence, or administrative or business management.

The reduction of modern office management to rules is deeply embedded in its very nature. The theory of modern public administration, for instance, assumes that the authority to order certain matters by decree – which has been legally granted to public authorities – does not entitle the bureau to regulate the matter by commands given for each case, but only to regulate the matter abstractly. This stands in extreme contrast to the regulation of all relationships through individual privileges and bestowals of favor, which is absolutely dominant in patrimonialism, at least in so far as such relationships are not fixed by sacred tradition.

Structures of Power

1: The Prestige and Power of the 'Great Powers'[2]

All political structures use force, but they differ in the manner in which and the extent to which they use or threaten to use it against other political organizations. These differences play a specific role in determining the form and destiny of political communities. Not all political structures are equally 'expansive.' They do not all strive for an outward expansion of their power, or keep their force in readiness for acquiring political power over other territories and communities by incorporating them or making them dependent. Hence, as structures of power, political organizations vary in the extent to which they are turned outward.

[...]

If the concept of 'nation' can in any way be defined unambiguously, it certainly cannot be stated in terms of empirical qualities common to those who count as members of the nation. In the sense of those using the term at a given time, the concept undoubtedly means, above all, that one may exact from certain groups of men a specific sentiment of solidarity in the face of other groups. Thus, the concept belongs in the sphere of values. Yet, there is no agreement on how these groups should be delimited or about what concerted action should result from such solidarity.

In ordinary language, 'nation' is, first of all, not identical with the 'people of a state,' that is, with the membership of a given polity. Numerous polities comprise groups among whom the independence of their 'nation' is emphatically asserted in the face of the other groups; or, on the other hand, they comprise parts of a group whose members declare this group to be one homogeneous 'nation' (Austria before 1918, for example). Furthermore, a 'nation' is not identical with a community speaking the same language; that this by no means always suffices is indicated by the Serbs and Croats, the North Americans, the Irish, and the English. On the contrary, a common language does not seem to be absolutely necessary to a 'nation.' In official documents, besides 'Swiss People' one also finds the phrase 'Swiss Nation.' And some language groups do not think of themselves as a separate 'nation,' for example, at least until recently, the white Russians. The pretension, however, to be considered a special 'nation' is regularly associated with a common language as a culture value of the masses; this is predominantly the case in the classic country of language conflicts, Austria, and equally so in Russia and in eastern Prussia. But this linkage of the common language and 'nation' is of varying intensity; for instance, it is very low in the United States as well as in Canada.

'National' solidarity among men speaking the same language may be just as well rejected as accepted. Solidarity, instead, may be linked with differences in the other great 'culture value of the masses,' namely, a religious creed, as is the case with the

Serbs and Croats. National solidarity may be connected with differing social structure and mores and hence with 'ethnic' elements, as is the case with the German Swiss and the Alsatians in the face of the Germans of the Reich, or with the Irish facing the British. Yet above all, national solidarity may be linked to memories of a common political destiny with other nations, among the Alsatians with the French since the revolutionary war which represents their common heroic age, just as among the Baltic Barons with the Russians whose political destiny they helped to steer.

It goes without saying that 'national' affiliation need not be based upon common blood. Indeed, everywhere the especially radical 'nationalists' are often of foreign descent. Furthermore, although a specific common anthropological type is not irrelevant to nationality, it is neither sufficient nor a prerequisite to found a nation. Nevertheless, the idea of the 'nation' is apt to include the notions of common descent and of an essential, though frequently indefinite, homogeneity. The nation has these notions in common with the sentiment of solidarity of ethnic communities, which is also nourished from various sources. But the sentiment of ethnic solidarity does not by itself make a 'nation.' Undoubtedly, even the white Russians in the face of the Great Russians have always had a sentiment of ethnic solidarity, yet even at the present time they would hardly claim to qualify as a separate 'nation.' The Poles of Upper Silesia, until recently, had hardly any feeling of solidarity with the 'Polish Nation.' They felt themselves to be a separate ethnic group in the face of the Germans, but for the rest they were Prussian subjects and nothing else.

Whether the Jews may be called a 'nation' is an old problem. The mass of the Russian Jews, the assimilating West-European-American Jews, the Zionists – these would in the main give a negative answer. In any case, their answers would vary in nature and extent. In particular, the question would be answered very differently by the peoples of their environment, for example, by the Russians on the one side and by the Americans on the other – or at least by those Americans who at the present time still maintain American and Jewish nature to be essentially similar, as an American President has asserted in an official document.

Those German-speaking Alsatians who refuse to belong to the German 'nation' and who cultivate the memory of political union with France do not thereby consider themselves simply as members of the French 'nation.' The Negroes of the United States, at least at present, consider themselves members of the American 'nation,' but they will hardly ever be so considered by the Southern Whites.

Class, Status, Party

1: Economically Determined Power and the Social Order

Law exists when there is a probability that an order will be upheld by a specific staff of men who will use physical or psychical compulsion with the intention of obtaining conformity with the order, or of inflicting sanctions for infringement of it.[3] The structure of every legal order directly influences the distribution of power, economic or otherwise, within its respective community. This is true of all legal orders and not only that of the state. In general, we understand by 'power' the chance of a man or of a number of men to realize their own will in a communal action even against the resistance of others who are participating in the action.

'Economically conditioned' power is not, of course, identical with 'power' as such. On the contrary, the emergence of economic power may be the consequence of power existing on other grounds. Man does not strive for power only in order to enrich himself economically. Power, including economic power, may be valued 'for its own sake.' Very frequently the striving for power is also conditioned by the social 'honor' it entails. Not all power, however, entails social honor: The typical American Boss, as well as the typical big speculator, deliberately relinquishes social honor. Quite generally, 'mere economic' power, and especially 'naked' money power, is by no means a recognized basis of social honor. Nor is power the only basis of social honor. Indeed, social honor, or prestige, may even be the basis of political or economic power, and very frequently has been. Power, as well as honor, may be guaranteed by the legal order, but, at least normally, it is not their primary source. The legal order is rather an additional factor that enhances the chance to hold power or honor; but it cannot always secure them.

The way in which social honor is distributed in a community between typical groups participating in this distribution we may call the 'social order.' The social order and the economic order are, of course, similarly related to the 'legal order.' However, the social and the economic order are not identical. The economic order is for us merely the way in which economic goods and services are distributed and used. The social order is of course conditioned by the economic order to a high degree, and in its turn reacts upon it.

Now: 'classes,' 'status groups,' and 'parties' are phenomena of the distribution of power within a community.

2: DETERMINATION OF CLASS-SITUATION BY MARKET-SITUATION

In our terminology, 'classes' are not communities; they merely represent possible, and frequent, bases for communal action. We may speak of a 'class' when (1) a number of people have in common a specific causal component of their life chances, in so far as (2) this component is represented exclusively by economic interests in the possession of goods and opportunities for income, and (3) is represented under the conditions of the commodity or labor markets. [These points refer to 'class situation,' which we may express more briefly as the typical chance for a supply of goods, external living conditions, and personal life experiences, in so far as this chance is determined by the amount and kind of power, or lack of such, to dispose of goods or skills for the sake of income in a given economic order. The term 'class' refers to any group of people that is found in the same class situation.]

It is the most elemental economic fact that the way in which the disposition over material property is distributed among a plurality of people, meeting competitively in the market for the purpose of exchange, in itself creates specific life chances. According to the law of marginal utility this mode of distribution excludes the non-owners from competing for highly valued goods; it favors the owners and, in fact, gives to them a monopoly to acquire such goods. Other things being equal, this mode of distribution monopolizes the opportunities for profitable deals for all those who, provided with goods, do not necessarily have to exchange them. It increases, at least generally, their power in price wars with those who, being propertyless, have nothing to offer but their services in native form or goods in a form constituted through their own labor, and who above all are compelled to get rid of these products in order barely to subsist. This mode of distribution gives to the propertied a monopoly on the possibility of transferring property from the sphere of use as a 'fortune,' to the sphere of 'capital goods'; that is, it gives them the entrepreneurial function and all chances to share directly or indirectly in returns on capital. All this holds true within the area in which pure market conditions prevail. 'Property' and 'lack of property' are, therefore, the basic categories of all class situations. It does not matter whether these two categories become effective in price wars or in competitive struggles.

Within these categories, however, class situations are further differentiated: on the one hand, according to the kind of property that is usable for returns; and, on the other hand, according to the kind of services that can be offered in the market. Ownership of domestic buildings; productive establishments; warehouses; stores; agriculturally usable land, large and small holdings – quantitative differences with possibly qualitative consequences –; ownership of mines; cattle; men (slaves); disposition over mobile instruments of production, or capital goods of all sorts, especially money or objects that can be exchanged for money easily and at any time; disposition over products of one's own labor or of others' labor differing according to their various distances from consumability; disposition over transferable monopolies of any kind – all these distinctions differentiate the class situations of the propertied just as does the 'meaning' which they can and do give to the utilization of property, especially to property which has money equivalence. Accordingly, the propertied, for instance, may belong to the class of rentiers or to the class of entrepreneurs.

Those who have no property but who offer services are differentiated just as much according to their kinds of services as according to the way in which they make use of these services, in a continuous or discontinuous relation to a recipient. But always this is the generic connotation of the concept of class: that the kind of chance in the *market* is the decisive moment which presents a common condition for the individual's fate. 'Class situation' is, in this sense, ultimately 'market situation.'

The Sociology of Charismatic Authority

1: THE GENERAL CHARACTER OF CHARISMA[4]

BUREAUCRATIC and patriarchal structures are antagonistic in many ways, yet they have in common a most important peculiarity: permanence. In this respect they are both institutions of daily routine. Patriarchal power especially is rooted in the provisioning of recurrent and normal needs of the workaday life. Patriarchal authority thus has its original locus in the economy, that is, in those branches of the economy that can be satisfied by means of normal routine. The patriarch is the 'natural leader' of the daily routine. And in this respect, the bureaucratic structure is only the counter-image of patriarchalism transposed into rationality. As a permanent structure with a system of rational rules, bureaucracy is fashioned to meet calculable and recurrent needs by means of a normal routine.

The provisioning of all demands that go beyond those of everyday routine has had, in principle, an entirely heterogeneous, namely, a *charismatic,* foundation; the further back we look in history, the more we find this to be the case. This means that the 'natural' leaders – in times of psychic, physical, economic, ethical, religious, political distress – have been neither officeholders nor incumbents of an 'occupation' in the present sense of the word, that is, men who have acquired expert knowledge and who serve for remuneration. The natural leaders in distress have been holders of specific gifts of the body and spirit; and these gifts have been believed to be supernatural, not accessible to everybody. The concept of 'charisma' is here used in a completely 'value-neutral' sense.

The capacity of the Irish culture hero, Cuchulain, or of the Homeric Achilles for heroic frenzy is a manic seizure, just as is that of the Arabian berserk who bites his shield like a mad dog – biting around until he darts off in raving bloodthirstiness. For a long time it has been maintained that the seizure of the berserk is artificially produced through acute poisoning. In Byzantium, a number of 'blond beasts,' disposed to such seizures, were kept about, just as war elephants were formerly kept. Shamanist ecstasy is linked to constitutional epilepsy, the possession and the testing of which represents a charismatic qualification. Hence neither is 'edifying' to our minds. They are just as little edifying to us as is the kind of 'revelation,' for instance, of the Sacred Book of the Mormons, which, at least from an evaluative standpoint, perhaps would have to be called a 'hoax.' But sociology is not concerned with such questions. In the faith of their followers, the chief of the Mormons has proved himself to be charismatically qualified, as have 'heroes' and 'sorcerers.' All of them have practiced their arts and ruled by virtue of this gift (charisma) and, where the idea of God has already been clearly conceived, by virtue of the divine mission lying therein. This holds for doctors and prophets, just as for judges and military leaders, or for leaders of big hunting expeditions.

It is to his credit that Rudolf Sohm brought out the sociological peculiarity of this category of domination-structure for a historically important special case, namely, the historical development of the authority of the early Christian church. Sohm performed this task with logical consistency, and hence, by necessity, he was one-sided from a purely historical point of view. In principle, however, the very same state of affairs recurs universally, although often it is most clearly developed in the field of religion.

In contrast to any kind of bureaucratic organization of offices, the charismatic structure knows nothing of a form or of an ordered procedure of appointment or dismissal. It knows no regulated 'career,' 'advancement,' 'salary,' or regulated and expert training of the holder of charisma or of his aids. It knows no agency of control or appeal, no local bailiwicks or exclusive functional jurisdictions; nor does it embrace permanent institutions like our bureaucratic 'departments,' which are independent of persons and of purely personal charisma.

Charisma knows only inner determination and inner restraint. The holder of charisma seizes the task that is adequate for him and demands obedience and a following by virtue of his mission. His success determines whether he finds them. His charismatic claim breaks down if his mission is not recognized by those to whom he feels he has been sent. If they recognize him, he is their master – so long as he knows how to maintain recognition through 'proving' himself. But he does not derive his 'right' from their will, in the manner of an election. Rather, the reverse holds: it is the *duty* of those to whom he addresses his mission to recognize him as their charismatically qualified leader.

In Chinese theory, the emperor's prerogatives are made dependent upon the recognition of the people. But this does not mean recognition of the sovereignty of the people any more than did the prophet's necessity of getting recognition from the believers in the early Christian community. The Chinese theory, rather, characterizes the charismatic nature of the *monarch's position,* which adheres to his *personal* qualification and to his *proved* worth.

Charisma can be, and of course regularly is, qualitatively particularized. This is an internal rather than an external affair, and results in the qualitative barrier of the charisma holder's mission and power. In meaning and in content the mission may be addressed to a group of men who are delimited locally, ethnically, socially, politically, occupationally, or in some other way. If the mission is thus addressed to a limited group of men, as is the rule, it finds its limits within their circle.

In its economic sub-structure, as in everything else, charismatic domination is the very opposite of bureaucratic domination. If bureaucratic domination depends upon regular income, and hence at least *a potiori* on a money economy and money taxes, charisma lives in, though not off, this world. This has to be properly understood. Frequently charisma quite deliberately shuns the possession of money and of pecuniary income *per se,* as did Saint Francis and many of his like; but this is of course not the rule. Even a pirate genius may exercise a 'charismatic' domination, in the value-neutral sense intended here. Charismatic political heroes seek booty and, above all, gold. But charisma, and this is decisive, always rejects as undignified any pecuniary gain that is methodical and rational. In general, charisma rejects all rational economic conduct.

The sharp contrast between charisma and any 'patriarchal' structure that rests upon the ordered base of the 'household' lies in this rejection of rational economic conduct. In its 'pure' form, charisma is never a source of private gain for its holders in the sense of economic exploitation by the making of a deal. Nor is it a source of income in the form of pecuniary compensation, and just as little does it involve an orderly taxation for the material requirements of its mission. If the mission is one of peace, individual patrons provide the necessary means for charismatic structures; or those to whom the charisma is addressed provide honorific gifts, donations, or other voluntary contributions. In the case of charismatic warrior heroes, booty represents one of the ends as well as the material means of the mission. 'Pure' charisma is contrary to all patriarchal domination (in the sense of the term used here). It is the opposite of all ordered economy. It is the very force that disregards economy. This also holds, indeed precisely, where the charismatic leader is after the acquisition of goods, as is the case with the charismatic warrior hero. Charisma can do this because by its very nature it is not an 'institutional' and permanent structure, but rather, where its 'pure' type is at work, it is the very opposite of the institutionally permanent.

[...]

Science as a Vocation

[...]
   Consider the historical and cultural sciences. They teach us how to understand and interpret political, artistic, literary, and social phenomena in terms of their origins. But they give us no answer to the question, whether the existence of these cultural phenomena have been and are *worth while*. And they do not answer the further question, whether it is worth the effort required to know them. They presuppose that there is an interest in partaking, through this procedure, of the community of 'civilized men.' But they cannot prove 'scientifically' that this is the case; and that they presuppose this interest by no means proves that it goes without saying. In fact it is not at all self-evident.
   Finally, let us consider the disciplines close to me: sociology, history, economics, political science, and those types of cultural philosophy that make it their task to interpret these sciences. It is said, and I agree, that politics is out of place in the lecture-room. It does not belong there on the part of the students. If, for instance, in the lecture-room of my former colleague Dietrich Schäfer in Berlin, pacifist students were to surround his desk and make an uproar, I should deplore it just as much as I should deplore the uproar which anti-pacifist students are said to have made against Professor Förster, whose views in many ways are as remote as could be from mine. Neither does politics, however, belong in the lecture-room on the part of the docents, and when the docent is scientifically concerned with politics, it belongs there least of all.
   To take a practical political stand is one thing, and to analyze political structures and party positions is another. When speaking in a political meeting about democracy, one does not hide one's personal standpoint; indeed, to come out clearly and take a stand is one's damned duty. The words one uses in such a meeting are not means of scientific analysis but means of canvassing votes and winning over others. They are not plow-shares to loosen the soil of contemplative thought; they are swords against the enemies: such words are weapons. It would be an outrage, however, to use words in this fashion in a lecture or in the lecture-room. If, for instance, 'democracy' is under discussion, one considers its various forms, analyzes them in the way they function, determines what results for the conditions of life the one form has as compared with the other. Then one confronts the forms of democracy with non-democratic forms of political order and endeavors to come to a position where the student may find the point from which, in terms of his ultimate ideals, he can take a stand. But the true teacher will beware of imposing from the platform any political position upon the student, whether it is expressed or suggested. 'To let the facts speak for themselves' is the most unfair way of putting over a political position to the student.

Why should we abstain from doing this? I state in advance that some highly esteemed colleagues are of the opinion that it is not possible to carry through this self-restraint and that, even if it were possible, it would be a whim to avoid declaring oneself. Now one cannot demonstrate scientifically what the duty of an academic teacher is. One can only demand of the teacher that he have the intellectual integrity to see that it is one thing to state facts, to determine mathematical or logical relations or the internal structure of cultural values, while it is another thing to answer questions of the *value* of culture and its individual contents and the question of how one should act in the cultural community and in political associations. These are quite heterogeneous problems. If he asks further why he should not deal with both types of problems in the lecture-room, the answer is: because the prophet and the demagogue do not belong on the academic platform.

To the prophet and the demagogue, it is said: 'Go your ways out into the streets and speak openly to the world,' that is, speak where criticism is possible. In the lecture-room we stand opposite our audience, and it has to remain silent. I deem it irresponsible to exploit the circumstance that for the sake of their career the students have to attend a teacher's course while there is nobody present to oppose him with criticism. The task of the teacher is to serve the students with his knowledge and scientific experience and not to imprint upon them his personal political views. It is certainly possible that the individual teacher will not entirely succeed in eliminating his personal sympathies. He is then exposed to the sharpest criticism in the forum of his own conscience. And this deficiency does not prove anything; other errors are also possible, for instance, erroneous statements of fact, and yet they prove nothing against the duty of searching for the truth. I also reject this in the very interest of science. I am ready to prove from the works of our historians that whenever the man of science introduces his personal value judgment, a full understanding of the facts *ceases*. But this goes beyond tonight's topic and would require lengthy elucidation.

I ask only: How should a devout Catholic, on the one hand, and a Freemason, on the other, in a course on the forms of church and state or on religious history ever be brought to evaluate these subjects alike? This is out of the question. And yet the academic teacher must desire and must demand of himself to serve the one as well as the other by his knowledge and methods. Now you will rightly say that the devout Catholic will never accept the view of the factors operative in bringing about Christianity which a teacher who is free of his dogmatic presuppositions presents to him. Certainly! The difference, however, lies in the following: Science 'free from presuppositions,' in the sense of a rejection of religious bonds, does not know of the 'miracle' and the 'revelation.' If it did, science would be unfaithful to its own 'presuppositions.' The believer knows both, miracle and revelation. And science 'free from presuppositions' expects from him no less – and no more – than acknowledgment that *if* the process can be explained without those supernatural interventions, which an empirical explanation has to eliminate as causal factors, the process has to be explained the way science attempts to do. And the believer can do this without being disloyal to his faith.

But has the contribution of science no meaning at all for a man who does not care to know facts as such and to whom only the practical standpoint matters? Perhaps science nevertheless contributes something.

The primary task of a useful teacher is to teach his students to recognize 'inconvenient' facts – I mean facts that are inconvenient for their party opinions. And for every party opinion there are facts that are extremely inconvenient, for my own opinion no less than for others. I believe the teacher accomplishes more than a mere intellectual task if he compels his audience to accustom itself to the existence of such facts. I would be so immodest as even to apply the expression 'moral achievement,' though perhaps this may sound too grandiose for something that should go without saying.

Thus far I have spoken only of practical reasons for avoiding the imposition of a personal point of view. But these are not the only reasons. The impossibility of 'scientifically' pleading for practical and interested stands – except in discussing the means for a firmly given and presupposed end – rests upon reasons that lie far deeper.

'Scientific' pleading is meaningless in principle because the various value spheres of the world stand in irreconcilable conflict with each other.

[...]

Fortunately, however, the contribution of science does not reach its limit with this. We are in a position to help you to a third objective: to gain *clarity*. Of course, it is presupposed that we ourselves possess clarity. As far as this is the case, we can make clear to you the following:

In practice, you can take this or that position when concerned with a problem of value – for simplicity's sake, please think of social phenomena as examples. *If* you take such and such a stand, then, according to scientific experience, you have to use such and such a *means* in order to carry out your conviction practically. Now, these means are perhaps such that you believe you must reject them. Then you simply must choose between the end and the inevitable means. Does the end 'justify' the means? Or does it not? The teacher can confront you with the necessity of this choice. He cannot do more, so long as he wishes to remain a teacher and not to become a demagogue. He can, of course, also tell you that if you want such and such an end, then you must take into the bargain the subsidiary consequences which according to all experience will occur. Again we find ourselves in the same situation as before. These are still problems that can also emerge for the technician, who in numerous instances has to make decisions according to the principle of the lesser evil or of the relatively best. Only to him one thing, the main thing, is usually given, namely, the end. But as soon as truly 'ultimate' problems are at stake for us this is not the case. With this, at long last, we come to the final service that science as such can render to the aim of clarity, and at the same time we come to the limits of science.

Besides we can and we should state: In terms of its meaning, such and such a practical stand can be derived with inner consistency, and hence integrity, from this or that ultimate *weltanschauliche* position. Perhaps it can only be derived from one such fundamental position, or maybe from several, but it cannot be derived from these or those other positions. Figuratively speaking, you serve this god and you offend the other god when you decide to adhere to this position. And if you remain faithful to yourself, you will necessarily come to certain final conclusions that subjectively make sense. This much, in principle at least, can be accomplished. Philosophy, as a special discipline, and the essentially philosophical discussions of principles in the other sciences attempt to achieve this. Thus, if we are competent in our pursuit (which must be presupposed here) we can force the individual, or at least we can help him, to give himself an *account of the ultimate meaning of his own conduct*. This appears to me as not so trifling a thing to do, even for one's own personal life. Again, I am tempted to say of a teacher who succeeds in this: he stands in the service of 'moral' forces; he fulfils the duty of bringing about self-clarification and a sense of responsibility. And I believe he will be the more able to accomplish this, the more conscientiously he avoids the desire personally to impose upon or suggest to his audience his own stand.

This proposition, which I present here, always takes its point of departure from the one fundamental fact, that so long as life remains immanent and is interpreted in its own terms, it knows only of an unceasing struggle of these gods with one another. Or speaking directly, the ultimately possible attitudes toward life are irreconcilable, and hence their struggle can never be brought to a final conclusion. Thus it is necessary to make a decisive choice. Whether, under such conditions, science is a worth while 'vocation' for somebody, and whether science itself has an objectively valuable 'vocation' are again value judgments about which nothing can be said in the lecture-room. To affirm the value of science is a presupposition for teaching there. I personally by my very work answer in the affirmative, and I also do so from precisely the standpoint that hates intellectualism as the worst devil, as youth does today, or usually only fancies it does. In that case the word holds for these youths: 'Mind you, the devil is old; grow old to understand him.' This does not mean age in the sense of the birth certificate. It means that if one wishes to settle with this devil, one must not take to flight before him as so many like to do nowadays. First of all, one has to see the devil's ways to the end in order to realize his power and his limitations.

Science today is a 'vocation' organized in special disciplines in the service of self-clarification and knowledge of interrelated facts. It is not the gift of grace of seers and prophets dispensing sacred values and revelations, nor does it partake of the contemplation of sages and philosophers about the meaning of the universe. This, to be sure, is the inescapable condition of our historical situation. We cannot evade it so long as we remain true to ourselves. And if Tolstoi's question recurs to you: as science does not, who is to answer the question: 'What shall we do, and, how shall we arrange our lives?' or, in the words used here tonight: 'Which of the warring gods should we serve? Or should we serve perhaps an entirely different god, and who is he?' then one can say that only a prophet or a savior can give the answers. If there is no such man, or if his message is no longer believed in, then you will certainly not compel him to appear on this earth by having thousands of professors, as privileged hirelings of the state, attempt as petty prophets in their lecture-rooms to take over his role. All they will accomplish is to show that they are unaware of the decisive state of affairs: the prophet for whom so many of our younger generation yearn simply does not exist. But this knowledge in its forceful significance has never become vital for them. The inward interest of a truly religiously 'musical' man can never be served by veiling to him and to others the fundamental fact that he is destined to live in a godless and prophetless time by giving him the *ersatz* of armchair prophecy. The integrity of his religious organ, it seems to me, must rebel against this.

NOTES

1 *Wirtschaft und Gesellschaft*, part III, chap. 6, pp. 650–78.
2 *Wirtschaft und Gesellschaft* (Tübingen, 1922 edition), part III, chap. 3, pp. 619–30; and *Gesammelte Aufraetze zur Soziologie und Sozialpolitik* (Tübingen, 1924), pp. 484–6. *Wirtschaft und Gesellschaft* appeared posthumously (1921) as part of the Grundriss für Sozialokonomik, handled by J.C.B. Mohr (P. Siebeck), Tübingen. Weber worked on the descriptive parts of *Wirtschaft und Gesellschaft* from 1910, and most of the chapters were essentially written before 1914.
3 *Wirtschaft und Gesellschaft*, part III, chap. 4, pp. 631–40. The first sentence in paragraph one and the several definitions in this chapter which are in brackets do not appear in the original text. They have been taken from other contexts of *Wirtschaft und Gesellschaft*.
4 *Wirtschaft und Gesellschaft*, part III, chap. 9, pp. 753–7.

PART II

STRUCTURAL FUNCTIONALISM, CONFLICT, AND EXCHANGE THEORIES

CHAPTER FOUR

STRUCTURAL FUNCTIONALISM

CHAPTER MENU

The classics in the sociological canon, most notably the writings of Weber and Durkheim, were introduced to American and other English-speaking scholars and students by the towering figure in post-World War II American sociology, Talcott Parsons in his first book, *The Structure of Social Action* (1937; based on his doctoral dissertation at the University of Heidleberg, Germany, where Weber had been a long-tenured professor). Born in Colorado in 1920, Parsons was a prolific sociologist and a founding member of Harvard University's department of social relations, where he spent his entire career (50 years) until his death in 1979. Though Parsons emphasized the necessary interrelation between theory and data, most of his writings were heavily theoretical as he elaborated his systems theory of society. For Parsons, society and all its constituent units (e.g. groups, institutions) are self-contained systems within which are specialized subsystems with discrete core functions, all arranged and working or functioning toward the order of the whole. His systems-thinking was influenced by Emile Durkheim whose construal of the organic interdependence of social institutions and social and occupational roles was derived from a biological-systems' understanding

Concise Reader in Sociological Theory: Theorists, Concepts, and Current Applications,
First Edition. Edited by Michele Dillon. Editorial material and organization
© 2021 John Wiley & Sons Ltd. Published 2021 by John Wiley & Sons Ltd.

of the body and the interdependence of its many specialized organs and functions. As Parsons elaborated in *The System of Modern Societies* (1971: 1-14) societal (and sub-societal or institutional) functions are: (1) Adaptation - economic productivity; (2) Goal attainment - political goals and rights; (3) Integration – consensual norms/laws; and (4) Latency, or values or cultural transmission, as accomplished through socialization. These functions are oriented to maintaining the societal system and its equilibrium or, in other words, social order.

For Parsons (1949/1954), any social system, including, for example, the (traditional) family is structured such as it is (or *was*, prior to the increase post-1970s in women's labor force participation) so that it functions to effectively meet the needs of its internal and external environment. Thus, in Parsonian terms, family social roles are differentiated by age and sex such that an age-based and a sexual division of labor is functional to family order and to the order of society as a whole. Men are primarily responsible for the adaptive function (work and political activity outside the home) while women are responsible for children's socialization and family integration. A slippage in any of these roles and functions presents the looming threat of family (and by extension, societal) dysfunction. Similarly, occupational differentiation, and a stratified status and economic rewards system relative to occupational roles (e.g. doctors earn more status and money than nurses) is functional to motivating some (well-socialized, high achieving) individuals to pursue more years of education and training than others and thus to defer immediate gratification for long-term increased gains while simultaneously meeting the differentiated needs of society (for doctors and nurses) (Parsons 1949/1954). Given the unintended political conservatism of Parsons's systems-thinking structural functionalism and its explicit pre-occupation with the maintenance of system equilibrium or social order, it is not surprising that his theorizing fell out of favor in the late 1970s and 1980s as the women's movement and other social protest movements sought to disrupt the social order (the status quo), and the gender and other forms of "normal" or allegedly "functional" inequality it perpetuated, including, not least, the gender inequality in sociology and academia more generally. That rupture opened the way for feminist and post-colonial theorizing, as well as for approaches that focused on the normalcy of conflict.

Criticisms of Parsons's theoretical conservatism aside, it is hard to cogently summarize Parsons's many contributions. But what is particularly helpful to sociological analysis is his elaboration of institutionalized pattern variables (Parsons 1951: 428–35), a schema of five different prototypical patterns or orientations (or attitudes) that can be applied to the empirical analysis of any social phenomenon, including comparative analysis of different societies or of different organizations, institutions, roles or occupational sectors. They are: (1) Universalistic versus particularistic; (2) Specificity versus diffuseness; (3) Achievement versus ascription; (4) Neutrality versus affectivity (emotion); and (5) Self versus collective orientation. This orientation schema basically reflects and can be used to basically anchor differences between the characteristics and expectations of (rational) modern societies (e.g. the US) compared to more traditional societies, and as such is the core of Parsons's modernization theory. Modernization theory was further elaborated by students of Parsons, such as Neil Smelser (1968), a sociologist whose research was highly influential in establishing the field of economic sociology, and more generally, Parsons's theory stimulated sociologists to examine social change in various western, Latin American, and African countries in the 1960s, 1970s, and 1980s in terms of their approximation to the expectations of modernization (with the US taken as the prototype of modernization).

The intellectual breadth of Parsons's influence is also evident in the work of many other sociologists including Robert Bellah (1967), another of Parsons's students, and someone who focused on the integrating role of culture, including forms of civil religion and political ritual, in modern secular societies. Bellah et al. (1985) also wrote extensively on how such integration and a shared sense of community and the communal good is increasingly frayed both by political conflict and narcissistic individualism. Both his and Parsons's work has been conceptually tweaked by a younger generation of scholars – neo-Functionalists such as, for example, Jeffrey Alexander (2006) who appraises the nature, functions and capacity of civil society in an increasingly diverse and multicultural context.

It is **Robert K. Merton** (1910–2003), however, who perhaps best exemplifies the enduring impact of Parsons's theorizing. Another of Parsons' students, Merton had a long life and an active career and is a prolific and impactful theorist in his own right especially in the field of deviance/criminology and in establishing the sociology of science. Like Durkheim and Parsons, Merton emphasized a functionalist analysis of society and of social structures. But, unlike Parsons, he was highly attentive to the empirical realities causing and resulting from the manifest and latent functions of particular structural practices and societal arrangements. The excerpt included here (*The Ethos of Science*) illuminates the social and cultural structure of science. Merton draws on Parsons's pattern variables to convey the distinctive ethos of science as being its universalism; this includes the expectation that the criteria used in doing and evaluating science are universal and impersonal, that is, they are standardized across diverse countries and policy and professional sectors regardless of societal or political context, and as such not subject to personal or political whims. Science is also, as he notes, collaborative (or communally owned), relying on the ongoing building upon of a progressively accumulating body of scientific knowledge and the sharing among scientists of new methods and data, as well as with the general public scientific findings pertaining to everyday individual (e.g. health and fitness) and societal functioning (e.g. climate change). Merton's analysis shows how the expectations or norms institutionalized in the scientific sector define what counts as science, and impact the methodology and professional practices of scientists as well as how science is received by the public.

REFERENCES

Alexander, Jeffrey. 2006. *The Civil Sphere*. New York: Oxford University Press.

Bellah, Robert. 1967. "Civil Religion in America." *Daedalus* 96: 1–21.

Bellah, Robert, Richard Madsen, William Sullivan, Ann Swidler, and Steven Tipton. 1985. *Habits of the Heart: Individualism and Commitment in American Life*. Berkeley: University of California Press.

Parsons, Talcott. 1937. *The Structure of Social Action*. New York: Free Press.

Parsons, Talcott. 1949/1954. *Essays in Sociological Theory*. Glencoe, IL: Free Press.

Parsons, Talcott. 1951. *The Social System*. Glencoe, IL: Free Press.

Parsons, Talcott. 1971. *The System of Modern Societies*. Englewood Cliffs, NJ: Prentice Hall.

Smelser, Neil. 1968. *Essays in Sociological Explanation*. Englewood Cliffs, NJ: Prentice Hall.

4A Robert K. Merton from *On Social Structure and Science*

Original publication details: Robert K. Merton, 1942/1944. "The Ethos of Science," in Robert K. Merton, *On Social Structure and Science*, edited by Piotr Sztompka, pp. 267–269, 271–272, 274–276. Chicago: University of Chicago Press, 1966.

The Ethos of Science

The ethos of science is that affectively toned complex of values and norms which is held to be binding on the man of science.[1] The norms are expressed in the form of prescriptions, proscriptions, preferences, and permissions. They are legitimatized in terms of institutional values. These imperatives, transmitted by precept and example and reinforced by sanctions are in varying degrees internalized by scientists, thus fashioning their scientific conscience or, if one prefers the latter-day phrase, their superego. Although the ethos of science has not been codified, it can be inferred from the moral consensus of scientists as expressed in use and wont, in countless writings on the scientific spirit and in moral indignation directed toward contraventions of the ethos.

An examination of the ethos of modern science is only a limited introduction to a larger problem: the comparative study of the institutional structure of science. Although detailed monographs assembling the needed comparative materials are few and scattered, they provide some basis for the provisional assumption that "science is afforded opportunity for development in a democratic order which is integrated with the ethos of science." This is not to say that the pursuit of science is confined to democracies. The most diverse social structures have provided some measure of support to science. [...]

The institutional goal of science is the extension of certified knowledge. The technical methods employed toward this end provide the relevant definition of knowledge: empirically confirmed and logically consistent statements of regularities (which are, in effect, predictions). The institutional imperatives (mores) derive from the goal and the methods. The entire structure of technical and moral norms implements the final objective. The technical norm of empirical evidence, adequate and reliable, is a prerequisite for sustained true prediction; the technical norm of logical consistency, a prerequisite for systematic and valid prediction. The mores of science possess a methodologic rationale but they are also binding, not only because they are procedurally efficient, but because they are believed right and good. They are moral as well as technical prescriptions.

Four sets of institutional imperatives – universalism, communism, disinterestedness, organized skepticism – are taken to comprise the ethos of modern science.

Universalism

Universalism[2] finds immediate expression in the canon that truth-claims, whatever their source, are to be subjected to *preestablished impersonal criteria:* consonant with observation and with previously confirmed knowledge. The acceptance or rejection of claims entering the lists of science is not to depend on the personal or social attributes of their protagonists; their race, nationality, religion, class, and personal qualities are as such irrelevant. Objectivity precludes particularism. The circumstance that scientifically verified formulations refer in that specific sense to objective sequences and correlations militates against all efforts to impose particularistic criteria of validity.

. . .The imperative of universalism is rooted deep in the impersonal character of science.

However, the institution of science is part of a larger social structure with which it is not always integrated. When the larger culture opposes universalism, the ethos of science is subjected to serious strain. Ethnocentrism is not compatible with universalism.

[. . .]

"Communism"

"Communism" in the nontechnical and extended sense of common ownership of goods, is a second integral element of the scientific ethos. The substantive findings of science are a product of social collaboration and are assigned to the community. They constitute a common heritage in which the equity of the individual producer is severely limited. An eponymous law or theory does not enter into the exclusive possession of the discoverer and heirs, nor do the mores bestow upon them special rights of use and disposition. Property rights in science are whittled down to a bare minimum by the rationale of the scientific ethic. Scientists' claims to "their" intellectual "property" are limited to those of recognition and esteem which, if the institution functions with a modicum of efficiency, are roughly commensurate with the significance of the increments brought to the common fund of knowledge. Eponymy – for example, the Copernican system, Boyle's law – is thus at once a mnemonic and a commemorative device.

[. . .]

Disinterestedness

Science, as is the case with the professions in general, includes disinterestedness as a basic institutional element. Disinterestedness is not to be equated with altruism nor interested action with egoism. Such equivalences confuse institutional and motivational levels of analysis.[3] A passion for knowledge, idle curiosity, altruistic concern with the benefit to humanity, and a host of other special motives have been attributed to the scientist. The quest for distinctive motives appears to have been misdirected. It is rather a distinctive pattern of institutional control of a wide range of motives which characterizes the behavior of scientists. For once the institution enjoins disinterested activity, it is to the interest of scientists to conform on pain of sanctions and, insofar as the norm has been internalized, on pain of psychological conflict.

The virtual absence of fraud in the annals of science, which appears exceptional when compared with the record of other spheres of activity, has at times been attributed to the personal qualities of scientists. By implication, scientists are recruited from the ranks of those who exhibit an unusual degree of moral integrity. There is, in fact, no satisfactory evidence that such is the case; a more plausible explanation may be found in certain distinctive characteristics of science itself. Involving as it does the verifiability of results, scientific research is under the exacting scrutiny of fellow experts. Otherwise put – and doubtless the observation can be interpreted as lese majesty – the activities of scientists are subject to rigorous policing, to a degree perhaps unparalleled in any other field of activity. The demand for disinterestedness has a firm basis in the public and testable character of science and this circumstance, it may be supposed, has contributed to the integrity of men of science. There is competition in the realm of science, competition that is intensified by the emphasis on priority as a criterion of achievement, and under competitive conditions there may well be generated incentives for eclipsing rivals by illicit means. But such impulses can find scant opportunity for expression in the field of scientific research. Cultism, informal cliques, prolific but trivial publications – these and other techniques may be used for self-aggrandizement.[4] But, in general, spurious claims appear to be negligible and ineffective. The translation of the norm of disinterestedness into practice is effectively supported by the ultimate accountability of scientists to their compeers. The dictates of socialized sentiment and of expediency largely coincide, a situation conducive to institutional stability.

In this connection, the field of science differs somewhat from that of other professions. The scientist does not stand vis-à-vis a lay clientele in the same fashion as do the physician and lawyer, for example. The possibility of exploiting the credulity, ignorance, and dependence of the layman is thus considerably reduced. Fraud, chicane, and irresponsible claims (quackery) are even less likely than among the "service" professions. To the extent that the scientist-layman relation does become paramount, there develop incentives for evading the mores of science. The abuse of expert authority and the creation of pseudosciences are called into play when the structure of control exercised by qualified compeers is rendered ineffectual.[5]

It is probable that the reputability of science and its lofty ethical status in the estimate of the layman is in no small measure due to technological achievements.[6] Every new technology bears witness to the integrity of the scientist. Science realizes its claims. However, its authority can be and is appropriated for interested purposes, precisely because the laity is often in no position to distinguish spurious from genuine claims to such authority. The presumably scientific pronouncements of totalitarian spokesmen on race or economy or history are for the uninstructed laity of the same order as newspaper reports of an expanding universe or wave mechanics. In both instances, they cannot be checked by the man in the street and in both instances, they may run counter to common sense. If anything, the myths will seem more plausible and are certainly more comprehensible to the general public than accredited scientific theories, since they are closer to common-sense experience and to cultural bias. Partly as a result of scientific achievements, therefore, the population at large becomes susceptible to new mysticisms expressed in apparently scientific terms. The borrowed authority of science bestows prestige on the unscientific doctrine.

Organized Skepticism

Organized skepticism is variously interrelated with the other elements of the scientific ethos. It is both a methodological and an institutional mandate. The temporary suspension of judgment and the detached scrutiny of beliefs in terms of empirical and logical criteria have periodically involved science in conflict with other institutions. Science which asks questions of fact, including potentialities, concerning every aspect of nature and society may come into conflict with other attitudes toward these same data which have been crystallized and often ritualized by other institutions. The scientific investigator does not preserve the cleavage between the sacred and the profane, between that which requires uncritical respect and that which can be objectively analyzed.

As we have noted, this appears to be the source of revolts against the so-called intrusion of science into other spheres. Such resistance on the part of organized religion has become less significant as compared with that of economic and political groups. The opposition may exist quite apart from the introduction of specific scientific discoveries which appear to invalidate particular dogmas of church, economy, or state. It is rather a diffuse, frequently vague apprehension that skepticism threatens the current distribution of power. Conflict becomes accentuated whenever science extends its research to new areas toward which there are institutionalized attitudes or whenever other institutions extend their control over science. In modern totalitarian society, antirationalism and the centralization of institutional control both serve to limit the scope provided for scientific activity.

NOTES

1 On the concept of ethos, see William Graham Sumner, *Folkways* (Boston: Ginn, 1906), 36 ff.; Hans Speier, "The Social Determination of Ideas," *Social Research* 5 (1938): 196 ff.; Max Scheler, *Schriften aus dem Nachlass* (1933; reprint, Bern, 1957), 1: 225–62. Albert Bayet, in his book on the subject, soon abandons description and analysis for homily; see his *La morale de la science* (Paris, 1931).

2 For a basic analysis of universalism in social relations, see Talcott Parsons, *The Social System* (Glencoe, Ill.: Free Press, 1951). For an expression of the belief that "science is wholly independent of national boundaries and races and creeds," see the resolution of the Council of the American Association for the Advancement of Science, *Science* 87 (1938): 10; also, "The Advancement of Science and Society: Proposed World Association," *Nature* 141 (1938): 169.

3 Talcott Parsons, "The Professions and Social Structure," *Social Forces* 17(1939): 458–9; cf. George Sarton, *The History of Science and the New Humanism* (1931; reprint, New Brunswick:

Transaction Books, 1988), 130 ff. The distinction between institutional compulsives and motives is a key, though largely implicit, conception of Marxist sociology.

4   See the account by Logan Wilson, *The Academic Man* (New York: Oxford University Press, 1941), 201 ff.

5   Cf. R. A. Brady, *The Spirit and Structure of German Fascism* (New York: Viking, 1937),

chap. 2; Martin Gardner, *In the Name of Science* (New York: Putnam's, 1953).

6   Francis Bacon set forth one of the early and most succinct statements of this popular pragmatism: "Now these two directions – the one active, the other contemplative – are one and the same thing; and what in operation is most useful, that in knowledge is most true" (*Novum Organum* [London: George Routledge and Sons, n.d.], 2: aphorism IV).

CHAPTER FIVE

CONFLICT AND DEPENDENCY THEORIES

CHAPTER MENU

Given the dominance of structural functionalism both in the sociology curriculum and as the overarching framework for a great deal of sociological research across several decades of the twentieth century, it's not surprising that some scholars were skeptical of the social order emphasis and overall systemic tidiness in Parsons, and were motivated to inject new ideas into the theoretical landscape. This section includes two excerpts, each conveying a distinct framework, an excerpt from **Ralf Dahrendorf**'s *Class and Class Conflict in Industrial Society* (1959), a conceptualization that is often equated with so-called "Conflict theory," and an excerpt from **Fernando Henrique Cardoso** and **Enzo Faletto**'s, *Dependency and Development in Latin America* (1979), a framework known as "Dependency theory."

Dahrendorf (1929–2017), was German-born but spent much of his career in England including as Director of the highly esteemed London School of Economics and was also an active politician serving in various parliamentary roles in Germany, the UK, and the European Union. He argues (see excerpt *5a Class and Class Conflict*) that Parsons's "integration theory" of society needs to complemented conceptually by

Concise Reader in Sociological Theory: Theorists, Concepts, and Current Applications,
First Edition. Edited by Michele Dillon. Editorial material and organization
© 2021 John Wiley & Sons Ltd. Published 2021 by John Wiley & Sons Ltd.

what he calls a "coercion theory of society" which among other things, fully recognizes that conflict is a prevalent and indeed normal part of society, and moreover, a driver of social change. Influenced by Max Weber's conceptualization of power and authority, Dahrendorf focuses on the authority relations that exist, especially in postindustrial society, between and among an array of occupational and other social groups as each vies to have its particular economic and non-economic interests given their due. As such, any and all interest groups (e.g. discrete trade unions, and political interest, social identity, local municipal, or university campus groups) are invariably conflict groups in competition (more or less) with one another in any given socio-political context. As such, conflict is democratized in that it is ubiquitous, not simply structured into an overarching antagonism, in Marxist terms, in the relations between the capitalist class and the proletariat. Indeed, what is functional about group conflict, Dahrendorf argues is that all interest/conflict groups are integrated as a normal part of contemporary society, and additionally, the varying conflicts are a driver of social change. The dialectic of conflict and resistance propels social change as the particular agendas of evolving interest groups lead to conflicts whose (partial) resolution through social policy, legislative and other institutional changes, produces a new reality (a new status quo) that in turn gives rise to new conflicts.

Parsons's modernization theory and the many empirical studies it influenced assumed a straightforward, linear understanding of economic development and its interrelated twinning with the growth of urbanization, education/literacy, political democratization, and the leaving behind of the pull of tradition (e.g. religion, ethnic loyalty). These assumptions were variously challenged by the empirical realities in specific western countries which demonstrated a more selective and uneven modernization, and especially so in non-western contexts such as Latin America. Andre Gunder Frank (1967) applied a neo-Marxist lens to argue, contrary to Parsons and others, that the sociology of development – modernization as more or less apparent in "developed" First World countries – necessarily rests on and is intertwined with the sociology of under-development (the reality of the Third World). In other words, the same capitalist profit logic and practices that produce economic development simultaneously produce under-development, and a related polarization of the core or the center and peripheral economies whereby the economic growth of the core is based on its exploitation of the periphery. Building on this (neo-Marxist) insight, Ferdinand Cardoso (who subsequently served as President of Brazil) and Enzo Faletto (see excerpt *5b Dependency and Development in Latin America*) focused not only on the inherent unequal economic relations between developed (e.g. the US, UK) and under-developed (e.g. Chile, Brazil) countries, but also on how the specific political and social context (e.g. the role of elites) in a given under-developed country provided additional mechanisms used in its economic and political subjugation vis-à-vis the developed world. For them, what is important is that these dynamics give rise to what they call "situations of dependency," dependency relations which are highly consequential economically and politically.

REFERENCES

Gunder Frank, Andre. 1967. *Capitalism and Underdevelopment in Latin America.* New York: Monthly Review Press.

Parsons, Talcott. 1951. *The Social System.* Glencoe, IL: Free Press.

5A Ralf Dahrendorf from *Class and Class Conflict in Industrial Society*

Original publication details: Ralf Dahrendorf, 1959. *Class and Class Conflict in Industrial Society*, 161–163, 167–169, 206–209. Stanford: Stanford University Press. Reproduced with permission of Stanford University Press.

The integration theory of society, as displayed by the work of Parsons and other structural-functionalists, is founded on a number of assumptions of the following type:

1   Every society is a relatively persistent, stable structure of elements.
2   Every society is a well-integrated structure of elements.
3   Every element in a society has a function, i.e., renders a contribution to its maintenance as a system.
4   Every functioning social structure is based on a consensus of values among its members.

In varying forms, these elements of (1) stability, (2) integration, (3) functional coordination, and (4) consensus recur in all structural-functional approaches to the study of social structure. They are, to be sure, usually accompanied by protestations to the effect that stability, integration, functional coordination, and consensus are only "relatively" generalized. Moreover, these assumptions are not metaphysical propositions about the essence of society; they are merely assumptions for purposes of scientific analysis. As such, however, they constitute a coherent view of the social process[1] which enables us to comprehend many problems of social reality.

However, it is abundantly clear that the integration approach to social analysis does not enable us to comprehend all problems of social reality. Let us look at two undeniably sociological problems of the contemporary world which demand explanation. (I) In recent years, an increasing number of industrial and commercial enterprises have introduced the position of personnel manager to cope with matters of hiring and firing, advice to employees, etc. Why? And: what are the consequences of the introduction of this new position? (2) On the 17th of June, 1953, the building workers of East Berlin put down their tools and went on a strike that soon led to a generalized revolt against the Communist regime of East Germany. Why? And: what are the consequences of this uprising? From the point of view of the integration model of society, the first of these problems is susceptible of a satisfactory solution. A special position to cope with personnel questions is functionally required by large enterprises in an age of rationalization and "social ethic"; the introduction of this position adapts the enterprise to the values of the surrounding society; its consequence is therefore of an integrative and stabilizing nature. But what about the second problem? Evidently, the uprising of the 17th of June is neither due to nor productive of integration in East German society. It documents and produces not stability, but instability. It contributes to the disruption, not the maintenance, of the existing system. It testifies to dissensus rather than consensus. The integration model tells us little more than that there are certain "strains" in the "system." In fact, in order to cope with problems of this kind we have to replace the integration theory of society by a different and, in many ways, contradictory model.

What I have called the coercion theory of society can also be reduced to a small number of basic tenets, although here again these assumptions oversimplify and overstate the case:

1   Every society is at every point subject to processes of change; social change is ubiquitous.
2   Every society displays at every point dissensus and conflict; social conflict is ubiquitous.
3   Every element in a society renders a contribution to its disintegration and change.
4   Every society is based on the coercion of some of its members by others.

If we return to the problem of the German workers' strike, it will become clear that this latter model enables us to deal rather more satisfactorily with its causes and consequences. The revolt of the building workers and their fellows in other industries can be explained in terms of coercion.[2] The revolting groups are engaged in a conflict which "functions" as an agent of change by disintegration. A ubiquitous phenomenon is expressed, in this case, in an exceptionally intense and violent way, and further explanation will have to account for this violence on the basis of the acceptance of conflict and change as universal features of social life. I need hardly add that, like the integration model, the coercion theory of society constitutes but a set of assumptions for purposes of scientific analysis and implies no claim for philosophical validity – although, like its counterpart, this model also provides a coherent image of social organization.

Now, I would claim that, in a sociological context, neither of these models can be conceived as exclusively valid or applicable. They constitute complementary, rather than alternative, aspects of the structure of total societies as well as of every element of this structure. We have to choose between them only for the explanation of specific problems, but in the conceptual arsenal of sociological analysis they exist side by side. Whatever criticism one may have of the advocates of one or the other of these models can therefore be directed only against claims for the exclusive validity of either.[3] Strictly speaking, both models are "valid" or, rather, useful and necessary for sociological analysis. We cannot conceive of society unless we realize the dialectics of stability and change, integration and conflict, function and motive force, consensus and coercion. In the context of this study, I regard this point as demonstrated by the analysis of the exemplary problems sketched above.

It is perhaps worth emphasizing that the thesis of the two faces of social structure does not require a complete, or even partial, revision of the conceptual apparatus that by now has become more or less generally accepted by sociologists in all countries. Categories like role, institution, norm, structure, even function are as useful in terms of the coercion model as they are for the analysis of social integration. In fact, the dichotomy of aspects can be carried through all levels of sociological analysis; that is, it can be shown that, like social structure itself, the notions of role and institution, integration and function, norm and substratum have two faces which may be expressed by two terms, but which may also in many cases be indicated by an extension of concepts already in use. "Interest and value," Radcliffe-Brown once remarked, "are correlative terms, which refer to the two sides of an asymmetrical relation" (221, p. 199). The notions of interest and value indeed seem to describe very well the two faces of the normative superstructure of society: what appears as a consensus of values on the basis of the integration theory can be regarded as a conflict of interests in terms of the coercion theory.

[. . .]

In conflict analysis we are concerned, *inter alia* with the generation of conflict groups by the authority relations obtaining in imperatively coordinated associations. Since imperative coordination, or authority, is a type of social relation, present in every conceivable social organization, it will be sufficient to describe such organizations simply as associations. Despite prolonged terminological discussions, no general agreement has been attained by sociologists on the precise meaning of the categories "organization," "association," and "institution." If I am not mistaken in my interpretation of the trend of terminological disputes, it appears justifiable to use the term "association" in such a way as to imply the coordination of organized aggregates of roles by domination and subjection. The state, a church, an enterprise, but also a political party, a trade union, and a chess club are associations in this sense. In all of them, authority relations exist; for all of them, conflict analysis is therefore applicable. If at a later stage we shall suggest restriction to the two great associations of the state and the industrial enterprise, this suggestion is dictated merely by considerations of empirical significance, not logical (or definitional) difference. In looking at social organizations not in terms of their integration and coherence but from the point of view of their structure of coercion and constraint, we regard them as (imperatively coordinated) associations rather than as social systems. Because social organizations are also associations, they generate conflicts of interest and become the birthplace of conflict groups.

I have assumed in the preceding remarks that authority is a characteristic of social organizations as general as society itself. Despite the assertion of Renner – and other modern sociologists – that in some contemporary societies the exercise of authority has been eliminated and replaced by the more anonymous "rule of the law" or other non-authoritative relations, I should indeed maintain that authority is a universal element of social structure. It is in this sense more general than, for example, property, or even status. With respect to post-capitalist industrial society, I hope to establish this position more unambiguously in the final chapters of this study. Generally speaking, however, the universality of authority relations would seem evident as soon as we describe these relations in a "passive" rather than in an "active" sense. Authority relations exist wherever there are people whose actions are subject to legitimate and sanctioned prescriptions that originate outside them but within social structure.

This formulation, by leaving open who exercises what kind of authority, leaves little doubt as to the omnipresence of some kind of authority somehow exercised. For it is evident that there are many forms and types of authority in historical societies. There are differences of a considerable order of magnitude between the relations of the citizen of classical Athens and his slaves, the feudal landlord and his villeins and serfs, the nineteenth-century capitalist and his workers, the secretary of a totalitarian state party and its members, the appointed manager of a modern enterprise and its employees, or the elected prime minister of a democratic country and the electorate. No attempt will be made in this study to develop a typology of authority. But it is assumed throughout that the existence of domination and subjection is a common feature of all possible types of authority and, indeed, of all possible types of association and organization.

[...]

Classes, understood as conflict groups arising out of the authority structure of imperatively coordinated associations, are in conflict. What are – so we must ask if we want to understand the lawfulness of this phenomenon – the social consequences, intended or unintended, of such conflicts? The discussion of this question involves, almost inevitably, certain value judgments. I think that R. Dubin is right in summarizing at least one prominent attitude toward the functions of social conflict as follows: "From the standpoint of the social order, conflict is viewed from two positions: (a) it may be destructive of social stability and therefore 'bad' because stability is good; (b) it may be evidence of the breakdown of social control and therefore symptomatic of an underlying instability in the social order. Both positions express a value preference for social stability" (77, p. 183). I would also agree with Dubin's own position: "Conflict may be labeled dysfunctional or symptomatic of an improperly integrated society. The empirical existence of conflict, however, is not challenged by the stability argument. . . . The fact of the matter is that group conflict cannot be wished out of existence. It is a reality with which social theorists must deal in constructing their general models of social behaviour" (p. 184). But I think that in two respects Dubin might have been rather less cautious. First, I should not hesitate, on the level of value judgments, to express a strong preference for the concept of societies that recognizes conflict as an essential feature of their structure and process. Secondly, and quite apart from value judgments, a strong case can be made for group conflict having consequences which, if not "functional," are utterly necessary for the social process. This case rests on the distinction between the two faces of society – a distinction which underlies our discussions throughout this study. It is perhaps the ultimate proof of the necessity of distinguishing these two faces that conflict itself, the crucial category in terms of the coercion model, has two faces, i.e., that of contributing to the integration of social "systems" and that of making for change.

Both these consequences have been admirably expressed by L. Coser. (Although, to my mind, Coser is rather too preoccupied with what he himself tends to call the "positive" or "integrative functions" of conflict.) On the one hand, Coser [1956] states in the unmistakable terminology of the integration theory of society (for which see my italics): "Conflict may serve to remove dissociating elements in a relationship and

to *re-establish* unity. Insofar as conflict is the resolution of tension between antago-
nists it has *stabilizing functions* and becomes an *integrating component* of the relationship. However, not all conflicts are *positively functional* for the relationship.... Loosely
structured groups, and open societies, by allowing conflicts, institute safeguards
against the type of conflict which would *endanger basic consensus* and thereby *minimize the danger of divergences* touching core values. The interdependence of antagonistic groups and the crisscrossing within such societies of conflicts, which *serve to
'sew the social system together'* by cancelling each other out, thus *prevent disintegration*
along one primary line of cleavage" (81, p. 80). On the other hand, Coser follows Sorel
in postulating "the idea that conflict . . . prevents the ossification of the social system
by exerting pressure for innovation and creativity" and states: "This conception seems
to be more generally applicable than to class struggle alone. Conflict within and
between groups in a society can prevent accommodations and habitual relations from
progressively impoverishing creativity. The clash of values and interests, the tension
between what is and what some groups feel ought to be, the conflict between vested
interests and new strata and groups demanding their share of power, wealth and status, have been productive of vitality" (80, pp. 197 f.).

Conflict may, indeed, from a Utopian point of view, be conceived as one of the patterns contributing to the maintenance of the *status quo*. To be sure, this holds only for
regulated conflicts, some of the conditions of which we shall try to explore presently.
Coser's analysis of Simmel (81) has convincingly demonstrated that there is no need
to abandon the integration theory of society simply because the phenomenon of conflict "cannot be wished away" but is a fact of observation. In this sense, conflict joins
role allocation, socialization, and mobility as one of the "tolerable" processes which
foster rather than endanger the stability of social systems. There seems little doubt,
however, that from this point of view we can barely begin to understand the phenomenon of group conflicts. Were it only for its "positive functions," for which Coser
found so many telling synonyms, class conflict would continue to be rather a nuisance which the sociologist would prefer to dispense with since it may, after all,
"endanger basic consensus." So far as the present study is concerned, "continuing
group conflict" will be regarded as "an important way of giving direction to social
change" (Dubin, 77, p. 194). Societies are essentially historical creatures, and, because
they are, they require the motive force of conflict – or, conversely, because there is
conflict, there is historical change and development. The dialectics of conflict and
history provide the ultimate reason of our interest in this phenomenon and at the
same time signify the consequences of social conflict with which we are concerned.

Dubin's observation that conflict is a stubborn fact of social life is undoubtedly
justified. Earlier, we have made the assertion explicit that social conflict is ubiquitous;
in fact, this is one of the premises of our analysis. Possibly, this premise permits even
further generalization. There has been in recent years some amount of interdisciplinary research on problems of conflict. In specific features the results of these interdisciplinary efforts remain as yet tentative; but one conclusion has been brought out by
them with impressive clarity: it appears that not only in social life, but wherever there
is life, there is conflict.[4] May we perhaps go so far as to say that conflict is a condition

necessary for life to be possible at all? I would suggest, in any case, that all that is creativity, innovation, and development in the life of the individual, his group, and his society is due, to no small extent, to the operation of conflicts between group and group, individual and individual, emotion and emotion within one individual. This fundamental fact alone seems to me to justify the value judgment that conflict is essentially "good" and "desirable."

If I here assume social conflict, and the particular type of group conflict with which we are concerned in the present study, to be ubiquitous, I want this statement to be understood more rigidly than is usual. At an earlier point I have intimated what I mean by rigidity in this sense. One or two remarks in addition to these earlier hints seem in order. In summarizing earlier research, Mack and Snyder state with some justice that by most authors "competition is not regarded as conflict or a form of conflict" (77, p. 217). The alleged difference between the two is identified differently by different authors. T. H. Marshall emphasizes common interests, rather than divergent interests, as characteristic of states of competition or conflict (59, p. 99). For Mack and Snyder, "competition involves striving for scarce objects . . . according to established rules which strictly limit what the competitors can do to each other in the course of striving; the chief objective is the scarce object, not the injury or destruction of an opponent per se" (77, p. 217). It seems to me, however, that it is not accidental if Mack and Snyder state a little later that "conflict arises from 'position scarcity' and 'resource scarcity,'" and that therefore "conflict relations always involve attempts to gain control of scarce resources and positions" (pp. 218 f.). Despite terminological traditions, I can see no reason why a conceptual distinction between competition and conflict should be necessary or, indeed, desirable.[5] Like competition, conflict involves a striving for scarce resources. From the point of view of linguistic usage, it is perfectly proper to say that conflicting interest groups compete for power. As far as the "established rules" of competition are concerned, they emphasize but one type of conflict, namely, regulated conflict. In the present study, the notion of conflict is intended to include relations such as have been described by many other authors *as competitive*.

NOTES

1 It is important to emphasize that "stability" as a tenet of the integration theory of society does not mean that societies are "static." It means, rather, that such processes as do occur (and the structural-functional approach is essentially concerned with processes) serve to maintain the patterns of the system as a whole. Whatever criticism I have of this approach, I do not want to be misunderstood as attributing to it a "static bias" (which has often been held against this approach without full consideration of its merits).

2 For purposes of clarity, I have deliberately chosen an example from a totalitarian state. But coercion is meant here in a very general sense, and the coercion model is applicable to all societies, independent of their specific political structure.

3 This, it seems to me, is the only – if fundamental – legitimate criticism that can be raised against Parsons' work on this general level. In *The Social System*, Parsons repeatedly advances, for the integration theory of society, a claim that it is the nucleus of "the general" sociological theory – a

claim which I regard as utterly unjustified. It is Lockwood's main concern also, in the essay quoted above, to reject this claim to universal validity.

4   This and numerous other statements in the present chapter are based on discussions with and publications of psychologists, anthropologists, lawyers, and social psychologists at the Center for Advanced Study in the Behavioral Sciences, Stanford, California. John Bowlby, M.D., and Professor Frank Newman, LL.D., have been particularly helpful in making suggestions. In support of the statement in the text I might also refer, however, to the symposium published in *Conflict*

Resolution (77), which includes contributions by economists, sociologists, social psychologists, anthropologists, and psychologists, and strongly supports my point.

5   At least, no such reason has been put forward. It might be argued, of course, that the concept of competition employed in economic theory is rather different from that defined by Marshall or Mack and Snyder, and does not carry any conflict connotation. I am not entirely sure that this argument is justified, but for purposes of the present analysis competition in a technical economic sense will be excluded.

REFERENCES

L.A. Coser. 1956. *The Functions of Social Conflict.* London.

L.A. Coser. 1957. "Social Conflict and Social Change." *British Journal of Sociology* VII (3), (September).

R. Dubin. 1957. "Approaches to the Study of Social Conflict: A Colloquium." *Conflict Resolution* 1(2) (June).

T.H. Marshall. 1938. "The Nature of Class Conflict," in T.H. Marshall, ed. *Class Conflict and Social Stratification.* London.

A.R. Radcliffe-Brown. 1952. "On Social Structure," in *Structure and Function in Primitive Society.* London.

Mack and Snyder. 1957. "Approaches to the Study of Social Conflict: A Colloquium." *Conflict Resolution* 1(2), (June).

5B Fernando Henrique Cardoso and Enzo Faletto from *Dependency and Development in Latin America*

Original publication details: Fernando H. Cardoso and Enzo Faletto, 1979. *Dependency and Development in Latin America*, translated by Marjory Mattingly Urquidi, pp. xx–xxv. Berkeley, CA: University of California Press. Reproduced with permission of University of California Press.

Theory of Dependency and Capitalistic Development

From the economic point of view a system is dependent when the accumulation and expansion of capital cannot find its essential dynamic component inside the system. In capitalistic economies the crucial component for the drive to expand is the capacity to enlarge the scale of capital. This cannot be done without the creation of new technologies and continuous expansion of the production of "capital goods," that is, machinery and equipment, to permit the continuing growth of enterprise expansion and capital accumulation. Furthermore, the expansion of a capitalistic economy requires financial support through a solid banking system. Of course, not all capitalist economies have these capabilities. Some of them have to find on a world scale the necessary complementarity to continue their march toward economic growth.

Almost all contemporary national economic systems are articulated in the international system. Superficial or apologetic analysts, in order to minimize exploitative aspects of the international economy, have merely assumed that "modern" economies are "interdependent." By stating this platitude, they often forget that the important question is what forms that "interdependency" takes. While some national economies need raw material produced by unskilled labor, or industrial goods produced by cheap labor, others need to import equipment and capital goods in general. While some economies become indebted to the financial capital cities of the world, others are creditors. Of course, bankers need clients, as much as clients need bankers. But the "interrelationship" between the two is qualitatively distinct because of the position held by each partner in the structure of the relationship. The same is true for the analysis of "interdependent" economies in world markets.

Capitalism is a world system. But some of its parts have more than their share of leadership and an almost exclusive possession of sectors crucial to production and capital accumulation, such as the technological or financial sectors. They require complementarity from dependent economies, but the crucial elements for the capital expansion on a cumulative and amplified scale are at their disposal.

Peripheral economies, even when they are no longer restricted to the production of raw material, remain dependent in a very specific form: their capital-goods production sectors are not strong enough to ensure continuous advance of the system, in financial as well as in technological and organizational terms. So, in order to go ahead with economic expansion, a dependent country has to play the "interdependency" game, but in a position similar to the client who approaches a banker. Of course, clients usually develop strategies of independence and can try to use the borrowed money in productive ways. But insofar as there are structural border lines, successful attempts are not an automatic output of the game. More often, rules of domination are enforced, and even if the dependent country becomes less poor after the first loan, a second one follows. In most cases, when such an economy flourishes, its roots have been planted by those who hold the lending notes.

Characterization of contemporary forms of dependent development could be perhaps the most significant contribution by "dependentistas" to the theory of capitalistic societies. If there is any novelty in this essay, it consists, together with the characterization of past forms of dependency, in the attempt to delineate what has been called "the new dependency." By means of this analysis it was foreseen how a general trend (industrial capitalism) creates concrete situations of dependency with features distinct from those of advanced capitalist societies. So, peripheral industrialization is based on products which in the center are *mass consumed*, but which are typically *luxurious consumption* in dependent societies. Industrialization in dependent economies enhances income concentration as it increases sharp differences in productivity without generalizing this trend to the whole of the economy: whereas the production of cars, televisions, refrigerators, and like types of goods is based on modern technology, important parts of food products, textiles, and other goods that constitute the basic consumption for the masses are still based on more traditional technology and relations of production. The wages of technicians, managers, and specialized workers, although not directly determined by productivity, are incomparably higher than those earned by peasants or workers employed in traditional sectors. Thus, industrialization in the periphery increases disparity of income among wage earners accentuating what has been called in Latin America the "structural heterogeneity."

These considerations stress that dependent capitalistic economies are not identical to central capitalistic economies. In spite of that, we do not subscribe to the attempts that have been made to propose a "theory of dependent capitalism." Of course, analyses of situations of dependency imply theories and require the use of methodologies. But – even by definition – it seems senseless to search for "laws of movement" specific to situations that *are dependent*, that is, that have their main features determined by the phases and trend of expansion of capitalism on a world scale. Attempts have to be made to enlarge and to give more specificity to the laws that have been developed and are being brought up to date by authors interested in the analysis of a general economic theory of capitalism. Our contribution, if there is one, goes in that direction without any pretentious aim to propose new theories that depart from the classical ones. To avoid misinterpretations, we refer to "situations of dependency" rather than to the "category" or to the "theory" of dependency.

A real process of dependent development does exist in some Latin American countries. By development, in this context, we mean "capitalist development." This form of development, in the periphery as well as in the center, produces as it evolves, in a cyclical way, wealth and poverty, accumulation and shortage of capital, employment for some and unemployment for others. So, we do not mean by the notion of "development" the achievement of a more egalitarian or more just society. These are not consequences expected from capitalist development, especially in peripheral economies.

By pointing to the existence of a process of capitalistic expansion in the periphery, we make a double criticism. We criticize those who expect permanent stagnation in underdeveloped dependent countries because of a constant decline in the rate of profit or the "narrowness of internal markets," which supposedly function as an insurpassable obstacle to capitalistic advancement. But we also criticize those who expect capitalistic development of peripheral economies to solve problems such as distribution of property, full employment, better income distribution, and better living conditions for people. Even in developed economies these problems remain unsolved, as Puerto Ricans, blacks, and poor whites testify in America. It would be unrealistic (if not apologetic) to believe that the existence of an actual process of capitalistic development in the peripheral economies will suppress social problems and conflicts around them. Development, in this context, means the progress of productive forces, mainly through the import of technology, capital accumulation, penetration of local economies by foreign enterprises, increasing numbers of wage-earning groups, and intensification of social division labor. It is realistic to expect either a shifting of the arena in which struggles are present or the unfolding of issues around which conflicts will be at stake. It is not realistic to imagine that capitalist development will solve basic problems for the majority of the population. In the end, what has to be discussed as an alternative is not the consolidation of the state and the fulfillment of "autonomous capitalism," but how to supercede them. The important question, then, is how to construct paths toward socialism.

We have limited our analyses to forms of dependency within capitalistic societies and, furthermore, to situations in which a nation-state has been formed. Although there are forms of dependent relationships between socialist countries, the structural context that permits an understanding of these is quite different from that within capitalist countries and requires specific analyses. The same is also true for economies like the Indian economy – and, to a lesser extent, that of Japan – which have historical patterns of formation that cannot be explained by the unfolding of European or American capitalistic economic expansion, although they also became linked, later on, to the international market.

We have not intended to discuss colonial types of contemporary situations of dependency in Latin America, such as, in the purest example, Puerto Rico. Considerable intellectual work has to be done to specify and render understandable, in the context of a more general view about dependency, the particularities of colonial or almost colonial situations.

CHAPTER SIX

SOCIAL EXCHANGE

CHAPTER MENU

The notion of exchange is central to everyday social life and not surprisingly is at the heart of a great deal of sociological theory. While Marx focuses on the centrality of unequal economic exchange in the macro context of capitalist relations (and the exploitation of workers by employers), other theorists highlight the micro-dynamics of exchange characteristic of all relationships. Georg Simmel notes that "Exchange is the purest and most concentrated form of all human interactions in which serious interests are at stake . . . every conversation, every love (even when requited unfavorably), every game, every act of looking one another over" (1907/1971: 43, 33). The net benefits or payoff in any interpersonal interaction between any two individuals – the assessment by the self and others of what one gives and what one gets – are, according

Concise Reader in Sociological Theory: Theorists, Concepts, and Current Applications,
First Edition. Edited by Michele Dillon. Editorial material and organization
© 2021 John Wiley & Sons Ltd. Published 2021 by John Wiley & Sons Ltd.

to George Homans (1910–89), the motivating source of all interaction and the basis of organizational and institutional life (Homans 1958). **Peter M. Blau**, a student of Homans, notes that "Two conditions must be met for behavior to lead to social exchange. It must be oriented toward ends [goals] that can only be achieved through interaction with other persons, and it must seek to adapt means to further the achievement of these ends" (Blau 1964: 5). Social (and economic) exchange relations, whether at the macro societal level (e.g. Marx) or at the micro-level (e.g. a particular friendship) are invariably characterized by power imbalances; and the micro dynamics of everyday life are grounded in the ongoing back and forth of who gives and gets more than the other in any given interaction or exchange. Blau (see excerpt *6a Exchange and Power in Social Life*) highlights that, unlike in economic exchange relationships (with money as the clear standard of cost/exchange), in social exchange the expectations of reciprocity and felt obligation are highly diffuse and unspecified, and thus the power imbalances created are typically unspoken and unacknowledged even as those tacit imbalances impact and shape the ongoing interactions in a given relationship. With such diffuseness, social exchange relies largely on trust that the other person will (eventually) reciprocate and meet the tacit obligation (e.g. to extend a return dinner invitation). Diffuseness injects ambiguity into the power and status imbalances in personal and friendship relationships, and at work and in organizational contexts more generally. Consequently, while the hierarchical bureaucratic structure of the workplace formally embeds specific power inequalities, the informal exchanges that occur on a daily basis – for example, when a supervisor relies on a savvy lower-level staff member for help in dealing with a computer problem (rather than contacting the designated computer staff expert), the pattern of exchange can create informal (though real and consequential) status and power imbalances that invert the formal status divisions.

Trust is a central component of personal and institutional relations; it is nurtured and protected by regulations and laws (e.g. the relationship between a bank and a customer who has a loan), but importantly, too, it is also embedded in peer and other social networks. As **James S. Coleman** notes (see excerpt *6b Social Capital*), personal relationships create social capital that can be deployed and used in all sorts of productive ways. And though Coleman emphasizes the significance of relatively tight networks with a high degree of trust, the social capital accumulated through loose networks of acquaintances is also highly productive; weak ties with an array of individuals who are not connected to one another can open a person's access to a much broader range of useful information than hanging out with just one tight set of friends, notwithstanding the benefits of such cliques (e.g. Granovetter 1973). While much of the social exchange literature tends to lean toward a focus on the individual (an individual's human capital) and what they bring to personal and work relationships, **Paula England** (see excerpt *6c Sometimes the Social Becomes Personal*) redirects attention to the sociological significance of social position (e.g. age, sex, gender, race, social class), and how social position and personal characteristics (e.g. skills, habits, attitudes) interact in direct and indirect ways to bring about certain outcomes. This line of reasoning is helpful in adding nuance to policy debates that are polarized by attributing the reasons for a given outcome (e.g. racial/ethnic differences in college dropout rates) to either solely the individual or solely the institutional or structural context.

REFERENCES

Blau, Peter M. 1964. *Exchange and Power in Social Life*. New York: John Wiley & Sons.

Granovetter, Mark. 1973. "The Strength of Weak Ties." *American Journal of Sociology* 78: 1360–80.

Homans, George Caspar. 1958. "Social Behavior as Exchange." *American Journal of Sociology* 63: 597–606.

Simmel, Georg. 1907/1971. *On Individuality and Social Forms*. Chicago: University of Chicago Press. Edited and with an introduction by Donald Levine.

6A Peter M. Blau from *Exchange and Power in Social Life*

Original publication details: Peter Blau, 1964. *Exchange and Power in Social Life*, pp. 91–95. Reproduced with permission of Taylor & Francis.

"Social exchange," as the term is used here, refers to voluntary actions of individuals that are motivated by the returns they are expected to bring and typically do in fact bring from others. Action compelled by physical coercion is not voluntary, although compliance with other forms of power can be considered a voluntary service rendered in exchange for the benefits such compliance produces, as already indicated. Whereas conformity with internalized standards does not fall under the definition of exchange presented, conformity to social pressures tends to entail indirect exchanges. Men make charitable donations, not to earn the gratitude of the recipients, whom they never see, but to earn the approval of their peers who participate in the philanthropic campaign. Donations are exchanged for social approval, though the recipients of the donations and the suppliers of the approval are not identical, and the clarification of the connection between the two requires an analysis of the complex structures of indirect exchange, which is reserved for chapters eight and ten. Our concern now is with the simpler direct exchanges.

The need to reciprocate for benefits received in order to continue receiving them serves as a "starting mechanism" of social interaction and group structure, as Gouldner has pointed out.[1] When people are thrown together, and before common norms or goals or role expectations have crystallized among them, the advantages to be gained from entering into exchange relations furnish incentives for social interaction, and the exchange processes serve as mechanisms for regulating social interaction, thus fostering the development of a network of social relations and a rudimentary group structure. Eventually, group norms to regulate and limit the exchange transactions emerge, including the fundamental and ubiquitous norm of reciprocity, which makes failure to discharge obligations subject to group sanctions. In contrast to Gouldner, however, it is held here that the norm of reciprocity merely reinforces and stabilizes tendencies inherent in the character of social exchange itself and that the fundamental starting mechanism of patterned social intercourse is found in the existential conditions of exchange, not in the norm of reciprocity. It is a necessary condition of exchange that individuals, in the interest of continuing to receive needed services, discharge their obligations for having received them in the past. Exchange processes utilize, as it were, the self-interests of individuals to produce a differentiated social structure within which norms tend to develop that require individuals to set aside some of their personal interests for the sake of those of the collectivity. Not all social constraints are normative constraints, and those imposed by the nature of social exchange are not, at least, not originally.

Social exchange differs in important ways from strictly economic exchange. The basic and most crucial distinction is that social exchange entails *unspecified* obligations. The prototype of an economic transaction rests on a formal contract that stipulates the exact quantities to be exchanged.[2] The buyer pays $30,000 for a specific house, or he signs a contract to pay that sum plus interest over a period of years. Whether the entire transaction is consummated at a given time, in which case the contract may never be written, or not, all the transfers to be made now or in the future are agreed upon at the time of sale. Social exchange, in contrast, involves the principle that one person does another a favor, and while there is a general expectation of some future return, its exact nature is definitely *not* stipulated in advance. The distinctive implications of such unspecified obligations are brought into high relief by the institutionalized form they assume in the Kula discussed by Malinowski:

> The main principle underlying the regulations of actual exchange is that the Kula consists in the bestowing of a ceremonial gift, which has to be repaid by an equivalent counter-gift after a lapse of time. . . . But it can never be exchanged from hand to hand, with the equivalence between the two objects being discussed, bargained about and computed. . . . The second very important principle is that the equivalence of the counter-gift is left to the giver, and it cannot be enforced by any kind of coercion. . . . If the article given as a counter-gift is not equivalent, the recipient will be disappointed and angry, but he has no direct means of redress, no means of coercing his partner. . . .[3]

Social exchange, whether it is in this ceremonial form or not, involves favors that create diffuse future obligations, not precisely specified ones, and the nature of the return cannot be bargained about but must be left to the discretion of the one who makes it. Thus, if a person gives a dinner party, he expects his guests to reciprocate at some future date. But he can hardly bargain with them about the kind of party to which they should invite him, although he expects them not simply to ask him for a quick lunch if he had invited them to a formal dinner. Similarly, if a person goes to some trouble in behalf of an acquaintance, he expects *some* expression of gratitude, but he can neither bargain with the other over how to reciprocate nor force him to reciprocate at all.

Since there is no way to assure an appropriate return for a favor, social exchange requires trusting others to discharge their obligations. While the banker who makes a loan to a man who buys a house does not have to trust him, although he hopes he will not have to foreclose the mortgage, the individual who gives another an expensive gift must trust him to reciprocate in proper fashion. Typically, however, exchange relations evolve in a slow process, starting with minor transactions in which little trust is required because little risk is involved. A worker may help a colleague a few times. If the colleague fails to reciprocate, the worker has lost little and can easily protect himself against further loss by ceasing to furnish assistance. If the colleague does reciprocate, perhaps excessively so out of gratitude for the volunteered help and in the hope of receiving more, he proves himself trustworthy of continued and extended favors. (Excessive reciprocation may be embarrassing, because it is a bid for a more extensive exchange relation than one may be willing to enter.) By discharging their obligations for services rendered, if only to provide inducements for the supply of more assistance, individuals demonstrate their trustworthiness, and the gradual expansion of mutual service is accompanied by a parallel growth of mutual trust. Hence, processes of social exchange, which may originate in pure self-interest, generate trust in social relations through their recurrent and gradually expanding character.

Only social exchange tends to engender feelings of personal obligation, gratitude, and trust; purely economic exchange as such does not. An individual is obligated to the banker who gives him a mortgage on his house merely in the technical sense of owing him money, but he does not feel personally obligated in the sense of experiencing a debt of gratitude to the banker, because all the banker's services, all costs and risks, are duly taken into account in and fully repaid by the interest on the loan he receives. A banker who grants a loan without adequate collateral, however, does make the recipient personally obligated for this favorable treatment, precisely because this act of trust entails a social exchange that is superimposed upon the strictly economic transaction.

In contrast to economic commodities, the benefits involved in social exchange do not have an exact price in terms of a single quantitative medium of exchange, which is another reason why social obligations are unspecific. It is essential to realize that this is a substantive fact, not simply a methodological problem. It is not just the social scientist who cannot exactly measure how much approval a given helpful action is worth; the actors themselves cannot precisely specify the worth of approval or of help in the absence of a money price. The obligations individuals incur in social exchange, therefore, are defined only in general, somewhat diffuse terms. Furthermore, the specific benefits exchanged are sometimes primarily valued as symbols of the supportiveness and friendliness they express, and it is the exchange of the underlying mutual support that is the main concern of the participants. Occasionally, a time-consuming service of great material benefit to the recipient might be properly repaid by mere verbal expressions of deep appreciation, since these are taken to signify as much supportiveness as the material benefits.[4] In the long run, however, the explicit efforts the associates in a peer relation make in one another's behalf tend to be in balance, if only because a persistent imbalance in these manifestations of good will raise questions about the reciprocity in the underlying orientations of support and congeniality.

NOTES

1 Alvin W. Gouldner. 1960. "The Norm of Reciprocity." *American Sociological Review* 25: 161–78, esp. p. 176.
2 This is not completely correct for an employment contract or for the purchase of professional services, since the precise services the employee or professional will be obligated to perform are not specified in detail in advance. Economic transac-tions that involve services generally are somewhat closer to social exchange than the pure type of economic exchange of commodities or *products* of services.
3 Bronislaw Malinowski. 1961. *Argonauts of the Western Pacific*. New York: Dutton, pp. 95–6.
4 See Erving Goffman. 1962. *Asylums*, Chicago: Aldine, pp. 274–86.

6B James S. Coleman from *Social Capital in the Creation of Human Capital*

Original publication details: James S. Coleman, 1988. "Social Capital in the Creation of Human Capital." *American Journal of Sociology* 94: 95–96, 97–99, 100–101, 102, 103–104. Reproduced with permission of University of Chicago Press.

There are two broad intellectual streams in the description and explanation of social action. One, characteristic of the work of most sociologists, sees the actor as socialized and action as governed by social norms, rules, and obligations. The principal virtues of this intellectual stream lie in its ability to describe action in social context and to explain the way action is shaped, constrained, and redirected by the social context.

The other intellectual stream, characteristic of the work of most economists, sees the actor as having goals independently arrived at, as acting independently, and as wholly self-interested. Its principal virtue lies in having a principle of action, that of maximizing utility. This principle of action, together with a single empirical generalization (declining marginal utility) has generated the extensive growth of neoclassical economic theory, as well as the growth of political philosophy of several varieties: utilitarianism, contractarianism, and natural rights.[1]

In earlier works (Coleman 1986a, 1986b), I have argued for and engaged in the development of a theoretical orientation in sociology that includes components from both these intellectual streams. It accepts the principle of rational or purposive action and attempts to show how that principle, in conjunction with particular social contexts, can account not only for the actions of individuals in particular contexts but also for the development of social organization. In the present paper, I introduce a conceptual tool for use in this theoretical enterprise: social capital. As background for introducing this concept, it is useful to see some of the criticisms of and attempts to modify the two intellectual streams.

[. . .]

Social Capital

Elements for these two intellectual traditions cannot be brought together in a pastiche. It is necessary to begin with a conceptually coherent framework from one and introduce elements from the other without destroying that coherence.

I see two major deficiencies in earlier work that introduced "exchange theory" into sociology, despite the pathbreaking character of this work. One was the limitation to microsocial relations, which abandons the principal virtue of economic theory, its ability to make the micro-macro transition from pair relations to system. This was evident both in Homans's (1961) work and in Blau's (1964) work. The other was the attempt to introduce principles in an ad hoc fashion, such as "distributive justice" (Homans 1964, p. 241) or the "norm of reciprocity" (Gouldner 1960). The former deficiency limits the theory's usefulness, and the latter creates a pastiche.

If we begin with a theory of rational action, in which each actor has control over certain resources and interests in certain resources and events, then social capital constitutes a particular kind of resource available to an actor.

Social capital is defined by its function. It is not a single entity but a variety of different entities, with two elements in common: they all consist of some aspect of social structures, and they facilitate certain actions of actors – whether persons or corporate actors – within the structure. Like other forms of capital, social capital is productive, making possible the achievement of certain ends that in its absence would not be possible. Like physical capital and human capital, social capital is not completely fungible but may be specific to certain activities. A given form of social capital that is valuable in facilitating certain actions may be useless or even harmful for others.

Unlike other forms of capital, social capital inheres in the structure of relations between actors and among actors. It is not lodged either in the actors themselves or in physical implements of production. Because purposive organizations can be actors ("corporate actors") just as persons can, relations among corporate actors can constitute social capital for them as well (with perhaps the best-known example being the sharing of information that allows price-fixing in an industry). However, in the present paper, the examples and area of application to which I will direct attention concern social capital as a resource for persons.

Before I state more precisely what social capital consists of, it is useful to give several examples that illustrate some of its different forms.

1. Wholesale diamond markets exhibit a property that to an outsider is remarkable. In the process of negotiating a sale, a merchant will hand over to another merchant a bag of stones for the latter to examine in private at his leisure, with no formal insurance that the latter will not substitute one or more inferior stones or a paste replica. The merchandise may be worth thousands, or hundreds of thousands, of dollars. Such free exchange of stones for inspection is important to the functioning of this market. In its absence, the market would operate in a much more cumbersome, much less efficient fashion.

Inspection shows certain attributes of the social structure. A given merchant community is ordinarily very close, both in the frequency of interaction and in ethnic and family ties. The wholesale diamond market in New York City, for example, is Jewish, with a high degree of intermarriage, living in the same community in Brooklyn, and going to the same synagogues. It is essentially a closed community.

Observation of the wholesale diamond market indicates that these close ties, through family, community, and religious affiliation, provide the insurance that is necessary to facilitate the transactions in the market. If any member of this community defected through substituting other stones or through stealing stones in his temporary possession, he would lose family, religious, and community ties. The strength of these ties makes possible transactions in which trustworthiness is taken for granted and trade can occur with ease. In the absence of these ties, elaborate and expensive bonding and insurance devices would be necessary – or else the transactions could not take place.

[. . .]

Human Capital and Social Capital

Probably the most important and most original development in the economics of education in the past 30 years has been the idea that the concept of physical capital as embodied in tools, machines, and other productive equipment can be extended to include human capital as well (see Schultz 1961; Becker 1964). Just as physical capital is created by changes in materials to form tools that facilitate production, human capital is created by changes in persons that bring about skills and capabilities that make them able to act in new ways.

Social capital, however, comes about through changes in the relations among persons that facilitate action. If physical capital is wholly tangible, being embodied in observable material form, and human capital is less tangible, being embodied in the skills and knowledge acquired by an individual, social capital is less tangible yet, for it exists in the *relations* among persons. Just as physical capital and human capital facilitate productive activity, social capital does as well. For example, a group within which there is extensive trustworthiness and extensive trust is able to accomplish much more than a comparable group without that trustworthiness and trust.

Forms of Social Capital

The value of the concept of social capital lies first in the fact that it identifies certain aspects of social structure by their functions, just as the concept "chair" identifies certain physical objects by their function, despite differences in form, appearance, and construction. The function identified by the concept of "social capital" is the value of these aspects of social structure to actors as resources that they can use to achieve their interests.

[. . .]

Obligations, Expectations, and Trustworthiness of Structures

If *A* does something for *B* and trusts *B* to reciprocate in the future, this establishes an expectation in *A* and an obligation on the part of *B*. This obligation can be conceived as a credit slip held by *A* for performance by *B*. If *A* holds a large number of these credit slips, for a number of persons with whom *A* has relations, then the analogy to financial capital is direct. These credit slips constitute a large body of credit that *A* can call in if necessary – unless, of course, the placement of trust has been unwise, and these are bad debts that will not be repaid.

In some social structures, it is said that "people are always doing things for each other." There are a large number of these credit slips outstanding, often on both sides of a relation (for these credit slips appear often not to be completely fungible across areas of activity, so that credit slips of *B* held by *A* and those of *A* held by *B* are not fully used to cancel each other out). . . . In . . . social structures where individuals are more self-sufficient and depend on each other less, there are fewer of these credit slips outstanding at any time.

This form of social capital depends on two elements: trustworthiness of the social environment, which means that obligations will be repaid, and the actual extent of obligations held. Social structures differ in both these dimensions, and actors within the same structure differ in the second. A case that illustrates the value of the trustworthiness of the environment is that of the rotating-credit associations of Southeast Asia and elsewhere. These associations are groups of friends and neighbors who typically meet monthly, each person contributing to a central fund that is then given to one of the members (through bidding or by lot), until, after a number of months, each of the *n* persons has made *n* contributions and received one payout. As Geertz (1962) points out, these associations serve as efficient institutions for amassing savings for small capital expenditures, an important aid to economic development.

But without a high degree of trustworthiness among the members of the group, the institution could not exist – for a person who receives a payout early in the sequence of meetings could abscond and leave the others with a loss. For example, one could not imagine a rotating-credit association operating successfully in urban areas marked by a high degree of social disorganization – or, in other words, by a lack of social capital.

Differences in social structures in both dimensions may arise for a variety of reasons. There are differences in the actual needs that persons have for help, in the existence of other sources of aid (such as government welfare services), in the degree of affluence (which reduces aid needed from others), in cultural differences in the tendency to lend aid and ask for aid (see Banfield 1967) in the closure of social networks, in the logistics of social contacts (see Festinger, Schachter, and Back 1963), and other factors. Whatever the source, however, individuals in social structures with high levels of obligations outstanding at any time have more social capital on which they can draw. The density of outstanding obligations means, in effect, that the overall usefulness of the tangible resources of that social structure is amplified by their availability to others when needed.

Individual actors in a social system also differ in the number of credit slips outstanding on which they can draw at any time. The most extreme examples are in hierarchically structured extended family settings, in which a patriarch (or "godfather") holds an extraordinarily large set of obligations that he can call in at any time to get what he wants done. Near this extreme are villages in traditional settings that are highly stratified, with certain wealthy families who, because of their wealth, have built up extensive credits that they can call in at any time.

Similarly, in political settings such as a legislature, a legislator in a position with extra resources (such as the Speaker of the House of Representatives or the Majority Leader of the Senate in the U.S. Congress) can, by effective use of resources, build up a set of obligations from other legislators that makes it possible to get legislation passed that would otherwise be stymied. This concentration of obligations constitutes social capital that is useful not only for this powerful legislator but useful also in getting an increased level of action on the part of a legislature. Thus, those members of legislatures among whom such credits are extensive should be more powerful than those without extensive credits and debits because they can use the credits to produce bloc voting on many issues. It is well recognized, for example, that in the U.S. Senate, some senators are members of what is called "the Senate Club," while others are not. This in effect means that some senators are embedded in the system of credits and debits, while others, outside the "Club," are not. It is also well recognized that those in the Club are more powerful than those outside it.

NOTE

1   For a discussion of the importance of the empirical generalization to economics, see Black, Coats, and Goodwin (1973).

REFERENCES

Banfield, Edward. 1967. *The Moral Basis of a Backward Society*. New York: Free Press.

Black, R.D.C., A.W. Coats, and C.D.W. Goodwin, eds. 1973. *The Marginal Revolution in Economics*. Durham, NC: Duke University Press.

Blau, Peter. 1964. *Exchange and Power in Social Life*. New York: Wiley.

Coleman, James S. 1986a. "Social Theory, Social Research, and a Theory of Action." *American Journal of Sociology* 91: 1309–35.

——1986b. *Individual Interests and Collective Action*. Cambridge: Cambridge University Press.

Festinger, Leon, Stanley Schachter, and Kurt Back. 1963. *Social Pressures in Informal Groups*. Stanford, CA: Stanford University Press.

Gouldner, Alvin. 1960. "The Norm of Reciprocity: A Preliminary Statement." *American Sociological Review* 25: 161–78.

Homans, George. 1974. *Social Behavior: Its Elementary Forms*, rev. ed. New York: Harcourt, Brace & World.

6C Paula England from *Sometimes the Social Becomes Personal: Gender, Class, and Sexualities*

Original publication details: Paula England, 2016. "Sometimes the Social Becomes Personal: Gender, Class, and Sexualities." *American Sociological Review* 81: 4–5, 5–7, 8–9, 14–15, 22. Reproduced with permission of Sage Publications, Inc.

Being in a social position affects one's outcomes. While it would be hard to find a statement less controversial among sociologists, there is substantial disagreement on the mechanisms through which this occurs. In recent decades, the idea that constraints directly delimit outcomes has been more popular among sociologists than the idea that constraints affect personal characteristics, which, in turn, affect outcomes. I argue here for the importance of being alert to both types of mechanisms through which social positions affect outcomes.

One type of mechanism is indirect and entails a two-step process. In the first step, being in a social position comes with constraints that affect personal characteristics – things people carry across situations, such as skills, habits, identities, worldviews, preferences, or values. These constraints change individuals' personal characteristics in a durable, although not necessarily permanent, way. In the second step of the process, personal characteristics affect outcomes. The first part of my title – "sometimes the social becomes personal" – summarizes the insight of models that see constraints as affecting outcomes by changing personal characteristics, which, in turn, affect outcomes.

[. . .]

My theoretical argument is that we should be alert to and investigate *both* types of mechanisms . . . I will discuss both, but spend more of my time on mechanisms involving personal characteristics, not because they are more important, but because I believe they are inappropriately suspect among sociologists.

[. . .]

Defining Terms

The social positions I focus on are gender and class background. But my theoretical point applies to any social position. "Social positions," as I use the term, encompass a broad array of phenomena. Examples include organizational membership, occupation, network position, neighborhood, nation, race, whether you are an immigrant, your sexual orientation, and whether you are cisgender or transgender. Some of these positions are roles or situations that can be defined independently of any characteristics of the individuals who occupy them. The class of your family of origin, an organization you belong to or work for, your occupation, your position in social networks, and your neighborhood or nation all fit this definition. However, I also consider race, whether you are an immigrant, gender, sexual orientation, and whether you are transgender to be social positions, although they are also seen as characteristics of individuals. I conceive of these individual characteristics as social positions if they are categories often used to classify, evaluate, and differentially treat people. For example, being a man or being a woman affects the constraints you face, and thus I see gender as a "social position." This is as true for gender, race, sexual orientation, immigrant status, or whether you are transgender as it is for occupation, class, network position, or geographic locale.

Being in a social position entails facing constraints. Constraints are important to the models I propose because, in the causal chain, constraints come between social positions and the outcomes of interest in both types of models. I use the word "constraint" very broadly. The narrowest notion of a constraint emanating from a social position is that it makes doing some things absolutely impossible. But social forces are on a continuum from gross physical coercion to nearly invisible processes, and I intend to include that entire range in what I call constraints. So constraints also include what a position makes it harder to do, or, the flip side, what a position gives you more resources or opportunities to do. Positions also differ in the incentives they create – in what carrots and sticks follow from what behavior; I consider these incentive structures to be constraints as well. Finally, constraints include the expectations others have of you because you are in this position.

By personal characteristics I refer to things individuals carry across situations, such as skills, habits, identities, worldviews, preferences, or values.[1] Characteristics must have some durability across situations and positions to count as personal. However, durable does not imply immutable; I am claiming that personal characteristics are molded by the constraints associated with social positions, and this implies that personal characteristics can change as one moves out of one social position into another. How durable effects of constraints on personal characteristics are probably depends on how long one is in the social position (with longer exposures yielding more durable characteristics) and whether the exposure to the constraint is at an age when humans have more or less plasticity. Although my emphasis is on social processes, many personal characteristics have some of their variance explained socially and some explained genetically, so I am not claiming that *all* variance in personal characteristics is explained by the constraints associated with social positions.

By "outcomes" I mean behaviors as well as rewards or punishments. Outcomes that are behaviors include such things as the extent to which one studies, continues or discontinues enrollment in school, engages in health-related behaviors, saves money, votes (at all or a particular way), or engages in crime.[2] Outcomes affected by constraints that are not behavioral (but may result in part from behavioral outcomes) include educational attainment, earnings, wealth, health, and psychological well-being. In my two empirical cases, behavioral outcomes include whether one has sex with a same-sex partner, engages in ridiculing others seen as gay, and uses birth control (contraception or abortion); having a nonmarital birth is a non-behavioral outcome.

Because I distinguish between theoretical mechanisms entailing constraints that affect outcomes directly, and mechanisms that affect outcomes indirectly via personal characteristics, I should clarify what I mean by "directly." A detailed look shows nearly all effects of any given factor on an outcome to be "indirect" through one or more mediating (i.e., intervening) variables. However, I use the term "direct" in the path-analytic sense, to mean "not through some mediator I have specified." In this address, "direct" means *not through personal characteristics*. Thus . . . effects of constraints on outcomes that are *not* mediated through personal characteristics will be called "direct" effects of constraints, even if they actually operate through other mediators. . . .

I turn now to how past theorizing about gender illuminates my core theoretical concern regarding how constraints affect outcomes, both directly and by affecting personal characteristics.[3] . . . As mentioned earlier, I treat gender as a social position because whether we are perceived to be men or women affects how individuals and institutions treat us.

In the 1960s and 1970s, sociologists and psychologists writing about gender stressed differences in orientations and preferences, and saw their origin in differential socialization by sex, through which cultural beliefs and values were internalized. Even though some now see this work as passé, the idea that internalized cultural beliefs affect outcomes never disappeared; in recent writings a number of sociologists argue that gendered ideals or dispositions affect choices of fields of study and occupations, thus helping to perpetuate job segregation and the pay gap (Cech 2013; Charles and Bradley 2009; England 2011; Okamoto and England 1999).

Yet much of gender sociology focuses on direct constraints. Even discussions of culture typically focus less on how internalized culture limits women's aspirations, and more on how cultural beliefs lead to biased underestimates of women's competence or overestimates of men's (Ridgeway and Correll 2004). The "doing gender" view (West and Zimmerman 1987), based in ethnomethodology, also emphasizes cultural beliefs as an external constraint rather than internalized preferences; in this view, what keeps us conforming to others' gendered expectations of us is our desire to make cognitive sense to them.[4] Other sociologists of gender emphasize direct effects of institutional constraints, such as governmental policies and employers' discrimination, on gender inequality (England 1992; Kanter 1977; Levanon, England, and Allison 2009; Reskin and Roos 1990). Some scholars have made broad theoretical statements arguing for the primacy of structural or macrosocial factors in causing gender inequality (Epstein 1988; Kanter 1976; Martin 2004).

As Risman (2004) reviews the literature, although some debates portrayed "structural" and "individual" approaches to gender as incompatible, many scholars now agree that we need an integrative approach that sees causal arrows between multiple levels – individual, interactional, and institutional (Browne and England 1997; England and Browne 1992; Ferree, Lorber, and Hess 1999; Ridgeway and Correll 2004; Risman 2004). This entails recognizing biological influences; how early socialization and later constraints shape identities, beliefs, and values; and direct effects of constraints resulting from how men and women are treated in interaction, and from organizational or governmental policies. This view is consistent with my claim that individuals' outcomes are affected by gender through direct effects of gendered constraints, as well as through such constraints affecting personal characteristics that, in turn, affect outcomes. Many scholars now agree on the need for a multilevel model, but claims about the role of gender differences in personal characteristics remain controversial among others. In discussion of my first empirical case, I will refer to the myriad effects – direct and indirect – as the "gender system" and examine some pathways through which it affects involvement in sex with same-sex partners.

[. . .]

Explaining the Gender Differences

Why do men participate less than women in sex with same-sex partners? I offer an explanation involving the gender system, and exemplifying the two types of theoretical mechanisms I introduced. The hypothesis I offer is social, but it in no way precludes genetic effects on whether one is attracted to or has sex with men, women, or both (for evidence regarding genetic effects on sexual orientation, see Bailey, Dunne, and Martin 2000; Bailey and Pillard 1991; Bailey et al. 1993; for a critical review of literature suggesting genetic effects, see Bearman and Brückner 2002).

Two distinct aspects of the gender system are needed for my argument. The first is the obvious point that people face social pressure to conform to what is expected of them as men or women. Gender conformity entails many things, such as that men should be strong and women nice. For both women and men it also entails being straight. You violate gender norms by not appearing to be straight, and violating gender norms is generally seen as negative.

A second aspect of the gender system concerns which gender is more valued. Everything associated with women – traits women are believed to have, or activities women often do – tends to be valued less. As one example of this, if you compare two distinct jobs, one filled mostly by men and another mostly by women, the pay for men and women is higher, on average, if they are in the male-dominated job. This is true even when the two distinct jobs require the same amount of education and skill (England 1992; England, Reid, and Kilbourne 1996; Kilbourne et al. 1994; Levanon et al. 2009; for debate, see England, Hermsen, and Cotter 2000; Tam 1997, 2000).

Putting these two aspects of the gender system together, both sexes face pressures to conform to gender norms, and thus to be straight, but I believe that men's gender nonconformity is *more* controversial precisely because the male gender is more valued. As a result, being a gay man is more stigmatized than being a lesbian (Watts 2015). Being bisexual is also less acceptable for men than for women. Analogous to the "one drop rule" of black racial identity, a man who is not 100 percent straight is seen in some quarters as gay (Anderson [2011:142–49] suggested this metaphor).

What we see here in the sexual arena parallels an asymmetry seen more broadly in the gender revolution, which mostly entailed women bucking gender conformity to enter spheres formerly reserved for men, not vice versa (England 2010). Many women entered male professions; few men have entered female jobs or become full-time homemakers. Girls now play sports, but fewer boys play with dolls. Women wear pants, but men wearing skirts has not caught on. Moreover, because women are more likely than men to violate gender norms, we get used to seeing women do these things, and the extent to which they register as "gender violations" lessens. It is consistent with this broader pattern that women are more likely than men to violate gender norms by having sex with a same-sex partner.[5]

The two types of theoretical mechanisms I introduced help make sense of why women feel freer than men to have sexual partners of the same sex. Consider models in which constraints do not change our personal characteristics but regulate our behavior more directly. As mentioned earlier, the "doing gender" perspective is an example (West and Zimmerman 1987). In this view, others' expectations summon our conformity, because we want to make sense to them. Applying this to sexuality, men "do gender" by "doing straight" to make sense to others as men. Other perspectives positing direct effects of constraints emphasize incentives – carrots and sticks.[6] Sticks are especially likely for men or boys perceived to be gay. Research documents ridicule, violence, and job discrimination for people who are not seen to be straight (on ridicule and violence against gay men, see Pascoe [2007] and Herek [2009]; on job discrimination, see Tilcsik [2011] who found discrimination for men and Bailey, Wallace, and Wright [2013] who did not). Queer women can experience these harms too,[7] but they are especially visited on men (Herek 2009).

In response to these expectations and incentives, men who are sexually interested in other men may avoid or hide gay behavior. I believe this is one reason that fewer men than women report having had sex with same-sex partners. Some of this difference probably reflects men actually being deterred from sex with men, and some may result from men underreporting more than women. Either is consistent with the argument that gay sex is more stigmatized for men. Men's motivation to look straight may also lead them to call others "fags" (Pascoe 2005, 2007). These expectations and incentives need not change personal characteristics to regulate behavior, and thus they represent conformity via direct effects of gender constraints.

But these very same constraints may also work in a longer-term way to change men's personal characteristics. The incentives and expectations may create internalized heterosexist values or solidify straight identities, even among men attracted to men. This is consistent with the evidence I showed that men are more likely than women to believe that sex with same-sex partners is wrong, and men are less likely than women to identify as bisexual. These personal characteristics – values and identities – further encourage men to avoid sex with same-sex partners. They also encourage another outcome – men policing other men's sexuality and thereby becoming part of the constraints pushing other men in a straight direction.

One reason to think that gendered constraints like these may really change personal characteristics is that they last a long time. If you are cisgender – that is, if you have not transitioned out of the sex category you were assigned at birth – then the sex you report is a good indicator of how the gender system has treated you your entire life.

[. . .]

As we go about our work as sociologists, my hope is that we will remain open to understanding both of the ways social positions and their constraints affect our outcomes. Sometimes constraints do not change our personal characteristics; they just change what we do and what happens to us. Other times, constraints change who we are in durable ways; sometimes the *social* becomes *personal*. When it does, studying the processes involved will enrich the science of sociology and its relevance to the social world.

NOTES

1   I am not treating individual characteristics, such as national origin, class background, race, sex, or sexual orientation, as "personal characteristics," although they may affect such characteristics through the constraints to which they (as social positions) subject us.

2   I consider internalized dispositions toward such behaviors to be personal characteristics, but the behaviors themselves to be outcomes.

3   Both the social structure and personality view and Bourdieu's theorizing are relevant to gender. In House and Mortimer's (1990) discussion of the

former they mention gender as a social structural location affecting personal characteristics, and Bourdieu (2001) applied his concept of "habitus" to what he called "masculine domination." Yet, few gender scholars writing on these issues have self-identified as following either Bourdieu or the social structure and personality view.

4   Ethnomethodological models do contain internalization of culture. But it is not Person I who "does gender" who is seen to be operating from beliefs about gender, but rather the Person 2, whose expectations of Person 1 are based on Person 1's gender. These expectations cause Person 1 to "do gender" to make sense to Person 2 (England and Browne 1992).

5   I know of two other hypotheses about why sex with same-sex partners is less common among men than women. First, Diamond (2008a, 2008b, 2014) suggests that women may have a greater biological propensity for sexual fluidity or bisexuality, but cautions that evidence is very preliminary and tentative. Second, in a personal communication, Leila Rupp (2015) has suggested that sex between two women is not stigmatized as gender-nonconforming in the same way that sex between men is, because sex between women is not seen as "real sex"; sex and sexual agency are defined in terms of the penis. Rupp (2012) points to a long history of women's sex with other women being seen as of little importance.

6   Incentives are key to rational choice perspectives, but they are used much more broadly in sociology, even among scholars not identifying with the rational choice perspective.

7   For example, Mishel (2015) found job discrimination against lesbians in an audit study.

REFERENCES

Anderson, Eric. 2011. *Inclusive Masculinity: The Changing Nature of Masculinities.* New York: Routledge.

Bailey, J. Michael, Michael P. Dunne, and Nicholas G. Martin. 2000. "Genetic and Environmental Influences on Sexual Orientation and Its Correlates in an Australian Twin Sample." *Journal of Personality and Social Psychology* 78(3): 524–36.

Bailey, J. Michael, and Richard C. Pillard. 1991. "A Genetic Study of Male Sexual Orientation." *Archives of General Psychiatry* 48(12): 1089–96.

Bailey, J. Michael, Richard C. Pillard, Michael C. Neale, and Yvonne Agyei. 1993. "Heritable Factors Influence Sexual Orientation in Women." *Archives of General Psychiatry* 50(3): 217–23.

Bailey, John, Michael Wallace, and Bradley Wright. 2013. "Are Gay Men and Lesbians Discriminated against When Applying for Jobs? A Four-City, Internet- Based Field Experiment." *Journal of Homosexuality* 60(6): 873–94.

Bearman, Peter S., and Hannah Brückner. 2002. "Opposite-Sex Twins and Adolescent Same-Sex Attraction." *American Journal of Sociology* 107(5): 1179–1205.

Browne, Irene, and Paula England. 1997. "Oppression from Within and Without in Sociological Theories: An Application to Gender." *Current Perspectives in Social Theory* 17: 77–104.

Cech, Erin A. 2013. "The Self-Expressive Edge of Occupational Sex Segregation." *American Journal of Sociology* 119(3):747–89.

Charles, Maria, and Karen Bradley. 2009. "Indulging Our Gendered Selves? Sex Segregation by Field of Study in 44 Countries." *American Journal of Sociology* 114(4): 924–76.

Diamond, Lisa M. 2008a. "Female Bisexuality from Adolescence to Adulthood: Results from a 10-Year Longitudinal Study." *Developmental Psychology* 44(1): 5–14.

Diamond, Lisa M. 2008b. *Sexual Fluidity: Understanding Women's Love and Desire.* Cambridge, MA: Harvard University Press.

Diamond, Lisa M. 2014. "Gender and Same-Sex Sexuality." pp. 629–52 in *APA Handbook of Sexuality and Psychology, Vol. 1, Person-Based Approaches,* edited by D. L. Tolman and L. M. Diamond. Washington, DC: American Psychological Association.

England, Paula. 1992. *Comparable Worth: Theories and Evidence*. Piscataway, NJ: Transaction Publishers.

England, Paula. 2010. "The Gender Revolution: Uneven and Stalled." *Gender & Society* 24(2): 149–66.

England, Paula. 2011. "Reassessing the Uneven Gender Revolution and Its Slowdown." *Gender & Society* 25(1): 113–23.

England, Paula, and Irene Browne. 1992. "Internalization and Constraint in Women's Subordination." *Current Perspectives in Social Theory* 12: 97–123.

England, Paula, Joan M. Hermsen, and David Cotter. 2000. "The Devaluation of Women's Work: A Comment on Tam." *American Journal of Sociology* 105(6): 1741–51.

England, Paula, Lori L. Reid, and Barbara Stanek Kilbourne. 1996. "The Effect of the Sex Composition of Jobs on Starting Wages in an Organization: Findings from the NLSY." *Demography* 33(4): 511–21.

Epstein, Cynthia Fuchs. 1988. *Deceptive Distinctions: Sex, Gender, and the Social Order*. New Haven, CT: Yale University Press.

Ferree, Myra M., Judith Lorber, and Beth B. Hess. 1999. "Introduction," pp. xv–xxxvi in *Revisioning Gender*, edited by M.M. Ferree, J. Lorber, and B.B. Hess. Thousand Oaks, CA: Sage.

Herek, Gregory M. 2009. "Hate Crimes and Stigma-Related Experiences among Sexual Minority Adults in the United States: Prevalence Estimates from a National Probability Sample." *Journal of Interpersonal Violence* 24(1): 54–74.

Kanter, Rosabeth M. 1976. "The Impact of Hierarchical Structures on the Work Behavior of Women and Men." *Social Problems* 23(4): 415–30.

Kanter, Rosabeth Moss. 1977. *Men and Women of the Corporation*. New York: Basic Books.

Kilbourne, Barbara Stanek, Paula England, George Farkas, Kurt Beron, and Dorothea Weir. 1994. "Returns to Skill, Compensating Differentials, and Gender Bias: Effects of Occupational Characteristics on the Wages of White Women and Men." *American Journal of Sociology* 100(3): 689–719.

Levanon, Asaf, Paula England, and Paul Allison. 2009. "Occupational Feminization and Pay: Assessing Causal Dynamics Using 1950–2000 U.S. Census Data." *Social Forces* 88(2):865–91.

Martin, Patricia Yancey. 2004. "Gender as Social Institution." *Social Forces* 82: 1249–73.

Okamoto, Dina, and Paula England. 1999. "Is There a Supply Side to Occupational Sex Segregation?" *Sociological Perspectives* 42(4): 557–82.

Pascoe, C. J. 2005. "'Dude, You're a Fag': Adolescent Masculinity and the Fag Discourse." *Sexualities* 8(3): 329–46.

Pascoe, C. J. 2007. *Dude, You're a Fag*. Berkeley: University of California Press.

Reskin, Barbara F., and Patricia A. Roos. 1990. *Job Queues, Gender Queues: Explaining Women's Inroads into Male Occupations*. Philadelphia: Temple University Press.

Ridgeway, Cecilia L., and Shelley J. Correll. 2004. "Unpacking the Gender System: A Theoretical Perspective on Gender Beliefs and Social Relations." *Gender & Society* 18(4): 510–31.

Risman, Barbara J. 2004. "Gender as a Social Structure: Theory Wrestling with Activism." *Gender & Society* 18(4):429–50.

Rupp, Leila J. 2012. "Sexual Fluidity 'Before Sex.'" *Signs* 37(4): 849–56.

Tam, Tony. 1997. "Sex Segregation and Occupational Gender Inequality in the United States: Devaluation or Specialized Training?" *American Journal of Sociology* 102(6): 1652–92.

Tam, Tony. 2000. "Occupational Wage Inequality and Devaluation: A Cautionary Tale of Measurement Error." *American Journal of Sociology* 105(6): 1752–60.

Tilcsik, András. 2011. "Pride and Prejudice: Employment Discrimination against Openly Gay Men in the United States." *American Journal of Sociology* 117(2): 586–626.

Watts, Alexander W. 2015. "Sexuality, Gender, and Morality: Testing an Integrated Theory of Anti-Gay Prejudice." Unpublished paper, Stanford University, Stanford, CA.

West, Candace, and Don H. Zimmerman. 1987. "Doing Gender." *Gender & Society* 1(2):125–51.

PART III

SYMBOLIC INTERACTION, PHENOMENOLOGY, AND ETHNOMETHODOLOGY

CHAPTER SEVEN

SYMBOLIC INTERACTION

CHAPTER MENU

Symbolic interaction focuses attention squarely on face-to-face interaction and on all the symbolic exchange – the totality of all kinds of information that is telegraphed and that must occur in any face-to-face encounter, whether in the co-presence of just one other individual or in a group activity or event; and how such inference across all forms of interpersonal interaction is structured and sustained. The face-to-face emphasis is important because it alerts us that a lot of interpersonal communication (whether in a classroom, a restaurant or a health clinic) is driven by non-verbal gestures, cues and miscues and their interpretation and reinterpretation. Today we are all highly accustomed to interacting with friends and family through social media, much of it devoid of "face time," and although much of this communication works well for us there is also a general concern that such communication may more likely (than in a face-to-face conversation) distort what we want to say and, or, undermine the meanings we want to convey. This is because while words matter, the tone with which we speak, the physical demeanor of our face and body, and the setting or situational context in which we speak and what its props and symbols convey – and how we

Concise Reader in Sociological Theory: Theorists, Concepts, and Current Applications,
First Edition. Edited by Michele Dillon. Editorial material and organization
© 2021 John Wiley & Sons Ltd. Published 2021 by John Wiley & Sons Ltd.

interpret all those elements in the cues and miscues other people communicate – are all pertinent to effective communication, and more specifically, effective role performance.

What occurs in face-to-face communication is deeply significant. As **George H. Mead** (see excerpt *7a Mind, Self, & Society*) elaborates, in child development, the initial face-to-face relationships which an infant experiences and engages form the Self. No one is born with a self already intact; rather the self can only emerge out of social interaction. This is largely accomplished as a result of the affirming reciprocity of the Other (e.g. a parent, other family members and, by extension, society in general) toward the infant, and through this process the Self is formed through the "I" and the "Me" taking on and internalizing the symbolic cues exchanged. We learn from early on to "read" others – their emotions, their demeanor, and their verbal and nonverbal responses to us, and we typically adjust our response to others as the interaction and its "I–Me" dynamic unfolds. This symbolic exchange is essential to the creation of the Self, the necessarily *social* self that is essential to human social functioning across the life course and, on any one day, across the numerous social situations we encounter and which we must necessarily engage and interact.

Erving Goffman builds on Mead's analysis to dissect social and institutional life as an ongoing series of self-presentations that the self must manage in the performance of their multiple and varied roles (see excerpt *7b The Presentation of Self in Everyday Life*). Although Goffman focuses on the detailed micro-dynamics of interpersonal face-to-face exchange, he emphasizes that role performances are highly structured – they are highly structured by society, and not spontaneously so-to-speak by the self. Roles are socially scripted; it is not the individual who makes up the role or the script as they interact (and even self-reflect) in a given situation. Rather, as in a play, individuals act out or perform the various parts and routines in a given role. They are socialized how to interpret cues and how to remedy a miscue; in short, we are socialized into how to define and interpret a given social situation (in the classroom, at work, at the doctor's office, at home, at a football game, at a religious worship site) and how to behave or to act in any given situation as we enact or perform the expected role(s) in that setting (and in other settings), and respond to the role performance(s) of others performing their respective roles. In short, in Goffman's dramaturgical approach, society – and its effective functioning (recall Emile Durkheim and Talcott Parsons) – is maintained, by the successful self-presentation and impression management strategies of socialized individuals successfully performing their expected social roles and the scripted duties and obligations associated with those roles.

The self-presentation and impression management work of some individuals and groups is made more difficult, Goffman (1963) elaborates, because they are carriers of a stigma. As with the self, which is formed by society (by and in social interaction), who and what is stigmatized are also collectively defined by society. Thus stigma, according to Goffman, is less of an attribute of a person than a marker of social relations and of social expectations in various interactions, that is, between the "normals" and the stigmatized. All those individuals and groups whom society stigmatizes, Goffman writes, have a "spoiled identity" that they must necessarily try to cover up in ongoing interactions and across multiple role settings in order to pass as "normal." Writing in the 1960s, he identified three categories of stigma, those relating to:

> (i) "physical deformities," (ii) "blemishes of character perceived as weak will, domineering or unnatural passions, treacherous and rigid beliefs, and dishonesty. . ..[associated with], mental disorder, imprisonment, addiction, alcoholism, homosexuality, unemployment, suicidal attempts, and radical political behavior," and (iii) "the tribal stigma of race, nation, and religion, these being stigma that can be transmitted through lineages and equally contaminate all members of a family" (Goffman 1963: 4).

Though socially defined and therefore not set in stone for all time, what specific identities and attributes are stigmatized can nonetheless endure over time even as social and legal changes may help to destigmatize certain individuals, groups, identities and conditions (e.g. gay sexuality, disabled people, mental illness).

In a similar vein Goffman (1961) also writes about how those whom society marginalizes or punishes are deprived of the sorts of scripts and props that they could use to try to reframe the societal definition of their situation, and by extension, how others interpret their situation or social identity and interact with them. Criminals, for example, are stripped of their self by the criminal justice system and, therefore, stripped of the opportunity to present as something other than a criminal (e.g. in their roles as fathers or mothers). He calls prisons and similarly regimented institutions "total institutions" (Goffman 1961) because their rituals and routines do not allow for any privacy for, or individuality on the part of, their inmates. Inmates, rather, are deprived, for example, of the boundary-setting markers (that separate front-stage from back-stage roles) and the array of props that individuals typically use to redefine or to subvert their own or another person's role performance. In sum, Goffman's focus on symbolic interaction is important because it highlights the fact that everyday social interaction, both formal and informal, demands a great deal of constant symbolic surveillance and interpretation on the part of the Self of our own and of others' interactions and of the many diverse micro-settings (e.g. an elevator) in which these interactions occur and which give us cues as to how we and others should self-present and perform and manage the social roles that comprise the totality of intra-personal (as we reflect on and anticipate our roles and how we were understood or misunderstood), interpersonal, group, institutional, and societal life.

REFERENCES

Goffman, Erving. 1961. *Asylums: Essays on the Social Situation of Mental Patients and Other Inmates.* Chicago: Aldine.

Goffman, Erving. 1963. *Stigma: Notes on the Management of Spoiled Identity.* New York: Simon and Schuster.

7A George H. Mead from *Mind, Self & Society*

Original publication details: George H. Mead, 1934. *Mind, Self, and Society*, pp. 135, 138–139, 173–176. Edited by Charles W. Morris. Chicago: University of Chicago Press. Reproduced with permission of University of Chicago Press.

From the Standpoint of a Social Behaviorist

The self is something which has a development; it is not initially there, at birth, but arises in the process of social experience and activity, that is, develops in the given individual as a result of his relations to that process as a whole and to other individuals within that process.

[. . .]

The individual experiences himself as such, not directly, but only indirectly, from the particular standpoints of other individual members of the same social group, or from the generalized standpoint of the social group as a whole to which he belongs. For he enters his own experience as a self or individual, not directly or immediately, not by becoming a subject to himself, but only in so far as he first becomes an object to himself just as other individuals are objects to him or in his experience; and he becomes an object to himself only by taking the attitudes of other individuals toward himself within a social environment or context of experience and behavior in which both he and they are involved.

The importance of what we term "communication" lies in the fact that it provides a form of behavior in which the organism or the individual may become an object to himself. It is that sort of communication which we have been discussing – not communication in the sense of the cluck of the hen to the chickens, or the bark of a wolf to the pack, or the lowing of a cow, but communication in the sense of significant symbols, communication which is directed not only to others but also to the individual himself. So far as that type of communication is a part of behavior it at least introduces a self. Of course, one may hear without listening; one may see things that he does not realize; do things that he is not really aware of. But it is where one does respond to that which he addresses to another and where that response of his own becomes a part of his conduct, where he not only hears himself but responds to himself, talks and replies to himself as truly as the other person replies to him, that we have behavior in which the individuals become objects to themselves.

[. . .]

Where in conduct does the "I" come in as over against the "me"? If one determines what his position is in society and feels himself as having a certain function and privilege, these are all defined with reference to an "I," but the "I" is not a "me" and cannot become a "me." We may have a better self and a worse self, but that again is not the "I" as over against the "me," because they are both selves. We approve of one and disapprove of the other, but when we bring up one or the other they are there for such approval as "me's." The "I" does not get into the limelight; we talk to ourselves, but do not see ourselves. The

"I" reacts to the self which arises through the taking of the attitudes of others. Through taking those attitudes we have introduced the "me" and we react to it as an "I."

The simplest way of handling the problem would be in terms of memory. I talk to myself, and I remember what I said and perhaps the emotional content that went with it. The "I" of this moment is present in the "me" of the next moment. There again I cannot turn around quick enough to catch myself. I become a "me" in so far as I remember what I said. The "I" can be given, however, this functional relationship. It is because of the "I" that we say that we are never fully aware of what we are, that we surprise ourselves by our own action. It is as we act that we are aware of ourselves. It is in memory that the "I" is constantly present in experience. We can go back directly a few moments in our experience, and then we are dependent upon memory images for the rest. So that the "I" in memory is there as the spokesman of the self of the second, or minute, or day ago. As given, it is a "me," but it is a "me" which was the "I" at the earlier time. If you ask, then, where directly in your own experience the "I" comes in, the answer is that it comes in as a historical figure. It is what you were a second ago that is the "I" of the "me." It is another "me" that has to take that rôle. You cannot get the immediate response of the "I" in the process.[1] The "I" is in a certain sense that with which we do identify ourselves. The getting of it into experience constitutes one of the problems of most of our conscious experience; it is not directly given in experience.

The "I" is the response of the organism to the attitudes of the others; the "me" is the organized set of attitudes of others which one himself assumes. The attitudes of the others constitute the organized "me," and then one reacts toward that as an "I." I now wish to examine these concepts in greater detail.

There is neither "I" nor "me" in the conversation of gestures; the whole act is not yet carried out, but the preparation takes place in this field of gesture. Now, in so far as the individual arouses in himself the attitudes of the others, there arises an organized group of responses. And it is due to the individual's ability to take the attitudes of these others in so far as they can be organized that he gets self-consciousness. The taking of all of those organized sets of attitudes gives him his "me"; that is the self he is aware of. He can throw the ball to some other member because of the demand made upon him from other members of the team. That is the self that immediately exists for him in his consciousness. He has their attitudes, knows what they want and what the consequence of any act of his will be, and he has assumed responsibility for the situation. Now, it is the presence of those organized sets of attitudes that constitutes that "me" to which he as an "I" is responding. But what that response will be he does not know and nobody else knows. Perhaps he will make a brilliant play or an error. The response to that situation as it appears in his immediate experience is uncertain, and it is that which constitutes the "I."

The "I" is his action over against that social situation within his own conduct, and it gets into his experience only after he has carried out the act. Then he is aware of it. He had to do such a thing and he did it. He fulfils his duty and he may look with pride at the throw which he made. The "me" arises to do that duty – that is the way in which it arises in his experience. He had in him all the attitudes of others, calling for a certain response; that was the "me" of that situation, and his response is the "I."

NOTE

1 The sensitivity of the organism brings parts of itself into the environment. It does not, however, bring the life-process itself into the environment, and the complete imaginative presentation of the organism is unable to present the living of the organism. It can conceivably present the conditions under which living takes place but not the unitary life-process. The physical organism in the environment always remains a thing.

7B Erving Goffman from *The Presentation of Self in Everyday Life*

Introduction

When an individual enters the presence of others, they commonly seek to acquire information about him or to bring into play information about him already possessed. They will be interested in his general socio-economic status, his conception of self, his attitude toward them, his competence, his trustworthiness, etc. Although some of this information seems to be sought almost as an end in itself, there are usually quite practical reasons for acquiring it. Information about the individual helps to define the situation, enabling others to know in advance what he will expect of them and what they may expect of him. Informed in these ways, the others will know how best to act in order to call forth a desired response from him.

For those present, many sources of information become accessible and many carriers (or "sign-vehicles") become available for conveying this information. If unacquainted with the individual, observers can glean clues from his conduct and appearance which allow them to apply their previous experience with individuals roughly similar to the one before them or, more important, to apply untested stereotypes to him. They can also assume from past experience that only individuals of a particular kind are likely to be found in a given social setting. They can rely on what the individual says about himself or on documentary evidence he provides as to who and what he is. If they know, or know of, the individual by virtue of experience prior to the interaction, they can rely on assumptions as to the persistence and generality of psychological traits as a means of predicting his present and future behavior.

However, during the period in which the individual is in the immediate presence of the others, few events may occur which directly provide the others with the conclusive information they will need if they are to direct wisely their own activity. Many crucial facts lie beyond the time and place of interaction or lie concealed within it. For example, the "true" or "real" attitudes, beliefs, and emotions of the individual can be ascertained only indirectly, through his avowals or through what appears to be involuntary expressive behavior. Similarly, if the individual offers the others a product or service, they will often find that during the interaction there will be no time and place immediately available for eating the pudding that the proof can be found in. They will be forced to accept some events as conventional or natural signs of something not directly available to the senses. In Ichheiser's terms,[1] the individual will have to act so that he intentionally or unintentionally *expresses* himself, and the others will in turn have to be *impressed* in some way by him.

The expressiveness of the individual (and therefore his capacity to give impressions) appears to involve two radically different kinds of sign activity: the expression that he *gives*, and the expression that he *gives off*. The first involves verbal symbols or their substitutes which he uses admittedly and solely to convey the information that he and the others are known to attach to these symbols. This is communication in the traditional and narrow sense. The second involves a wide range of action that others can treat as symptomatic of the actor, the expectation being that the action was performed for reasons other than the information conveyed in this way. As we shall have to see, this distinction has an only initial validity. The individual does of course intentionally convey misinformation by means of both of these types of communication, the first involving deceit, the second feigning.

Taking communication in both its narrow and broad sense, one finds that when the individual is in the immediate presence of others, his activity will have a promissory character. The others are likely to find that they must accept the individual on faith, offering him a just return while he is present before them in exchange for something whose true value will not be established until after he has left their presence. (Of course, the others also live by inference in their dealings with the physical world, but it is only in the world of social interaction that the objects about which they make inferences will purposely facilitate and hinder this inferential process.) The security that they justifiably feel in making inferences about the individual will vary, of course, depending on such factors as the amount of information they already possess about him, but no amount of such past evidence can entirely obviate the necessity of acting on the basis of inferences. As William I. Thomas suggested:

> It is also highly important for us to realize that we do not as a matter of fact lead our lives, make our decisions, and reach our goals in everyday life either statistically or scientifically. We live by inference. I am, let us say, your guest. You do not know, you cannot determine scientifically, that I will not steal your money or your spoons. But inferentially I will not, and inferentially you have me as a guest.[2]

Let us now turn from the others to the point of view of the individual who presents himself before them. He may wish them to think highly of him, or to think that he thinks highly of them, or to perceive how in fact he feels toward them, or to obtain no clear-cut impression; he may wish to ensure sufficient harmony so that the interaction can be sustained, or to defraud, get rid of, confuse, mislead, antagonize, or insult them. Regardless of the particular objective which the individual has in mind and of his motive for having this objective, it will be in his interests to control the conduct of the others, especially their responsive treatment of him.[3] This control is achieved largely by influencing the definition of the situation which the others come to formu-late, and he can influence this definition by expressing himself in such a way as to give them the kind of impression that will lead them to act voluntarily in accordance with his own plan. Thus, when an individual appears in the presence of others, there will usually be some reason for him to mobilize his activity so that it will convey an impression to others which it is in his interests to convey. Since a girl's dormitory mates will glean evidence of her popularity from the calls she receives on the phone, we can suspect that some girls will arrange for calls to be made, and Willard Waller's finding can be anticipated:

> It has been reported by many observers that a girl who is called to the telephone in the dormitories will often allow herself to be called several times, in order to give all the other girls ample opportunity to hear her paged.[4]

Of the two kinds of communication – expressions given and expressions given off – this report will be primarily concerned with the latter, with the more theatrical and contextual kind, the non-verbal, presumably unintentional kind, whether this communication be purposely engineered or not.

[. . .]

When we allow that the individual projects a definition of the situation when he appears before others, we must also see that the others, however passive their role may seem to be, will themselves effectively project a definition of the situation by virtue of their response to the individual and by virtue of any lines of action they initi-ate to him. Ordinarily the definitions of the situation projected by the several differ-ent participants are sufficiently attuned to one another so that open contradiction will not occur. I do not mean that there will be the kind of consensus that arises when each individual present candidly expresses what he really feels and honestly agrees with the expressed feelings of the others present. This kind of harmony is an optimis-tic ideal and in any case not necessary for the smooth working of society. Rather, each participant is expected to suppress his immediate heartfelt feelings, conveying a view of the situation which he feels the others will be able to find at least temporarily acceptable. The maintenance of this surface of agreement, this veneer of consensus, is facilitated by each participant concealing his own wants behind statements which assert values to which everyone present feels obliged to give lip service. Further, there is usually a kind of division of definitional labor. Each participant is allowed to estab-lish the tentative official ruling regarding matters which are vital to him but not immediately important to others, e.g., the rationalizations and justifications by which he accounts for his past activity. In exchange for this courtesy he remains silent or non-committal on matters important to others but not immediately important to him. We have then a kind of interactional *modus vivendi*. Together the participants contribute to a single over-all definition of the situation which involves not so much a real agreement as to what exists but rather a real agreement as to whose claims concerning what issues will be temporarily honored. Real agreement will also exist concerning the desirability of avoiding an open conflict of definitions of the situation.[5] I will refer to this level of agreement as a "working consensus." It is to be understood that the working consensus established in one interaction setting will be quite different in content from the working consensus established in a different type of setting. Thus, between two friends at lunch, a reciprocal show of affection, respect, and concern for the other is maintained. In service occupations, on the other hand, the specialist often maintains an image of disinterested involvement in the problem of the client, while the client responds with a show of respect for the competence and integrity of the specialist. Regardless of such differences in content, however, the general form of these working arrangements is the same.

In noting the tendency for a participant to accept the definitional claims made by the others present, we can appreciate the crucial importance of the information that the individual *initially* possesses or acquires concerning his fellow participants, for it is on the basis of this initial information that the individual starts to define the situation and starts to build up lines of responsive action. The individual's initial projection commits him to what he is proposing to be and requires him to drop all pretenses of being other things. As the interaction among the participants progresses, additions and modifications in this initial informational state will of course occur, but it is essential that these later developments be related without contradiction to, and even built up from, the initial positions taken by the several participants. It would seem that an individual can more easily make a choice as to what line of treatment to demand from and extend to the others present at the beginning of an encounter than he can alter the line of treatment that is being pursued once the interaction is underway.

In everyday life, of course, there is a clear understanding that first impressions are important. Thus, the work adjustment of those in service occupations will often hinge upon a capacity to seize and hold the initiative in the service relation, a capacity that will require subtle aggressiveness on the part of the server when he is of lower socio-economic status than his client.

[...]

To summarize, then, I assume that when an individual appears before others he will have many motives for trying to control the impression they receive of the situation. This report is concerned with some of the common techniques that persons employ to sustain such impressions and with some of the common contingencies associated with the employment of these techniques. The specific content of any activity presented by the individual participant, or the role it plays in the interdependent activities of an on-going social system, will not be at issue; I shall be concerned only with the participant's dramaturgical problems of presenting the activity before others. The issues dealt with by stagecraft and stage management are sometimes trivial but they are quite general; they seem to occur everywhere in social life, providing a clear-cut dimension for formal sociological analysis.

It will be convenient to end this introduction with some definitions that are implied in what has gone before and required for what is to follow. For the purpose of this report, interaction (that is, face-to-face interaction) may be roughly defined as the reciprocal influence of individuals upon one another's actions when in one another's immediate physical presence. An interaction may be defined as all the interaction which occurs throughout any one occasion when a given set of individuals are in one another's continuous presence; the term "an encounter" would do as well. A "performance" may be defined as all the activity of a given participant on a given occasion which serves to influence in any way any of the other participants. Taking a particular participant and his performance as a basic point of reference, we may refer to those who contribute the other performances as the audience, observers, or co-participants. The pre-established pattern of action which is unfolded during a performance and which may be presented or played through on other occasions may be called a "part" or "routine."[6] These situational terms can easily be related to conventional structural ones. When an individual or performer plays the same part to the same audience on different occasions, a social relationship is likely to arise. Defining social role as the enactment of rights and duties attached to a given status, we can say that a social role will involve one or more parts and that each of these different parts may be presented by the performer on a series of occasions to the same kinds of audience or to an audience of the same persons.

NOTES

1 Gustav Ichheiser, "Misunderstandings in Human Relations," Supplement to *The American Journal of Sociology*, LV (September, 1949), pp. 6–7.

2 Quoted in E.H. Volkart, editor, *Social Behavior and Personality*, Contributions of W.I. Thomas to Theory and Social Research (New York: Social Science Research Council, 1951), p. 5.

3 Here I owe much to an unpublished paper by Tom Burns of the University of Edinburgh. He presents the argument that in all interaction a basic underlying theme is the desire of each participant to guide and control the responses made by the others present. A similar argument has been advanced by Jay Haley in a recent unpublished paper, but in regard to a special kind of control, that having to do with defining the nature of the relationship of those involved in the interaction.

4 Willard Waller, "The Rating and Dating Complex," *American Sociological Review*, II, p. 730.

5 An interaction can be purposely set up as a time and place for voicing differences in opinion, but in such cases participants must be careful to agree not to disagree on the proper tone of voice, vocabulary, and degree of seriousness in which all arguments are to be phrased, and upon the mutual respect which disagreeing participants must carefully continue to express toward one another. This debaters' or academic definition of the situation may also be invoked suddenly and judiciously as a way of translating a serious conflict of views into one that can be handled within a framework acceptable to all present.

6 For comments on the importance of distinguishing between a routine of interaction and any particular instance when this routine is played through, see John von Neumann and Oskar Morgenstern, *The Theory of Games and Economic Behaviour*, 2nd ed. Princeton: Princeton University Press, 1947, p. 49.

CHAPTER EIGHT

PHENOMENOLOGY

CHAPTER MENU

Social reality is something that sociologists, by definition, problematize. Most nota-bly, Karl Marx challenges us to rethink and to reassess with a skeptical or critical eye all that we take for granted about life in capitalist consumer society and how capital-ism works. Though much more influenced by Durkheim and Weber than by Marx, **Peter L. Berger** (1919–2017) and **Thomas Luckmann** (1927–2016) problematize what counts as reality and who defines it and, by extension, what and whose knowl-edge is relevant and matters to the crafting of society (see excerpt *8a The Social Construction of Reality*). Their work points to the mutual interdependence of micro intra-subjective and inter-subjective (or interpersonal) experiences and lived practi-cal knowledge with macro institutional and broader societal processes. In particular, they draw attention to how ordinary everyday reality and its associated everyday common sense knowledge is produced, maintained, and, or, reworked to construct and reflect new objective institutional realities. Central to Berger and Luckmann's focus is the significance of the individual's *experience* of their very particular, highly localized everyday reality. The elevation of subjective experience and subjective knowledge as core components of societal life – and of theorizing and inquiry – is

Concise Reader in Sociological Theory: Theorists, Concepts, and Current Applications,
First Edition. Edited by Michele Dillon. Editorial material and organization
© 2021 John Wiley & Sons Ltd. Published 2021 by John Wiley & Sons Ltd.

referred to as phenomenology. With a long tradition in German philosophy, especially the ideas of Edmund Husserl (1859–1938) and the writings of Alfred Schutz (1899–1959), phenomenology takes as its starting point the assumption that individuals have an intentional consciousness of the world of everyday life and of the immediate, particular things (phenomena) in their lifeworld. The lifeworld refers to the respective individuals' salient everyday experiences; it is not a generalized consciousness of an abstract world at large but a highly specific here-and-now consciousness of a highly immediate and highly relevant here-and-now set of practical tasks and people and activities (cf. Schutz 1970).

Berger and Luckmann elaborated on, extended, and popularized the insights of Schutz. Although the title of their book *The Social Construction of Reality* (see excerpt *8a*) might convey that reality, because it is socially constructed, is arbitrary and fluid and essentially anything we want it to be, such an inference is, in fact, the opposite of what Berger and Luckmann's theory articulates. Rather, in focusing on the sociology of everyday life or of everyday knowledge, they draw on and simultaneously integrate both Max Weber's dictum that sociologists should apprehend the subjective meanings motivating all social action, and Emile Durkheim's dictum that sociologists must consider social facts as things (Berger and Luckmann 1966: 18). Using empirical examples of ordinary practical tasks and everyday routines, Berger and Luckmann show how subjective experiences and meanings are informed and constrained by the objective facts – the macro and micro structural realities (social institutions, language) – of a particular socio-historical context and how, at the same time, individuals' subjective experiences in and of the objectively imposing reality may lead them to push back against that reality and create new ways of thinking about and dealing with the gaps or inconsistencies between their subjective knowledge of a specific personally experienced reality and the institutional definition of what comprises that reality.

Importantly, as Berger and Luckmann also emphasize (see excerpt *8a*), the subjective experience of reality is not personally idiosyncratic. Rather, as emphasized by G.H. Mead (1934), the self is a thoroughly social self and, therefore, even what might appear as a personally unique thought or experience is informed by the world of everyday life of that individual, a world that necessarily includes other relevant people and their shared apprehension of its relevant institutional realities, language, norms, etc. Thus, objective reality and the subjective experience of it are necessarily inter-subjective realities and experiences; common sense is not just my common sense, but the common sense that makes practical sense to me and others in my immediate reality given our subjective (and inter-subjective) experiences. The dialectic between objective and subjective realities produces a dynamic social order that despite objective forces of resistance, facilitates the emergence of new ways of doing things (new habits) and naming things and thus a new objective reality that in turn legitimates a new common sense and associated practices. In short, society (social institutions, laws, common sense) is made the objective reality that it is and that we know it to be by the inter-subjective and collectively shared experiences, meanings and practices of individuals in particular lived contexts. The recent transformation in the cultural and legal status of same-sex marriage offers a helpful illumination of the dynamic dialectical relation between objective and subjective realities. The objective legal and other institutional constructions (e.g. in religious and media discourse) of gay sexuality as deviant objectively stigmatized gays and lesbians. Yet their subjective experiences of their sexuality gave them personally a different – and once shared with others (e.g. through lesbian, gay, bisexual [LGB+] support groups) – an intersubjective understanding that being gay was not abnormal (but the experience of many others like them). This opened up for them a collectively shared universe of experience and meaning that empowered them to advocate for sexual equality, and which once eventually won (e.g. legal same-sex marriage – objectively affirmed for both LGB and all others the objective reality of the normalcy of gay sexuality/gay marriage/gay families.

REFERENCES

Berger, Peter and Thomas Luckmann. 1966. *The Social Construction of Reality*. Garden City, NY: Doubleday.

Mead, G.H. 1934. *Mind, Self & Society*. Ed. and with an introduction by Charles W. Morris. Chicago: University of Chicago Press.

Schutz, Alfred. 1970. *On Phenomenology and Social Relations: Selected Writings*. Ed. and with an introduction by Helmut Wagner. Chicago: University of Chicago Press.

8A Peter L. Berger and Thomas Luckmann from *The Social Construction of Reality: A Treatise in the Sociology of Knowledge*

Original publication details: Peter L. Berger and Thomas Luckmann, 1966. *The Social Construction of Reality*, pp. 19–25, 52–62, 81–82, 85–88. Garden City, NY: Doubleday. © 1966 by Peter L. Berger and Thomas Luckmann. Reproduced with permission of Doubleday, an imprint of the Knopf Doubleday Publishing Group, a division of Penguin Random House LLC. All rights reserved.

The Reality of Everyday Life

Everyday life presents itself as a reality interpreted by men and subjectively meaningful to them as a coherent world. As sociologists we take this reality as the object of our analyses. Within the frame of reference of sociology as an empirical science it is possible to take this reality as given, to take as data particular phenomena arising within it, without further inquiring about the foundations of this reality, which is a philosophical task. However, given the particular purpose of the present treatise, we cannot completely bypass the philosophical problem. The world of everyday life is not only taken for granted as reality by the ordinary members of society in the subjectively meaningful conduct of their lives. It is a world that originates in their thoughts and actions, and is maintained as real by these. Before turning to our main task we must, therefore, attempt to clarify the foundations of knowledge in everyday life, to wit, the objectivations of subjective processes (and meanings) by which the *inter*subjective commonsense world is constructed.

For the purpose at hand, this is a preliminary task, and we can do no more than sketch the main features of what we believe to be an adequate solution to the philosophical problem – adequate, let us hasten to add, only in the sense that it can serve as a starting point for sociological analysis. The considerations immediately following are, therefore, of the nature of philosophical prolegomena and, in themselves, pre-sociological. The method we consider best suited to clarify the foundations of knowledge in everyday life is that of phenomenological analysis, a purely descriptive method and, as such, "empirical" but not "scientific" – as we understand the nature of the empirical sciences.[1]

The phenomenological analysis of everyday life, or rather of the subjective experience of everyday life, refrains from any causal or genetic hypotheses, as well as from assertions about the ontological status of the phenomena analyzed. It is important to remember this. Commonsense contains innumerable pre and quasi-scientific interpretations about everyday reality, which it takes for granted. If we are to describe the reality of commonsense we must refer to these interpretations, just as we must take account of its taken-for-granted character –but we do so within phenomenological brackets.

Consciousness is always intentional; it always intends or is directed toward objects. We can never apprehend some putative substratum of consciousness as such, only consciousness of something or other. This is so regardless of whether the object of consciousness is experienced as belonging to an external physical world or apprehended as an element of an inward subjective reality. Whether I (the first person singular, here as in the following illustrations, standing for ordinary self-consciousness in everyday life) am viewing the panorama of New York City or whether I become conscious of an inner anxiety, the processes of consciousness involved are intentional in both instances. The point need not be belabored that the consciousness of the Empire State Building differs from the awareness of anxiety. A detailed phenomenological analysis would uncover the various layers of experience, and the different structures of meaning involved in, say, being bitten by a dog, remembering having been bitten by a dog, having a phobia about all dogs, and so forth. What interests us here is the common intentional character of all consciousness.

Different objects present themselves to consciousness as constituents of different spheres of reality. I recognize the fellowmen I must deal with in the course of everyday life as pertaining to a reality quite different from the disembodied figures that appear in my dreams. The two sets of objects introduce quite different tensions into my consciousness and I am attentive to them in quite different ways. My consciousness, then, is capable of moving through different spheres of reality. Put differently, I am conscious of the world as consisting of multiple realities. As I move from one reality to another, I experience the transition as a kind of shock. This shock is to be understood as caused by the shift in attentiveness that the transition entails. Waking up from a dream illustrates this shift most simply.

Among the multiple realities there is one that presents itself as the reality par excellence. This is the reality of everyday life. Its privileged position entitles it to the designation of paramount reality. The tension of consciousness is highest in everyday life, that is, the latter imposes itself upon consciousness in the most massive, urgent and intense manner. It is impossible to ignore, difficult even to weaken in its imperative presence. Consequently, it forces me to be attentive to it in the fullest way. I experience everyday life in the state of being wide-awake. This wide-awake state of existing in and apprehending the reality of everyday life is taken by me to be normal and self-evident, that is, it constitutes my natural attitude.

I apprehend the reality of everyday life as an ordered reality. Its phenomena are prearranged in patterns that seem to be independent of my apprehension of them and that impose themselves upon the latter. The reality of everyday life appears already objectified, that is, constituted by an order of objects that have been designated *as* objects before my appearance on the scene. The language used in everyday life continuously provides me with the necessary objectifications and posits the order within which these make sense and within which everyday life has meaning for me. I live in a place that is geographically designated; I employ tools, from can openers to sports cars, which are designated in the technical vocabulary of my society; I live within a web of human relationships, from my chess club to the United States of America, which are also ordered by means of vocabulary. In this manner language marks the co-ordinates of my life in society and fills that life with meaningful objects.

The reality of everyday life is organized around the "here" of my body and the "now" of my present. This "here and now" is the focus of my attention to the reality of everyday life. What is "here and now" presented to me in everyday life is the *realissimum* of my consciousness. The reality of everyday life is not, however, exhausted by these immediate presences, but embraces phenomena that are not present "here and now." This means that I experience everyday life in terms of differing degrees of closeness and remoteness, both spatially and temporally. Closest to me is the zone of everyday life that is directly accessible to my bodily manipulation. This zone contains the world within my reach, the world in which I act so as to modify its reality, or the world in which I work. In this world of working my consciousness is dominated by the pragmatic motive, that is, my attention to this world is mainly determined by what I am doing, have done or plan to do in it In this way it is my world par excellence. I know, of course, that the reality of everyday life contains zones that are not accessible to me in this manner. But either I have no pragmatic interest in these zones or my interest in them is indirect insofar as they may be, potentially, manipulative zones for me. Typically, my interest in the far zones is less intense and certainly less urgent. I am intensely interested in the cluster of objects involved in my daily occupation – say, the world of the garage, if I am a mechanic. I am interested, though less directly, in what goes on in the testing laboratories of the automobile industry in Detroit – I am unlikely ever to be in one of these laboratories, but the work done there will eventually affect my everyday life. I may also be interested in what goes on at Cape Kennedy or in outer space, but this interest is a matter of private, "leisure-time" choice rather than an urgent necessity of my everyday life.

The reality of everyday life further presents itself to me as an intersubjective world, a world that I share with others. This intersubjectivity sharply differentiates everyday life from other realities of which I am conscious. I am alone in the world of my dreams, but I know that the world of everyday life is as real to others as it is to myself. Indeed, I cannot exist in everyday life without continually interacting and communicating with others. I know that my natural attitude to this world corresponds to the natural attitude of others, that they also comprehend the objectifications by which this world is ordered, that they also organize this world around the "here and now" of *their* being in it and have projects for working in it. I also know, of course, that the others have a perspective on this common world that is not identical with mine. My "here" is their "there." My "now" does not fully overlap with theirs. My projects differ from and may even conflict with theirs. All the same, I know that I live with them in a common world. Most importantly, I know that there is an ongoing correspondence between *my* meanings and *their* meanings in this world, that we share a common sense about its reality. The natural attitude is the attitude of commonsense consciousness precisely because it refers to a world that is common to many men. Commonsense knowledge is the knowledge I share with others in the normal, self-evident routines of everyday life.

The reality of everyday life is taken for granted as reality. It does not require additional verification over and beyond its simple presence. It is simply *there*, as self-evident and compelling facticity. I *know* that it is real. While I am capable of engaging in doubt about its reality, I am obliged to suspend such doubt as I routinely exist in everyday life. This suspension of doubt is so firm that to abandon it, as I might want to do, say, in theoretical or religious contemplation, I have to make an extreme transition. The world of everyday life proclaims itself and, when I want to challenge the proclamation, I mast engage in a deliberate, by no means easy effort. The transition from the natural attitude to the theoretical attitude of the philosopher or scientist illustrates this point. But not all aspects of this reality are equally unproblematic. Everyday life is divided into sectors that are apprehended routinely, and others that present me with problems of one kind or another. Suppose that 1 am an automobile mechanic who is highly knowledgeable about all American-made cars. Everything that pertains to the latter is a routine, unproblematic facet of my everyday life. But one day someone appears in the garage and asks me to repair his Volkswagen. I am now compelled to enter the problematic world of foreign-made cars. I may do so reluctantly or with professional curiosity, but in either case I am now faced with problems that I have not yet routinized. At the same time, of course, I do not leave the reality of everyday life. Indeed, the latter becomes enriched as I begin to incorporate into it the knowledge and skills required for the repair of foreign-made cars. The reality of everyday life encompasses both kinds of sectors, as long as what appears as a problem does not pertain to a different reality altogether (say, the reality of theoretical physics, or of nightmares). As long as the routines of everyday life continue without interruption they are apprehended as unproblematic.

But even the unproblematic sector of everyday reality is so only until further notice, that is, until its continuity is interrupted by the appearance of a problem. When this happens, the reality of everyday life seeks to integrate the problematic sector into what is already unproblematic. Commonsense knowledge contains a variety of instructions as to how this is to be done. For instance, the others with whom I work are unproblematic to me as long as they perform their familiar, taken -for-granted routines – say, typing away at desks next to mine in my office. They become problematic if they interrupt these routines – say, huddling together in a comer and talking in whispers. As I inquire about the meaning of this unusual activity, there is a variety of possibilities that my common-sense knowledge is capable of reintegrating into the unproblematic routines of everyday life: they may be consulting on how to fix a broken typewriter, or one of them may have some urgent instructions from the boss, and so on. On the other hand, I may find that they are discussing a union directive to go on strike, something as yet outside my experience but still well within the range of problems with which my commonsense knowledge can deal. It will deal with it, though, *as* a problem, rather than simply reintegrating it into the unproblematic sector of everyday life. If, however, I come to the conclusion that my colleagues have gone collectively mad, the problem that presents itself is of yet another kind. I am now faced with a problem that transcends the boundaries of the reality of everyday life and points to an altogether different reality. Indeed, my conclusion that my colleagues have gone mad implies *ipso facto* that they have gone off into a world that is no longer the common world of everyday life.

Compared to the reality of everyday life, other realities appear as finite provinces of meaning, enclaves within the paramount reality marked by circumscribed meanings and modes of experience. The paramount reality envelops them on all sides, as it were, and consciousness always returns to the paramount reality as from an excursion.

[...]

One may ask in what manner social order itself arises.

The most general answer to this question is that social order is a human product, or, more precisely, an ongoing human production. It is produced by man in the course of his ongoing externalization. Social order is not biologically given or derived from any biological *data* in its empirical manifestations. Social order, needless to add, is also not given in man's natural environment, though particular features of this may be factors in determining certain features of a social order (for example, its economic or technological arrangements). Social order is not part of the "nature of things," and it cannot be derived from the "laws of nature."[2] Social order exists *only* as a product of human activity.

[...]

Origins of Institutionalization

All human activity is subject to habitualization. Any action that is repeated frequently becomes cast into a pattern, which can then be reproduced with an economy of effort and which, *ipso facto*, is apprehended by its performer *as* that pattern. Habitualization further implies that the action in question may be performed again in the future in the same manner and with the same economical effort. This is true of non-social as well as of social activity. Even the solitary individual on the proverbial desert island habitualizes his activity. When he wakes up in the morning and resumes his attempts to construct a canoe out of matchsticks, he may mumble to himself, "There I go again," as he starts on step one of an operating procedure consisting of, say, ten steps. In other words, even solitary man has at least the company of his operating procedures.

Habitualized actions, of course, retain their meaningful character for the individual although the meanings involved become embedded as routines in his general stock of knowledge, taken for granted by him and at hand for his projects into the future.[3] Habitualization carries with it the important psychological gain that choices are narrowed. While in theory there may be a hundred ways to go about the project of building a canoe out of matchsticks, habitualization narrows these down to one. This frees the individual from the burden of "all those decisions," providing a psychological relief that has its basis in man's undirected instinctual structure. Habitualization provides the direction and the specialization of activity that is lacking in man's biological equipment, thus relieving the accumulation of tensions that result from undirected drives.[4] And by providing a stable background in which human activity may proceed with a minimum of decision-making most of the time, it frees energy for such decisions as may be necessary on certain occasions. In other words, the background of habitualized activity opens up a foreground for deliberation and innovation.[5]

In terms of the meanings bestowed by man upon his activity, habitualization makes it unnecessary for each situation to be defined anew, step by step.[6] A large variety of situations may be subsumed under its predefinitions. The activity to be undertaken in these situations can then be anticipated. Even alternatives of conduct can be assigned standard weights.

These processes of habitualization precede any institutionalization, indeed can be made to apply to a hypothetical solitary individual detached from any social interaction. The fact that even such a solitary individual, assuming that he has been formed as a self (as we would have to assume in the case of our matchstick-canoe builder), will habitualize his activity in accordance with biographical experience of a world of social institutions preceding his solitude need not concern us at the moment. Empirically, the more important part of the habitualization of human activity is coextensive with the latter's institutionalization. The question then becomes how do institutions arise.

Institutionalization occurs whenever there is a reciprocal typification of habitualized actions by types of actors. Put differently, any such typification is an institution.[7] What must be stressed is the reciprocity of institutional typifications and the typicality of not only the actions but also the actors in institutions. The typifications of habitualized actions that constitute institutions are always shared ones. They are *available* to all the members of the particular social group in question, and the institution itself typifies individual actors as well as individual actions. The institution posits that actions of type X will be performed by actors of type X. For example, the institution of the law posits that heads shall be chopped off in specific ways under specific circumstances, and that specific types of individuals shall do the chopping (executioners, say, or members of an impure caste, or virgins under a certain age, or those who have been designated by an oracle).

Institutions further imply historicity and control. Reciprocal typifications of actions are built up in the course of a shared history. They cannot be created instantaneously. Institutions always have a history, of which they are the products. It is impossible to understand an institution adequately without an understanding of the historical process in which it was produced. Institutions also, by the very fact of their existence, control human conduct by setting up predefined patterns of conduct, which channel it in one direction as against the many other directions that would theoretically be possible. It is important to stress that this controlling character is inherent in institutionalization as such, prior to or apart from any mechanisms of sanctions specifically set up to support an institution. These mechanisms (the sum of which constitute what is generally called a system of social control) do, of course, exist in many institutions and in all the agglomerations of institutions that we call societies. Their controlling efficacy, however, is of a secondary or supplementary kind. As we shall see again later, the primary social control is given in the existence of an institution as such. To say that a segment of human activity has been institutionalized is already to say that this segment of human activity has been subsumed under social control. Additional control mechanisms are required only insofar as the processes of institutionalization are less than completely successful. Thus, for instance, the law may provide that anyone who breaks the incest taboo will have his head chopped off. This provision may be necessary because there have been cases when individuals offended against the taboo. It is unlikely that this sanction will have to be invoked continuously (unless the institution delineated by the incest taboo is itself in the course of disintegration, a special case that we need not elaborate here). It makes little sense, therefore, to say that human sexuality is socially controlled by beheading certain individuals. Rather, human sexuality is socially controlled by its institutionalization in the course of the particular history in question. One may add, of course, that the incest taboo itself is nothing but the negative side of an assemblage of typifications, which define in the first place which sexual conduct is incestuous and which is not.

In actual experience institutions generally manifest themselves in collectivities containing considerable numbers of people. It is theoretically important, however, to emphasize that the institutionalizing process of reciprocal typification would occur even if two individuals began to interact *de novo*. Institutionalization is incipient in every social situation continuing in time. Let us assume that two persons from entirely different social worlds begin to interact. By saying "persons" we presuppose that the two individuals have formed selves, something that could, of course, have occurred only in a social process. We are thus for the moment excluding the cases of Adam and Eve, or of two "feral" children meeting in a clearing of a primeval jungle. But we are assuming that the two individuals arrive at their meeting place from social worlds that have been historically produced in segregation from each other, and that the interaction therefore takes place in a situation that has not been institutionally defined for either of the participants. It may be possible to imagine a Man Friday joining our matchstick-canoe builder on his desert island, and to imagine the former as a Papuan and the latter as an American. In that case, however, it is likely that the American will have read or at least have heard about the story of Robinson Crusoe, which will introduce a measure of predefinition of the situation at least for him. Let us, then, simply call our two persons *A* and *B*.

As *A* and *B* interact, in whatever manner, typifications will be produced quite quickly. *A* watches *B* perform. He attributes motives to *B*'s actions and, seeing the actions recur, typifies the motives as recurrent. As B goes on performing, A is soon able to say to himself, "Aha, there he goes again." At the same time, A may assume that B is doing the same thing with regard to him. From the beginning, both A and B assume this reciprocity of typification. In the course of their interaction these typifications will be expressed in specific patterns of conduct. That is, A and B will begin to play roles *vis-à-vis* each other. This will occur even if each continues to perform actions different from those of the other. The possibility of taking the role of the other will appear with regard to the same actions performed by both. That is, A will inwardly appropriate B's reiterated roles and make them the models for his own role-playing. For example, B's role in the activity of preparing food is not only typified as such by A, but enters as a constitutive element into A's own food-preparation role. Thus a collection of reciprocally typified actions will emerge, habitualized for each in roles, some of which will be performed separately and some in common.[8] While this reciprocal typification is not yet institutionalization (since, there only being two individuals, there is no possibility of a typology of actors), it is clear that institutionalization is already present *in nucleo*.

At this stage one may ask what gains accrue to the two individuals from this development. The most important gain is that each will be able to predict the other's actions. Concomitantly, the interaction of both becomes predictable. The "There he goes again" becomes a "There *we* go again." This relieves both individuals of a considerable amount of tension. They save time and effort, not only in whatever external tasks they might be engaged in separately or jointly, but in terms of their respective psychological economies. Their life together is now defined by a widening sphere of taken-for-granted routines. Many actions are possible on a low level of attention. Each action of one is no longer a source of astonishment and potential danger to the other. Instead, much of what goes on takes on the triviality of what, to both, will be everyday life. This means that the two individuals are constructing a background, in the sense discussed before, which will serve to stabilize both their separate actions and their interaction. The construction of this background of routine in turn makes possible a division of labor between them, opening the way for innovations, which demand a higher level of attention. The division of labor and the innovations will lead to new habitualizations, further widening the background common to both individuals. In other words, a social world will be in process of construction, containing within it the roots of an expanding institutional order.

Generally, all actions repeated once or more tend to be habitualized to some degree, just as all actions observed by another necessarily involve some typification on his part. However, for the kind of reciprocal typification just described to occur there must be a continuing social situation in which the habitualized actions of two or more individuals interlock. Which actions are likely to be reciprocally typified in this manner?

The general answer is, those actions that are relevant to both A and B within their common situation. The areas likely to be relevant in this way will, of course, vary in different situations. Some will be those facing A and B in terms of their previous biographies, others may be the result of the natural, presocial circumstances of the situation. What will in all cases have to be habitualized is the communication process between *A* and *B*. Labor, sexuality and territoriality are other likely foci of typification and habitualization. In these various areas the situation of *A* and *B* is paradigmatic of the institutionalization occurring in larger societies.

Let us push our paradigm one step further and imagine that *A* and *B* have children. At this point the situation changes qualitatively. The appearance of a third party changes the character of the ongoing social interaction between *A* and *B*, and it will change even further as additional individuals continue to be added.[9] The institutional world, which existed *in statu nascendi* in the original situation of *A* and *B*, is now passed on to others. In this process institutionalization perfects itself. The habitualizations and typifications undertaken in the common life of *A* and *B*, formations that until this point still had the quality of *ad hoc* conceptions of two individuals, now become historical institutions. With the acquisition of historicity, these formations also acquire another crucial quality, or, more accurately, perfect a quality that was incipient as soon as *A* and *B* began the reciprocal typification of their conduct: this quality is objectivity. This means that the institutions that have now been crystallized (for instance, the institution of paternity as it is encountered by the children) are experienced as existing over and beyond the individuals who "happen to" embody them at the moment. In other words, the institutions are now experienced as possessing a reality of their own, a reality that confronts the individual as an external and coercive fact.[10]

As long as the nascent institutions are constructed and maintained only in the interaction of *A* and *B*, their objectivity remains tenuous, easily changeable, almost playful, even while they attain a measure of objectivity by the mere fact of their formation. To put this a little differently, the routinized background of *A*'s and *B*'s activity remains fairly accessible to deliberate intervention by *A* and *B*. Although the routines, once established, carry within them a tendency to persist, the possibility of changing them or even abolishing them remains at hand in consciousness. *A* and *B* alone are responsible for having constructed this world. *A* and *B* remain capable of changing or abolishing it. What is more, since they themselves have shaped this world in the course of a shared biography which they can remember, the world thus shaped appears fully transparent to them. They understand the world that they themselves have made. All this changes in the process of transmission to the new generation. The objectivity of the institutional world "thickens" and "hardens," not only for the children, but (by a mirror effect) for the parents as well. The "There we go again" now becomes "This is how these things are done." A world so regarded attains a firmness in consciousness; it becomes real in an ever more massive way and it can no longer be changed so readily. For the children, especially in the early phase of their socialization into it, it becomes *the* world. For the parents, it loses its playful quality and becomes "serious." For the children, the parentally transmitted world is not fully transparent. Since they had no part in shaping it, it confronts them as a given reality that, like nature, is opaque in places at least.

Only at this point does it become possible to speak of a social world at all, in the sense of a comprehensive and given reality confronting the individual in a manner analogous to the reality of the natural world. Only in this way, *as* an objective world, can the social formations be transmitted to a new generation. In the early phases of socialization the child is quite incapable of distinguishing between the objectivity of natural phenomena and the objectivity of the social formations.[11] To take the most important item of socialization, language appears to the child as inherent in the nature of things, and he cannot grasp the notion of its conventionality. A thing *is* what it is called, and it could not be called anything else. All institutions appear in the same way, as given, unalterable and self-evident. Even in our empirically unlikely example of parents having constructed an institutional world *de novo*, the objectivity of this world would be increased for them by the socialization of their children, because the objectivity experienced by the children would reflect back upon their own experience of this world. Empirically, of course, the institutional world transmitted by most parents already has the character of historical and objective reality. The process of transmission simply strengthens the parents' sense of reality, if only because, to put it crudely, if one says, "This is how these things are done," often enough one believes it oneself.[12]

An institutional world, then, is experienced as an objective reality. It has a history that antedates the individual's birth and is not accessible to his biographical recollection. It was there before he was born, and it will be there after his death. This history itself, as the tradition of the existing institutions, has the character of objectivity. The individual's biography is apprehended as an episode located within the objective history of the society. The institutions, as historical and objective facticities, confront the individual as undeniable facts. The institutions are *there*, external to him, persistent in their reality, whether he likes it or not. He cannot wish them away. They resist his attempts to change or evade them. They have coercive power over him, both in themselves, by the sheer force of their facticity, and through the control mechanisms that are usually attached to the most important of them. The objective reality of institutions is not diminished if the individual does not understand their purpose or their mode of operation. He may experience large sectors of the social world as incomprehensible, perhaps oppressive in their opaqueness, but real nonetheless. Since institutions exist as external reality, the individual cannot understand them by introspection. He must "go out" and learn about them, just as he must to learn about nature. This remains true even though the social world, as a humanly produced reality, is potentially understandable in a way not possible in the case of the natural world.[13]

It is important to keep in mind that the objectivity of the institutional world, however massive it may appear to the individual, is a humanly produced, constructed objectivity. The process by which the externalized products of human activity attain the character of objectivity is objectivation.[14] The institutional world is objectivated human activity, and so is every single institution. In other words, despite the objectivity that marks the social world in human experience, it does not thereby acquire an ontological status apart from the human activity that produced it. The paradox that man is capable of producing a world that he then experiences as something other than a human product will concern us later on. At the moment, it is important to emphasize that the relationship between man, the producer, and the social world, his product, is and remains a dialectical one. That is, man (not, of course, in isolation but in his collectivities) and his social world interact with each other. The product acts back upon the producer. Externalization and objectivation are moments in a continuing dialectical process. The third moment in this process, which is internalization (by which the objectivated social world is retrojected into consciousness in the course of socialization), will occupy us in considerable detail later on. It is already possible, however, to see the fundamental relationship of these three dialectical moments in social reality. Each of them corresponds to an essential characterization of the social world. *Society is a human product. Society is an objective reality. Man is a social product*. It may also already be evident than an analysis of the social world that leaves out any one of these three moments will be distortive.[15] One may further add that only with the transmission of the social world to a new generation (that is, internalization as effectuated in socialization) does the fundamental social dialectic appear in its totality. To repeat, only with the appearance of a new generation can one properly speak of a social world.

At the same point, the institutional world requires legitimation, that is, ways by which it can be "explained" and justified. This is not because it appears less real. As we have seen, the reality of the social world gains in massivity in the course of its transmission. This reality, however, is a historical one, which comes to the new generation as a tradition rather than as a biographical memory. In our paradigmatic example, A and B, the original creators of the social world, can always reconstruct the circumstances under which their world and any part of it was established. That is, they can arrive at the meaning of an institution by exercising their powers of recollection. A's and B's children are in an altogether different situation. Their knowledge of the institutional history is by way of "hearsay." The original meaning of the institutions is inaccessible to them in terms of memory. It, therefore, becomes necessary to interpret this meaning to them in various legitimating formulas. These will have to be consistent and comprehensive in terms of the institutional order, if they are to carry conviction to the new generation. The same story, so to speak, must be told to all the children. It follows that the expanding institutional order develops a corresponding canopy of legitimations, stretching over it a protective cover of both cognitive and normative interpretation. These legitimations are learned by the new generation during the same process that socializes them into the institutional order. This, again, will occupy us in greater detail further on.

The development of specific mechanisms of social controls also becomes necessary with the historicization and objectivation of institutions. Deviance from the institutionally "programmed" courses of action becomes likely once the institutions have become realities divorced from their original relevance in the concrete social processes from which they arose. To put this more simply, it is more likely that one will deviate from programs set up for one by others than from programs that one has helped establish oneself. The new generation posits a problem of compliance, and its socialization into the institutional order requires the establishment of sanctions. The institutions must and do claim authority over the individual, independently of the subjective meanings he may attach to any particular situation. The priority of the institutional definitions of situations must be consistently maintained over individual temptations at redefinition. The children must be "taught to behave" and, once taught, must be "kept in line." So, of course, must the adults. The more conduct is institutionalized, the more predictable and thus the more controlled it becomes. If socialization into the institutions has been effective, outright coercive measures can be applied economically and selectively. Most of the time, conduct will occur "spontaneously" within the institutionally set channels. The more, on the level of meaning, conduct is taken for granted, the more possible alternatives to the institutional "programs" will recede, and the more predictable and controlled conduct will be.

[. . .]

Institutionalization is not, however, an irreversible process, despite the fact that institutions, once formed, have a tendency to persist.[16] For a variety of historical reasons, the scope of institutionalized actions may diminish; deinstitutionalization may take place in certain areas of social life.[17] For example, the private sphere that has emerged in modern industrial society is considerably deinstitutionalized as compared to the public sphere.[18]

A further question, with respect to which institutional orders will vary historically, is: What is the relationship of the various institutions to each other, on the levels of performance and meaning?[19] In the first extreme type discussed above, there is a unity of institutional performances and meanings in each subjective biography. The entire social stock of knowledge is actualized in every individual biography. Everybody *does* everything and *knows* everything. The problem of the integration of meanings (that is, of the meaningful relationship of the various institutions) is an exclusively subjective one. The objective sense of the institutional order presents itself to each individual as given and generally known, socially taken for granted as such. If there is any problem at all, it is because of subjective difficulties the individual may have internalizing the socially agreed-upon meanings.

With increasing deviance from this heuristic model (that is, of course, with all actual societies, though not to the same degree) there will be important modifications in the givenness of the institutional meanings. The first two of these we have already indicated: a segmentation of the institutional order, with only certain types of individuals performing certain actions, and, following that, a social distribution of knowledge, with role-specific knowledge coming to be reserved to certain types. With these developments, however, a new configuration appears on the level of meaning. There will now be an *objective* problem with respect to an encompassing integration of meanings within the entire society. This is an altogether different problem from the merely subjective one of harmonizing the sense one makes of one's biography with the sense ascribed to it by society. The difference is as great as that between producing propaganda that will convince others and producing memoirs that will convince oneself.

[. . .]

Another consequence of institutional segmentation is the possibility of socially segregated subuniverses of meaning. These result from accentuations of role specialization to the point where role-specific knowledge becomes altogether esoteric as against the common stock of knowledge. Such subuniverses of meaning may or may not be submerged from the common view. In certain cases, not only are the cognitive contents of the subuniverse esoteric, but even the existence of the subuniverse and of the collectivity that sustains it may be a secret. Subuniverses of meaning may be socially structured by various criteria – sex, age, occupation, religious inclination, aesthetic taste, and so on. The chance of subuniverses appearing, of course, increases steadily with progressive division of labor and economic surplus. A society with a subsistence economy can have cognitive segregation between men and women, or between old and young warriors, as in the "secret societies" common in Africa and among American Indians. It may still be able to afford the esoteric existence of a few priests and magicians. Full-blown subuniverses of meaning such as characterized, say, Hindu castes, the Chinese literary bureaucracy, or the priestly coteries of ancient Egypt require much more developed solutions of the economic problem.

Like all social edifices of meaning, the subuniverses must be "carried" by a particular collectivity,[20] that is, by the group that ongoingly produces the meanings in question and within which these meanings have objective reality. Conflict or competition may exist between such groups. On the simplest level, there may be conflict over the allocation of surplus resources to the specialists in question, for example, over exemption from productive labor. Who is to be officially exempt, *all* medicine men, or only those who perform services in the household of the chief? Or, who is to receive a fixed stipend from the authorities, those who cure the sick with herbs or those who do it by going into a trance? Such social conflicts are readily translated into conflicts between rival schools of thought, each seeking to establish itself and to discredit if not liquidate the competitive body of knowledge. In contemporary society, we continue to have such conflicts (socio-economic as well as cognitive) between orthodox medicine and such rivals as chiropractic, homeopathy or Christian Science. In advanced industrial societies, with their immense economic surplus allowing large numbers of individuals to devote themselves full-time to even the obscurest pursuits, pluralistic competition between subuniverses of meaning of every conceivable sort becomes the normal state of affairs.[21]

With the establishment of subuniverses of meaning a variety of perspectives on the total society emerges, each viewing the latter from the angle of one subuniverse. The chiropractor has a different angle on society than the medical school professor, the poet than the businessman, the Jew than the gentile, and so on. It goes without saying that this multiplication of perspectives greatly increases the problem of establishing a stable symbolic canopy for the *entire* society. Each perspective, with whatever appendages of theories or even *Weltanschauungen*, will be related to the concrete social interests of the group that holds it. This does *not* mean, however, that the various perspectives, let alone the theories or *Weltanschauungen*, are nothing but mechanical reflections of the social interests. Especially on the theoretical level it is quite possible for knowledge to attain a great deal of detachment from the biographical and social interests of the knower. Thus there may be tangible social reasons why Jews have become preoccupied with certain scientific enterprises, but it is impossible to predict scientific positions in terms of their being held by Jews or non-Jews. In other words, the scientific universe of meaning is capable of attaining a good deal of autonomy as against its own social base. Theoretically, though in practice there will be great variations, this holds with any body of knowledge, even with cognitive perspectives on society.

What is more, a body of knowledge, once it is raised to the level of a relatively autonomous subuniverse of meaning, has the capacity to act back upon the collectivity that has produced it. For instance, Jews may become social scientists because they have special problems in society *as* Jews. But once they have been initiated into the social-scientific universe of discourse, they may not only look upon society from an angle that is no longer distinctively Jewish, but even their social activities *as* Jews may change as a result of their newly acquired social-scientific perspectives. The extent of such detachment of knowledge from its existential origins depends upon a considerable number of historical variables (such as the urgency of the social interests involved, the degree of theoretical refinement of the knowledge in question, the social relevance or irrelevance of the latter, and others). The important principle for our general considerations is that the relationship between knowledge and its social base is a dialectical one, that is, knowledge is a social product *and* knowledge is a factor in social change.[22] This principle of the dialectic between social production and the objectivated world that is its product has already been explicated; it is especially important to keep it in mind in any analysis of concrete subuniverses of meaning.

The increasing number and complexity of subuniverses make them increasingly inaccessible to outsiders. They become esoteric enclaves, "hermetically sealed" (in the sense classically associated with the Hermetic corpus of secret lore) to all but those who have been properly initiated into their mysteries. The increasing autonomy of subuniverses makes for special problems of legitimation *vis-à-vis* both outsiders and insiders. The outsiders have to be *kept out*, sometimes even kept ignorant of the existence of the subuniverse. If, however, they are not so ignorant, and if the subuniverse requires various special privileges and recognitions from the larger society, there is the problem of keeping out the outsiders and at the same time having them acknowledge the legitimacy of this procedure. This is done through various techniques of intimidation, rational and irrational propaganda (appealing to the outsiders' interests and to their emotions), mystification and, generally, the manipulation of prestige symbols. The insiders, on the other hand, have to be *kept in*. This requires the development of both practical and theoretical procedures by which the temptation to escape from the subuniverse can be checked. . . . It is not enough to set up an esoteric subuniverse of medicine. The lay public must be convinced that this is right and beneficial, and the medical fraternity must be held to the standards of the subuniverse. Thus the general population is intimidated by images of the physical doom that follows "going against doctor's advice"; it is persuaded *not* to do so by the pragmatic benefits of compliance, and by its own horror of illness and death. To underline its authority the medical profession shrouds itself in the age-old symbols of power and mystery, from outlandish costume to incomprehensible language, all of which, of course, are legitimated to the public and to itself in pragmatic terms. Meanwhile the fully accredited inhabitants of the medical world are kept from "quackery" (that is, from stepping outside the medical subuniverse in thought or action) not only by the powerful external controls available to the profession, but by a whole body of professional knowledge that offers them "scientific proof" of the folly and even wickedness of such deviance. In other words, an entire legitimating machinery is at work so that laymen will *remain* laymen, and doctors doctors, and (if at all possible) that both will do so happily.

NOTES

1   This entire section of our treatise is based on Alfred Schutz and Thomas Luckmann, *Die Struktuzen der Lebenswelt*, . . . Our argument here is based on Schutz, as developed by Luckmann in the afore-mentioned work, in *toto*. The reader wishing to acquaint himself with Schutz's work published to date may consult Alfred Schutz, *Der sinnhafte Aufbau der sozialen Welt* (Vienna, Springer, 1960); *Collected Papers*, Vols. I and II. The reader interested in Schutz's adaptation of the phenomenological method to the analysis of the social world may consult especially his *Collected Papers*, Vol. I, pp. 99 ff., and Maurice Natanson (ed.), *Philosophy of the Social Sciences* (New York, Random House, 1963), pp. 183 ff.

2   In insisting that social order is not based on any "laws of nature" we are not *ipso facto* taking a position on a metaphysical conception of "natural law." Our statement is limited to such facts of nature as are empirically available.

3   The term "stock of knowledge" is taken from Schutz.

4   Gehlen refers to this point in his concepts of *Triebüberschuss* and *Entlastung*.

5   Gehlen refers to this point in his concept of *Hintergrundserfüllung*.

6   The concept of the definition of the situation was formed by W. I. Thomas and developed throughout his sociological work.

7   We are aware of the fact that this concept of institution is broader than the prevailing one in contemporary sociology. We think that such a broader concept is useful for a comprehensive analysis of basic social processes. On social control, *cf.* Friedrich Tenbruck, "Soziale Kontrolle," *Staatslexikon der Goerres-Gesellschaft* (1962), and Heinrich Popitz, "Soziale Normen," *European Journal of Sociology*.

8   The term "taking the role of the other" is taken from Mead. We are here taking Mead's paradigm of socialization and applying it to the broader problem of institutionalization. The argument combines key features of both Mead's and Gehlen's approaches.

9   Simmel's analysis of the expansion from the dyad to the triad is important in this connection. The following argument combines Simmel's and Durkheim's conceptions of the objectivity of social reality.

10   In Durkheim's terms this means that, with the expansion of the dyad into a triad and beyond, the original formations become genuine "social facts," that is, they attain *choséité*.

11   Jean Piaget's concept of infantile "realism" may be compared here.

12   For an analysis of this process in the contemporary family, *cf.* Peter L. Berger and Hansfried Kellner, "Marriage and the Construction of Reality," *Diogenes* 46 (1964), 1 ff.

13   The preceding description closely follows Durkheim's analysis of social reality. This does *not* contradict the Weberian conception of the meaningful character of society. Since social reality always originates in meaningful human actions, it continues to carry meaning even if it is opaque to the individual at a given time. The original may be *reconstructed*, precisely by means of what Weber called *Verstehen*.

14   The term "objectivation" is derived from the Hegelian/Marxian *Versachlichung*.

15   Contemporary American sociology tends towards leaving out the first moment. Its perspective on society thus tends to be what Marx called a reification (*Verdinglichung*), that is, an undialectical distortion of social reality that obscures the latter's character as an ongoing

human production, viewing it instead in thing-like categories appropriate only to the world of nature. That the dehumanization implicit in this is mitigated by values deriving from the larger tradition of the society is, presumably, morally fortunate, but is irrelevant theoretically.

16   The tendency of institutions to persist was analyzed by Georg Simmel in terms of his concept of "faithfulness." *Cf.* his *Soziologie* (Berlin, Duncker und Humblot, 1958), pp. 438 ff.

17   This concept of deinstitutionalization is derived from Gehlen.

18   The analysis of deinstitutionalization in the private sphere is a central problem of Gehlen's social psychology of modern society. *Cf.* his *Die Seele im technischen Zeitalter* (Hamburg, Rowohlt, 1957).

19   If one were willing to put up with further neologisms, one could call this the question about the degree of "fusion" or "segmentation" of the institutional order. On the face of it, this question would seem to be identical with the structural-functional concern about the "functional integration" of societies. The latter term, however, presupposes that the "integration" of a society can be determined by an outside observer who investigates the external functioning of the society's institutions. We would contend, on the contrary, that both "functions" and "disfunctions" can only be analyzed by way of the level of meaning. Consequently, "functional integration," if one wants to use this term at all, means the integration of the institutional order by way of various legitimating processes. In other words, *the integration lies not in the institutions but in their legitimation.* This implies, as against the structural-functionalists, that an institutional order cannot adequately be understood as a "system."

20   Weber repeatedly refers to various collectivities as "carriers" (*Tidger*) of what we have called here subuniverses of meaning, especially in his comparative sociology of religion. The analysis of this phenomenon is, of course, related to Marx's *Unterbau/Ueberbau* scheme.

21   The pluralistic competition between subuniverses of meaning is one of the most important problems for an empirical sociology of knowledge of contemporary society. We have dealt with this problem elsewhere in our work in the sociology of religion, but see no point in developing an analysis of this in the present treatise.

22   This proposition can be put into Marxian terms by saying that there is a dialectical relationship between substructure (*Unterbau*) and superstructure (*Ueberbau*) – a Marxian insight that has been widely lost in main-line Marxism until very recently. The problem of the possibility of socially detached knowledge has, of course, been a central one for the sociology of knowledge as defined by Scheler and Mannheim. We are not giving it such a central place for reasons inherent in our general theoretical approach. The important point for a theoretical sociology of knowledge is the dialectic between knowledge and its social base. Questions such as Mannheim's concerning the "unattached intelligentsia" are applications of the sociology of knowledge to concrete historical and empirical phenomena. Propositions about these will have to be made on a level of much lesser theoretical generality than interests us here. Questions concerning the autonomy of social-scientific knowledge, on the other hand, should be negotiated in the context of the methodology of the social sciences. This area we have excluded in our definition of the scope of the sociology of knowledge, for theoretical reasons stated in our introduction.

CHAPTER NINE

ETHNOMETHODOLOGY

CHAPTER MENU

While symbolic interaction draws attention to the micro-dynamics of the ongoing work required in daily life, Goffman (see Chapter 7) is very clear that such interpretive work is highly scripted and, as such, structured into role socialization and role expectations and performances. Consequently, despite the opportunity for, and actual occurrence of, miscues and misinterpretations in the ongoing process of interpersonal (verbal and non-verbal) symbolic exchange, role performances generally follow and result in social order, rather than social disorder. Ethnomethodology, a theoretical paradigm developed by **Harold Garfinkel** focuses specifically on showing how social order is accomplished in everyday life (see excerpt *9a Studies in Ethnomethodology*). For Garfinkel, reality should not simply be assumed as an objective reality or as a thing external to and independent of individuals (as argued by

Concise Reader in Sociological Theory: Theorists, Concepts, and Current Applications,
First Edition. Edited by Michele Dillon. Editorial material and organization
© 2021 John Wiley & Sons Ltd. Published 2021 by John Wiley & Sons Ltd.

Emile Durkheim). Instead, he problematizes what comprises everyday reality, and draws attention to the practical work that ordinary individuals do across an array of roles and across an array of familial and institutional settings, work that must be done to bring about and affirm the societal reality. This perspective is called ethnomethodology because it literally focuses on the methods that people (*ethnos* is the Greek word for people) use to produce an ordered social reality, one that is reasonable in terms of the context in which people live and that makes sense not only to the individual but to all those to whom the individual is accountable. As Garfinkel (see excerpt 9*a*) notes, what societal members do "is always somebody else's business" and consequently we, as individual societal members always need to be able to account for what we are doing and why we are doing it the way we are doing it (or did it). We have to have a coherent and reasonable account, reasonable enough that for all intents and purposes our account of what *really* happened or of why one *really* made the decision one made is persuasive to all those diverse stakeholders (or busybodies!) who take an interest in our decisions and the reasonableness of the process used to get to that decision (regardless of the decision's outcomes). Garfinkel uses the example of the work of a coroner's office, and elsewhere discusses how jurors in a trial make sense of what really happened in the circumstances of a death or a crime, respectively. But regardless of the specific problem or issue, this is the sort of account-making all of us are necessarily engaged in on an ongoing basis.

The *doing* work entailed in accomplishing reality extends to and includes how we perform gender, sexuality, race, class and other of our multiple intersecting identities. In this view, gender for example is not merely a sociological variable (as for Durkheim or Parsons), or merely a social role (that of a woman or a man with its respective role expectations and routines, as for Goffman), but a process, an ongoing process of actually doing gender as an ongoing series of practical activities. Long before transgender identity became a topic of increased public conversation, Garfinkel focused on a specific clinical case, that of "Agnes" (excerpt 9*a*) who was born a boy but who felt they were a natural girl, and thus had to accomplish this different sexual/gendered reality in opposition to the objective perceived normalness of what a boy and what a girl is/does. Building on Garfinkel, Candace West and Sarah Fenstermaker (1995a) extended the ethnomethodological discussion to the practical work of "doing difference" more generally (see excerpt 9*b Doing Gender, Doing Difference*). Their work was somewhat controversial among sociologists because of a perception that they were downplaying the structural and historical forces that produce (and structurally reproduce) gender, sexual, racial, and other forms of inequality. **Fenstermaker and West** address these misapprehensions. They make the counterclaim that while macro structures determine the unequal circumstances and opportunities available to individuals and groups differently located within society (invariably a highly stratified society; see Marx and Weber), individuals employ the particular methods in their everyday practices that accomplish in an ongoing manner what is understood as a reasonable and normal reality. They reproduce (and/or to some extent resist and may alter) the micro and the larger societal expectations of what is taken as making sense in a given (heavily structured) societal context. For example, despite equality of opportunity, and regulations and laws that seek to ensure equal treatment at work for women and men, women, as "normal" societal members, accomplish and account for reality in particular ways – when a woman faculty member naturally feels the urge to clear coffee cups from the seminar room table and automatically acts on that practice because that's what she and women in general tend to do (and are tacitly expected to do) no matter the setting or their status. In this way, women perform gender and accomplish a gendered reality.

9A Harold Garfinkel from *Studies in Ethnomethodology*

Original publication details: Harold Garfinkel, 1967. *Studies in Ethnomethodology*, pp. 11–18, 120–124. Englewood Cliffs, NJ: Prentice Hall.

I use the term "ethnomethodology" to refer to the investigation of the rational properties of indexical expressions and other practical actions as contingent ongoing accomplishments of organized artful practices of everyday life. They seek to specify its problematic features, to recommend methods for its study, but above all to consider what we might learn definitely about it. My purpose in the remainder of this chapter is to characterize ethnomethodology.

Practical Sociological Reasoning: Doing Accounts in "Common Sense Situations of Choice"

The Los Angeles Suicide Prevention Center (SPC) and the Los Angeles Medical Examiner-Coroner's Office joined forces in 1957 to furnish Coroner's Death Certificates the warrant of scientific authority "within the limits of practical certainties imposed by the state of the art." Selected cases of "sudden, unnatural death" that were equivocal between "suicide" and other modes of death were referred by the Medical Examiner-Coroner to the SPC with the request that an inquiry, called a "psychological autopsy,"[1] be done.

The practices and concerns by SPC staff to accomplish their inquiries in common sense situations of choice repeated the features of practical inquiries that were encountered in other situations: studies of jury deliberations in negligence cases; clinic staff in selecting patients for out-patient psychiatric treatment; graduate students in sociology coding the contents of clinic folders into a coding sheet by following detailed coding instructions; and countless professional procedures in the conduct of anthropological, linguistic, social psychiatric, and sociological inquiry. The following features in the work at SPC were recognized by staff with frank acknowledgement as prevailing conditions of their work and as matters to consider when assessing the efficacy, efficiency, or intelligibility of their work – and added SPC testimony to that of jurors, survey researchers, and the rest:

(1) An abiding concern on the part of all parties for the temporal concerting of activities; (2) a concern for the practical question *par excellence*: "What to do next?"; (3) a concern on the inquirer's part to give evidence of his grasp of "What Anyone Knows" about how the settings work in which he had to accomplish his inquiries, and

his concern to do so in the actual occasions in which the decisions were to be made by his exhibitable conduct in choosing; (4) matters which at the level of talk might be spoken of as "production programs," "laws of conduct," "rules of rational decision-making," "causes," "conditions," "hypothesis testing," "models," "rules of inductive and deductive inference" in the actual situation were taken for granted and were depended upon to consist of recipes, proverbs, slogans, and partially formulated plans of action; (5) inquirers were required to know and be skilled in dealing with situations "of the sort" for which "rules of rational decision-making" and the rest were intended in order to "see" or by what they did to insure the objective, effective, consistent, completely, empirically adequate, *i.e.,* rational character of recipes, prophecies, proverbs, partial descriptions in an actual occasion of the use of rules; (6) for the practical decider the "actual occasion" as a phenomenon in its own right exercised overwhelming priority of relevance to which "decision rules" or theories of decision-making were without exception subordinated in order to assess their rational features rather than *vice versa;* (7) finally, and perhaps most characteristically, all of the foregoing features, together with an inquirer's "system" of alternatives, his "decision" methods, his information, his choices, and the rationality of his accounts and actions were constituent parts of the same practical circumstances in which inquirers did the work of inquiry – a feature that inquirers if they were to claim and recognize the practicality of their efforts knew of, required, counted on, took for granted, used, and glossed.

The work by SPC members of conducting their inquiries was part and parcel of the day's work. Recognized by staff members as constituent features of the day's work, their inquiries were thereby intimately connected to the terms of employment, to various internal and external chains of reportage, supervision, and review, and to similar organizationally supplied "priorities of relevances" for assessments of what "realistically," "practically," or "reasonably" needed to be done and could be done, how quickly, with what resources, seeing whom, talking about what, for how long, and so on. Such considerations furnished "We did what we could, and for all reasonable interests here is what we came out with" its features of organizationally appropriate sense, fact, impersonality, anonymity of authorship, purpose, reproducibility – *i.e.,* of a *properly* and *visibly* rational account of the inquiry.

Members were required in their occupational capacities to formulate accounts of how a death *really*-for-all-practical-purposes-happened. "Really" made unavoidable reference to daily, ordinary, occupational workings. Members alone were entitled to invoke such workings as appropriate grounds for recommending the reasonable character of the result *without necessity for furnishing specifics.* On occasions of challenge, ordinary occupational workings would be cited explicitly, in "relevant part." Otherwise those features were disengaged from the product. In their place an account of how the inquiry was done made out the how-it-was-actually-done as appropriate to usual demands, usual attainments, usual practices, *and* to usual talk by SPC personnel talking as *bona fide* professional practitioners about usual demands, usual attainments, and usual practices.

One of several titles (relating to mode of death) had to be assigned to each case. The collection consisted of legally possible combinations of four elementary possibilities – natural death, accident, suicide, and homicide.[2] *All* titles were so administered as to not only withstand the varieties of equivocation, ambiguity, and improvisation that arose in every actual occasion of their use, but these titles were so administered as to *invite* that ambiguity, equivocality, and improvisation. It was part of the work not *only* that equivocality is a trouble – is *perhaps* a trouble – but also the practitioners were directed to those circumstances in order to *invite* the ambiguity or the equivocality, to invite the improvisation, or to invite the temporizing, and the rest. It is not that the investigator, having a list of titles performed an inquiry that proceeded stepwise to establish the grounds for electing among them. The formula was not, "Here is what we did, and among the titles as goals of our research *this* title finally interprets in a best fashion what we found out." Instead titles were continually postdicted and foretold. An inquiry was apt to be heavily guided by the inquirer's use of imagined settings in which the title will have been "used" by one or another interested party, including the deceased, and this was done by the inquirers in order to decide, using whatever "datum" might have been searched out, that *that* "datum" could be used to mask if masking needed to be done, or to equivocate, or gloss, or lead, or exemplify if they were needed. The prevailing feature of an inquiry was that nothing about it remained assured aside from the organized occasions of its uses. Thus a routine inquiry was one that the investigator used particular contingencies to accomplish, and depended upon particular contingencies to recognize and to recommend the practical adequacy of his work. When assessed by a member, *i.e.* viewed with respect to actual practices for making it happen, a routine inquiry is not one that is accomplished by rule, or according to rules. It seemed much more to consist of an inquiry that is openly recognized to have fallen short, but in the same ways it falls short its adequacy is acknowledged and for which no one is offering or calling particularly for explanations.

What members are *doing* in their inquiries is always somebody else's business in the sense that particular, organizationally located, locatable persons acquire an interest in light of the SPC member's account of whatever it is that will have been reported to have "really happened." Such considerations contributed heavily to the perceived feature of investigations that they were directed in their course by an account for which the claim will have been advanced that for all practical purposes it is correct. Thus over the path of his inquiry the investigator's task consisted of an account of how a particular person died in society that is adequately told, sufficiently detailed, clear, etc., for all practical purposes.

"What really happened," over the course of arriving at it, as well as after the "what really happened" has been inserted into the file and the title has been decided, may be chronically reviewed as well as chronically foretold in light of what might have been done, or what will have been done with those decisions. It is hardly news that on the way to a decision what a decision will have come to was reviewed and foretold in light of the anticipated consequences of a decision. *After* a recommendation had been made and the coroner had signed the death certificate the result can yet be, as they say, "revised." It can still be made a decision which needs to be reviewed "once more."

Inquirers wanted very much to be able to assure that they could come out at the end with an account of how the person died that would permit the coroner and his staff to withstand claims arguing that that account was incomplete or that the death happened differently than – or in contrast to or in contradiction of – what the members to the arrangement "claimed." The reference is neither only nor entirely to the complaints of the survivors. Those issues are dealt with as a succession of episodes, most being settled fairly quickly. The great contingencies consisted of enduring processes that lay in the fact that the coroner's office is a political office. The coroner's office activities produce continuing records of his office's activities. These records are subject to review as the products of the scientific work of the coroner, his staff, and his consultant. Office activities are methods for accomplishing reports that are scientific-for-all-practical-purposes. This involved "writing" as a warranting procedure in that a report, by reason of being written, is put into a file. That the investigator "does" a report is thereby made a matter for public record for the use of only partially identifiable other persons. Their interests in why or how or what the inquirer did would have in some relevant part to do with his skill and entitlement as a professional. But investigators know too that other interests will inform the "review," for the inquirer's work will be scrutinized to see its scientific-adequacy-for-all-practical-purposes as professionals' socially managed claims. Not only for investigators, but on all sides there is the relevance of "What was really found out for-all-practical-purposes?" which consists unavoidably of how much can you find out, how much can you disclose, how much can you gloss, how much can you conceal, how much can you hold as none of the business of some important persons, *investigators* included. All of them acquired an interest by reason of the fact that investigators, as a matter of occupationalduty,werecomingupwithwrittenreportsofhow,for-all-practical-purposespersons-really-died-and-are-really-dead-*in*-the-society.

Decisions had an unavoidable consequentiality. By this is meant that investigators needed to say *in so many words*, "What really happened?" The important words were the titles that were assigned to a text to recover that text as the title's "explication." But what an assigned title consists of as an "explicated" title is at any particular time for no one to say with any finality even when it is proposed "in so many words." In fact, *that* it is proposed "in so many words," *that* for example a written text was inserted "into the file of the case," furnishes entitling grounds that can be invoked in order to make something of the "so many words" that will have been used as an account of the death. Viewed with respect to patterns of use, titles and their accompanying texts have an open set of consequences. Upon any occasion of the use of texts it can remain to be seen what can be done with them, or what they will have come to, or what remains done "for the time being" pending the ways in which the environment of that decision may organize itself to "reopen the case," or "issue a complaint," or "find an issue" and so on. Such ways for SPC'ers are, as patterns, certain; but as particular processes for making them happen are in every actual occasion indefinite.

SPC inquiries begin with a death that the coroner finds equivocal as to *mode* of death. That death they use as a precedent with which various ways of living in society that could have terminated with that death are searched out and read "in the remains"; in the scraps of this and that like the body and its trappings, medicine bottles, notes, bits and pieces of clothing, and other memorabilia – stuff that can be photographed, collected, and packaged. Other "remains" are collected too: rumors, passing remarks, and stories – materials in the "repertoires" of whosoever might be consulted via the common work of conversations. These *whatsoever* bits and pieces that a story or a rule or a proverb might make intelligible are used to formulate a recognizably coherent, standard, typical, cogent, uniform, planful, *i.e.*, a professionally defensible, and thereby, for members, a *recognizably* rational account of how the society worked to produce those remains. This point will be easier to make if the reader will consult any standard textbook in forensic pathology. In it he will find the inevitable photograph of a victim with a slashed throat. Were the coroner to use that "sight" to recommend the equivocality of the mode of death he might say something like this: "In the case where a body looks like the one in that picture, you are looking at a suicidal death because the wound shows the 'hesitation cuts' that accompany the great wound. One can imagine these cuts are the remains of a procedure whereby the victim first made several preliminary trials of a hesitating sort and then performed the lethal slash. Other courses of action are imaginable, too, and so cuts that look like hesitation cuts can be produced by other mechanisms. One needs to start with the actual display and imagine how different courses of actions could have been organized such that *that* picture would be compatible with it. One might think of the photographed display as a phase-of-the-action. In any actual display is there a course of action with which that phase is uniquely compatible? *That* is the coroner's question."

The coroner (and SPC'ers) ask this with respect to each *particular* case, and thereby their work of achieving practical decidability seems almost unavoidably to display the following prevailing and important characteristic. SPC'ers must accomplish that decidability with respect to the "this's": they have to start with *this* much; *this* sight; *this* note; *this* collection of whatever is at hand. And *whatever* is there is good enough in the sense that *whatever* is there not only *will* do, but *does*. One makes whatever is there *do*. I do not mean by "making do" that an SPC investigator is too easily content, or that he does not look for more when he should. Instead, I mean: the *whatever* it is that he has to deal with, *that* is what will have been used to have found out, to have made decidable, the way in which the society operated to have produced *that* picture, to have come to *that* scene as its end result. In this way the remains on the slab serve not only as a precedent but as a goal of SPC inquiries. *Whatsoever* SPC members are faced with must serve as the precedent with which to read the remains so as to see how the society could have operated to have produced what it is that the inquirer has "in the end," "in the final analysis," and "in *any* case." What the inquiry can come to is what the death came to.

NOTES

1   The following references contain reports on the "psychological autopsy" procedure developed at the Los Angeles Suicide Prevention Center: Theodore J. Curphey, "The Forensic Pathologist and the Multi-Disciplinary Approach to Death," in *Essays in Self-Destruction*, ed. Edwin S. Shneidman (International Science Press, 1967); Theodore J. Curphey, "The Role of the Social Scientist in the Medico-Legal Certification of Death from Suicide," in *The Cry for Help*, ed. Norman L. Farberow and Edwin S. Shneidman (New York: McGraw-Hill Book Company, 1961);

Edwin S. Shneidman and Norman L. Farberow, "Sample Investigations of Equivocal Suicidal Deaths," in *The Cry for Help*; Robert E. Litman, Theodore J. Curphey, Edwin S. Shneidman, Norman L. Farberow, and Norman D. Tabachnick, "Investigations of Equivocal Suicides," *Journal of the American Medical Association*, 184 (1963), 924–9; and Edwin S. Shneidman, "Orientations Toward Death: A Vital Aspect of the Study of Lives," in *The Study of Lives*, ed. Robert W. White

(New York: Atherton Press, 1963), reprinted in the *International Journal of Psychiatry*, 2 (1966), 167–200.

2   The possible combinations include the following: natural; accident; suicide; homicide; possible accident; possible suicide; possible natural; (between) accident or suicide, undetermined; (between) natural or suicide, undetermined; (between) natural or accident, undetermined; and (among) natural or accident or suicide, undetermined.

9B Sarah Fenstermaker and Candace West from *Doing Gender, Doing Difference: Inequality, Power, and Institutional Change*

Original publication details: Sarah Fenstermaker and Candace West, 2002. "'Doing Difference' Revisited: Problems, Prospects, and the Dialogue in Feminist Theory" in *Doing Gender, Doing Difference: Inequality, Power, and Institutional Change*, edited by Sarah Fenstermaker and Candace West, pp. 206–211. New York: Routledge. Reproduced with permission of Taylor & Francis.

"Difference" as an Ongoing Interactional Accomplishment

In 1995, we observed a peculiar trend in feminist scholarship, namely, a tendency to use mathematical metaphors in descriptions of relationships among gender, race, and class (West and Fenstermaker 1995a). In some cases, scholarship seemed to draw on addition, summing up the effects of each "variable" in order to characterize the whole. In other cases, analyses invoked multiplication, using expressions such as "double negative" and "triple disadvantage" to describe their compound effects. Even geometry came into play, in turns of phrase like "intersecting systems" and "interlocking categories" describing relationships among gender, race, and class. We noted that the very existence of these distinctive metaphors seemed premonitory of the problems scholars were experiencing in coming to terms with the topic. . . .

We began "Doing Difference" (West and Fenstermaker 1995a) by asking how feminist scholarship came to draw on mathematical metaphors in the first place. One reason for these metaphors, we suggested, was the white middle-class preoccupation of much feminist thought. But we also proposed that existing conceptualizations of gender contributed to the problem by offering no alternatives but those mathematical metaphors. What was lacking, we contended, was a way of thinking about gender that provided for understanding how gender, race, and class operate *simultaneously* with one another. This would allow us to see how the importance of these socially relevant, organizing experiences might differ across interactional contexts. Moreover, this would give us a way to address the mechanisms that produce power and inequality in social life. We proposed a conceptual mechanism, the "doing" of difference, to illuminate "the relations between individual and institutional practice, and among forms of domination" (1995a, 19).

With the publication of "Doing Difference" (West and Fenstermaker 1995a), we completed a trilogy of papers advancing our proposition that class-, race-, and gender-based inequalities result from the ongoing interactional accomplishments of class, race, and gender (see also Fenstermaker, West, and Zimmerman 1991; West and Fenstermaker 1993, 1995a). We have asserted that whatever the inequality they produce, these accomplishments are seemingly infinitely adaptable to specific social circumstances. Although their relative standing in any given interaction may vary, they are nonetheless governed by the same underlying interactional mechanisms. We have argued that each of us, specifically located in groups, institutions, relationships, and human activities, is held accountable – in varying ways and to differing degrees – to particular "classed," "raced," and "gendered" expectations. These expectations are informed by the past outcomes of interactions, which, in turn, resulted in historical and institutional practices. Through these means, we not only produce "natural" differences among human beings, but also reaffirm inequality based on such differences as an "only natural" state of affairs. Class, race, and gender are related to one another *as accomplishments*: dynamic, adaptable, mutable, and deriving their particular meaning through social interaction.

By way of summary: People "do" difference by creating invidious distinctions among themselves – for example, as members of different sex categories, different race categories, and different class categories – differences that are hardly "natural." These far-from-"natural" distinctions are then brought forward to affirm and reaffirm the "essentially different natures" of different category members and institutional arrangements based on these. The accomplishment of class, race, and gender makes social arrangements based on category membership understandable as normal and natural (i.e., as *legitimate*) modes of social organization. Thus, distinctions that are generated through this process are seen as basic and enduring dispositions of persons. In the end, patriarchy, racism, and class oppression are seen as *responses* to those dispositions – as if the social order were merely a rational accommodation to "natural differences" among social beings.

Each of the *theoretical* assertions in the foregoing summary rightfully garnered comments and criticisms, and we organize this article around the ones that are consequential for further theory development. Yet it also bears mention that, in each of our three more recent attempts to advance our formulation, we called for concerted attention to the *empirical* manifestations of the dynamics of gender, race, and class. We made clear that for us the utility of the theoretical formulation would be realized only if it facilitated understanding of the empirical actualities of social inequality. For example, we concluded "Doing Difference" (1995a) by urging that "empirical evidence must be brought to bear on the question of variation in the salience of categorical memberships, while still allowing for the simultaneous influence of these memberships on interaction" (33). Since the original formulation of "Doing Gender" (West and Zimmerman 1987), and the extensions that followed (Fenstermaker, West, and Zimmerman 1991; West and Fenstermaker 1993), scores of empirical analyses have employed the formulation in one way or another – usually as a device to make post hoc theoretical sense of empirical findings.[1]

Despite the apparent attraction of the formulation among researchers, the 1995 publication of "Doing Difference" stirred a good deal of controversy, primarily among feminist sociologists of race and gender. A symposium in the feminist sociology journal *Gender & Society* only added to the number of comments we had already received from colleagues in response to the work. In the symposium other scholars raised a number of issues central to our framework, and we briefly responded to them. In this article we return to our response and the central doubts raised about "Doing Difference," and we employ the text of the others' commentary in a way that grounds our comments in the original feminist dialogue. In so doing we hope both to clarify our position and to point to issues yet unresolved.

We hope that this contribution to the ongoing debate will dispel several common misapprehensions surrounding the notion that social inequality is the outcome of ongoing interactional doings. People – *we* – function in interaction not only as individuals, but also as purveyors of institutional action and as defenders of the sensibilities of and rationales for past action. One great achievement of social science has been the detailed description and systematic measurement of the outcomes of social domination and oppression. We proceed on the premise that a clear sense of the ways in which such outcomes actually happen – how they are brought into being and made material through interaction – would greatly enhance our understanding of power, inequality, and social change.

Common Misapprehensions

We have found that in any discussion of the "doing" of race, class, or gender, we must first turn to the inevitable confusion between process and outcome, and restate our interest in unearthing the mechanisms *by which inequality outcomes obtain*. Yet no number of italicized words, phrases, or sentences appears to do the trick. Our work is often interpreted as suggesting that the inequalities surrounding race, class, and gender oppression are equivalent. Perhaps this stems from sociology's historical (and often rightful) preoccupation with the compelling details of race, class, and gender domination. What we argue, however, is that the *accomplishment* of race, class, and gender is what lies at the heart of social inequality and what allows us to understand how forms of oppression intersect and overlap (West and Fenstermaker 1995b). . . .

The likelihood of this misapprehension coloring readers' more general understanding of our formulation has had the unfortunate effect of preoccupying us with repeated discussions of the nature of gender, race, and class. We have been rightly criticized (Schwalbe 2000) in this regard. Schwalbe argues that sociology is fixated on the reifications of gender, race, and class as *things* – characteristics, attributes, discrete "variables" – rather than pursuing these as active social accomplishments. In regard to our work, he argues that even we are sometimes seduced into such language, generating little forward motion in articulating the processes we assert. Perhaps so: The common confusion of the results of inequality with the workings of it has surely taken its toll on the productive elaboration of our theoretical framework.

Another misapprehension that follows from a misreading of our original theorizing about gender (West and Zimmerman 1987; Fenstermaker et al. 1991) – and perhaps, from a broader confusion over social constructionism – is that we are proposing
a social science version of Judith Butler's theory of gender performativity
(Butler 1990, 1993): a kind of "inequality as performance" theory. For us, the doing of
difference is certainly not a set of performances nor a simple combination of gender,
race, and class displays. However, the very notion of accomplishment allows for attention to the performative aspects of communicating difference and complying with (or
defying) normative expectations for members of particular race, class, and sex
categories.[3]

From this conflation of our work and Butler's springs another misreading: a view of
our formulation as a kind of poststructural erasure of differences that are consequential to people's lives. Patricia Hill Collins (1995) has put this charge most forcefully:

> Recasting racism, patriarchy, and class exploitation solely in social constructionist terms
> reduces race, class, and gender to performances, interactions between people embedded
> in a never ending string of equivalent relations, all containing race, class, and gender in
> some form, but a chain of equivalences devoid of power relations. (493)

We could never provide an adequate response to this charge, since the ideas within
it so obviously conflict with our argument: the idea that social construction necessarily implies the reduction of raced, classed, and gendered social dynamics to performances; the idea that the doing of difference is confined to face-to-face interactions;
the idea that interactions appear in never ending strings of "equivalent relations"; and
the idea that the interactions we speak of are even conceivable when "devoid of power
relations." . . .

But within Collins's criticism lie extremely productive questions about the nature
of social accomplishment, the nature of difference, and how we are conceptualizing
such processes. First is the notion that the "doing" of gender, race, and class are phenomena best confined to face-to-face interaction. Second (and immediately related to
the first) are time-worn questions concerning the relationship of social structure and
the individual (sometimes packaged as the "micro/macro" problem that seems to
plague so many sociologists). Obviously related to these questions is how historically
repeated patterns of inequality bequeath their legacy to present-day processes. Thus,
a crucial third question is how, within this formulation, resistance might operate and
social change might occur. To clarify both critique and response, we will briefly
return to these three concerns.

The Dynamics of Doing Difference

In her recent attempt to offer an integrative framework for the concepts of racial and
gender formation Evelyn Nakano Glenn (1999) proposes that scholars focus on the
processes of racialization and gendering rather than the reified and static categories

of race and gender. She asserts that *both* social structure and expressions of cultural representation are implicated in what we would call the "doing" of race, class, and gender. She argues that "these processes take place at multiple levels, including *representation . . . micro-interaction . . . and social structure*" (9). Other scholars have also reconsidered the distinction between micro and macro phenomena and some have begun to adapt Anthony Giddens's (1984) earlier model of structuration to social processes. For example, Harvey Molotch, William Freudenburg, and Krista Paulsen (2000) argue:

> In their structure-making actions, humans draw, per force, from existing conditions – that is, from structures resulting from their prior actions. Thus, as people take actions they make structures, and every action is both enabled and constrained by the prior structures. (793)

Likewise, and long ago, Philip Abrams (1972) called for a greater sensitivity to the ambiguities of such multiple levels in a "sociology of process," wherein "society must be understood as a process constructed historically by individuals who are constructed historically by society" (227). If we allow for the logic of individual agency *in interaction* with the accumulated decisions of history, the patterned practices of individuals as institutional actors, and the legacies of prior individual decisions, the "doing" of social inequality can take on far more meaningful proportions than Collins (1995) described, or those that Lynn Weber (1995) reduced to "a few unremarkable actors in everyday interactions" (501). Indeed, we would argue that those "few unremarkable actors in everyday interactions" are responsible for the force of history, the exercise of institutional power, and enduring social structures.[4]

Sociologists may also draw on Dorothy Smith's (1987) work to make greater sense of the ways in which these multiple levels may be apprehended. We would argue that viewing the "micro/macro" problem as a useful and accurate depiction of the world is only a variation on the theme of a "bifurcated consciousness," where multiple standpoints are kept systematically from official view. If we allow for the constant confluence of what we have called "situated social action" and social structure, how race, class, and gender are done is informed both by past practice and by a response to the normative order of the moment. As we said in the symposium on "Doing Difference" (West and Fenstermaker 1995b),

> Our focus on ever-changing, variously situated social relationships as the sites for the doing of difference does not denude those relationships of the powerful contexts in which they unfold. We argue only that the impact of the forces of social structure and history is realized *in the unfolding of those relationships*. (509)

This claim, that individual action and social structure are only different aspects of the daily – and often unremarkable – social accomplishment of race, class, and gender, raises the question of how we might conceive of resistance and opposition to those structures daily brought into being, reaffirmed, and reproduced.

NOTES

1   Even an inexhaustive and haphazard collection of empirical pieces employing the framework covers a wide variety of topics (e.g. men's and women's prisons, women surgeons, rock music, the Internet, crime and violence, coal mines, and firehouses).

2   Butler's theories cannot be reduced to the dramaturgical either. Elsewhere. . . we explore the convergences and divergences between the two theoretical formulations.

3   Joan Acker's work (e.g., 1992a, 1992b) demonstrates that the presence of gender in work organizations is certainly ubiquitous and takes on a variety of aspects. The operational mechanisms *behind* these manifestations, we would argue, point directly to the accomplishment of difference as an everyday yet powerful feature of organizations.

REFERENCES

Abrams, P. 1972. *Historical sociology.* Ithaca, NY: Cornell University Press.

Acker, Joan. 1992a. Gendered institutions: From sex roles to gendered institutions. *Contemporary Sociology* 21: 565–9.

_____ 1992b. Gendering organizational theory. In *Gendering organizational theory*, edited by Albert J. Mills and Peta Tancred. London: Sage.

Butler, J. 1990. *Gender trouble: Feminism and the subversion of identity.* New York: Routledge.

_____ 1993. *Bodies that matter: On the discursive limits of "sex."* New York: Routledge. Collins, P.H.

_____ 1995. Symposium: On West and Fenstermaker's "Doing difference." *Gender & Society* 9: 491–4.

Fenstermaker, S., C. West, and D. H. Zimmerman. 1991. Gender inequality: New conceptual terrain. In *Gender, family and economy: The triple overlap*, edited by Rae Lesser Blumberg. Newbury Park, CA: Sage.

Giddens, A. 1984. *The constitution of society.* Berkeley: University of California Press. Glenn, E.N. 1999. The social construction and institutionalization of gender and race: An integrative framework. In *Revisioning gender*, edited by Myra Marx Ferree, Judith Lorber, and Beth B. Hess. Thousand Oaks, CA: Sage.

Molotch, H., W. Freudenburg, and K. E. Paulsen. 2000. History repeats itself, but how? City character, urban tradition, and the accomplishment of place. *American Sociological Review* 65: 791–823.

Schwalbe, M. 2000. Charting futures for sociology: Inequality mechanisms, *intersections and global change. Contemporary Sociology* 29: 275–81.

Smith, D. E. 1987. *The everyday world as problematic: A feminist sociology.* Boston: Northeastern University Press.

Weber, L. 1995. Symposium: On West and Fenstermaker's "Doing Difference." *Gender & Society* 9: 499–503.

West, C. and S. Fenstermaker. 1993. Power, inequality, and the accomplishment of gender: An ethnomethdological view. In *Theory on Gender/ Feminism on Theory*, edited by Paula England. New York: Aldine dc Gruyter.

_____ 1995a. Doing difference. *Gender & Society* 9: 8–37.

_____ 1995b. (Re)Doing difference: A reply. *Gender & Society* 9: 506–13.

West, C. and D. H. Zimmerman. 1997. Doing gender. *Gender & Society* 1: 125–51.

PART IV

MAJOR POSTWAR EUROPEAN
INFLUENCES ON SOCIOLOGICAL
THEORY

CHAPTER TEN

CRITICAL THEORY: THE FRANKFURT SCHOOL

CHAPTER MENU

Critical theory is a term used broadly to include a range of largely Marxist-inspired theorizing characteristic of an array of post-World War II, mostly European-born, theorists as well as in later decades encompassing feminist, postcolonial, and cultural theorists. In this sense, it includes scholars who critique the dominant institutional arrangements in society – capitalism, patriarchy, white privilege – and how the multiple forms of everyday inequality are reproduced and perpetuated. More narrowly, critical theory is the term used (including in this *Reader*) to refer to the writings of theorists associated with the Frankfurt School, so-called because of the original association of these scholars with the influential Institute for Social Research in Frankfurt. Frankfurt School theorists individually address an array of specific themes (from jazz to literature, art, and high culture, to Freudian psychoanalysis), but share in common a commitment to systematically critiquing the multilayered intersection of capitalist profit, the packaging of culture as a commodity, and the deployment of culture and politics in the service of both capitalism and the dilution of democratic ideals. Their work reflects a strong Marxist influence but, importantly too, they also are heavily

Concise Reader in Sociological Theory: Theorists, Concepts, and Current Applications,
First Edition. Edited by Michele Dillon. Editorial material and organization
© 2021 John Wiley & Sons Ltd. Published 2021 by John Wiley & Sons Ltd.

indebted to Weber. In particular, they extend Weber's pessimism – especially explicit toward the end of his analysis of *The Protestant Ethic and the Spirit of Capitalism*, where he talks of the "iron cage" of rationality, and the increased prominence at the end of the nineteenth century of the institutionalization of instrumental rationality in and across all spheres of society (and its related displacement of values other than material acquisitiveness).

What is distinctive about critical theory is that it squarely places attention on the significance of culture – especially everyday consumer and pop culture and entertainment – as a tool in the suppression of critical thinking by corporate media owners (who, in turn, are owned by even larger corporations with economic stakes in multiple products and services). The core thesis of Frankfurt School theorists is that Enlightenment values and ideals – the gift of human reason and its relevance to human emancipation and ideals of human equality, democratic participation, and solidarity – have been subverted by capitalist interests and the mutual alliance of economic and political actors, and used to control and disempower individuals intellectually, economically, and politically so as to ensure the maintenance of the (unequal) status quo. Thus **Max Horkheimer** and **Theodor W. Adorno** write about the "dialectic of enlightenment" (see excerpt 10a *The Dialectic of Enlightenment*). Instead of the human and social freedom promised by the Enlightenment's understanding of the individual as a being endowed with reason, and thus the ability to self-govern and, with others, to collectively govern and build a society that would institutionalize human and social equality, rational principles and procedures (e.g. scientific management, surveillance) are used in an instrumental manner to dominate individuals and groups, as well as the natural environment, to advance particular interests at the expense of the common good. In other words, reason has been eclipsed by power – by the decisions and actions of powerful corporations, business lobbying groups, and the politicians they financially support and, indeed, control. According to Horkheimer and Adorno, the notion of technological and social progress is defined in ways that increase and deepen inequality rather than improving the lives of all individuals and advancing their access to and participation in the benefits that technological progress can provide (e.g. breakthroughs in medicine, or in expanding education). Mass media news, entertainment, and advertising are especially impactful in suppressing critical awareness of the inequalities in society as a result of how they intentionally elevate simplistic and homogenized views of the "good life," a "good life," not anchored by the search for truth or based on concern for others, but equated with consumerist lifestyles, and with fashion and art that commodifies (for profit) rather than reflects individual personalities or creative choices. They argue that the mass media reduces all content to that which fits a formula of sameness (whether comedy or tragedy), a sameness that generates profit (and not critical thinking or an active engagement with the content). Similarly, their colleague Herbert Marcuse (1964) writes about "one-dimensional man," a phrase that captures the claim that not only individuals, but political parties and political and cultural discourse have become stripped of everything but the most superficial veneer of personality and interest, and are incapable of engaging in any kind of thoughtful or meaningful reflection and conversation that would challenge the dominance of one-sided ideas, whether about politics, movies, or fashion.

Marcuse, Horkheimer, Adorno, and other Frankfurt School theorists elaborated their critique of politics and consumer culture and its suppression of enlightened, critical thought in the wake of World War II, and thus were urgently responding to the authoritarianism and dehumanization perpetuated by a populist politics that fueled Nazism, Fascism, and the Holocaust. We now live in a different historical moment, one in which technology has become exponentially more pervasive in everyday life, and consumerism a truly global phenomenon and consumer brand names (not coincidentally linked to or promoted by global technology companies such as Apple and Google) the dominant vocabulary we all share. The expansion of technology can have a democratizing function; most of us have the ability to access Twitter and express our opinions, or to use YouTube to present our personally curated views on a host of issues. Yet, despite the new possibilities for deepening democratic participation in society and working across geographical and cultural divides to build a more egalitarian society, the use of social media and political conversation in general has become even more one-sided and, at the same time, polarizing. Critique of the existing structures and of the inequalities they perpetuate is undermined by the mass media, the ever expanding culture industry – and fueled today by mobile social media and technology corporations such as Facebook and Google – with deception and manipulation rather than illumination the driving, profit infused, goals. Thus Facebook connects you to numerous friends, and Amazon is amazingly efficient in finding and delivering whatever goods you *need* (underpinned by *wants* cultivated by advertising), and Google gives you answers to anything you want to know – but as they smoothly do all this, they also efficiently mine all the vast personal data you (and your friends) happily share. In turn, they use these data to specifically target you personally with additional customized advertising to further expand the scope of your consumption habits. Accordingly, as Horkheimer and Adorno presciently elaborated (see excerpt *10a Dialectic of Enlightenment*), technology is used to follow and to control individuals, and as such to colonize and dominate them, and it does so while yielding a lot of money for corporations while simultaneously providing personal, private data to the government and its various surveillance agencies (e.g. the FBI).

The sharp critique of society elaborated by Horkheimer and Adorno (and Marcuse) can be criticized for its deep pessimism, notwithstanding the salience of its extensive applicability to the present day. They fail to articulate a way forward that would build on the positive aspects of modernity while taming the more negative consequences of society's deviation from and subversion of Enlightenment principles. **Jürgen Habermas,** born in Cologne, Germany in 1928, a later, second-generation Frankfurt School theorist, does precisely this. Like his predecessors, Habermas writes extensively on the impediments to an engaged and participatory democracy in late capitalism. In particular, in *Legitimation Crisis* (1975), he identifies the economic and social integration crises endemic in society owing to the inability of governments and other actors to resolve the steering problems associated with structural economic problems (e.g., fiscal crises, the collapse of financial risk management practices). Related to this, he identifies depoliticization processes such as the elimination of an economic, class-based activism displaced by the rise of consumer culture and a corporate shareholder society (whereby pension funds and ordinary individuals' economic assets are increasingly invested in and thus reliant on the profit-maximization success of financial, industrial and technological corporations).

Long a proponent of the importance of a vibrant public sphere in which media and other institutions facilitate lively intellectual conversations and political debate (Habermas 1989), Habermas's writings seek to revive the emancipatory potential of reason (as envisioned by Enlightenment thinkers) as a positive force to be used in articulating the common good and pathways toward its realization. He seeks to recover reason from its one-sided deployment as a strategic, instrumental tool used to dominate people and social processes, and instead retrieve its communicative potential to resist the colonization of the lifeworld – by domineering economic, technological, political and cultural actors – and to actively chart a more equal and just society (McCarthy 1984). Habermas thus focuses on reason (and reasonableness) as a means of argumentation. In his two-volume *Theory of Communicative Action* (see excerpt *10b Theory of Communicative Action*), Habermas outlines the necessary steps entailed in communicative action and how the process of assessing competing validity claims can move social actors forward to a cooperative and dynamic consensus that forms the basis for specific action outcomes (and their ongoing assessment and re-assessment) vis-à-vis the common good. Importantly, communication itself, notwithstanding its inherent dialogical value, is not the equivalent of communicative action. Rather, the communicative action process must invariably be oriented to identifying and carrying through on executing a particular action outcome based on the objective and subjective claims articulated and assessed (in an ongoing manner) by the conversation partners. Communicative action entails individuals in dialogue giving sincere and straightforward reasons for, and reasons against, any given claim or counterclaim, and a commitment accordingly to use communicative reason to achieve action outcomes that can chart a path forward in a given situation. In Habermas's ideal speech situation, reason is used to critique the status quo and to move beyond its coercive forces to achieve a more argumentatively consensual and a more participatory, democratic society. In the contemporary context of globalizing capitalist inequality, political polarization, and cultural exclusion (e.g. of immigrants, refugees, asylum seekers), the articulation of an emancipatory agenda based on a revival of Enlightenment ideas of equality, freedom, and solidarity, is clearly complicated by the multilayered strategic interests and power inequalities that characterize late modernity. Strategic interests so nakedly prevail in all kinds of contexts (even in personal relationships) that it is difficult to think of using reason and rationality to work with others to attain a common goal and, relatedly, that we be open to reassessing the goal itself relative to how it advances emancipatory values (e.g. equality of participation) rather than any one party's (strategic) interests. Yet, we must embrace this task if we are to build a better society.

REFERENCES

Habermas, Jürgen. 1975. *Legitimation Crisis*. Boston: Beacon Press.

Habermas, Jürgen. 1989. *The Structural Transformation of the Public Sphere*. Cambridge, MA: MIT Press.

Marcuse, Herbert. 1964. *One-Dimensional Man: Studies in the Ideology of Advanced Industrial Society*. Boston: Beacon Press.

McCarthy, Thomas. 1984. "Translator's Introduction," pp. v–xlii in Jürgen Habermas, *The Theory of Communicative Action*, vol. 1. Boston: Beacon Press.

10A Max Horkheimer and Theodor W. Adorno from *Dialectic of Enlightenment*

Original publication details: Max Horkheimer and Theodor W. Adorno, 1944/1994. *The Dialectic of Enlightenment: Philosophical Fragments*, edited by Gunzelin Schmid Noerr, pp. xi–xv, 121–124, 126–127, 134–135. Redwood City, CA: Stanford University Press. English translation © 2002 by the Board of Trustees of the Leland Stanford Junior University. All rights reserved.

When public opinion has reached a state in which thought inevitably becomes a commodity, and language the means of promoting that commodity, then the attempt to trace the course of such depravation has to deny any allegiance to current linguistic and conceptual conventions, lest their world-historical consequences thwart it entirely.

If it were only a question of the obstacles resulting from the self-oblivious instrumentalization of science, then a critique of social problems could at least attach itself to trends opposed to the accepted scientific mode; yet even these are affected by the total process of production. They have changed no less than the ideology to which they referred. They suffer what triumphant thought has always suffered. If it willingly emerges from its critical element to become a mere means at the disposal of an existing order, then despite itself it tends to convert the positive it elected to defend into something negative and destructive. The philosophy which put the fear of death into infamy in the eighteenth century, despite all the book-burnings and piles of corpses, chose to serve that very infamy under Napoleon. Ultimately, Comte's school of apologetic usurped the succession to the inflexible Encyclopedists, and joined hands with everything that the latter had formerly rejected. The metamorphoses of criticism into affirmation do not leave the theoretical content untouched, for its truth evaporates. Now, of course, a mechanized history outstrips such intellectual developments, and the official apologists – who have other concerns – liquidate the history that helped them to their place in the sun, before it can prostitute itself.

When examining its own guilty conscience, thought has to forgo not only the affirmative use of scientific and everyday conceptual language, but just as much that of the opposition. There is no longer any available form of linguistic expression which has not tended toward accommodation to dominant currents of thought; and what a devalued language does not do automatically is proficiently executed by societal mechanisms. There are analogies in all areas for the censors voluntarily maintained by film companies faced otherwise with the threat of increased overheads. The process which a literary text has to undergo, if not in the anticipatory maneuvers of its author, then certainly in the combined efforts of readers, editors, subeditors and ghost writers in and outside publishing houses, exceeds any censorship in thoroughness. To make its functions wholly superfluous would seem to be the ambition of the educational system, despite all salutary reforms. Believing that without strict limitation to the verification of facts and probability theory, the cognitive spirit would prove all too susceptible to charlatanism and superstition, it makes a parched ground ready and avid for charlatanism and superstition. Just as prohibition has always offered access to the poisonous product, so the obstruction of the theoretical faculty paved the way for political error and madness. And even so far as men have not yet succumbed to political delusion, the mechanisms of censorship – both internal and external – will deprive them of the means of resistance.

The dilemma that faced us in our work proved to be the first phenomenon for investigation: the self-destruction of the Enlightenment. We are wholly convinced – and therein lies our *petitio principii* – that social freedom is inseparable from enlightened thought. Nevertheless, we believe that we have just as clearly recognized that the notion of this very way of thinking, no less than the actual historic forms – the social institutions – with which it is interwoven, already contains the seed of the reversal universally apparent today. If enlightenment does not accommodate reflection on this recidivist element, then it seals its own fate. If consideration of the destructive aspect of progress is left to its enemies, blindly pragmatized thought loses its transcending quality and, its relation to truth. In the enigmatic readiness of the technologically educated masses to fall under the sway of any despotism, in its self-destructive affinity to popular paranoia, and in all uncomprehended absurdity, the weakness of the modern theoretical faculty is apparent.

We believe that these fragments will contribute to the health of that theoretical understanding, insofar as we show that the prime cause of the retreat from enlightenment into mythology is not to be sought so much in the nationalist, pagan and other modern mythologies manufactured precisely in order to contrive such a reversal, but in the Enlightenment itself when paralyzed by fear of the truth. In this respect, both concepts are to be understood not merely as historico-cultural (*geistesgeschichtlich*) but as real. Just as the Enlightenment expresses the actual movement of civil society as a whole in the aspect of its idea as embodied in individuals and institutions, so truth is not merely the rational consciousness but equally the form that consciousness assumes in actual life. The dutiful child of modern civilization is possessed by a fear of departing from the facts which, in the very act of perception, the dominant conventions of science, commerce, and politics – cliché-like – have already molded; his anxiety is none other than the fear of social deviation. The same conventions define the notion of linguistic and conceptual clarity which the art, literature and philosophy of the present have to satisfy. Since that notion declares any negative treatment of the facts or of the dominant forms of thought to be obscurantist formalism or – preferably – alien, and therefore taboo, it condemns the spirit to increasing darkness. It is characteristic of the sickness that even the best-intentioned reformer who uses an impoverished and debased language to recommend renewal, by his adoption of the insidious mode of categorization and the bad philosophy it conceals, strengthens the very power of the established order he is trying to break. False clarity is only another name for myth; and myth has always been obscure and enlightening at one and the same time: always using the devices of familiarity and straightforward dismissal to avoid the labor of conceptualization.

The fallen nature of modern man cannot be separated from social progress. On the one hand the growth of economic productivity furnishes the conditions for a world of greater justice; on the other hand it allows the technical apparatus and the social groups which administer it a disproportionate superiority to the rest of the population. The individual is wholly devalued in relation to the economic powers, which at the same time press the control of society over nature to hitherto unsuspected heights. Even though the individual disappears before the apparatus which he serves, that apparatus provides for him as never before. In an unjust state of life, the impotence and pliability of the masses grow with the quantitative increase in commodities allowed them. The materially respectable and socially deplorable rise in the living standard of the lower classes is reflected in the simulated extension of the spirit. Its true concern is the negation of reification; it cannot survive where it is fixed as a cultural commodity and doled out to satisfy consumer needs. The flood of detailed information and candy-floss entertainment simultaneously instructs and stultifies mankind.

The issue is not that of culture as a value, which is what the critics of civilization, Huxley, Jaspers, Ortega y Gasset and others, have in mind. The point is rather that the Enlightenment *must consider itself*, if men are not to be wholly betrayed. The task to be accomplished is not the conservation of the past, but the redemption of the hopes of the past. Today, however, the past is preserved as the destruction of the past. Whereas a worthwhile education was a privilege until the nineteenth century, and one paid for by the increased suffering of the uneducated, in the twentieth century factory space has been purchased by melting down all cultural values in a gigantic crucible. Perhaps that would not be so high a price as the defenders of culture suppose, if the selling-out of culture did not contribute to the conversion of economic triumphs into their opposite.

Under existing conditions the gifts of fortune themselves become elements of misfortune. Their quantity, in default of a social subject, operated during the internal economic crises of times past as so-called "surplus production"; today, because of the enthronement of power-groups as that social subject, it produces the international threat of Fascism: progress becomes regression.

[. . .]

Interested parties explain the culture industry in technological terms. It is alleged that because millions participate in it, certain reproduction processes are necessary that inevitably require identical needs in innumerable places to be satisfied with identical goods. The technical contrast between the few production centers and the large number of widely dispersed consumption points is said to demand organization and planning by management. Furthermore, it is claimed that standards were based in the first place on consumers' needs, and for that reason were accepted with so little resistance. The result is the circle of manipulation and retroactive need in which the unity of the system grows ever stronger. No mention is made of the fact that the basis on which technology acquires power over society is the power of those whose economic hold over society is greatest. A technological rationale is the rationale of domination itself. It is the coercive nature of society alienated from itself. Automobiles, bombs, and movies keep the whole thing together until their leveling element shows its strength in the very wrong which it furthered. It has made the technology of the culture industry no more than the achievement of standardization and mass production, sacrificing whatever involved a distinction between the logic of the work and that of the social system. This is the result not of a law of movement in technology as such but of its function in today's economy. The need which might resist central control has already been suppressed by the control of the individual consciousness. The step from the telephone to the radio has clearly distinguished the roles. The former still allowed the subscriber to play the role of subject, and was liberal. The latter is democratic: it turns all participants into listeners and authoritatively subjects them to broadcast programs which are all exactly the same. No machinery of rejoinder has been devised, and private broadcasters are denied any freedom. They are confined to the apocryphal field of the "amateur," and also have to accept organization from above. But any trace of spontaneity from the public in official broadcasting is controlled and absorbed by talent scouts, studio competitions and official programs of every kind selected by professionals. Talented performers belong to the industry long before it displays them; otherwise they would not be so eager to fit in. The attitude of the public, which ostensibly and actually favors the system of the culture industry, is a part of the system and not an excuse for it. If one branch of art follows the same formula as one with a very different medium and content; if the dramatic intrigue of broadcast soap operas becomes no more than useful material for showing how to master technical problems at both ends of the scale of musical experience – real jazz or a cheap imitation; or if a movement from a Beethoven symphony is crudely "adapted" for a film sound-track in the same way as a Tolstoy novel is garbled in a film script: then the claim that this is done to satisfy the spontaneous wishes of the public is no more than hot air. We are closer to the facts if we explain these phenomena as inherent in the technical and personnel apparatus which, down to its last cog, itself forms part of the economic mechanism of selection. In addition there is the agreement – or at least the determination – of all executive authorities not to produce or sanction anything that in any way differs from their own rules, their own ideas about consumers, or above all themselves.

In our age the objective social tendency is incarnate in the hidden subjective purposes of company directors, the foremost among whom are in the most powerful sectors of industry – steel, petroleum, electricity, and chemicals. Culture monopolies are weak and dependent in comparison. They cannot afford to neglect their appeasement of the real holders of power if their sphere of activity in mass society (a sphere producing a specific type of commodity which anyhow is still too closely bound up with easygoing liberalism and Jewish intellectuals) is not to undergo a series of purges. The dependence of the most powerful broadcasting company on the electrical industry, or of the motion picture industry on the banks, is characteristic of the whole sphere, whose individual branches are themselves economically interwoven. All are in such close contact that the extreme concentration of mental forces allows demarcation lines between different firms and technical branches to be ignored. The ruthless unity in the culture industry is evidence of what will happen in politics. Marked differentiations such as those of A and B films, or of stories in magazines in different price ranges, depend not so much on subject matter as on classifying, organizing, and labeling consumers. Something is provided for all so that none may escape; the distinctions are emphasized and extended. The public is catered for with a hierarchical range of mass-produced products of varying quality, thus advancing the rule of complete quantification. Everybody must behave (as if spontaneously) in accordance with his previously determined and indexed level, and choose the category of mass product turned out for his type. Consumers appear as statistics on research organization charts, and are divided by income groups into red, green, and blue areas; the technique is that used for any type of propaganda.

How formalized the procedure is can be seen when the mechanically differentiated products prove to be all alike in the end. That the difference between the Chrysler range and General Motors products is basically illusory strikes every child with a keen interest in varieties. What connoisseurs discuss as good or bad points serve only to perpetuate the semblance of competition and range of choice. The same applies to the Warner Brothers and Metro Goldwyn Mayer productions. But even the differences between the more expensive and cheaper models put out by the same firm steadily diminish: for automobiles, there are such differences as the number of cylinders, cubic capacity, details of patented gadgets; and for films there are the number of stars, the extravagant use of technology, labor, and equipment, and the introduction of the latest psychological formulas. The universal criterion of merit is the amount of "conspicuous production," of blatant cash investment. The varying budgets in the culture industry do not bear the slightest relation to factual values, to the meaning of the products themselves. Even the technical media are relentlessly forced into uniformity. Television aims at a synthesis of radio and film, and is held up only because the interested parties have not yet reached agreement, but its consequences will be quite enormous and promise to intensify the impoverishment of aesthetic matter so drastically, that by tomorrow the thinly veiled identity of all industrial culture products can come triumphantly out into the open, derisively fulfilling the Wagnerian dream of the *Gesamtkunstwerk* – the fusion of all the arts in one work. The alliance of word, image, and music is all the more perfect than in *Tristan* because the sensuous elements which all approvingly reflect the surface of social reality are in principle embodied in the same technical process, the unity of which becomes its distinctive content. This process integrates all the elements of the production, from the novel (shaped with an eye to the film) to the last sound effect. It is the triumph of invested capital, whose title as absolute master is etched deep into the hearts of the dispossessed in the employment line; it is the meaningful content of every film, whatever plot the production team may have selected.

[...]

Real life is becoming indistinguishable from the movies. The sound film, far surpassing the theater of illusion, leaves no room for imagination or reflection on the part of the audience, who is unable to respond within the structure of the film, yet deviate from its precise detail without losing the thread of the story; hence the film forces its victims to equate it directly with reality. The stunting of the mass-media consumer's powers of imagination and spontaneity does not have to be traced back to any psychological mechanisms; he must ascribe the loss of those attributes to the objective nature of the products themselves, especially to the most characteristic of them, the sound film. They are so designed that quickness, powers of observation, and experience are undeniably needed to apprehend them at all; yet sustained thought is out of the question if the spectator is not to miss the relentless rush of facts. Even though the effort required for his response is semi-automatic, no scope is left for the imagination. Those who are so absorbed by the world of the movie – by its images, gestures, and words – that they are unable to supply what really makes it a world, do not have to dwell on particular points of its mechanics during a screening. All the other films and products of the entertainment industry which they have seen have taught them what to expect; they react automatically. The might of industrial society is lodged in men's minds. The entertainments manufacturers know that their products will be consumed with alertness even when the customer is distraught, for each of them is a model of the huge economic machinery which has always sustained the masses, whether at work or at leisure – which is akin to work. From every sound film and every broadcast program the social effect can be inferred which is exclusive to none but is shared by all alike. The culture industry as a whole has molded men as a type unfailingly reproduced in every product. All the agents of this process, from the producer to the women's clubs, take good care that the simple reproduction of this mental state is not nuanced or extended in any way.

[...]

The industry submits to the vote which it has itself inspired. What is a loss for the firm which cannot fully exploit a contract with a declining star is a legitimate expense for the system as a whole. By craftily sanctioning the demand for rubbish it inaugurates total harmony. The connoisseur and the expert are despised for their pretentious claim to know better than the others, even though culture is democratic and distributes its privileges to all. In view of the ideological truce, the conformism of the buyers and the effrontery of the producers who supply them prevail. The result is a constant reproduction of the same thing.

A constant sameness governs the relationship to the past as well. What is new about the phase of mass culture compared with the late liberal stage is the exclusion of the new. The machine rotates on the same spot. While determining consumption it excludes the untried as a risk. The movie-makers distrust any manuscript which is not reassuringly backed by a bestseller. Yet for this very reason there is never-ending talk of ideas, novelty, and surprise, of what is taken for granted but has never existed. Tempo and dynamics serve this trend. Nothing remains as of old; everything has to run incessantly, to keep moving. For only the universal triumph of the rhythm of mechanical production and reproduction promises that nothing changes, and nothing unsuitable will appear. Any additions to the well-proven culture inventory are too much of a speculation. The ossified forms – such as the sketch, short story, problem film, or hit song – are the standardized average of late liberal taste, dictated with threats from above. The people at the top in the culture agencies, who work in harmony as only one manager can with another, whether he comes from the rag trade or from college, have long since reorganized and rationalized the objective spirit. One might think that an omnipresent authority had sifted the material and drawn up an official catalog of cultural commodities to provide a smooth supply of available mass-produced lines.

10B Jürgen Habermas from *The Theory of Communicative Action: Reason and the Rationalization of Society*

Original publication details: Jürgen Habermas, 1984. *The Theory of Communicative Action*, Vol. 1, pp. 94–96, 98–101. Boston: Beacon Press. Reproduced with permission of Beacon Press and Polity Press Ltd.

With the concept of communicative action there comes into play the additional presupposition of a *linguistic medium* that reflects the actor's relations to the world as such. At this level of concept formation the rationality problematic, which until now has arisen only for the social scientist, moves into the perspective of the agent himself. We have to make clear in what sense achieving understanding in language is thereby introduced as a mechanism for coordinating action. Even the strategic model of action *can* be understood in such a way that participants' actions, directed through egocentric calculations of utility and coordinated through interest situations, are mediated through speech acts. In the cases of normatively regulated and dramaturgical action we even *have to* suppose a consensus formation among participants that is in principle of a linguistic nature. Nevertheless, in these three models of action language is conceived *one-sidedly* in different respects.

The teleological model of action takes language as one of several media through which speakers oriented to their own success can influence one another in order to bring opponents to form or to grasp beliefs and intentions that are in the speakers' own interest. This concept of language – developed from the limit case of indirect communication aimed at *getting* someone to form a belief, an intention, or the like – is, for instance, basic to intentionalist semantics. The normative model of action presupposes language as a medium that transmits cultural values and carries a consensus that is merely reproduced with each additional act of understanding. This culturalist concept of language is widespread in cultural anthropology and content-oriented linguistics.[1] The dramaturgical model of action presupposes language as a medium of self-presentation; the cognitive significance of the propositional components and the interpersonal significance of the illocutionary components are thereby played down in favor of the expressive functions of speech acts. Language is assimilated to stylistic and aesthetic forms of expression.[2] Only the communicative model of action presupposes language as a medium of uncurtailed communication whereby speakers and hearers, out of the context of their preinterpreted lifeworld, refer simultaneously to things in the objective, social, and subjective worlds in order to negotiate common definitions of the situation. This interpretive concept of language lies behind the various efforts to develop a formal prgamatics.[3]

The one-sidedness of the first three concepts of language can be seen in the fact that the corresponding types of communication singled out by them prove to be limit cases of communicative action: *first*, the indirect communication of those who have only the realization of their own ends in view; *second*, the consensual action of those who simply actualize an already existing normative agreement; and *third*, presentation of self in relation to an audience. In each case only one function of language is thematized: the release of perlocutionary effects, the establishment of interpersonal relations, and the expression of subjective experiences. By contrast, the communicative model of action, which defines the traditions of social science connected with Mead's symbolic interactionism, Wittgenstein's concept of language games, Austin's theory of speech acts, and Gadamer's hermeneutics, takes all the functions of language equally into consideration. As can be seen in the ethnomethodological and hermeneutic approaches, there is a danger here of reducing social *action* to the interpretive accomplishments of participants in communication, of assimilating action to speech, interaction to conversation. In the present context I can introduce this concept of communicative action only in a provisional way.

[. . .]

For the communicative model of action, language is relevant only from the pragmatic viewpoint that speakers, in employing sentences with an orientation to reaching understanding, take up relations to the world, not only directly as in teleological, normatively regulated or dramaturgical action, but in a reflective way. Speakers integrate the three formal world-concepts, which appear in the other models of action either singly or in pairs, into a system and presuppose this system in common as a framework of interpretation within which they can reach an understanding. They no longer relate *straightaway* to something in the objective, social, or subjective worlds; instead they relativize their utterances against the possibility that their validity will be contested by other actors. Reaching an understanding functions as a mechanism for coordinating actions only through the participants in interaction coming to an agreement concerning the claimed *validity* of their utterances, that is, through intersubjectively recognizing the *validity claims* they reciprocally raise. A speaker puts forward a criticizable claim in relating with his utterance to at least one "world"; he thereby uses the fact that this relation between actor and world is in principle open to objective appraisal in order to call upon his opposite number to take a rationally motivated position. The concept of communicative action presupposes language as the medium for a kind of reaching understanding, in the course of which participants, through relating to a world, reciprocally raise validity claims that can be accepted or contested.

With this model of action we are supposing that participants in interaction can now mobilize the rationality potential – which according to our previous analysis resides in the actor's three relations to the world – expressly for the cooperatively pursued goal of reaching understanding. If we leave to one side the well-formedness of the symbolic expressions employed, an actor who is oriented to understanding in this sense must raise at least three validity claims with his utterance, namely:

1   That the statement made is true (or that the existential presuppositions of the propositional content mentioned are in fact satisfied);
2   That the speech act is right with respect to the existing normative context (or that the normative context that it is supposed to satisfy is itself legitimate); and
3   That the manifest intention of the speaker is meant as it is expressed.

Thus the speaker claims truth for statements or existential presuppositions, rightness for legitimately regulated actions and their normative context, and truthfulness or sincerity for the manifestation of subjective experiences. We can easily recognize therein the three relations of actor to world presupposed *by the social scientist* in the previously analyzed concepts of action; but in the concept of communicative action they are ascribed to the perspective of *the speakers and hearers themselves*. It is the actors themselves who seek consensus and measure it against truth, rightness, and sincerity, that is, against the "fit" or "misfit" between the speech act, on the one hand, and the three worlds to which the actor takes up relations with his utterance, on the other. Such relations hold between an utterance and;

1   The objective world (as the totality of all entities about which true statements are possible);
2   The social world (as the totality of all legitimately regulated interpersonal relations);
3   The subjective world (as the totality of the experiences of the speaker to which he has privileged access).

Every process of reaching understanding takes place against the background of a culturally ingrained preunderstanding. This background knowledge remains unproblematic as a whole; only that part of the stock of knowledge that participants make use of and thematize at a given time is put to the test. To the extent that definitions of situations are negotiated by participants *themselves*, this thematic segment of the lifeworld is at their disposal with the negotiation of each new definition of the situation.

A definition of the situation establishes an order. Through it, participants in communication assign the various elements of an action situation to one of the three worlds and thereby incorporate the actual action situation into their preinterpreted lifeworld. A definition of the situation by another party that prima facie diverges from one's own presents a problem of a peculiar sort; for in cooperative processes of interpretation no participant has a monopoly on correct interpretation. For both parties the interpretive task consists in incorporating the other's interpretation of the situation into one's own in such a way that in the revised version "his" external world and "my" external world can – against the background of "our" lifeworld – be relativized in relation to "the" world, and the divergent situation definitions can be brought to coincide sufficiently. Naturally this does not mean that interpretation must lead in every case to a stable and unambiguously differentiated assignment. Stability and absence of ambiguity are rather the exception in the communicative practice of everyday life. A more realistic picture is that drawn by ethnomethodologists – of a diffuse, fragile, continuously revised and only momentarily successful communication in which participants rely on problematic and unclarified presuppositions and feel their way from one occasional commonality to the next.

To avoid misunderstanding I would like to repeat that the communicative model of action does not equate action with communication. Language is a medium of communication that serves understanding, whereas actors, in coming to an understanding with one another so as to coordinate their actions, pursue their particular aims. In this respect the teleological structure is fundamental to *all* concepts of action.[4] Concepts of *social action* are distinguished, however, according to how they specify the *coordination* among the goal-directed actions of different participants: as the interlacing of egocentric calculations of utility (whereby the degree of conflict and cooperation varies with the given interest positions): as a socially integrating agreement about values and norms instilled through cultural tradition and socialization; as a consensual relation between players and their publics; or as reaching understanding in the sense of a cooperative process of interpretation. In all cases the teleological structure of action is presupposed, inasmuch as the capacity for goal-setting and goal-directed action is ascribed to actors, as well as an interest in carrying out their plans of action. But only the strategic model of action *rests content* with an explication of the features of action oriented directly to success; whereas the other models of action specify conditions under which the actor pursues his goals – conditions of legitimacy, of self-presentation, or of agreement arrived at in communication, under which alter can "link up" his actions with those of ego. In the case of communicative action the interpretive accomplishments on which cooperative processes of interpretation are based represent the mechanism for *coordinating* action; communicative action is *not exhausted* by the act of reaching understanding in an interpretive manner. If we take as our unit of analysis a simple speech act carried out by S, to which at least one participant in interaction can take up a "yes" or "no" position, we can clarify the conditions for the communicative coordination of action by stating what it means for a hearer to understand what is said. But communicative action designates a type of interaction that is *coordinated through* speech acts and does *not coincide with* them.

NOTES

1   Benjamin Lee Whorf, *Language, Thought and Reality* (Cambridge, Mass., 1956); H Gipper. *Gibt es ein sprachliches Relalivilälsprinzip?* (Frankfurt, 1972); P. Henle, ed., *Sprache, Denken, Kultur* (Frankfurt, 1969).

2   Harré and Secord. *Explanation of Behavior,* pp. 215ff.; *see* especially Charles Taylor. *Language and Human Nature* (Carleton, Montreal, 1978).

3   F. Schütze, *Sprache,* 2 vols. (Munich. 1975).

4   R. Bubner, *Handlung, Sprache und Vernunft,* pp. 168ff.

CHAPTER ELEVEN

PIERRE BOURDIEU

CHAPTER MENU

Pierre Bourdieu (1930–2002) is the dominant French sociological theorist of the post-World War II era. A trained ethnographer who did his PhD dissertation research on everyday culture and social relations among the Kabylia in Algeria, he maintained a keen eye for everyday cultural nuances and strong appreciation for empirical data across his career. Bourdieu is primarily regarded as a theorist of social stratification and inequality, though the breadth of the subjects he addresses in his writings means that there is much conceptual richness in, and many angles of entry to, his body of work regardless of one's specialization or subfield. The excerpts included here capture the core of Bourdieu's theory. Bourdieu's overarching interest is in the reproduction of inequality; in other words, what institutional mechanisms and everyday habits and practices make it possible for inequality to be actively produced and sustained across generations and across various aspects of everyday life even as economic and status mobility, both upward and downward, are available and relatively accessible pathways

Concise Reader in Sociological Theory: Theorists, Concepts, and Current Applications,
First Edition. Edited by Michele Dillon. Editorial material and organization
© 2021 John Wiley & Sons Ltd. Published 2021 by John Wiley & Sons Ltd.

(e.g. through education) to any given individual. The notion of capital is key for Bourdieu and, influenced by Weber, he identifies and differentiates among multiple forms of capital (see excerpt, *11a The Forms of Capital*). Specifically, he distinguishes between economic capital, cultural capital, and social capital and elaborates on how each of these discrete types of capital are at once objective, stratifying forces and subjectively apprehended and used by individuals and groups in the execution of daily life across its multiple institutional fields or sectors: in schools and universities, at work, in art, in the family, at church.

Bourdieu argues that all forms of capital can be acquired (though at any given time their volume can vary), that they take time to accumulate, that they are relatively durable and also relatively enduring in their impact, and that they need to be actively and purposefully used, that is, exchanged for other forms of capital. For example, wealthy individuals can use their (high volume) economic capital to pay for a prestigious education for their children (thus enhancing their children's cultural capital) or to buy a culturally coveted piece of art that their friends and business partners can admire and by extension thus enhance their symbolic capital (their reputation). Similarly, someone with low economic capital can actively use their social capital, particularly if their friendship network includes an individual or two with high economic capital, to access a competitive internship or to meet other economically privileged friends the results of which in turn might open up new economic, social and cultural opportunities for them. The use and exchange of capital is an agential and dynamic process; individuals and social classes and class fractions actively use (and must use) their varying forms of capital across a range of settings; moreover, the volume of the different forms of capital at play in any one-to-one or class fraction-to-class fraction social relation can vary in all sorts of multiple combinations. (Someone with high economic capital may have little cultural capital; someone with a lot of cultural capital may have low economic and /or social capital.)

Yet, notwithstanding the multiple flows across and among the varying types and amounts of capital, Bourdieu argues that the outcomes are more likely to reproduce existing economic, cultural, and social hierarchies and attendant inequalities than to create a more equal distribution of capital. This is largely because hierarchical distinctions, are not only structurally determining, but additionally, are embodied, literally, in individuals. All of us as individuals acquire and embody habits, practices, and dispositions (what Bourdieu calls the habitus) that in our everyday choices and decisions make us active carriers of the social class, gender and other hierarchical distinctions that are inscribed into us through our socialization in a particular social class and gendered family context (see excerpt *11b Distinction: A Social Critique of the Judgement of Taste*). And these inscribed experiences, reproduced through natural habits of practice on a regular basis, predispose us to behave in certain ways, and these habits and predispositions endure even as our social setting and our social class location might change. As Bourdieu (1984: 6) notes, "We distinguish ourselves by the distinctions we make." And many of the everyday distinctions we make – for example, what type of food we choose to eat, how much, and how we eat it, and where we sit at the table and how we set the table; or the kinds of music we like – are based on judgments of taste – or more accurately, deeply inculturated embodied experiences that make some choices, some tastes and some smells and some art and some music much more palatable to us than others (even when we may have acquired the economic capital to act on more expensive tastes).

Bourdieu's illumination of the multiplicity of tastes and preferences may convey that taste is a very democratic thing: different people, and different genders and different class factions simply like different things. The rub, however, is that different habits and subjective tastes are symbolically coded and as such objectively reflect and reproduce the objective hierarchy of inequality that rewards certain habits and tastes more highly than others. There is, for example, a gender habitus that women and men through their everyday tastes and everyday habits subjectively reproduce and in the process reinforce the objective gender hierarchy in which men receive more rewards than women (literally, bigger helpings of food!). And there is a differentiated class habitus that in objective social space (contemporary society) differentially allocates rewards to the occupants of the respective classes and class fractions. Because we embody habits that are grounded in inscribed everyday differences and practices of inequality, this means that some individuals and groups have a better "feel for the game" than others (Bourdieu 1984: 54). In a stratified society, moreover all games are competitive, with winners and losers. Those who play a game best are usually those who have a playful seriousness, a disposition habituated from their immersion in the culture of the game over a long time, and who can feign and afford to feign indifference over whether they win or lose. They know what works and don't need to worry about what works. This Bourdieusian insight about the enduring significance of cultural dispositions underpins college initiatives that seek to make first-generation students (those whose parents did not go to college) acclimate to the game of college. Specially designed programs help First Gen students learn to navigate not only the formal curriculum but, equally important, to understand the hidden curriculum, the formal and informal ways to interact with faculty, as well as how to engage with other students whether in the classroom, the dorm, or the dining halls, etc.

REFERENCE

Bourdieu, Pierre. 1984. *Distinction: A Social Critique of the Judgment of Taste*. Cambridge, MA: Harvard University Press.

11A Pierre Bourdieu from *The Forms of Capital*

Original publication details: Pierre Bourdieu, 1986. "The Forms of Capital," pp. 242–243, 245, 249–250 in *Handbook of Theory and Research for the Sociology of Education*, edited by John Richardson. New York: Greenwood Press. Reproduced with permission of ABC-CLIO, Inc.

Economic theory has allowed to be foisted upon it a definition of the economy of practices which is the historical invention of capitalism; and by reducing the universe of exchanges to mercantile exchange, which is objectively and subjectively oriented toward the maximization of profit, i.e., (economically) *self-interested*, it has implicitly defined the other forms of exchange as noneconomic, and therefore *disinterested*. In particular, it defines as disinterested those forms of exchange which ensure the *transubstantiation* whereby the most material types of capital – those which are economic in the restricted sense – can present themselves in the immaterial form of cultural capital or social capital and vice versa. Interest, in the restricted sense it is given in economic theory, cannot be produced without producing its negative counterpart, disinterestedness. The class of practices whose explicit purpose is to maximize monetary profit cannot be defined as such without producing the purposeless finality of cultural or artistic practices and their products; the world of bourgeois man, with his double-entry accounting, cannot be invented without producing the pure, perfect universe of the artist and the intellectual and the gratuitous activities of art-for-art's sake and pure theory. In other words, the constitution of a science of mercantile relationships which, inasmuch as it takes for granted the very foundations of the order it claims to analyze – private property, profit, wage labor, etc. – is not even a science of the field of economic production, has prevented the constitution of a general science of the economy of practices, which would treat mercantile exchange as a particular case of exchange in all its forms.

It is remarkable that the practices and assets thus salvaged from the "icy water of egotistical calculation" (and from science) are the virtual monopoly of the dominant class – as if economism had been able to reduce everything to economics only because the reduction on which that discipline is based protects from sacrilegious reduction everything which needs to be protected. If economics deals only with practices that have narrowly economic interest as their principle and only with goods that are directly and immediately convertible into money (which makes them quantifiable), then the universe of bourgeois production and exchange becomes an exception and can see itself and present itself as a realm of disinterestedness. As everyone knows, priceless things have their price, and the extreme difficulty of converting certain practices and certain objects into money is only due to the fact that this conversion is refused in the very intention that produces them, which is nothing other than the denial (*Verneinung*) of the economy. A general science of the economy of practices, capable of reappropriating the totality of the practices which, although objectively economic, are not and cannot be socially recognized as economic, and which can be performed only at the cost of a whole labor of dissimulation or, more precisely, *euphemization*, must endeavor to grasp capital and profit in all their forms and to establish the laws whereby the different types of capital (or power, which amounts to the same thing) change into one another.[1]

Depending on the field in which it functions, and at the cost of the more or less expensive transformations which are the precondition for its efficacy in the field in question, capital can present itself in three fundamental guises: as *economic capital*, which is immediately and directly convertible into money and may be institutionalized in the form of property rights; as *cultural capital*, which is convertible, on certain conditions, into economic capital and may be institutionalized in the form of educational qualifications; and as *social capital*, made up of social obligations ("connections"), which is convertible, in certain conditions, into economic capital and may be institutionalized in the form of a title of nobility.[2]

Cultural Capital

Cultural capital can exist in three forms: in the *embodied* state, i.e., in the form of long-lasting dispositions of the mind and body; in the *objectified* state, in the form of cultural goods (pictures, books, dictionaries, instruments, machines, etc.), which are the trace or realization of theories or critiques of these theories, problematics, etc.; and in the *institutionalized* state, a form of objectification which must be set apart because, as will be seen in the case of educational qualifications, it confers entirely original properties on the cultural capital which it is presumed to guarantee.

[. . .]

Cultural capital can be acquired, to a varying extent, depending on the period, the society, and the social class, in the absence of any deliberate inculcation, and therefore quite unconsciously. It always remains marked by its earliest conditions of acquisition which, through the more or less visible marks they leave (such as the pronunciations characteristic of a class or region), help to determine its distinctive value. It cannot be accumulated beyond the appropriating capacities of an individual agent; it declines and dies with its bearer (with his biological capacity, his memory, etc.). Because it is thus linked in numerous ways to the person in his biological singularity and is subject to a hereditary transmission which is always heavily disguised, or even invisible, it defies the old, deep-rooted distinction the Greek jurists made between inherited properties (*ta patroa*) and acquired properties (*epikteta*), i.e., those which an individual adds to his heritage. It thus manages to combine the prestige of innate property with the merits of acquisition. Because the social conditions of its transmission and acquisition are more disguised than those of economic capital, it is predisposed to function as symbolic capital, i.e., to be unrecognized as capital and recognized as legitimate competence, as authority exerting an effect of (mis)recognition, e.g., in the matrimonial market and in all the markets in which economic capital is not fully recognized, whether in matters of culture, with the great art collections or great cultural foundations, or in social welfare, with the economy of generosity and the gift. Furthermore, the specifically symbolic logic of distinction additionally secures material and symbolic profits for the possessors of a large cultural capital: any given cultural competence (e.g., being able to read in a world of illiterates) derives a scarcity value from its position in the distribution of cultural capital and yields profits of distinction for its owner. In other words, the share in profits which scarce cultural capital secures in class-divided societies is based, in the last analysis, on the fact that all agents do not have the economic and cultural means for prolonging their children's education beyond the minimum necessary for the reproduction of the labor-power least valorized at a given moment.[3]

[. . .]

Social Capital

Social capital is the aggregate of the actual or potential resources which are linked to possession of a durable network of more or less institutionalized relationships of mutual acquaintance and recognition – or in other words, to membership in a group[4] – which provides each of its members with the backing of the collectivity-owned capital, a "credential" which entitles them to credit, in the various senses of the word. These relationships may exist only in the practical state, in material and/or symbolic exchanges which help to maintain them. They may also be socially instituted and guaranteed by the application of a common name (the name of a family, a class, or a tribe or of a school, a party, etc.) and by a whole set of instituting acts designed simultaneously to form and inform those who undergo them; in this case, they are more or less really enacted and so maintained and reinforced, in exchanges. Being based on indissolubly material and symbolic exchanges, the establishment and maintenance of which presuppose reacknowledgment of proximity, they are also partially irreducible to objective relations of proximity in physical (geographical) space or even in economic and social space.[5]

The volume of the social capital possessed by a given agent thus depends on the size of the network of connections he can effectively mobilize and on the volume of the capital (economic, cultural or symbolic) possessed in his own right by each of those to whom he is connected.[6] This means that, although it is relatively irreducible to the economic and cultural capital possessed by a given agent, or even by the whole set of agents to whom he is connected, social capital is never completely independent of it because the exchanges instituting mutual acknowledgment presuppose the reacknowledgment of a minimum of objective homogeneity, and because it exerts a multiplier effect on the capital he possesses in his own right.

The profits which accrue from membership in a group are the basis of the solidarity which makes them possible.[7] This does not mean that they are consciously pursued as such, even in the case of groups like select clubs, which are deliberately organized in order to concentrate social capital and so to derive full benefit from the multiplier effect implied in concentration and to secure the profits of membership – material profits, such as all the types of services accruing from useful relationships, and symbolic profits, such as those derived from association with a rare, prestigious group.

The existence of a network of connections is not a natural given, or even a social given, constituted once and for all by an initial act of institution, represented, in the case of the family group, by the genealogical definition of kinship relations, which is the characteristic of a social formation. It is the product of an endless effort at institution, of which institution rites – often wrongly described as rites of passage – mark the essential moments and which is necessary in order to produce and reproduce lasting, useful relationships that can secure material or symbolic profits (see Bourdieu 1982). In other words, the network of relationships is the product of investment strategies, individual or collective, consciously or unconsciously aimed at establishing or reproducing social relationships that are directly usable in the short or long term, i.e., at transforming contingent relations, such as those of neighborhood, the workplace, or even kinship, into relationships that are at once necessary and elective, implying durable obligations subjectively felt (feelings of gratitude, respect, friendship, etc.) or institutionally guaranteed (rights).

NOTES

1 This is true of all exchanges between members of different fractions of the dominant class, possessing different types of capital These range from sales of expertise, treatment, or other services which take the form of gift exchange and dignify themselves with the most decorous names that can be found (honoraria, emoluments, etc.) to matrimonial exchanges, the prime example of a transaction that can only take place insofar as it is not perceived or defined as such by the contracting parties. It is remarkable that the apparent extensions of economic theory beyond the limits constituting, the discipline have left intact the asylum of the sacred, apart from a few sacrilegious incursions. Gary S. Becker, for example, who was one of the first to take explicit account of the types of capital that are usually ignored, never considers anything other than monetary costs and profits, forgetting the nonmonetary investments (*inter alia,* the affective ones) and the material and symbolic profits that education provides in a deferred, indirect way, such as the added value which the dispositions produced or reinforced by schooling (bodily or verbal manners, tastes, etc.) or the relationships established with fellow students can yield in live matrimonial market (Becker 1964a).

2 *Symbolic capital,* that is to say, capital – in whatever form – insofar as it is represented. i.e., apprehended symbolically, in a relationship of knowledge or, more precisely, of misrecognition and recognition, presupposes the intervention of the habitus, as a socially constituted cognitive capacity.

3 In a relatively undifferentiated society, in which access to the means of appropriating the cultural heritage is very equally distributed, embodied culture does not function as cultural capital, i.e., as a means of acquiring exclusive advantages.

4 Here, too, the notion of cultural capital did not spring from pure theoretical work, still less from an analogical extension of economic concepts. It arose from the need to identify the principle of social effects which, although they can be seen clearly at the level of singular agents – where statistical inquiry inevitably operates – cannot be reduced to the set of properties individually possessed by a given agent. These effects, in which spontaneous sociology readily perceives the work of "connections," are particularly visible in all cases in which different individuals obtain very unequal profits from virtually equivalent (economic or cultural) capital, depending on the extent to which they can mobilize by proxy the capital of a group (a family, the alumni of an elite school, a select club, the aristocracy, etc.) that is more or less constituted as such and more or less rich in capital.

5 Neighborhood relationships may of course, receive an elementary form of institutionalization, as in the Beam – or the Basque region – where neighbors, *lous besis* (a word which, in old texts, is applied to the legitimate inhabitants of the village, the rightful members of the assembly), are explicitly designated, in accordance with fairly codified rules, and are assigned functions which are differentiated according to their rank (there is a "first neighbor," a "second neighbor," and so on), particularly for the major social ceremonies (funerals, marriages, etc.). But even in this case, the relationships actually used by no means always coincide with the relationships socially instituted.

6 Manners (bearing pronunciation, etc.) may be included in social capital insofar us, through the mode of acquisition they point to, they indicate initial membership of a more or less prestigious group.

7   National liberation movements or nationalist ideologies cannot be accounted for solely by reference to strictly economic profits, i.e., anticipation of the profits which may be derived from redistribution of a proportion of wealth to the advantage of the nationals nationalization) and the recovery of highly paid jobs . . . To these specifically economic antici-pated profits, which would only explain the nationalism of the privileged classes, must be added the very real and very immediate profits derived from membership (social capital) which are proportionately greater for those who are lower town the social hierarchy ("poor whites") or, more precisely, more threatened by economic and social decline.

REFERENCE

Pierre Bourdieu. 1982. "Les rites d'institution." *Actes de la recherché en sciences sociales* 43: 58–63.

11B Pierre Bourdieu from *Distinction: A Social Critique of the Judgement of Taste*

Original publication details: Pierre Bourdieu, 1984. *Distinction: A Social Critique of the Judgment of Taste,* translated by Richard Nice, pp. 56–58, 101–102, 169–172, 190–196. Cambridge, Mass.: Harvard University Press. © 1984 by the President and Fellows of Harvard College and Routledge and Kegan Paul, Ltd.

THE AESTHETIC SENSE AS THE SENSE OF DISTINCTION   Thus, the aesthetic disposition is one dimension of a distant, self-assured relation to the world and to others which presupposes objective assurance and distance. It is one manifestation of the system of dispositions produced by the social conditionings associated with a particular class of conditions of existence when they take the paradoxical form of the greatest freedom conceivable, at a given moment, with respect to the constraints of economic necessity. But it is also a distinctive expression of a privileged position in social space whose distinctive value is objectively established in its relationship to expressions generated from different conditions. Like every sort of taste, it unites and separates. Being the product of the conditionings associated with a particular class of conditions of existence, it unites all those who are the product of similar conditions while distinguishing them from all others. And it distinguishes in an essential way, since taste is the basis of all that one has – people and things – and all that one is for others, whereby one classifies oneself and is classified by others.

Tastes (i.e., manifested preferences) are the practical affirmation of an inevitable difference. It is no accident that, when they have to be justified, they are asserted purely negatively, by the refusal of other tastes.[1] In matters of taste, more than anywhere else, all determination is negation;[2] and tastes are perhaps first and foremost distastes, disgust provoked by horror or visceral intolerance ('sick-making') of the tastes of others. 'De gustibus non est disputandum': not because 'tous les goûts sont dans la nature', but because each taste feels itself to be natural – and so it almost is, being a habitus – which amounts to rejecting others as unnatural and therefore vicious. Aesthetic intolerance can be terribly violent. Aversion to different life-styles is perhaps one of the strongest barriers between the classes; class endogamy is evidence of this. The most intolerable thing for sacrilegious reuniting of tastes which taste dictates shall be separated. This means that the games of artists and aesthetes and their struggles for the monopoly of artistic legitimacy are less innocent than they seem. At stake in every struggle over art there is also the imposition of an art of living, that is, the transmutation of an arbitrary way of living into the legitimate way of life which casts every other way of living into arbitrariness.[3] The artist's life-style is always a challenge thrown at the bourgeois life-style, which it seeks to condemn as unreal and even absurd, by a sort of practical demonstration of the emptiness of the values and powers it pursues. The neutralizing relation to the world which defines the aesthetic disposition potentially implies a subversion of the spirit of seriousness required by bourgeois investments. Like the visibly ethical judgements of those who lack the means to make art the basis of their art of living, to see the world and other people through literary reminiscences and pictorial references, the 'pure' and purely aesthetic judgements of the artist and the aesthete spring from the dispositions of an ethos;[4] but because of the legitimacy which they command so long as their relationship to the dispositions and interests of a group defined by strong cultural capital and weak economic capital remains unrecognized, they provide a sort of absolute reference point in the necessarily endless play of mutually self-relativizing tastes. By a paradoxical reversal, they thereby help to legitimate the bourgeois claim to 'natural distinction' as difference made absolute.

Objectively and subjectively aesthetic stances adopted in matters like cosmetics, clothing or home decoration are opportunities to experience or assert one's position in social space, as a rank to be upheld or a distance to be kept. It goes without saying that the social classes are not equally inclined and prepared to enter this game of refusal and counter-refusal; and that the strategies aimed at transforming the basic dispositions of a life-style into a system of aesthetic principles, objective differences into elective distinctions, passive options (constituted externally by the logic of the distinctive relationships) into conscious, elective choices are in fact reserved for members of the dominant class, indeed the very top bourgeoisie, and for artists, who as the inventors and professionals of the 'stylization of life' are alone able to make their art of living one of the fine arts. By contrast, the entry of the petite bourgeoisie into the game of distinction is marked, inter alia, by the anxiety of exposing oneself to classification by offering to the taste of others such infallible indices of personal taste as clothes or furniture, even a simple pair of armchairs, as in one of Nathalie Sarraute's novels. As for the working classes, perhaps their sole function in the system of aesthetic positions is to serve as a foil, a negative reference point, in relation to which all aesthetics define themselves, by successive negations.[5] Ignoring or ignorant of manner and style, the 'aesthetic' (in itself) of the working classes and culturally most deprived fractions of the middle classes defines as 'nice', pretty', 'lovely' (rather than 'beautiful') things that are already defined as such in the 'aesthetic' of calendars and postcards: a sunset, a little girl playing with a cat, a folk dance, an old master, a first communion, a children's procession. The striving towards distinction comes in with petit-bourgeois aestheticism, which delights in all the cheap substitutes for chic objects and practices – driftwood and painted pebbles, cane and raffia, 'art' handicrafts and art photography.

This aestheticism defines itself against the 'aesthetic' of the working classes, refusing their favourite subjects, the themes of 'views', such as mountain landscapes, sunsets and woods, or souvenir photos, such as the first communion, the monument or the old master. In photography, this taste prefers objects that are close to those of the popular aesthetic but semi-neutralized by more or less explicit reference to a pictorial tradition or by a visible stylistic intention combining the human picturesque (weaver at his loom, tramps quarrelling, folk dance) with gratuitous form (pebbles, rope, tree bark). [...]

One only has to ask the question, which economists strangely ignore, of the economic conditions of the production of the dispositions demanded by the economy, i.e., in this case,[6] the question of the economic and social determinants of tastes, to see the necessity of including in the complete definition of the product the differential experiences which the consumers have of it as a function of the dispositions they derive from their position in economic space. These experiences do not have to be felt in order to be understood with an understanding which may owe nothing to lived experience, still less to sympathy. The habitus, an objective relationship between two objectivities, enables an intelligible and necessary relation to be established between practices and a situation, the meaning of which is produced by the habitus through categories of perception and appreciation that are themselves produced by an observable social condition.

Class Condition and Social Conditioning

Because it can only account for practices by bringing to light successively the series of effects which underlie them, analysis initially conceals the structure of the life-style characteristic of an agent or class of agents, that is, the unity hidden under the diversity and multiplicity of the set of practices performed in fields governed by different logics and therefore inducing different forms of realization, in accordance with the formula: [(habitus) (capital)] + field = practice. It also conceals the structure of the symbolic space marked out by the whole set of these structured practices, all the distinct and distinctive life-styles which are always defined objectively and sometimes subjectively in and through their mutual relationships. So it is necessary to reconstruct what has been taken apart, first by way of verification but also in order to rediscover the kernel of truth in the approach characteristic of common-sense knowledge, namely, the intuition of the systematic nature of life-styles and of the whole set which they constitute. To do this, one must return to the practice-unifying and practice-generating principle, i.e., class habitus, the internalized form of class condition and of the conditionings it entails. One must therefore construct the *objective class*, the set of agents who are placed in homogeneous conditions of existence imposing homogeneous conditionings and producing homogeneous systems of dispositions capable of generating similar practices; and who possess a set of common properties, objectified properties, sometimes legally guaranteed (as possession of goods and

power) or properties embodied as class habitus (and, in particular, systems of classificatory schemes).[7]

VARIABLES AND SYSTEMS OF VARIABLES   In designating these classes (classes of
agents or, which amounts to the same thing in this context, classes of conditions of
existence) by the name of an occupation, one is merely indicating that the position in
the relations of production governs practices, in particular through the mechanisms
which control access to positions and produce or select a particular class of habitus.
But this is not a way of reverting to a pre-constructed variable such as 'socio-occupa-
tional category'. The individuals grouped in a class that is constructed in a particular
respect (that is, in a particularly determinant respect) always bring with them, in
addition to the pertinent properties by which they are classified, secondary properties which are thus smuggled into the explanatory model.[8] This means that a class or
class fraction is defined not only by its position in the relations of production, as
identified through indices such as occupation, income or even educational level, but
also by a certain sex-ratio, a certain distribution in geographical space (which is never
socially neutral) and by a whole set of subsidiary characteristics which may function,
in the form of tacit requirements, as real principles of selection or exclusion without
ever being formally stated (this is the case with ethnic origin and sex). A number of
official criteria in fact serve as a mask for hidden criteria: for example, the requiring
of a given diploma can be a way of demanding a particular social origin.
[...]

The Habitus and the Space of Life-Styles

The mere fact that the social space described here can be presented as a diagram
indicates that it is an abstract representation, deliberately constructed, like a map, to
give a bird's-eye view, a point of view on the whole set of points from which ordinary
agents (including the sociologist and his reader, in their ordinary behaviour) see the
social world. Bringing together in simultaneity, in the scope of a single glance – this
is its heuristic value – positions which the agents can never apprehend in their totality
and in their multiple relationships, social space is to the practical space of everyday
life, with its distances which are kept or signalled, and neighbours who may be more
remote than strangers, what geometrical space is to the 'travelling space' (*espace
bodologique*) of ordinary experience, with its gaps and discontinuities.

But the most crucial thing to note is that the question of this space is raised within
the space itself – that the agents have points of view on this objective space which
depend on their position within it and in which their will to transform or conserve it
is often expressed. Thus many of the words which sociology uses to designate the
classes it constructs are borrowed from ordinary usage, where they serve to express
the (generally polemical) view that one group has of another. As if carried away by
their quest for greater objectivity, sociologists almost always forget that the 'objects'
they classify produce not only objectively classifiable practices but also classifying
operations that are no less objective and are themselves classifiable. The division into

classes performed by sociology leads to the common root of the classifiable practices which agents produce and of the classificatory judgements they make of other agents' practices and their own. The habitus is both the generative principle of objectively classifiable judgements and the system of classification (*principium divisionis*) of these practices. It is in the relationship between the two capacities which define the habitus, the capacity to produce classifiable practices and works, and the capacity to differentiate and appreciate these practices and products (taste), that the represented social world, i.e., the space of life-styles, is constituted.

The relationship that is actually established between the pertinent characteristics of economic and social condition (capital volume and composition, in both synchronic and diachronic aspects) and the distinctive features associated with the corresponding position in the universe of life-styles only becomes intelligible when the habitus is const[r]ucted as the generative formula which makes it possible to account both for the classifiable practices and products and for the judgements, themselves classified, which make these practices and works into a system of distinctive signs. When one speaks of the aristocratic asceticism of teachers or the pretension of the petite bourgeoisie, one is not only describing these groups by one, or even the most important, of their properties, but also endeavouring to name the principle which generates all their properties and all their judgements of their, or other people's, properties. The habitus is necessity internalized and converted into a disposition that generates meaningful practices and meaning-giving perceptions; it is a general, transposable disposition which carries out a systematic, universal application – beyond the limits of what has been directly learnt – of the necessity inherent in the learning conditions. That is why an agent's whole set of practices (or those of a whole set of agents produced by similar conditions) are both systematic, inasmuch as they are the product of the application of identical (or interchangeable) schemes, and systematically distinct from the practices constituting another life-style.

Because different conditions of existence produce different habitus – systems of generative schemes applicable, by simple transfer, to the most varied areas of practice – the practices engendered by the different habitus appear as systematic configurations of properties expressing the differences objectively inscribed in conditions of existence in the form of systems of differential deviations which, when perceived by agents endowed with the schemes of perception and appreciation necessary in order to identify, interpret and evaluate their pertinent features, function as lifestyles.[9]

The habitus is not only a structuring structure, which organizes practices and the perception of practices, but also a structured structure: the principle of division into logical classes which organizes the perception of the social world is itself the product of internalization of the division into social classes. Each class condition is defined, simultaneously, by its intrinsic properties and by the relational properties which it derives from its position in the system of class conditions, which is also a system of differences, differential positions, i.e., by everything which distinguishes it from what it is not and especially from everything it is opposed to; social identity is defined and asserted through difference. This means that inevitably inscribed within the dispositions of the habitus is the whole structure of the system of conditions, as it presents itself in the experience of a life-condition occupying a particular position within that structure. The most fundamental oppositions in the structure (high/low, rich/poor etc.) tend to establish themselves as the fundamental structuring principles of practices and the perception of practices. As a system of practice-generating schemes which expresses systematically the necessity and freedom inherent in its class condition and the difference constituting that position, the habitus apprehends differences between conditions, which it grasps in the form of differences between classified, classifying practices (products of other habitus), in accordance with principles of differentiation which, being themselves the product of these differences, are objectively attuned to them and therefore tend to perceive them as natural.

[...]

Tastes in food also depend on the idea each class has of the body and of the effects of food on the body, that is, on its strength, health and beauty; and on the categories it uses to evaluate these effects, some of which may be important for one class and ignored by another, and which the different classes may rank in very different ways. Thus, whereas the working classes are more attentive to the strength of the (male) body than its shape, and tend to go for products that are both cheap and nutritious, the professions prefer products that are tasty, health-giving, light and not fattening. Taste, a class culture turned into nature, that is, *embodied*, helps to shape the class body. It is an incorporated principle of classification which governs all forms of incorporation, choosing and modifying everything that the body ingests and digests and assimilates, physiologically and psychologically. It follows that the body is the most indisputable materialization of class taste, which it manifests in several ways. It does this first in the seemingly most natural features of the body, the dimensions (volume, height, weight) and shapes (round or square, stiff or supple, straight or curved) of its visible forms, which express in countless ways a whole relation to the body, i.e., a way of treating it, caring for it, feeding it, maintaining it, which reveals the deepest dispositions of the habitus. It is in fact through preferences with regard to food which may be perpetuated beyond their social conditions of production (as, in other areas, an accent, a walk etc.)[10] and also, of course, through the uses of the body in work and leisure which are bound up with them, that the class distribution of bodily properties is determined.

The quasi-conscious representation of the approved form of the perceived body, and in particular its thinness or fatness, is not the only mediation through which the social definition of appropriate foods is established. At a deeper level, the whole body schema, in particular the physical approach to the act of eating, governs the selection of certain foods. For example, in the working classes, fish tends to be regarded as an unsuitable food for men, not only because it is a light food, insufficiently 'filling', which would only be cooked for health reasons, i.e., for invalids and children, but also because, like fruit (except bananas) it is one of the 'fiddly' things which a man's hands cannot cope with and which make him childlike (the woman, adopting a maternal role, as in all similar cases, will prepare the fish on the plate or peel the pear); but above all, it is because fish has to be eaten in a way which totally contradicts the masculine way of eating, that is, with restraint, in small mouthfuls, chewed gently, with the front of the mouth, on the tips of the teeth (because of the bones). The whole masculine identity – what is called virility – is involved in these two ways of eating, nibbling and picking, as befits a woman, or with whole-hearted male gulps and mouthfuls, just as it is involved in the two (perfectly homologous) ways of talking, with the front of the mouth or the whole mouth, especially the back of the mouth, the throat (in accordance with the opposition, noted in an earlier study, between the manners symbolized by *la bouche* and *la gueule*).[11]

This opposition can be found in each of the uses of the body, especially in the most insignificant-looking ones, which, as such, are predisposed to serve as 'memory joggers' charged with the group's deepest values, its most fundamental 'beliefs'. It would be easy to show, for example, that Kleenex tissues, which have to be used delicately, with a little sniff from the tip of the nose, are to the big cotton handkerchief, which is blown into sharply and loudly, with the eyes closed and the nose held tightly, as repressed laughter is to a belly laugh, with wrinkled nose, wide-open mouth and deep breathing ('doubled up with laughter'), as if to amplify to the utmost an experience which will not suffer containment, not least because it has to be shared, and therefore clearly manifested for the benefit of others.

And the practical philosophy of the male body as a sort of power, big and strong, with enormous, imperative, brutal needs, which is asserted in every male posture, especially when eating, is also the principle of the division of foods between the sexes, a division which both sexes recognize in their practices and their language. It behooves a man to drink and eat more, and to eat and drink stronger things. Thus, men will have two rounds of aperitifs (more on special occasions), big ones in big glasses (the success of Ricard or Pernod is no doubt partly due to its being a drink both strong and copious – not a dainty 'thimbleful'), and they leave the tit-bits (savoury biscuits, peanuts) to the children and the women, who have a small measure (not enough to 'get tipsy') of homemade aperitif (for which they swap recipes). Similarly, among the hors d'oeuvres, the *charcuterie* is more for the men, and later the cheese, especially if it is strong, whereas the *crudités* (raw vegetables) are more for the women, like the salad; and these affinities are marked by taking a second helping or sharing what is left over. Meat, the nourishing food par excellence, strong and strong-making, giving vigour, blood, and health, is the dish for the men, who take a second helping, whereas the women are satisfied with a small portion. It is not that they are stinting themselves; they really don't want what others might need, especially the men, the natural meat-eaters, and they derive a sort of authority from what they do not see as a privation. Besides, they don't have a taste for men's food, which is reputed to be harmful when eaten to excess (for example, a surfeit of meat can 'turn the blood', over-excite, bring you out in spots etc.) and may even arouse a sort of disgust.

Strictly biological differences are underlined and symbolically accentuated by differences in bearing, differences in gesture, posture and behaviour which express a whole relationship to the social world. To these are added all the deliberate modifications of appearance, especially by use of the set of marks – cosmetic (hairstyle, make-up, beard, moustache, whiskers etc.) or vestimentary – which, because they depend on the economic and cultural means that can be invested in them, function as social markers deriving their meaning and value from their position in the system of distinctive signs which they constitute and which is itself homologous with the system of social positions. The sign-bearing, sign-wearing body is also a producer of signs which are physically marked by the relationship to the body: thus the valorization of virility, expressed in a use of the mouth or a pitch of the voice, can determine the whole of working-class pronunciation. The body, a social product which is the only tangible manifestation of the 'person', is commonly perceived as the most natural expression of innermost nature. There are no merely 'physical' facial signs; the colour and thickness of lipstick, or expressions, as well as the shape of the face or the mouth, are immediately read as indices of a 'moral' physiognomy, socially characterized, i.e., of a 'vulgar' or 'distinguished' mind, naturally 'natural' or naturally 'cultivated'. The signs constituting the perceived body, cultural products which differentiate groups by their degree of culture, that is, their distance from nature, seem grounded in nature. The legitimate use of the body is spontaneously perceived as an index of moral uprightness, so that its opposite, a 'natural' body, is seen as an index of *laisser-aller* ('letting oneself go'), a culpable surrender to facility.

Thus one can begin to map out a universe of class bodies, which (biological accidents apart) tends to reproduce in its specific logic the universe of the social structure. It is no accident that bodily properties are perceived through social systems of classification which are not independent of the distribution of these properties among the social classes. The prevailing taxonomies tend to rank and contrast the properties most frequent among the dominant (i.e., the rarest ones) and those most frequent among the dominated.[12] The social representation of his own body which each agent has to reckon with,[13] from the very beginning, in order to build up his subjective image of his body and his bodily hexis, is thus obtained by applying a social system of classification based on the same principle as the social products to which it is applied. Thus, bodies would have every likelihood of receiving a value strictly corresponding to the positions of their owners in the distribution of the other fundamental properties – but for the fact that the logic of social heredity sometimes endows those least endowed in all other respects with the rarest bodily properties, such as beauty (sometimes 'fatally' attractive, because it threatens the other hierarchies), and, conversely, sometimes denies the 'high and mighty' the bodily attributes of their position, such as height or beauty.

UNPRETENTIOUS OR UNCOUTH?　It is clear that tastes in food cannot be considered in complete independence of the other dimensions of the relationship to the world, to others and to one's own body, through which the practical philosophy of each class is enacted. To demonstrate this, one would have to make a systematic comparison of the working-class and bourgeois ways of treating food, of serving, presenting and offering it, which are infinitely more revelatory than even the nature of the products involved (especially since most surveys of consumption ignore differences in quality). The analysis is a difficult one, because each life-style can only really be constructed in relation to the other, which is its objective and subjective negation, so that the meaning of behaviour is totally reversed depending on which point of view is adopted and on whether the common words which have to be used to name the conduct (e.g., 'manners') are invested with popular or bourgeois connotations.

Considerable misunderstanding can result from ignorance of this mechanism in all surveys by questionnaire, which are always an exchange of words. The confusions are made even worse when the interviewer tries to collect opinions about words or reactions to words (as in the 'ethical test' in which the respondents were presented with the same lists of adjectives to describe an ideal friend, garment or interior). The responses he records in this case have in fact been defined in relation to stimuli which, beyond their nominal identity (that of the words offered), vary in their perceived reality, and therefore their practical efficacy, in accordance with the very principles of variation (and firstly, social class) whose effects one is seeking to measure (which can lead to literally meaningless encounters between opposing classes). Groups invest themselves totally, with everything that opposes them to other groups, in the common words which express their social identity, i.e., their difference. Behind their apparent neutrality, words as ordinary as 'practical', 'sober', 'clean', 'functional', 'amusing', 'delicate', 'cosy', 'distinguished' are thus divided against themselves, because the different classes either give them different meanings, or give them the same meaning but attribute opposite values to the things named. Some examples: *soigné* (neat, trim, careful, well-groomed, well-kept), so strongly appropriated by those who use it to express their taste for a job well done, properly finished, or for the meticulous attention they devote to their personal appearance, that it no doubt evokes for those who reject it the narrow or 'up-tight' rigour they dislike in the petit-bourgeois style; or *drôle* (amusing, funny, droll), whose social connotations, associated with a socially marked pronunciation, bourgeois or snobbish,[14] clash with the values expressed, putting off those who would certainly respond to a popular equivalent of *drôle*, such as *bidonnant, marrant* or *rigolo*; or, again, *sobre*, which, applied to a garment or an interior, can mean radically different things when expressing the prudent, defensive strategies of a small craftsman, the aesthetic asceticism of a teacher or the austerity-in-luxury of the old-world *grand bourgeois*. It can be seen that every attempt to produce an ethical organon common to all classes is condemned from the start, unless, like every 'universal' morality or religion, it plays systematically on the fact that language is both common to the different classes and capable of receiving different, even opposite, meanings in the particular, and sometimes antagonistic, uses that are made of it.

Plain speaking, plain eating: the working-class meal is characterized by plenty (which does not exclude restrictions and limits) and above all by freedom. 'Elastic' and 'abundant' dishes are brought to the table – soups or sauces, pasta or potatoes (almost always included among the vegetables) – and served with a ladle or spoon, to avoid too much measuring and counting, in contrast to everything that has to be cut and divided, such as roasts.[15] This impression of abundance, which is the norm on special occasions, and always applies, so far as is possible, for the men, whose plates are filled twice (a privilege which marks a boy's accession to manhood), is often balanced, on ordinary occasions, by restrictions which generally apply to the women, who will share one portion between two, or eat the left-overs of the previous day; a girl's accession to womanhood is marked by doing without. It is part of men's status to eat and to eat well (and also to drink well); it is particularly insisted that they should eat, on the grounds that 'it won't keep', and there is something suspect about a refusal.

On Sundays, while the women are on their feet, busily serving, clearing the table, washing up, the men remain seated, still eating and drinking. These strongly marked differences of social status (associated with sex and age) are accompanied by no practical differentiation (such as the bourgeois division between the dining room and the kitchen, where the servants eat and sometimes the children), and strict sequencing of the meal tends to be ignored. Everything may be put on the table at much the same time (which also saves walking), so that the women may have reached the dessert, and also the children, who will take their plates and watch television, while the men are still eating the main dish and the 'lad', who has arrived late, is swallowing his soup.

This freedom, which may be perceived as disorder or slovenliness, is adapted to its function. Firstly, it is labour-saving, which is seen as an advantage. Because men take no part in housework, not least because the women would not allow it – it would be a dishonour to see men step outside their rôle – every economy of effort is welcome. Thus, when the coffee is served, a single spoon may be passed around to stir it. But these short cuts are only permissible because one is and feels at home, among the family, where ceremony would be an affectation. For example, to save washing up, the dessert may be handed out on improvised plates torn from the cake-box (with a joke about 'taking the liberty', to mark the transgression), and the neighbour invited in for a meal will also receive his piece of cardboard (offering a plate would exclude him) as a sign of familiarity. Similarly, the plates are not changed between dishes. The soup plate, wiped with bread, can be used right through the meal. The hostess will certainly offer to 'change the plates', pushing back her chair with one hand and reaching with the other for the plate next to her, but everyone will protest ('It all gets mixed up inside you') and if she were to insist it would look as if she wanted to show off her crockery (which she is allowed to if it is a new present) or to treat her guests as strangers, as is sometimes deliberately done to intruders or 'scroungers' who never return the invitation. These unwanted guests may be frozen out by changing their plates despite their protests, not laughing at their jokes, or scolding the children for their behaviour ('No, no, *we* don't mind', say the guests; 'They ought to know better by now', the parents respond). The common root of all these 'liberties' is no doubt the sense that at least there will not be self-imposed controls, constraints and restrictions – especially not in eating, a primary need and a compensation – and especially not in the heart of domestic life, the one realm of freedom, when everywhere else, and at all other times, necessity prevails.

In opposition to the free-and-easy working-class meal, the bourgeoisie is concerned to eat with all due form. Form is first of all a matter of rhythm, which implies expectations, pauses, restraints; waiting until the last person served has started to eat, taking modest helpings, not appearing over-eager. A strict sequence is observed and all coexistence of dishes which the sequence separates, fish and meat, cheese and dessert, is excluded: for example, before the dessert is served, everything left on the table, even the salt-cellar, is removed, and the crumbs are swept up. This extension of rigorous rules into everyday life (the bourgeois male shaves and dresses first thing every morning, and not just to 'go out'), refusing the division between home and the exterior, the quotidian and the extra-quotidian, is not explained solely by the presence of strangers – servants and guests – in the familiar family world. It is the expression of a habitus of order, restraint and propriety which may not be abdicated. The relation to food – *the* primary need and pleasure – is only one dimension of the bourgeois relation to the social world. The opposition between the immediate and the deferred, the easy and the difficult, substance (or function) and form, which is exposed in a particularly striking fashion in bourgeois ways of eating, is the basis of all aestheticization of practice and every aesthetic. Through all the forms and formalisms imposed on the immediate appetite, what is demanded – and inculcated – is not only a disposition to discipline food consumption by a conventional structuring which is also a gentle, indirect, invisible censorship (quite different from enforced privations) and which is an element in an art of living (correct eating, for example, is a way of paying homage to one's hosts and to the mistress of the house, a tribute to her care and effort). It is also a whole relationship to animal nature, to primary needs and the populace who indulge them without restraint; it is a way of denying the meaning and primary function of consumption, which are essentially common, by making the meal a social ceremony, an affirmation of ethical tone and aesthetic refinement. The manner of presenting and consuming the food, the organization of the meal and setting of the places, strictly differentiated according to the sequence of dishes and arranged to please the eye, the presentation of the dishes, considered as much in terms of shape and colour (like works of art) as of their consumable substance, the etiquette governing posture and gesture, ways of serving oneself and others, of using the different utensils, the seating plan, strictly but discreetly hierarchical, the censorship of all bodily manifestations of the act or pleasure of eating (such as noise or haste), the very refinement of the things consumed, with quality more important than quantity – this whole commitment to stylization tends to shift the emphasis from substance and function to form and manner, and so to deny the crudely material reality of the act of eating and of the things consumed, or, which amounts to the same thing, the basely material vulgarity of those who indulge in the immediate satisfactions of food and drink.[16]

NOTES

1 Two examples, chosen from among hundreds, but paradigmatic, of explicit use of the scheme 'something other than': 'La Fiancée du pirate is one of those very rare French films that are *really* satirical, *really* funny, because it does not resort to the carefully defused, prudently inoffensive comedy one finds in *la Grande Vadrouille* and *le Petit Baigneur.*. . . In short, it is *something other than* the dreary hackwork of boulevard farce' (J. L. Bory, *Le Nouvel Observateur*, 8 December 1969; italics mine). 'Through distance, or at least, through difference, to endeavour to present a text

on pictorial modernity *other than* the hackneyed banalities of *a certain style of art criticism. Between* verbose aphasia, the textual transcription of pictures, exclamations of recognition, *and* the works of specialized aesthetics, perhaps *marking* some of the ways in which conceptual, theoretical work gets to grips with contemporary plastic production' (G. Gassiot-Talabot et ah. *Figurations* 1960–1973 [Paris, Union générale des éditions, 1973], p. 7; italics mine).

2 This essential negativity, which is part of the very logic of the constitution of taste and its change,

explains why, as Gombrich points out, 'the terminology of art history was so largely built on words denoting some principle of exclusion. Most movements in art erect some new taboo, some new negative principle, such as the banishing from painting by the impressionists of all "anecdotal" elements. The positive slogans and shibboleths which we read in artists' or critics' manifestos past or present are usually much less well defined' (E. H. Gombrich, *Norm and Form: Studies in the Art of the Renaissance* [London, New York; Phaidon Press, 1966], p. 89).

3 This is seen clearly in the case of the theatre, which touches more directly and more overtly on the implicit or explicit principles of the art of living. Especially in the case of comedy, it presupposes common values or interests or, more precisely, a complicity and connivance based on immediate assent to the same self-evident propositions, those of the *doxa*, the totality of opinions accepted at the level of pre-reflexive belief. (This explains why the institutions supplying the products, and the products themselves, are more sharply differentiated in the theatre than in any other art.)

4 For an analysis of 'art for art's sake' as the expression of the artistic life-style, see P. Bourdieu, 'L'invention de la vie d'artiste,' *Actes,* 2 (1975), 67–93.

5 This is true despite the apparent exception in which some artists return to certain popular preferences, which had a totally different meaning in a cultural configuration dominated by choices which for them would be quite improbable or even impossible. These returns to the 'popular' style, which often pass for a return to the 'people', are determined not by any genuine relationship to the working classes, who are generally spurned – even in idealization, which is a form of refusal – but by the internal relations of the field of artistic production or the field of the dominant class. (This point has a general validity, and one would need to examine what the writings of intellectuals on the working classes owe to the specific interests of intellectuals in struggles in which what is at stake, if not the people, is the legitimacy conferred, in certain conditions, by appearing as the spokesman for popular interests.)

6 For another example of this paradoxical neglect, see P. Bourdieu, *Travail et travailleurs en Algérie* (Paris, Mouton. 1963), and *Algeria 1960* (Cambridge, Cambridge University Press, 1979).

7 The objective class must not be confused with the mobilized class, the set of individuals brought together, on the basis of the homogeneity of the objectified or embodied properties which define the objective class, for the purpose of the struggle to preserve or modify the structure of the distribution of objectified properties.

8 Jean Benzécri puts this well: Let us assume individuals $\alpha\beta_1\gamma_1$, $\alpha\beta_2$, γ_2, . . ., $\alpha\beta_n$ γ_n, each described as possessing three features. Leaving aside the last two elements in each description, we can say that all the individuals belong to a single species defined by feature α, which we can call species α. But although feature α enables us to define this species and recognize its individuals, we cannot study the former without considering features β, γ, of the latter. From this standpoint, if we call B the sum of β modalities which the second feature can assume, and C the sum of the γ modalities of the third feature, then studying species α means studying αBC, i.e., in addition to the first, stable feature, every form which the first (B) or the second (C) may take; and also the possible associations between the latter (e g., β with γ rather than with γ^1 or γ^2).' J. Benzécri, 'Définition logique et définition statistique: notes de lecture sur un chapitre de Ernst Cassirer'. *Cahiers de l'Analyse des Données,* 3 (1978), 239–42.

9 It follows from this that the relationship between conditions of existence and practices or the meaning of practices is not to be understood in terms either of the logic of mechanism or of the logic of consciousness.

10 That is why the body designates not only present position but also trajectory.

11 In 'The Economics of Linguistic Exchanges', *Social Science Information,* 26 (December 1977), 643–68, Bourdieu develops the opposition between two ways of speaking, rooted in two relations to the body and the world, which have a lexical reflection in the many idioms based on two words for 'mouth': *la bouche* and *la gueule.*

La bouche is the 'standard' word for the mouth; but in opposition to *la gueule* – a slang or 'vulgar' word except when applied to animals – it tends to be restricted to the lips, whereas *la gueule* can include the whole face or the throat. Most of the idioms using *la bouche* imply fastidiousness, effeminacy or disdain; those with *la gueule* connote vigour, strength or violence (translator's note).

12 This means that the taxonomies applied to the perceived body (fat/thin, strong/weak, big/small etc.) are, as always, at once arbitrary (e g., the ideal female body may be fat or thin, in different economic and social contexts) and necessary, i.e., grounded in the specific reason of a given social order.

13 More than ever, the French possessive pronouns – which do not mark the owner's gender – ought to be translated 'his or her'. The 'sexism' of the text results from the male translator's reluctance to defy the dominant use of a sexist symbolic system (translator).

14 Oddly but accurately over-determined in English by droll/drawl (translator).

15 One could similarly contrast the bowl, which is generously filled and held two-handed for unpretentious drinking, and the cup, into which a little is poured, and more later ('Would you care for a little more coffee?'), and which is held between two fingers and sipped from.

16 Formality is a way of denying the truth of the social world and of social relations. Just as popular 'functionalism' is refused as regards food, so too there is a refusal of the realistic vision which leads the working classes to accept social exchanges for what they are (and, for example, to say, without cynicism, of someone who has done a favour or rendered a service, 'She knows I'll pay her back'). Suppressing avowal of the calculation which pervades social relations, there is a striving to sec presents, received or given, as 'pure' testimonies of friendship, respect, affection, and equally 'pure' manifestations of generosity and moral worth.

CHAPTER TWELVE

MICHEL FOUCAULT AND QUEER THEORY

CHAPTER MENU

Michel Foucault (1926–84) is another major French theorist who has hugely impacted intellectual thought. Unlike Pierre Bourdieu who is the more towering figure in sociology, Foucault's impact is more keenly felt in literary theory, philosophy, and interdisciplinary Queer Studies. At a broad level, Foucault is interested in the production of truth. He shows how the truths produced by the various disciplines, whether literature, philosophy, psychiatry (Foucault 1965), medicine (Foucault 1975), criminology (Foucault 1979), or sexuality (Foucault 1978), are embedded in power relations that can never be escaped. As such, the very notion of Truth as a lofty goal to be striven toward is a fool's errand because all knowledge, even that which seems to be bare of power interests, is in fact contaminated by power relations. What we mean by Truth, and how we categorize and what we call all things, is for Foucault, inherently arbitrary (Foucault 1974). Yet such arbitrariness cannot be resisted because the very claims that we might use to challenge the arbitrariness of the categories used in everyday and institutional practices are themselves products of and entangled in the power-infused discourse that has developed to name things; the DSM (Diagnostic and Statistical Manual of the American Psychiatric Association) categorizations of sexual deviance and mental and behavioral pathology

Concise Reader in Sociological Theory: Theorists, Concepts, and Current Applications,
First Edition. Edited by Michele Dillon. Editorial material and organization
© 2021 John Wiley & Sons Ltd. Published 2021 by John Wiley & Sons Ltd.

are a partial illumination of this process even as, or precisely because, its categorizations of pathology change. As such, language, and all discourse – including silence as a form of resistance to discourse – are techniques of power. As Foucault succinctly notes:

> Truth isn't outside power, or lacking in power: contrary to a myth whose history and functions would repay further study, truth isn't the reward of free spirits, the child of protracted solitude, nor the privilege of those who have succeeded in liberating themselves. Truth is a thing of this world: it is produced only by virtue of multiple forms of constraint ... Each society has its regime of truth, its general politics of truth: that is, the types of discourse which it accepts and makes function as true ... The political question, to sum up, is not error, illusion, alienated consciousness, or ideology; it is truth itself. (Foucault 1984: 72–3, 75)

For sociologists, Foucault's particular relevance is his insightfully rigorous analysis of the institutional disciplining of the body, and thus the disciplining of individuals. His impact derives largely from the originality he brings to interrogating the history or "the birth" of social categories and institutional processes and procedures; an excavation that uncovers how such things as madness, sexuality, confession, the prison, the clinic, the asylum are constructed and structured through an institutionally embedded, multilayered scaffolding. He illuminates a social archaeology that entwines the particular interests of the nation state and of its political economic development in the everyday regulation of its citizens, and specifically of body practices that are also within the purview of religious institutions (e.g. specifically in the European historical context, the post-Reformation Catholic Church). Thus across multiple settings, a multi-tentacle institutional bedrock surveys, surveils, regulates and controls bodies, what bodies do, and what they do to and with other bodies/ individuals. Biopolitics (see excerpt *12a The History of Sexuality*, pp. xx–xx), the intertwining of government, economic, medical, criminological, and religious institutions' explicit interests in the biology of the body (e.g. fertility and its control), marks the birth of sex as not just something to be controlled but, relatedly, a topic to be categorized and elaborated on in all its many manifest uses and practices (e.g. see the reports from the Centers for Disease Control, and census categories of types of births and types of families). Sex, therefore, was/is no longer "a deadly secret," but became/is a discourse, and a discourse used as an instrument of biopower. Thus multiple disciplinary practices are deployed on the body/bodies to ensure their capitulation to institutional control. These disciplinary practices, as identified by Foucault, are not merely concerned with the body as a whole – in the more conventional sociological sense of the way in which bureaucratic structures (cf. Weber), laws and conventions (cf. Durkheim), and social roles (e.g. Durkheim, Parsons, Goffman) regulate individual behavior. Rather, as Foucault elaborates, "Discipline is a political anatomy of detail" (Foucault 1979: 139), wherein body desires, movements, gestures, attitudes, and behavior are subject to "a policy of coercions that act upon the body" with calculated manipulation (1979: 137–8), a manipulation that produces docile bodies:

"A body is docile that may be subjected, used, transformed and improved" (1979: 136). Such disciplinary techniques and procedures and their effects are illuminated in the discourses/practices across many institutional and cultural spheres today, including those deployed by the media, advertising and fashion industries that sustain global consumerism.

The manipulation and production of docile bodies, whether in prison, the confessional, or on the cat-walk cannot be resisted because the specific points of power (and thus of resistance) can never be pinned down. This is because, as Foucault elaborates (see excerpt, *History of Sexuality*, pp. 90-96), power is fluid and in constant motion. Again, unlike Weber's and conventional sociological definitions of power, for Foucault, power is not structural; it is not hierarchical or socially located in particular positions, roles and places, but is everywhere, always circulating within and ubiquitously infusing any and all social relations and any and all discourses.

Not surprisingly, Foucault's attentiveness to sexuality, and to the fact that it has a history, a history, moreover, that is underpinned by a regime of truth production focused on the institutional control of sexual desires and sexual acts, opened up the attention of sociologists and others to the societal construction of what is natural or normal sex and what are its deviants – specifically, the assumed "normalcy" of heterosexuality and the "aberration" presented by homosexuality. Coinciding with the gay rights activism of the late 1960s (e.g. Stonewall riots) and through the 1970s and subsequent decades, Foucault's work was instrumental in problematizing the labeling of gay sexuality as deviant and pathological (see the revised DSM). As scholarly and public debates raged over whether being gay is a natural biological state or a personally chosen social identity (e.g. Epstein 1987), some scholars argued that rather than thinking about sexuality in set binary terms (homosexuality versus heterosexuality), it was more emancipatory in terms of achieving sexual equality – and more empirically accurate – to regard sexuality as fluid and as an identity and a constellation of erotic desires experienced as being variable along a continuum. Queer Theory was the name adopted by scholars such as **Steven Seidman** who embraced this paradigm and who sought to advance an alternative practical understanding of sexuality that went "beyond the binary," even as other scholars and activists lauded institutional attempts to treat lesbian, gay, bisexual, and transsexual (LGBT) individuals and heterosexuals as equals (and who in doing so, unintentionally reproduced the normalcy of the either/or sexual binary). Queer Theorists argue for the queering of all institutions, and of all disciplines (including sociology; see excerpt *12b Queer Theory/Sociology*), and thus for the abandonment of binary categorical analysis that invariably undermines sexual fluidity. In the Queer view, the legalization and increased cultural acceptance of same-sex marriage is not a victory for sexual equality but affirmation of the sexual binary and the domestication of queer sexuality within the conventional institutional structure of marriage (and which itself is grounded in/biased toward a heterosexist model of desire and relationships).

REFERENCES

Epstein, Steven. 1987. "Gay Politics, Ethnic Identity: The Limits of Social Constructionism." *Socialist Review* 93–94: 9–54.

Foucault, Michel. 1965. *Madness and Civilization: A History of Insanity in the Age of Reason*. New York: Random House.

Foucault, Michel. 1975. *The Birth of the Clinic: An Archaeology of Medical Perception*. New York: Pantheon.

Foucault, Michel. 1978. *The History of Sexuality*, vol. 1. New York: Random House.

Foucault, Michel. 1979. *Discipline and Punish: The Birth of the Prison*. New York: Penguin.

Foucault, Michel. 1984. "Truth and Power," pp. 51–75 in Paul Rabinow, ed. *The Foucault Reader*. New York: Pantheon.

12A Michel Foucault from *The History of Sexuality*

Original publication details: Michel Foucault, 1978. *The History of Sexuality*, Vol. 1, pp. 90–96, 26–28. New York: Vintage.

Of course, it had long been asserted that a country had to be populated if it hoped to be rich and powerful; but this was the first time that a society had affirmed, in a constant way, that its future and its fortune, were tied not only to the number and the uprightness of its citizens, to their marriage rules and family organization, but to the manner in which each individual made use of his sex. Things went from ritual lamenting over the unfruitful debauchery of the rich, bachelors, and libertines to a discourse in which the sexual conduct of the population was taken both as an object of analysis and as a target of intervention; there was a progression from the crudely populationist arguments of the mercantilist epoch to the much more subtle and calculated attempts at regulation that tended to favor or discourage – according to the objectives and exigencies of the moment – an increasing birthrate. Through the political economy of population there was formed a whole grid of observations regarding sex. There emerged the analysis of the modes of sexual conduct, their determinations and their effects, at the boundary line of the biological and the economic domains. There also appeared those systematic campaigns which, going beyond the traditional means – moral and religious exhortations, fiscal measures – tried to transform the sexual conduct of couples into a concerted economic and political behavior. In time these new measures would become anchorage points for the different varieties of racism of the nineteenth and twentieth centuries. It was essential that the state know what was happening with its citizens' sex, and the use they made of it, but also that each individual be capable of controlling the use he made of it. Between the state and the individual, sex became an issue, and a public issue no less; a whole web of discourses, special knowledges, analyses, and injunctions settled upon it.

The situation was similar in the case of children's sex. It is often said that the classical period consigned it to an obscurity from which it scarcely emerged before the *Three Essays* or the beneficent anxieties of Little Hans. It is true that a longstanding "freedom" of language between children and adults, or pupils and teachers, may have disappeared. No seventeenth-century pedagogue would have publicly advised his disciple, as did Erasmus in his *Dialogues,* on the choice of a good prostitute. And the boisterous laughter that had accompanied the precocious sexuality of children for so long – and in all social classes, it seems – was gradually stifled. But this was not a plain and simple imposition of silence. Rather, it was a new regime of discourses. Not any less was said about it; on the contrary. But things were said in a different way; it was different people who said them, from different points of view, and in order to obtain different results. Silence itself – the things one declines to say, or is forbidden to name, the discretion that is required between different speakers – is less the absolute limit of discourse, the other side from which it is separated by a strict boundary, than an element that functions alongside the things said, with them and in relation to them within over-all strategies. There is no binary division to be made between what one says and what one does not say; we must try to determine the different ways of not saying such things, how those who can and those who cannot speak of them are distributed, which type of discourse is authorized, or which, form of discretion is required in either case. There is not one but many silences, and they are an integral part of the strategies that underlie and permeate discourses.

Take the secondary schools of the eighteenth century, for example. On the whole, one can have the impression that sex was hardly spoken of at all in these institutions. But one only has to glance over the architectural layout, the rules of discipline, and their whole internal organization: the question of sex was a constant preoccupation. The builders considered it explicitly. The organizers took it permanently into account. All who held a measure of authority were placed in a state of perpetual alert, which the fixtures, the precautions taken, the interplay of punishments and responsibilities, never ceased to reiterate. The space for classes, the shape of the tables, the planning of the recreation lessons, the distribution of the dormitories (with or without partitions, with or without curtains), the rules for monitoring bedtime and sleep periods – all this referred, in the most prolix manner, to the sexuality of children.[1] What one might call the internal discourse of the institution – the one it employed to address itself, and which circulated among those who made it function – was largely based on the assumption that this sexuality existed, that it was precocious, active, and ever present. But this was not all: the sex of the schoolboy became in the course of the eighteenth century – and quite apart from that of adolescents in general – a public problem. Doctors counseled the directors and professors of educational establishments, but they also gave their opinions to families; educators designed projects which they submitted to the authorities; schoolmasters turned to students, made recommendations to them, and drafted for their benefit books of exhortation, full of moral and medical examples. Around the schoolboy and his sex there proliferated a whole literature of precepts, opinions, observations, medical advice, clinical cases, outlines for reform, and plans for ideal institutions.

[. . .]

This history of sexuality, or rather this series of studies concerning the historical relationships of power and the discourse on sex, is, I realize, a circular project in the sense that it involves two endeavors that refer back to one another. We shall try to rid ourselves of a juridical and negative representation of power, and cease to conceive of it in terms of law, prohibition, liberty, and sovereignty. But how then do we analyze what has occurred in recent history with regard to this thing – seemingly one of the most forbidden areas of our lives and bodies – that is sex? How, if not by way of prohibition and blockage, does power gain access to it? Through which mechanisms, or tactics, or devices? But let us assume in turn that a somewhat careful scrutiny will show that power in modern societies has not in fact governed sexuality through law and sovereignty; let us suppose that historical analysis has revealed the presence of a veritable "technology" of sex, one that is much more complex and above all much more positive than the mere effect of a "defense" could be; this being the case, does this example – which can only be considered a privileged one, since power seemed in this instance, more than anywhere else, to function as prohibition – not compel one to discover principles for analyzing power which do not derive from the system of right and the form of law? Hence it is a question of forming a different grid of historical decipherment by starting from a different theory of power; and, at the same time, of advancing little by little toward a different conception of power through a closer examination of an entire historical material. We must at the same time conceive of sex without the law, and power without the king.

Method

Hence the objective is to analyze a certain form of knowledge regarding sex, not in terms of repression or law, but in terms of power. But the word *power* is apt to lead to a number of misunderstandings – misunderstandings with respect to its nature, its form, and its unity. By power, I do not mean "Power" as a group of institutions and mechanisms that ensure the subservience of the citizens of a given state. By power, I do not mean, either, a mode of subjugation which, in contrast to violence, has the form of the rule. Finally, I do not have in mind a general system of domination exerted by one group over another, a system whose effects, through successive derivations, pervade the entire social body. The analysis, made in terms of power, must not assume that the sovereignty of the state, the form of the law, or the over-all unity of a domination are given at the outset; rather, these are only the terminal forms power takes. It seems to me that power must be understood in the first instance as the multiplicity of force relations immanent in the sphere in which they operate and which constitute their own organization; as the process which, through ceaseless struggles and confrontations, transforms, strengthens, or reverses them; as the support which these force relations find in one another, thus forming a chain or a system, or on the contrary, the disjunctions and contradictions which isolate them from one another; and lastly, as the strategies in which they take effect, whose general design or institutional crystallization is embodied in the state apparatus, in the formulation of the law, in the various social hegemonies. Power's condition of possibility, or in any case the viewpoint which permits one to understand its exercise, even in its more "peripheral" effects, and which also makes it possible to use its mechanisms as a grid of intelligibility of the social order, must not be sought in the primary existence of a central point, in a unique source of sovereignty from which secondary and descendent forms would emanate; it is the moving substrate of force relations which, by virtue of their inequality, constantly engender states of power, but the latter are always local and unstable. The omnipresence of power: not because it has the privilege of consolidating everything under its invincible unity, but because it is produced from one moment to the next, at every point, or rather in every relation from one point to another. Power is everywhere; not because it embraces everything, but because it comes from everywhere. And "Power," insofar as it is permanent, repetitious, inert, and self-reproducing, is simply the over-all effect that emerges from all these mobilities, the concatenation that rests on each of them and seeks in turn to arrest their movement. One needs to be nominalistic, no doubt: power is not an institution, and not a structure; neither is it a certain strength we are endowed with; it is the name that one attributes to a complex strategical situation in a particular society.

Should we turn the expression around, then, and say that politics is war pursued by other means? If we still wish to maintain a separation between war and politics, perhaps we should postulate rather that this multiplicity of force relations can be coded – in part but never totally – either in the form of "war," or in the form of "politics"; this would imply two different strategies (but the one always liable to switch into the other) for integrating these unbalanced, heterogeneous, unstable, and tense force relations.

Continuing this line of discussion, we can advance a certain number of propositions:

- Power is not something that is acquired, seized, or shared, something that one holds on to or allows to slip away; power is exercised from innumerable points, in the interplay of nonegalitarian and mobile relations.
- Relations of power are not in a position of exteriority with respect to other types of relationships (economic processes, knowledge relationships, sexual relations), but are immanent in the latter; they are the immediate effects of the divisions, inequalities, and disequilibriums which occur in the latter, and conversely they are the internal conditions of these differentiations; relations of power are not in superstructural positions, with merely a role of prohibition or accompaniment; they have a directly productive role, wherever they come into play.
- Power comes from below; that is, there is no binary and all-encompassing opposition between rulers and ruled at the root of power relations, and serving as a general matrix – no such duality extending from the top down and reacting on more and more limited groups to the very depths of the social body. One must suppose rather that the manifold relationships of force that take shape and come into play in the machinery of production, in families, limited groups, and institutions, are the basis for wide-ranging effects of cleavage that run through the social body as a whole. These then form a general line of force that traverses the local oppositions and links them together; to be sure, they also bring about redistributions, realignments, homogenizations, serial arrangements, and convergences of the force relations. Major dominations are the hegemonic effects that are sustained by all these confrontations.
- Power relations are both intentional and nonsubjective. If in fact they are intelligible, this is not because they are the effect of another instance that "explains" them, but rather because they are imbued, through and through, with calculation: there is no power that is exercised without a series of aims and objectives. But this does not mean that it results from the choice or decision of an individual subject;

let us not look for the headquarters that presides over its rationality; neither the caste which governs, nor the groups which control the state apparatus, nor those who make the most important economic decisions direct the entire network of power that functions in a society (and makes *it* function); the rationality of power is characterized by tactics that are often quite explicit at the restricted level where they are inscribed (the local cynicism of power), tactics which, becoming connected to one another, attracting and propagating one another, but finding their base of support and their condition elsewhere, end by forming comprehensive systems: the logic is perfectly clear, the aims decipherable, and yet it is often the case that no one is there to have invented them, and few who can be said to have formulated them: an implicit characteristic of the great anonymous, almost unspoken strategies which coordinate the loquacious tactics whose "inventors" or decisionmakers are often without hypocrisy.

- Where there is power, there is resistance, and yet, or rather consequently, this resistance is never in a position of exteriority in relation to power. Should it be said that one is always "inside" power, there is no "escaping" it, there is no absolute outside where it is concerned, because one is subject to the law in any case? Or that, history being the ruse of reason, power is the ruse of history, always emerging the winner? This would be to misunderstand the strictly relational character of power relationships. Their existence depends on a multiplicity of points of resistance: these play the role of adversary, target, support, or handle in power relations. These points of resistance are present everywhere in the power network. Hence there is no single locus of great Refusal, no soul of revolt, source of all rebellions, or pure law of the revolutionary. Instead there is a plurality of resistances, each of them a special case: resistances that are possible, necessary, improbable; others that are spontaneous, savage, solitary, concerted, rampant, or violent; still others that are quick to compromise, interested, or sacrificial; by definition, they can only exist in the strategic field of power relations. But this does not mean that they are only a reaction or rebound, forming with respect to the basic domination an underside that is in the end always passive, doomed to perpetual defeat. Resistances do not derive from a few heterogeneous principles; but neither are they a lure or a promise that is of necessity betrayed. They are the odd term in relations of power; they are inscribed in the latter as an irreducible opposite. Hence they too are distributed in irregular fashion: the points, knots, or focuses of resistance are spread over time and space at varying densities, at times mobilizing groups or individuals in a definitive way, inflaming certain points of the body, certain moments in life, certain types of behavior. Are there no great radical ruptures, massive binary divisions, then? Occasionally, yes. But more often one is dealing with mobile and transitory points of resistance, producing cleavages in a society that shift about, fracturing unities and effecting regroupings, furrowing across individuals themselves, cutting them up and remolding them, marking off irreducible regions in them, in their bodies and minds. Just as the network of power relations ends by forming a dense web that passes through apparatuses and institutions, without being exactly localized in them, so too the swarm of points of resistance traverses social stratifications and individual unities.

NOTE

1   *Règlement de police pour les lycées* (1809), art. 67: "There shall always be, during class and study hours, an instructor watching the exterior, so as to prevent students who have gone out to relieve themselves from stopping and congregating. art. 68: "After the evening prayer, the students will be conducted back to the dormitory, where the schoolmasters will put them to bed at once.

art. 69: "The masters will not retire except after having made certain that every student is in bed. art. 70: "The beds shall be separated by partitions two meters in height. The dormitories shall be illuminated during the night."

12B Steven Seidman from *Queer Theory/Sociology*

Original publication details: Steven Seidman, 1996. *Queer Theory/Sociology*, pp. 7–13. Malden, MA: Blackwell. Reproduced with permission of John Wiley & Sons, Inc.

The sociology of homosexuality from the early 1970s through the 1980s has not played a major role in recent lesbian and gay theory debates, in part because sociologists did not critically investigate the categories of sexuality, heterosexuality, and homosexuality. They did not question the social functioning of the hetero/homosexual binary as the master category of a modern regime of sexuality. Moreover, many sociologists lacked an historical perspective while perpetuating an approach that isolated the question of homosexuality from dynamics of social modernization and politics.

As sociologists were beginning to approach sex as a social fact, there were [...] social perspectives on sexuality that were developed by the women's and gay movements. With the formation of homophile groups in the 1950s (e.g. the Mattachine Society and the Daughters of Bilitis), homosexuality was alternatively theorized as a property of all individuals or as a property of a segment of the human population. Viewing homosexuality as natural was intended to legitimate it. Moreover, despite the radicalization of gay theory in lesbian feminism and gay liberation in the seventies, few challenged the view of homosexuality as a basis of individual and social identity. A good deal of lesbian-feminist and gay liberationist theory aimed to reverse dominant sexual views by asserting the naturalness and normality of homosexuality. The notion of homosexuality as a universal category of the self and sexual identity was rarely questioned in the homophile, lesbian-feminist, and gay liberationist discourses (exceptions include c

As the initial wave of a gay affirmative politics, roughly from 1968–73, passed into a period of community building, personal empowerment, and local struggles, we can speak of a new period in lesbian and gay theory – the age of "social constructionism." Drawing from labeling and phenomenological theory, and influenced heavily by Marxism and feminism, social constructionists had roots in both academia and political activism. Social-constructionist perspectives challenge the antithesis of sex and society. Sex is viewed as fundamentally social; the modern categories of sexuality, most importantly, those of heterosexuality and homosexuality, are understood as social and historical creations. Social constructionist perspectives suggested that "homosexuality" was not a uniform, identical phenomenon but that its meaning and social role varied historically. In particular, constructionists argued that instead of assuming that "the homosexual" is a trans-historical identity or a universal human type, the idea that homosexual desire reveals a distinctive human type or social identity is said to be unique to modern Western societies. Michel Foucault (1980) provided the classic statement. "As defined by ancient civil or canonical codes, sodomy was a category of forbidden acts; their perpetrator was nothing more than the juridical subject of them. The nineteenth-century homosexual became a personage, a past, a case history, a life form . . . Nothing that went into total composition was unaffected by his sexuality. It was everywhere present in him: at the root of all his actions . . . because it was a secret that always gave itself away" (p. 43). Foucault's thesis of the social construction of "the homosexual" found support in the concurrent work of Jeffrey Weeks (1977), Jonathan Katz (1976), Carroll Smith-Rosenberg (1975), and Randolph Trumbach (1977).

Social constructionism emerged in the context of prodigious efforts at lesbian and gay community building in the seventies. Constructionist studies sought to explain the origin, social meaning, and changing forms of the modern homosexual (e.g. D'Emilio 1983; Plummer 1981; Faderman 1981). As much as these perspectives challenged essentialist or universalistic understandings of homosexuality, they contributed to a politics of the making of a homosexual minority. Instead of asserting the homosexual as a natural fact made into a political minority by social prejudice, constructionists traced the social factors that produced a homosexual identity which functioned as the foundation for homosexuals as a new ethnic minority (e.g. D'Emilio 1983; Faderman 1981). Social-constructionist studies legitimated a model of lesbian and gay subcultures as ethnic-like minorities (Epstein 1987; Seidman 1993).[1]

Social-constructionist perspectives dominated analyses of homosexuality through the eighties and have been institutionalized in lesbian and gay studies programs in the nineties. Debates about essentialism (Stein 1992) and the rise, meaning, and changing social forms of homosexual identities and communities, are at the core of lesbian and gay studies. However, since the late eighties aspects of this constructionist perspective have been contested. In particular, discourses that sometimes circulate under the rubric of Queer theory, though often impossible to differentiate from constructionist texts, have sought to shift the debate somewhat away from explaining the modern homosexual to questions of the operation of the hetero/homosexual binary, from an exclusive preoccupation with homosexuality to a focus on heterosexuality as a social and political organizing principle, and from a politics of minority interest to a politics of knowledge and difference (Seidman 1995).

What is the social context of the rise of Queer theory?

By the end of the seventies, the gay and lesbian movement had achieved such a level of subcultural elaboration and general social tolerance, at least in the US, that a gay politics focused on social assimilation far overshadowed the liberationist politics of the previous decade. Thus, Dennis Altman (1982), a keen observer of the gay movement in the seventies, could speak of the homosexualization of America. And yet at this very historical moment events were conspiring to put lesbian and gay life into crisis.

A backlash against homosexuality, spearheaded by the New Right but widely supported by neoconservatives and mainstream Republicans, punctured illusions of a coming era of tolerance and sexual pluralism (Adam 1987; Seidman 1992). The AIDS epidemic energized an anti-gay backlash and put lesbians and gay men on the defensive as religious and medicalized models which discredited homosexuality were rehabilitated. While the AIDS crisis also demonstrated the strength of established gay institutions, for many lesbians and gay men it underscored the limits of a politics of minority rights and inclusion. Both the backlash and the AIDS crisis prompted a renewal of radical activism, of a politics of confrontation, coalition building, and the need for a critical theory that links gay affirmation to broad institutional change.

Internal developments within gay and lesbian subcultures also prompted a shift in gay theory and politics. Social differences within the gay and lesbian communities erupted into public conflict around the issues of race and sex. By the early eighties, a public culture fashioned by lesbian and gay people of color registered sharp criticisms of mainstream gay culture for its devaluation and exclusion of their experiences, interests, values, and unique forms of life – e.g., their writing, political perspectives, relationships, and particular modes of oppression. The concept of a lesbian and gay identity that served as the foundation for building a community and organizing politically was criticized as reflecting a white, middle-class experience (Anzaldua and Moraga 1983; Lorde 1984; Beam 1986; Moraga 1983). The categories of "lesbian" and "gay" were criticized for functioning as disciplining political forces. Simultaneously, lesbian feminism was further put into crisis by challenges to its foundational concept of sexuality and sexual ethics. At the heart of lesbian feminism, especially in the late seventies, was an understanding of the difference between men and women anchored in a spiritualized concept of female sexuality and an eroticization of the male that imagined male desire as revealing a logic of misogyny and domination. Being a woman and a lesbian meant exhibiting in one's desires and behaviors a lesbian-feminist sexual and social identity. Many lesbians, and feminists in general, criticized lesbian feminism for stigmatizing their own erotic and intimate lives as deviant or male-identified (e.g. Rubin 1984; Allison 1981; Bright 1984; Califia 1979, 1981). In the course of the feminist "sex wars," a virtual parade of female and lesbian sexualities entered the public life of lesbian culture, e.g., butch-fems, sadomasochists, sexualities of all kinds mocking the idea of a unified lesbian sexual identity (Phelan 1989; Ferguson 1989; Seidman 1992). If the intent of people of color and sex rebels was to encourage social differences to surface in gay and lesbian life, one consequence was to raise questions about the very idea of a lesbian or gay identity as the foundations of gay culture and politics.

Some in the lesbian and gay communities reacted to the "crisis" by reasserting a natural foundation for homosexuality (e.g., the gay brain) in order to unify homosexuals in the face of a political backlash, to defend themselves against attacks prompted by the plague, and to overcome growing internal discord. However, many activists and intellectuals moved in the opposite direction, affirming a stronger thesis of the social construction of homosexuality that took the form of a radical politics of difference. Although people of color and sex rebels pressured gay culture in this direction, there appeared a new cadre of "Queer" theorists. Influenced profoundly by French poststructuralism and Lacanian psychoanalysis, they have altered the terrain of gay theory and politics (e.g. Sedgwick 1991; Butler 1991; Fuss 1991; de Lauretis 1991; Warner 1993; Doty 1993).

Queer theory has accrued multiple meanings, from a merely useful shorthand way to speak of all gay, lesbian, bisexual, and transgendered experiences to a theoretical sensibility that pivots on transgression or permanent rebellion. I take as central to Queer theory its challenge to what has been the dominant foundational concept of both homophobic and affirmative homosexual theory: the assumption of a unified homosexual identity. I interpret Queer theory as contesting this foundation and therefore the very telos of Western homosexual politics.

Modern Western homophobic and gay-affirmative theory has assumed a homosexual subject. Dispute revolved around its origin (natural or social), changing social forms and roles, its moral meaning, and political strategies of repression and resistance. There has been little serious disagreement regarding the assumption that homosexual theory and politics has as its object "the homosexual" as a stable, unified, and identifiable human type. Drawing from the critique of unitary identity politics by people of color and sex rebels, and from the poststructural critique of "representational" models of language, Queer theorists argue that identities are always multiple or at best composites with literally an infinite number of ways in which "identity-components" (e.g., sexual orientation, race, class, nationality, gender, age, able-ness) can intersect or combine. Any specific identity construction, moreover, is arbitrary, unstable, and exclusionary. Identity constructions necessarily entail the silencing or exclusion of some experiences or forms of life. For example, asserting a black, middle-class, American lesbian identity silences differences that relate to religion, regional location, subcultural identification, relation to feminism, age, or education. Identity constructs are necessarily unstable since they elicit opposition or resistance by people whose experiences or interests are submerged by a particular assertion of identity. Finally, rather than viewing the affirmation of identity as necessarily liberating, Queer theorists view them as, in part, disciplinary and regulatory structures. Identity constructions function as templates defining selves and behaviors and therefore excluding a range of possible ways to frame the self, body, desires, actions, and social relations.

Approaching identities as multiple, unstable, and regulatory may suggest to critics the undermining of gay theory and politics, but, for Queer theorists, it presents new and productive possibilities. Although I detect a strain of anti-identity politics in some Queer theory, the aim is not to abandon identity as a category of knowledge and politics but to render it permanently open and contestable as to its meaning and political role. In other words, decisions about identity categories become pragmatic, related to concerns of situational advantage, political gain, and conceptual utility. The gain, say Queer theorists, of figuring identity as permanently open as to its meaning and political use is that it encourages the public surfacing of differences or a culture where multiple voices and interests are heard and shape gay life and politics.

Queer theory articulates a related objection to a homosexual theory and politics organized on the foundation of the homosexual subject: This project reproduces the hetero/homosexual binary, a code that perpetuates the heterosexualization of society. Modern Western affirmative homosexual theory may naturalize or normalize the gay subject or even register it as an agent of social liberation, but it has the effect of consolidating heterosexuality and homosexuality as master categories of sexual and social identity; it reinforces the modern regime of sexuality. Queer theory wishes to challenge the regime of sexuality itself, that is, the knowledges that construct the self as sexual and that assume heterosexuality and homosexuality as categories marking the truth of sexual selves. The modern system of sexuality organized around the heterosexual or homosexual self is approached as a system of knowledge, one that structures the institutional and cultural life of Western societies. In other words, Queer theorists view heterosexuality and homosexuality not simply as identities or social statuses but as categories of knowledge, a language that frames what we know as bodies, desires, sexualities, identities. This is a normative language as it shapes moral boundaries and political hierarchies. Queer theorists shift their focus from an exclusive preoccupation with the oppression and liberation of the homosexual subject to an analysis of the institutional practices and discourses producing sexual knowledges and the ways they organize social life, attending in particular to the way these knowledges and social practices repress differences. In this regard, Queer theory is suggesting that the study of homosexuality should not be a study of a minority – the making of the lesbian/gay/bisexual subject – but a study of those knowledges and social practices that organize "society" as a whole by sexualizing – heterosexualizing or homosexualizing – bodies, desires, acts, identities, social relations, knowledges, culture, and social institutions. Queer theory aspires to transform homosexual theory into a general social theory or one standpoint from which to analyze social dynamics.

NOTE

1   The index of the *American Journal of Sociology* indicates that between 1895 and 1965 there was 1 article printed on homosexuality and 13 articles listed under the heading of "Sex," most of which addressed issues of gender, marriage, or lifestyle. The index of the *American Sociological Review* indicates that between 1936 and 1960 there were 14 articles published under the heading of "Sexual Behavior," most of which did not address issues of sexuality. One journal article commented on the absence of a sociology of sexuality. "The sociology of sex is quite undeveloped, although sex is a social force of the first magnitude. Sociologists have investigated the changing roles of men and women ... [and] the sexual aspects of marriage. . . . Occasionally a good study on illegitimacy or prostitution appears. However, when it is stated that a sociology of sex does not exist, I mean that our discipline has not investigated, in any substantial manner, the social causes, conditions and consequences of heterosexual and homosexual activities of all types" (Bowman 1949). Another sociologist, one who later became President of the American Sociological Association, also studied sexuality, Kingsley Davis (1937, 1939). Some twenty years after Bowman lamented the absence of a sociology of sexuality, Edward Sagarin (1971) reiterated this lament. "Here and there an investigation, a minor paper, a little data, particularly in the literature of criminology . . . and what at the time was called social disorganization . . . marked the totality of sex literature in sociology (p. 384).

REFERENCES

Adam, Barry. 1987. *The Rise of a Gay and Lesbian Movement*. Boston: G. K. Hall.

Allison, Dorothy. 1981. "Lesbian Politics in the '80s." *New York Native*. Dec. 7–20.

Altman, Dennis. 1971. *Homosexual Liberation and Oppression*. New York: Avon.

——. 1982. The *Homosexualization of America*. Boston: Beacon.

Anzaldua, Gloria and Moraga, Cherrie (eds). 1983. *This Bridge Called My Back*. New York: Kitchen Table Press.

Beam, Joseph (ed.) 1986. *In the Life*. Boston: Allyson.

Bowman, Claude 1949. "Cultural Ideology and Heterosexual Reality: A Preface to Sociological Research." *American Sociological Review*, 14: 624–33.

Bright, Susie. 1984. "The Year of the Lustful Lesbian." *New York Native*, July 30–Aug. 12.

Butler, Judith. 1991. *Gender Trouble*. New York: Routledge.

Califia, Pat. 1981. "What is Gay Liberation?" *The Advocate*, June 25.

——. 1979. "A Secret Side of Lesbian Sexuality." *The Advocate*, Dec. 27.

Chauncey, George, Jr. 1982. "From Sexual Inversion to Homosexuality: Medicine and the Changing Conceptualization of Female Deviance." *Salmagundi*, 58/59: 114–46.

Davis, Kingsley, 1937. "The Sociology of Prostitution." *American Sociological Review*, 2: 744–55.

——. 1939. "Illegitimacy and the Social Structure." *American Journal of Sociology*, 45: 215–33.

D'Emilio, John. 1983. *Sexual Politics, Sexual Communities*. Chicago: University of Chicago Press.

de Lauretis, Teresa. 1991. "Queer Theory: Lesbian and Gay Sexualities." *Differences*, 3: iii–xviii.

Doty, Alexander. 1993. *Making Things Perfectly Queer*. Minneapolis: University of Minnesota Press.

Epstein, Steven. 1987. "Gay Politics, Ethnie Identity: The Limits of Social Constructionism." *Socialist Review*, 93/94 (May–Aug.): 9–54.

Faderman, Lillian. 1981. *Surpassing the Love of Men*. New York: Morrow.

Ferguson, Ann. 1989. *Blood at the Root*. Boston: Pandora Press.

Foucault, Michel. 1980. *The History of Sexuality, Volume 1*. New York: Vintage.

Fuss, Diana (ed). 1991. *Inside/Out*. New York: Routledge.

Katz, Jonathan. 1976. *Gay American History*. New York: Thomas Y. Crowell.

——. 1983. *Gay/Lesbian Almanac*. New York: Harper &: Row.

Lorde, Audre. 1984. *Sister Outsider*. Freedom, Calif: The Crossing Press.

McIntosh, Mary. 1968. "The Homosexual Role."

Moraga, Cherrie. 1983. *Loving in the War Years*. Boston: South End Press.

Phelan, Shane. 1989. *Identity Politics*. Philadelphia: Temple University Press.

Plummer, Ken (ed.) 1981. *The Making of the Modern Homosexual*. London: Hutchinson.

Rubin Gayle, 1984. "Thinking Sex." C. Vance (ed.), *Pleasure and Danger*. Boston: Routledge, pp. 267–319.

Sedgwick, Eve. 1991. The Epistemology of the Closet. Berkeley: University of California Press.

Seidman, Steven, 1992. *Embattled Eros*. New York: Routledge.

——. 1993. "Identity and Politics in a Postmodern Gay Culture: Some Conceptual and Historical Notes." In M. Warner (ed.), *Fear of a Queer Planet*. Minneapolis: University of Minnesota Press.

——. 1995. "Deconstructing Queer Theory or the Under-Theorizing of the Social and the Ethical." In L. Nicholson and S. Seidman (eds), *Social Postmodernism*. Cambridge: Cambridge University Press.

Smith-Rosenberg, Carroll. 1975. "The Female World of Love and Ritual-Relations Between Women in Nineteenth-Century America." *Signs*, 9: 1–29.

——. 1990. "Discourses of Sexuality and Subjectivity: The New Women, 1870–1936." In M. Duberman et al. (eds), *Hidden from History*. New York Penguin, pp. 264–80.

Stein, Edward (ed.). 1992. *Forms of Desire*. New York: Routledge.

Trumbach, Randolph, 1977. "London's Sodomites: Homosexual Behavior and Western Culture in the Eighteenth Century." *Journal of Social History*, 11: 1–33.

Warner, Michael (ed.). 1993. Fear of a Queen Planet. Minneapolis: University of Minnesota Press.

Weeks, Jeffrey. 1977. *Coming Out*. London: Quartet.

PART V

STANDPOINT THEORIES AMID GLOBALIZATION

CHAPTER THIRTEEN

FEMINIST THEORIES

CHAPTER MENU

Concise Reader in Sociological Theory: Theorists, Concepts, and Current Applications,
First Edition. Edited by Michele Dillon. Editorial material and organization
© 2021 John Wiley & Sons Ltd. Published 2021 by John Wiley & Sons Ltd.

Of all the many advances in sociological theory since its founding in the late nineteenth century, the emergence of feminist theories is the most transformative in impacting how we think about the social world. Though encompassing an array of different perspectives with various particular nuances, common to feminist theory is the core argument that women's work in the domestic (family) and public world needs to be fully recognized; that the personhood of women and men are equal even as history and the man-made institutions that have evolved convey otherwise. An androcentric culture – the product of a patriarchal society – as **Charlotte Perkins Gilman** (1860–1935) elaborates (see excerpt *13a The Man-Made World or Our Androcentric Culture*), presents women as a subspecies, essentially inferior to men. Though writing in 1911, Gilman's argument resonates even today as women confront a social reality in which women's activities, whether in the home, in the workplace, or in leisure arenas still contend to be treated on a par with men's. Notwithstanding the major achievements of women across all spheres of society, women are nonetheless frequently treated as the "second sex" – as captured by the French feminist writer Simone de Beauvoir (1949/1953) – whose interests, desires, aspirations, feelings, experiences, and accomplishments are invariably less important than those of men.

In 1979, **Arlie Hochschild** first articulated her now well-known, highly impactful theory of emotion management or emotion work (subsequently published as *The Managed Heart*) in which she drew attention to the fact that feelings and specifically feeling rules, are socially structured. Feeling rules, expectations and conventions about who may and, indeed, should feel and express certain emotions, are gendered, she elaborated – and are grounded in assumptions about the allegedly different, essential natures of women and men, a stance that the gender equality movement has sought to change and thus to open up the breadth of socially legitimate emotions available to women and men alike.

Feminist theorists not only open up our understanding of women and of gender equality and inequality, but they also instruct us how to study the social world through a lens that at once disrupts taken-for-granted knowledge and plumbs women's diverse experiences for new knowledges. The Canadian sociologist **Dorothy E. Smith** elaborates (see excerpt *13c The Conceptual Practices of Power*) on what is entailed in studying the standpoint of women in society. She argues that women's experiences are both marginalized and devalued across the broad spectrum of ruling texts (e.g. laws, policies and regulations, religious texts, advertising and other media discourses) and across the multiplicity of ruling institutional practices (e.g. how work is organized, how illnesses and diagnoses are categorized and studied) that define women's and men's reality. Drawing on a phenomenological framework, she illuminates how the embodiment and institutionalization of these established texts and practices create ways of seeing that do not fully acknowledge or apprehend the specific ways in which women directly experience the everyday and the everynight world in ways that are very different to men's experiences, nor how these differences that are their respective realities underpin and circumscribe gender relations and all relations of power. Women's experiences in two different worlds, the domestic (home and family) and the public/work, yield realities that are unaligned and frequently contradictory, thus

necessarily bifurcating the consciousness of women as they move between and negotiate these divergent realities and their attendant experiences. The standpoint of
women, Smith argues, needs to be taken seriously and taken deep account of in any
knowledge-gathering enterprise. This requires sociologists (and others) to enter into
the locally situated everyday worlds of women and to apprehend those worlds from
those women's experiences of how their particular here-and-now world works – or
doesn't, due to established practices that, however well-intentioned, are inept in dealing with the experiences (e.g. sexual abuse) women bring to the institutional authorities established to respond to their experiences (e.g. the police, social workers,
doctors). Feminist standpoint theory, with its emphasis on "knowing from within"
individuals' particular localized experiences is applicable, by extension, to understanding the everyday/everynight experiences of all those groups whose subjective
ways of knowing, of experiencing daily life amid oppression, have been similarly marginalized (e.g. African Americans, LGBTQ+) or excluded (e.g. Indigenous peoples)
across history by the established, objective knowledge (socially constructed by privileged white men) and the practices that it underpins and legitimates.

The reassessment of feminist theory to specifically pay attention to the exclusion of
minority racialized voices and experiences was the critical task undertaken by
Patricia Hill Collins who introduced intersectionality theory to sociology. Her
highly impactful book, *Black Feminist Thought: Knowledge, Consciousness and the
Politics of Empowerment*, first published in 1990, is a forceful analysis of the historical,
institutional, and cultural degradation of Black women in a society which privileges
whiteness, including the privileging of white women over Black women. Collins
highlights (see excerpt *13d Black Feminist Thought*) how Black women's experiences
of both the domestic and the public worlds are invariably different to those of white
women largely because Black women have a long history of work activity in and
across both worlds simultaneously, as well as an experientially driven, strong sense of
shared community solidarity with other Black women. Notwithstanding their shared
structural and cultural position of intersecting racial and gender inequality, Collins
(1990: 24) emphasizes the diversity of Black women's experiences and thus challenges
the essentialist claim that all Black women have similar experiences and, or, ideas
about those experiences; consequently, she argues, it makes better sense to talk of "a
Black women's standpoint" than "a Black woman's standpoint."

As Collins (1990: 67–8) elaborates, the subjugation of Black women in, for
example, media representations and political discourses that portray them as "ste-
reotypical mammies, matriarchs, welfare recipients, and hot mommas," is far from
being benign. Rather, such representations function as "controlling images" that
contribute to sustaining the oppression of Black women, even as Black women as
exemplified by their accomplished and agential lives have a strong history of
debunking and fighting back against such disempowering representations. Collins
argues that Black feminist knowledge is grounded in the experiences and writings
and artistry of Black women such as Toni Morrison who use their artistry and
their work to give voice to experiences that are both particular to individual Black
women and also especially common to Black women; today, I consider Beyoncé

and her video-album *Lemonade* as exemplary of the kind of knowledge and empowerment conveyed by the Black feminist thought that Collins celebrates as Black women's standpoint. It narrates images and words that reflect and point to the impact of intersecting gender and racial power inequalities, and to how those grounded identities position Black women to be exposed to specific everyday/everynight experiences as well as, importantly, how they use those experiences to act back on their oppressors.

The concept of intersectionality aims to capture the dynamic array of unequal identity positions that a given individual may occupy in a particular societal context – not just gender and race, but also sexuality, social class, religion, geography, nationality, etc. The dynamism of the concept, and its analytical and empirical scope, makes it, on the surface, a highly accessible term to invoke. And indeed the current popularity of the construct is a testament to the powerful analytical insight first brought to notice by Collins and other race and feminist theorists; identity is never and can never be a singular entity and nor can identity be detached from its embedding in a complex comingling of historical, cultural, and biographical forces. Yet, intersectionality has also come under some criticism, in large part, for the ways in which some scholars detach the concept from the expected political activism that its initial deployment assumed. As Collins explains (see excerpt *13e Intersectionality's Definitional Dilemmas*), scholarship or theorizing grounded in intersectionality must necessarily have a political goal: it must always be intertwined with a commitment to actual practices that seek to ameliorate the macro-structural and micro-relational power inequalities within which any/all intersectional identities are grounded.

The accomplishment of feminist theory to illuminate that gender, gender hierarchies, gender relations and gendered experiences are social structured and socially structuring, also led to a deeper understanding of *masculinities* and of how societal expectations of men and of men's roles and self-presentation(s) are similarly entangled in structures of social practice (Connell 1995). As **R.W. Connell** and **James W. Messerschmidt** discuss (see excerpt *13f Hegemonic Masculinity*), masculinity is not a singular paradigm even though a hegemonic masculinity exerts an overarching powerful force in social relations and institutional practices. Comingling with the socially dominant masculinity, are variations grounded in different class-based, racialized, and non-heteronormative masculinities, and depending on the specific, local sociohistorical context, they can prevail and act back against, complicate and destabilize the (culturally superior) hegemonic masculinity. In reassessing the theoretical validity of hegemonic masculinity, Connell and Messerschmidt argue for a more fluid understanding of masculinity and of its polar concept, femininity, as well as avoidance of systemically seeing gender relations in terms of domination/subordination. Thus they argue that the idea of men's collective dominance over women needs to be reassessed in light of women's personal and collective agency against male domination. Today, the #MeToo movement conveys women's energized collective push for transformative change in how social attitudes and institutional practices cultivate collusion in male domination, and allow its maintenance both structurally as well as in personal relationships at work and at home. Connell and Messerschmidt also point out the tensions that inhere in the gap between theoretical constructs of masculinity and of gender hierarchies more generally, and their empirical relevance across an array of local, national, and transnational societal contexts.

REFERENCES

Collins, Patricia Hill. 1990. *Black Feminist Thought: Knowledge, Consciousness, and the Politics of Empowerment.* New York: Routledge. 2nd ed. 2000.

Connell, R.W. 1995. *Masculinities.* New York: Cambridge University Press.

De Beauvoir, Simone. 1949/1953. *The Second Sex.* Harmondsworth: Penguin.

Hochschild, Arlie. 1983. *The Managed Heart. Commercialization of Human Feeling.* Berkeley: University of California Press.

13A Charlotte Perkins Gilman from *The Man-Made World or Our Androcentric Culture*

Original publication details: Charlotte Perkins Gilman, 1911. *The Man-Made World or Androcentric Culture*, pp. 17–22. New York: Charlton Company. Public domain.

Our historic period is not very long. Real written history only goes back a few thousand years, beginning with the stone records of ancient Egypt. During this period we have had almost universally what is here called an Androcentric Culture. The history, such as it was, was made and written by men.

The mental, the mechanical, the social development, was almost wholly theirs. We have, so far, lived and suffered and died in a man-made world. So general, so unbroken, has been this condition, that to mention it arouses no more remark than the statement of a natural law. We have taken it for granted, since the dawn of civilization, that "mankind" meant men-kind, and the world was theirs.

Women we have sharply delimited. Women were a sex; "the sex," according to chivalrous toasts; they were set apart for special services peculiar to femininity. As one English scientist put it, in 1888, "Women are not only not the race – they are not even half the race, but a subspecies told off for reproduction only."

This mental attitude toward women is even more clearly expressed by Mr. H. B. Marriot-Watson in his article on "The American Woman" in the "Nineteenth Century" for June, 1904, where he says: "Her constitutional restlessness has caused her to abdicate those functions which alone excuse or explain her existence." This is a peculiarly happy and condensed expression of the relative position of women during our androcentric culture. The man was accepted as the race type without one dissentient voice; and the woman – a strange, diverse creature, quite disharmonious in the accepted scheme of things – was excused and explained only as a female.

She has needed volumes of such excuse and explanation; also, apparently, volumes of abuse and condemnation. In any library catalogue we may find books upon books about women: physiological, sentimental, didactic, religious – all manner of books about women, as such. Even to-day in the works of Marholm – poor young Weininger, Moebius, and others, we find the same perpetual discussion of women – as such.

This is a book about men – as such. It differentiates between the human nature and the sex nature. It will not go so far as to allege man's masculine traits to be all that excuse or explain his existence; but it will point out what are masculine traits as distinct from human ones, and what has been the effect on our human life of the unbridled dominance of one sex.

We can see at once, glaringly, what would have been the result of giving all human affairs into female hands. Such an extraordinary and deplorable situation would have "feminized" the world. We should have all become "effeminate."

See how in our use of language the case is clearly shown. The adjectives and derivatives based on woman's distinctions are alien and derogatory when applied to human affairs; "effeminate" – too female, connotes contempt, but has no masculine analogue; whereas "emasculate" – not enough male, is a term of reproach, and has no feminine analogue. "Virile" – manly, we oppose to "puerile" – childish, and the very word "virtue" is derived from "vir" – a man.

Even in the naming of other animals we have taken the male as the race type, and put on a special termination to indicate "his female," as in lion, lioness; leopard, leopardess; while all our human scheme of things rests on the same tacit assumption; man being held the human type; woman a sort of accompaniment and subordinate assistant, merely essential to the making of people.

She has held always the place of a preposition in relation to man. She has been considered above him or below him, before him, behind him, beside him, a wholly relative existence – "Sydney's sister," "Pembroke's mother" – but never by any chance Sydney or Pembroke herself.

Acting on this assumption, all human standards have been based on male characteristics, and when we wish to praise the work of a woman, we say she has "a masculine mind."

It is no easy matter to deny or reverse a universal assumption. The human mind has had a good many jolts since it began to think, but after each upheaval it settles down as peacefully as the vine-growers on Vesuvius, accepting the last lava crust as permanent ground.

What we see immediately around us, what we are born into and grow up with, be it mental furniture or physical, we assume to be the order of nature.

If a given idea has been held in the human mind for many generations, as almost all our common ideas have, it takes sincere and continued effort to remove it; and if it is one of the oldest we have in stock, one of the big, common, unquestioned world ideas, vast is the labor of those who seek to change it.

Nevertheless, if the matter is one of importance, if the previous idea was a palpable error, of large and evil effect, and if the new one is true and widely important, the effort is worth making.

The task here undertaken is of this sort. It seeks to show that what we have all this time called "human nature" and deprecated, was in great part only male nature, and good enough in its place; that what we have called "masculine" and admired as such, was in large part human, and should be applied to both sexes; that what we have called "feminine" and condemned, was also largely human and applicable to both. Our androcentric culture is so shown to have been, and still to be, a masculine culture in excess, and therefore undesirable.

In the preliminary work of approaching these facts it will be well to explain how it can be that so wide and serious an error should have been made by practically all men. The reason is simply that they were men. They were males, and saw women as females – and not otherwise.

13B Arlie Hochschild from *Emotion Work, Feeling Rules, and Social Structure*

Original publication details: Arlie Hochschild, 1979. "Emotion Work, Feeling Rules, and Social Structure." *American Journal of Sociology* 85: 566–568. Reproduced with permission of University of Chicago Press.

Like other rules, feeling rules can be obeyed halfheartedly or boldly broken, the latter at varying costs. A feeling rule can be in varying proportions external or internal. Feeling rules differ curiously from other types of rules in that they do not apply to action but to what is often taken as a precursor to action. Therefore they tend to be latent and resistant to formal codification.

Feeling rules reflect patterns of social membership. Some rules may be nearly universal, such as the rule that one should not enjoy killing or witnessing the killing of a human being, including oneself.[1] Other rules are unique to particular social groups and can be used to distinguish among them as alternate governments or colonizers of individual internal events.

Framing Rules and Feeling Rules: Issues in Ideology

Rules for managing feeling are implicit in any ideological stance; they are the "bottom side" of ideology. Ideology has often been construed as a flatly cognitive framework, lacking systematic implications for how we manage feelings, or, indeed, for how we feel. Yet, drawing on Durkheim (1961),[2] Geertz (1964), and in part on Goffman (1974), we can think of ideology as an interpretive framework that can be described in terms of framing rules and feeling rules. By "framing rules" I refer to the rules according to which we ascribe definitions or meanings to situations. For example, an individual can define the situation of getting fired as yet another instance of capitalists' abuse of workers or as yet another result of personal failure. In each case, the frame may reflect a more general rule about assigning blame. By "feeling rules" I refer to guidelines for the assessment of fits and misfits between feeling and situation. For example, according to one feeling rule, one can be legitimately angry at the boss or company; according to another, one cannot. Framing and feeling rules are back to back and mutually imply each other.

It follows that when an individual changes an ideological stance, he or she drops old rules and assumes new ones for reacting to situations, cognitively and emotively. A sense of rights and duties applied to feelings in situations is also changed. One uses emotion sanctions differently and accepts different sanctioning from others. For example, feeling rules in American society have differed for men and women because of the assumption that their natures differ basically. The feminist movement brings with it a new set of rules for framing the work and family life of men and women: the same balance of priorities in work and family now ideally applies to men as to women. This carries with it implications for feeling. A woman can now as legitimately (as a man) become angry (rather than simply upset or disappointed) over abuses at work, since her heart is supposed to be in that work and she has the right to hope, as much as a man would, for advancement. Or, a man has the right to feel angry at the loss of custody if he has shown himself the fitter parent. "Old-fashioned" feelings are now as subject to new chidings and cajolings as are "old-fashioned" perspectives on the same array of situations.

One can defy an ideological stance not simply by maintaining an alternative frame on a situation but by maintaining an alternative set of feeling rights and obligations. One can defy an ideological stance by inappropriate affect and by refusing to perform the emotion management necessary to feel what, according to the official frame, it would seem fitting to feel. Deep acting or emotion work, then, can be a form of obeisance to a given ideological stance, lax emotion management a clue to an ideology lapsed or rejected.

As some ideologies gain acceptance and others dwindle, contending sets of feeling rules rise and fall.[3] Sets of feeling rules contend for a place in people's minds as a governing standard with which to compare the actual lived experience of, say, the senior prom, the abortion, the wedding, the birth, the first job, the first layoff, the divorce. What we call "the changing climate of opinion" partly involves a changed framing of the "same" sorts of events. For example, each of two mothers may feel guilty about leaving her small child at day care while working all day. One mother, a feminist, may feel that she should not feel as guilty as she does. The second, a traditionalist, may feel that she should feel more guilty than, in fact, she does feel.

Part of what we refer to as the psychological effects of "rapid social change," or "unrest," is a change in the relation of feeling rule to feeling and a lack of clarity about what the rule actually is, owing to conflicts and contradictions between contending sets of rules. Feelings and frames are deconventionalized, but not yet reconventionalized. We may, like the marginal man, say, "I don't know how I should feel."

NOTES

1   But this, too, seems to be culturally variable. Erving Goffman points out that hangings in the 16th century were a social event that the participant was "supposed to enjoy," a rule that has since disappeared in civilian society.

2   Durkheim, in *The Elementary Forms of Religious Life*, conveys just this understanding of the relation of world view to feeling rules: "When the Christian, during the ceremonies commemorating the Passion, and the Jew, on the anniversary of the fall of Jerusalem, fast and mortify themselves, it is not in giving way to a sadness which they feel spontaneously. Under these circumstances, the internal state of the believer is out of all proportion to the severe

abstinences to which they submit themselves. If he is sad, it is primarily because he consents to being sad. And he consents to it in order to affirm his faith" (Durkheim 1961, p. 224). Again, "An individual . . . if he is strongly attached to the society of which he is a member, feels that he is morally held to participating in its sorrows and joys; not to be interested in them would be equivalent to breaking the bonds uniting him to the group; it would be renouncing all desire for it and contradicting himself" (1961, p. 446, emphases mine).

3   Collins suggests that ideology functions as a weapon in the conflict between contending elites. Groups contend not only for access to the means of economic production or the means of violence but also for access to the means of "emotion production" (1975, p. 59). Rituals are seen as useful tools for forging emotional solidarity (that can be used against others) and for setting up status hierarchies (that can dominate those who find that the new ideals have denigrating effects on themselves).

REFERENCES

Randall Collins. 1975. *Conflict Sociology*. New York: Academic Press.

Emile Durkheim. 1961. *The Elementary Forms of the Religious Life*. New York: Collier.

Clifford Geertz. 1964. "Ideology as a Cultural System," in *The Interpretation of Cultures*. London: Hutchinson, pp. 49–76.

Erving Goffman. 1974. *Frame Analysis*. New York: Harper & Row.

13C Dorothy E. Smith from *The Conceptual Practices of Power: A Feminist Sociology of Knowledge*

Original publication details: Dorothy E. Smith, 1990. *The Conceptual Practices of Power*, pp. 12–14, 18–21, 22, 28. Boston: Northeastern University Press.

The enterprise of this book has a double character. It begins with the discovery of learning how to explore the social from within without allowing it to be swallowed up into the wholly subjective. That means exploring as insiders the socially organized practices that constitute objectified forms of knowledge. It means exploring what we already know how to do and participate in, and that, of course, means finding methods of exploration that don't fall into the same objectifying mode. Thus we look for a method of inquiry where inquiry itself is a critique of socially organized practices of knowing and hence is itself an exploration of method.

The opening up of women's experience gives sociologists access to social realities previously unavailable, indeed repressed. But can a feminist sociology be content to describe these realities in the terms of our discipline, merely extending our field of interest to include work on gender roles, the women's movement, women in the labor force, sexuality, the social psychology of women, and so forth? Thinking more boldly or perhaps just thinking the whole thing through further brings us to ask how a sociology might look if it began from women's standpoint and what might happen to a sociology that attempts to deal seriously with that standpoint. Following this line of thought has consequences larger than they seem at first.

It is not enough to supplement an established sociology by addressing ourselves to what has been left out or overlooked, or by making women's issues into sociological issues. That does not change the standpoint built into existing sociological procedures, but merely makes the sociology of women an addendum to the body of objectified knowledge.

The first difficulty is that how sociology is thought – its methods, conceptual schemes, and theories – has been based on and built up within the male social universe, even when women have participated in its doing. This sociology has taken for granted not only an itemized inventory of issues or subject matters (industrial sociology, political sociology, social stratification, and so forth) but the fundamental social and political structures under which these become relevant and are ordered. There is thus a disjunction between how women experience the world and the concepts and theoretical schemes by which society's self-consciousness is inscribed. My early explorations of these issues included a graduate seminar in which we discussed the possibility of a women's sociology. Two students expressed their sense that theories of the emergence of leadership in small groups just did not apply to what had happened in an experimental group situation they had participated in. They could not find the correlates of the theory in their experiences.

A second difficulty is that the worlds opened up by speaking from the standpoint of women have not been and are not on a basis of equality with the objectified bodies of knowledge that have constituted and expressed the standpoint of men. The worlds of men have had, and still have, an authority over the worlds that are traditionally women's and still are predominantly women's – the worlds of household, children, and neighborhood. And though women do not inhabit only these worlds, for the vast majority of women they are the primary ground of our lives, shaping the course of our lives and our participation in other relations. Furthermore, objectified knowledges are part of the world from which our kind of society is governed. The domestic world stands in a dependent relation to that other, and its whole character is subordinate to it.

The two difficulties are related to each other in a special way. The effect of the second interacting with the first is to compel women to think their world in the concepts and terms in which men think theirs. Hence the established social forms of consciousness alienate women from their own experience.

The profession of sociology has been predicated on a universe grounded in men's experience and relationships and still largely appropriated by men as their "territory." Sociology is part of the practice by which we are all governed; that practice establishes its relevances. Thus the institutions that lock sociology into the structures occupied by men are the same institutions that lock women into the situations in which we have found ourselves oppressed. To unlock the latter leads logically to an unlocking of the former. What follows, then, or rather what then becomes possible – for it is of course by no means inevitable – is less a shift in the subject matter than a different conception of how sociology might become a means of understanding our experience and the conditions of our experience (both women's and men's) in contemporary capitalist society.

Relations of Ruling and Objectified Knowledge

When I speak here of governing or ruling I mean something more general than the notion of government as political organization. I refer rather to that total complex of activities, differentiated into many spheres, by which our kind of society is ruled, managed, and administered. It includes what the business world calls *management*, it includes the professions, it includes government and the activities of those who are selecting, training, and indoctrinating those who will be its governors. The last includes those who provide and elaborate the procedures by which it is governed and develop methods for accounting for how it is done – namely, the business schools, the sociologists, the economists. These are the institutions through which we are ruled and through which we, and I emphasize this *we*, participate in ruling.

Sociology, then, I conceive as much more than a gloss on the enterprise that justifies and rationalizes it, and at the same time as much less than "science." The governing of our kind of society is done in abstract concepts and symbols, and sociology helps create them by transposing the actualities of people's lives and experience into the conceptual currency with which they can be governed.

[. . .]

Women's Exclusion from the Governing Conceptual Mode

The suppression of the local and particular as a site of knowledge has been and remains gender organized. The domestic sites of women's work, traditionally identified with women, are outside and subservient to this structure. Men have functioned as subjects in the mode of governing, women have been anchored in the local and particular phase of the bifurcated world. It has been a condition of a man's being able to enter and become absorbed in the conceptual mode, and to forget the dependence of his being in that mode upon his bodily existence, that he does not have to focus his activities and interests upon his bodily existence. Full participation in the abstract mode of action requires liberation from attending to needs in the concrete and particular. The organization of work in managerial and professional circles depends upon the alienation of subjects from their bodily and local existence. The structure of work and the structure of career take for granted that these matters have been provided for in such a way that they will not interfere with a man's action and participation in that world. Under the traditional gender regime, providing for a man's liberation from Bierstedt's Aristotelian categories is a woman who keeps house for him, bears and cares for his children, washes his clothes, looks after him when he is sick, and generally provides for the logistics of his bodily existence.

Women's work in and around professional and managerial settings performs analogous functions. Women's work mediates between the abstracted and conceptual and the material form in which it must travel to communicate. Women do the clerical work, the word processing, the interviewing for the survey; they take messages, handle the mail, make appointments, and care for patients. At almost every point women mediate for men at work the relationship between the conceptual mode of action and the actual concrete forms in which it is and must be realized, and the actual material conditions upon which it depends.

Marx's concept of alienation is applicable here in a modified form. The simplest formulation of alienation posits a relation between the work individuals do and an external order oppressing them in which their work contributes to the strength of the order that oppresses them. This is the situation of women in this relation. The more successful women are in mediating the world of concrete particulars so that men do not have to become engaged with (and therefore conscious of) that world as a condition to their abstract activities, the more complete men's absorption in it and the more effective its authority. The dichotomy between the two worlds organized on the basis of gender separates the dual forms of consciousness; the governing consciousness dominates the primary world of a locally situated consciousness but cannot cancel it; the latter is a subordinated, suppressed, absent, but absolutely essential ground of the governing consciousness. The gendered organization of subjectivity dichotomizes the two worlds, estranges them, and silences the locally situated consciousness by silencing women.

Women Sociologists and the Contradiction between Sociology and Experience

Bifurcation of consciousness is experienced as women move between these two modes with a working consciousness active in both. We are situated as sociologists across a contradiction in our discipline's relationship to our experience of the world. Traditional gender roles deny the existence of the contradiction; suppression makes it invisible, as it has made other contradictions between women and men invisible. Recognizing, exploring, and working within it means finding alternative ways of thinking and inquiry to those that would implicate us in the sociological practice of the relations of ruling.

The theories, concepts, and methods of our discipline claim to be capable of accounting for the world we experience directly. But they have been organized around and built up from a way of knowing the world that takes for granted and subsumes without examining the conditions of its own existence. It is not capable of analyzing its relation to its conditions because the sociological subject as an actual person in an actual concrete setting has been canceled in the procedures that objectify and separate her from her knowledge. Thus the linkage that points back to its conditions is obliterated.

For women those conditions are a direct practical problem to be somehow solved in doing sociological work and following a sociological career. How are we to manage career and children (including of course negotiating sharing that work with a man)? How is domestic work to get done? How is career time to be coordinated with family caring time? How is the remorseless structure of the children's school schedule to be coordinated with the equally exigent scheduling of professional and managerial work? Rarely are these problems solved by the full sharing of responsibilities between women and men. But for the most part these claims, these calls, these somehow unavoidable demands, are still ongoingly present and pressing for women, particularly, of course, for those with children. Thus the relation between ourselves as practicing sociologists and ourselves as working women is always there for us as a practical matter, an ordinary, unremarked, yet pervasive aspect of our experience of the world. The bifurcation of consciousness becomes for us a daily chasm to be crossed, on the one side of which is this special conceptual activity of thought, research, teaching, and administration, and on the other the world of localized activities oriented toward particular others, keeping things clean, managing somehow the house and household and the children – a world in which the particularities of persons in their full organic immediacy (feeding, cleaning up the vomit, changing the diapers) are inescapable. Even if this isn't something that currently preoccupies us, as it no longer preoccupies me, our present is given shape by a past that was thus.

We have learned, as women in sociology, that the discipline has not been one that we could enter and occupy on the same terms as men. We do not fully appropriate its authority, that is, the right to author and authorize the acts of knowing and thinking that are the knowing and thinking of the discipline. Feminist theory in sociology is still *feminist* theory and not just plain sociological theory. The inner principles of our theoretical work remain lodged outside us. The frames of reference that order the terms upon which inquiry and discussion are conducted have originated with men. The subjects of sociological sentences (if they have a subject) are still male, even though protocol now calls for a degendering of pronouns. Even before we became conscious of our sex as the basis of an exclusion (they have not been talking about us), we nonetheless could not fully enter ourselves as the subjects of its statements. The problem remains; we must suspend our sex and suspend our knowledge of who we are as well as who it is that in fact is speaking and of whom. Even now, we do not fully participate in the declarations and formulations of its mode of consciousness. The externalization of sociology as a profession is for women an estrangement both in suppressing dimensions of our experience as women and in creating for our use systems of interpreting and understanding our society that enforce that suppression.

Women who move between these two worlds have access to an experience that displays for us the structure of the bifurcated consciousness. For those of us who are sociologists, it undermines our commitment to a sociology aimed at an externalized body of knowledge based on an organization of experience that excludes ours.

[. . .]

The only way of knowing a socially constructed world is knowing it from within. We can never stand outside it. A relation in which sociological phenomena are objectified and presented as external to and independent of the observer is itself a special social practice also known from within. The relation of observer and object of observation, of sociologist to "subject," is a specialized social relationship. Even to be a stranger is to enter a world constituted from within as strange. The strangeness itself is the mode in which it is experienced.

[. . .]

The Standpoint of Women as a Place to Start

The standpoint of women situates the inquirer in the site of her bodily existence and in the local actualities of her working world. It is a standpoint that positions inquiry but has no specific content. Those who undertake inquiry from this standpoint begin always from women's experience as it is for women. We are the authoritative speakers of our experience. The standpoint of women situates the sociological subject prior to the entry into the abstracted conceptual mode, vested in texts, that is the order of the relations of ruling. From this standpoint, we know the everyday world through the particularities of our local practices and activities, in the actual places of our work and the actual time it takes. In making the everyday world problematic we also problematize the everyday localized practices of the objectified forms of knowledge organizing our everyday worlds.

A bifurcated consciousness is an effect of the actual social relations in which we participate as part of a daily work life. Entry as subject into the social relations of an objectified consciousness is itself an organization of actual everyday practices. The sociology that objectifies society and social relations and transforms the actualities of people's experience into the synthetic objects of its discourse is an organization of actual practices and activities. We know and use practices of thinking and inquiring sociologically that sever our knowledge of society from the society we know as we live and practice it. The conceptual practices of an alienated knowledge of society are also in and of the everyday world. In and through its conceptual practices and its everyday practices of reading and writing, we enter a mode of consciousness outside the everyday site of our bodily existence and experiencing. The standpoint of women, or at least, *this* standpoint of women at work, in the traditional ways women have worked and continue to work, exposes the alienated knowledge of the relations of ruling as the everyday practices of actual individuals. Thus, though an alienated knowledge also alienates others who are not members of the dominant white male minority, the standpoint of women distinctively opens up for exploration the conceptual practices and activities of the extralocal, objectified relations of ruling as what actual people do.

13D Patricia Hill Collins from *Black Feminist Thought: Knowledge, Consciousness, and the Politics of Empowerment*

Original publication details: Patricia Hill Collins, 1990/2009. *Black Feminist Thought*, 3rd ed, pp. 8–12, 22–24, 266–271. New York: Routledge. Reproduced with permission of Taylor & Francis.

Black Feminist Thought as Critical Social Theory

Even if they appear to be otherwise, situations such as the suppression of Black women's ideas within traditional scholarship and the struggles within the critiques of that established knowledge are inherently unstable. Conditions in the wider political economy simultaneously shape Black women's subordination and foster activism. On some level, people who are oppressed usually know it. For African-American women, the knowledge gained at intersecting oppressions of race, class, and gender provides the stimulus for crafting and passing on the subjugated knowledge[1] of Black women's critical social theory (Collins 1998, 3–10).

As an historically oppressed group, U.S. Black women have produced social thought designed to oppose oppression. Not only does the form assumed by this thought diverge from standard academic theory – it can take the form of poetry, music, essays, and the like – but the *purpose* of Black women's collective thought is distinctly different. Social theories emerging from and/or on behalf of U.S. Black women and other historically oppressed groups aim to find ways to escape from, survive in, and/or oppose prevailing social and economic injustice. In the United States, for example, African-American social and political thought analyzes institutionalized racism, not to help it work more efficiently, but to resist it. Feminism advocates women's emancipation and empowerment, Marxist social thought aims for a more equitable society, while queer theory opposes heterosexism. Beyond U.S. borders, many women from oppressed groups also struggle to understand new forms of injustice. In a transnational, postcolonial context, women within new and often Black-run nation-states in the Caribbean, Africa, and Asia struggle with new meanings attached to ethnicity, citizenship status, and religion. In increasingly multicultural European nation-states, women migrants from former colonies encounter new forms of subjugation (Yuval-Davis 1997). Social theories expressed by women emerging from these diverse groups typically do not arise from the rarefied atmosphere of their imaginations. Instead, social theories reflect women's efforts to come to terms with lived experiences within intersecting oppressions of race, class, gender, sexuality, ethnicity, nation, and religion (see, e.g., Alexander and Mohanty 1997; Mirza 1997).

Black feminist thought, U.S. Black women's critical social theory, reflects similar power relationships. For African-American women, critical social theory encompasses bodies of knowledge and sets of institutional practices that actively grapple with the central questions facing U.S. Black women as a collectivity. The need for such thought arises because African-American women as a *group* remain oppressed within a U.S. context characterized by injustice. This neither means that all African-American women within that group are oppressed in the same way, nor that some U.S. Black women do not suppress others. Black feminist thought's identity as a "critical" social theory lies in its commitment to justice, both for U.S. Black women as a collectivity and for that of other similarly oppressed groups.

Historically, two factors stimulated U.S. Black women's critical social theory. For one, prior to World War II, racial segregation in urban housing became so entrenched that the majority of African-American women lived in self-contained Black neighborhoods where their children attended overwhelmingly Black schools, and where they themselves belonged to all-Black churches and similar community organizations. Despite the fact that ghettoization was designed to foster the political control and economic exploitation of Black Americans (Squires 1994), these all-Black neighborhoods simultaneously provided a separate space where African-American women and men could use African-derived ideas to craft distinctive oppositional knowledges designed to resist racial oppression.

Every social group has a constantly evolving worldview that it uses to order and evaluate its own experiences (Sobel 1979). For African-Americans this worldview originated in the cosmologies of diverse West African ethnic groups (Diop 1974). By retaining and reworking significant elements of these West African cultures, communities of enslaved Africans offered their members explanations for slavery alternative to those advanced by slave owners (Gutman 1976; Webber 1978; Sobel 1979). These African-derived ideas also laid the foundation for the rules of a distinctive Black American civil society. Later on, confining African-Americans to all-Black areas in the rural South and Northern urban ghettos fostered the solidification of a distinctive ethos in Black civil society regarding language (Smitherman 1977), religion (Sobel 1979; Paris 1995), family structure (Sudarkasa 1981), and community politics (Brown 1994). While essential to the survival of U.S. Blacks as a group and expressed differently by individual African-Americans, these knowledges remained simultaneously hidden from and suppressed by Whites. Black oppositional knowledges existed to resist injustice, but they also remained subjugated.

As mothers, othermothers, teachers, and churchwomen in essentially all-Black rural communities and urban neighborhoods, U.S. Black women participated in constructing and reconstructing these oppositional knowledges. Through the lived experiences gained within their extended families and communities, individual African-American women fashioned their own ideas about the meaning of Black womanhood. When these ideas found collective expression, Black women's self-definitions enabled them to refashion African-influenced conceptions of self and community. These self-definitions of Black womanhood were designed to resist the negative controlling images of Black womanhood advanced by Whites as well as the discriminatory social practices that these controlling images supported. In all, Black women's participation in crafting a constantly changing African-American culture fostered distinctively Black and women-centered worldviews.

Another factor that stimulated U.S. Black women's critical social theory lay in the common experiences they gained from their jobs. Prior to World War II, U.S. Black women worked primarily in two occupations – agriculture and domestic work. Their ghettoization in domestic work sparked an important contradiction. Domestic work fostered U.S. Black women's economic exploitation, yet it simultaneously created the conditions for distinctively Black and female forms of resistance. Domestic work allowed African-American women to see White elites, both actual and aspiring, from perspectives largely obscured from Black men and from these groups themselves. In their White "families," Black women not only performed domestic duties but frequently formed strong ties with the children they nurtured, and with the employers themselves. On one level this insider relationship was satisfying to all concerned. Accounts of Black domestic workers stress the sense of self-affirmation the women experienced at seeing racist ideology demystified. But on another level these Black women knew that they could never belong to their White "families." They were economically exploited workers and thus would remain outsiders. The result was being placed in a curious *outsider-within* social location (Collins 1986), a peculiar marginality that stimulated a distinctive Black women's perspective on a variety of themes (see, e.g., Childress 1986).

Taken together, Black women's participation in constructing African-American culture in all-Black settings and the distinctive perspectives gained from their outsider-within placement in domestic work provide the material backdrop for a unique Black women's standpoint. When armed with cultural beliefs honed in Black civil society, many Black women who found themselves doing domestic work often developed distinct views of the contradictions between the dominant group's actions and ideologies. Moreover, they often shared their ideas with other African-American women. Nancy White, a Black inner-city resident, explores the connection between experience and beliefs:

> Now, I understand all these things from living. But you can't lay up on these flowery beds of ease and think that you are running your life, too. Some women, white women, can run their husband's lives for a while, but most of them have to . . . see what he tells them there is to see. If he tells them that they ain't seeing what they know they *are* seeing, then they have to just go on like it wasn't there! (in Gwaltney 1980, 148)

Not only does this passage speak to the power of the dominant group to suppress the knowledge produced by subordinate groups, but it illustrates how being in outsider-within locations can foster new angles of vision on oppression. Ms. White's Blackness makes her a perpetual outsider. She could never be a White middle-class woman lying on a "flowery bed of ease." But her work of caring for White women allowed her an insider's view of some of the contradictions between White women thinking that they are running their lives and the patriarchal power and authority in their households.

Practices such as these, whether experienced oneself or learned by listening to African-American women who have had them, have encouraged many U.S. Black women to question the contradictions between dominant ideologies of American womanhood and U.S. Black women's devalued status. If women are allegedly passive and fragile, then why are Black women treated as "mules" and assigned heavy cleaning chores? If good mothers are supposed to stay at home with their children, then why are U.S. Black women on public assistance forced to find jobs and leave their children in day care? If women's highest calling is to become mothers, then why are Black teen mothers pressured to use Norplant and Depo Provera? In the absence of a viable Black feminism that investigates how intersecting oppressions of race, gender, and class foster these contradictions, the angle of vision created by being deemed devalued workers and failed mothers could easily be turned inward, leading to internalized oppression. But the legacy of struggle among U.S. Black women suggests that a collectively shared, Black women's oppositional knowledge has long existed. This collective wisdom in turn has spurred U.S. Black women to generate a more specialized knowledge, namely, Black feminist thought as critical social theory. Just as fighting injustice lay at the heart of U.S. Black women's experiences, so did analyzing and creating imaginative responses to injustice characterize the core of Black feminist thought.

Historically, while they often disagreed on its expression – some U.S. Black women were profoundly reformist while more radical thinkers bordered on the revolutionary – African-American women intellectuals who were nurtured in social conditions of racial segregation strove to develop Black feminist thought as critical social theory. Regardless of social class and other differences among U.S. Black women, all were in some way affected by intersecting oppressions of race, gender, and class. The economic, political, and ideological dimensions of U.S. Black women's oppression suppressed the intellectual production of individual Black feminist thinkers. At the same time, these same social conditions simultaneously stimulated distinctive patterns of

U.S. Black women's activism that also influenced and was influenced by individual Black women thinkers. Thus, the dialectic of oppression and activism characterizing U.S. Black women's experiences with intersecting oppressions also influenced the ideas and actions of Black women intellectuals.

[...]

Why U.S. Black Feminist Thought?

Black feminism remains important because U.S. Black women constitute an oppressed group. As a collectivity, U.S. Black women participate in a *dialectical* relationship linking African-American women's oppression and activism. Dialectical relationships of this sort mean that two parties are opposed and opposite. As long as Black women's subordination within intersecting oppressions of race, class, gender, sexuality, and nation persists, Black feminism as an activist response to that oppression will remain needed.

In a similar fashion, the overarching purpose of U.S. Black feminist thought is also to resist oppression, both its practices and the ideas that justify it. If intersecting oppressions did not exist, Black feminist thought and similar oppositional knowledges would be unnecessary. As a critical social theory, Black feminist thought aims to empower African-American women within the context of social injustice sustained by intersecting oppressions. Since Black women cannot be fully empowered unless intersecting oppressions themselves are eliminated, Black feminist thought supports broad principles of social justice that transcend U.S. Black women's particular needs.

Because so much of U.S. Black feminism has been filtered through the prism of the U.S. context, its contours have been greatly affected by the specificity of American multiculturalism (Takaki 1993). In particular, U.S. Black feminist thought and practice respond to a fundamental contradiction of U.S. society. On the one hand, democratic promises of individual freedom, equality under the law, and social justice are made to all American citizens. Yet on the other hand, the reality of differential group treatment based on race, class, gender, sexuality, and citizenship status persists. Groups organized around race, class, and gender in and of themselves are not inherently a problem. However, when African-Americans, poor people, women, and other groups discriminated against see little hope for group-based advancement, this situation constitutes social injustice.

Within this overarching contradiction, U.S. Black women encounter a distinctive set of social practices that accompany our particular history within a unique matrix of domination characterized by intersecting oppressions. Race is far from being the only significant marker of group difference – class, gender, sexuality, religion, and citizenship status all matter greatly in the United States (Andersen and Collins 1998). Yet for African-American women, the effects of institutionalized racism remain visible and palpable. Moreover, the institutionalized racism that African-American women encounter relies heavily on racial segregation and accompanying discriminatory practices designed to deny U.S. Blacks equitable treatment. Despite important strides to desegregate U.S. society since 1970, racial segregation remains deeply entrenched in housing, schooling, and employment (Massey and Denton 1993). For many African-American women, racism is not something that exists in the distance. We encounter racism in everyday situations in workplaces, stores, schools, housing, and daily social interaction (St. Jean and Feagin 1998). Most Black women do not have the opportunity to befriend White women and men as neighbors, nor do their children attend school with White children. Racial segregation remains a fundamental feature of the U.S. social landscape, leaving many African-Americans with the belief that "the more things change, the more they stay the same" (Collins 1998, 11–43). Overlaying these persisting inequalities is a rhetoric of color blindness designed to render these social inequalities invisible. In a context where many believe that to talk of race fosters racism, equality allegedly lies in treating everyone the same. Yet as Kimberle Crenshaw (1997) points out, "it is fairly obvious that treating different things the same can generate as much inequality as treating the same things differently" (p. 285).

Although racial segregation is now organized differently than in prior eras (Collins 1998, 11–43), being Black and female in the United States continues to expose African-American women to certain common experiences. U.S. Black women's similar work and family experiences as well as our participation in diverse expressions of African-American culture mean that, overall, U.S. Black women as a group live in a different world from that of people who are not Black and female. For individual women, the particular experiences that accrue to living as a Black woman in the United States can stimulate a distinctive consciousness concerning our own experiences and society overall. Many African-American women grasp this connection between what one does and how one thinks.

[. . .]

Black Women as Agents of Knowledge

Social movements of the 1950s, 1960s, and 1970s stimulated a greatly changed intellectual and political climate in the United States. Compared to the past, many more U.S. Black women became legitimated agents of knowledge. No longer passive objects of knowledge manipulated within prevailing knowledge validation processes, African-American women aimed to speak for ourselves.

African-American women in the academy and other positions of authority who aim to advance Black feminist thought now encounter the often conflicting epistemological standards of three key groups. First, Black feminist thought must be validated by ordinary African-American women who, in the words of Hannah Nelson, grow to womanhood "in a world where the saner you are, the madder you are made to appear" (Gwaltney 1980, 7). To be credible in the eyes of this group, Black feminist intellectuals must be personal advocates for their material, be accountable for the consequences of their work, have lived or experienced their material in some fashion, and be willing to engage in dialogues about their findings with ordinary, everyday people.

Historically, living life as an African-American woman facilitated this endeavor because knowledge validation processes controlled in part or in full by Black women occurred in particular organizational settings. When Black women were in charge of our own self-definitions, these four dimensions of Black feminist epistemology – lived experience as a criterion of meaning, the use of dialogue, the ethic of personal accountability, and the ethic of caring – came to the forefront. When the core themes and interpretive frameworks of Black women's knowledge were informed by Black feminist epistemology, a rich tradition of Black feminist thought ensued.

Traditionally women engaged in this overarching intellectual and political project were blues singers, poets, autobiographers, storytellers, and orators. They became Black feminist intellectuals both by doing intellectual work and by being validated as such by everyday Black women. Black women in academia could not openly join their ranks without incurring a serious penalty. In racially segregated environments that routinely excluded the majority of African-American women, only a select few were able to defy prevailing norms and explicitly embrace Black feminist epistemology. Zora Neale Hurston was one such figure. Consider Alice Walker's description of Hurston:

> In my mind, Zora Neale Hurston, Billie Holiday, and Bessie Smith form a sort of unholy trinity. Zora *belongs* in the tradition of black women singers, rather than among "the literati." . . . Like Billie and Bessie she followed her own road, believed in her own gods, pursued her own dreams, and refused to separate herself from "common" people. (Walker 1977, xvii–xviii)

For her time, Zora Neale Hurston remains an exception, for prior to 1950, few African-American women earned advanced degrees, and most of those who did complied with prevailing knowledge validation processes.

The community of Black women scholars constitutes a second constituency whose epistemological standards must be met. As the number of Black women academics grows, this heterogeneous collectivity shares a similar social location in higher education, yet finds a new challenge in building group solidarities across differences. African-American women scholars place varying amounts of importance on furthering Black feminist scholarship. However, despite this new-found diversity, since more African-American women earn advanced degrees, the range of Black feminist scholarship has expanded. Historically, African-American women may have brought sensibilities gained from Black feminist epistemology to their scholarship. But gaining legitimacy often came with the cost of rejecting such an epistemology. Studying Black women's lives at all placed many careers at risk. More recently, increasing numbers of African-American women scholars have chosen to study Black women's experiences, and to do so by relying on elements of Black feminist epistemology in framing their work. For example, Valerie Lee's (1996) study of African-American midwives in the South deploys an innovative merger of Black women's fiction, ethnographic method, and personal narrative, to good effect.

A third group whose epistemological standards must be met consists of dominant groups who still control schools, graduate programs, tenure processes, publication outlets, and other mechanisms that legitimate knowledge. African-American women academics who aim to advance Black feminist thought typically must use dominant Eurocentric epistemologies for this group. The difficulties these Black women now face lie less in demonstrating that they could master White male epistemologies than in resisting the hegemonic nature of these patterns of thought in order to see, value, and use existing alternative Black feminist ways of knowing. For Black women who are agents of knowledge within academia, the marginality that accompanies outsider-within status can be the source of both frustration and creativity. In an attempt to minimize the differences between the cultural context of African-American communities and the expectations of mainstream social institutions, some women dichotomize their behavior and become two different people. Over time, the strain of doing this can be enormous. Others reject Black women's accumulated wisdom and work against their own best interests by enforcing the dominant group's specialized thought. Still others manage to inhabit both contexts but do so critically, using perspectives gained from their outsider-within social locations as a source of insights and ideas. But while such women can make substantial contributions as agents of knowledge, they rarely do so without substantial personal cost. "Eventually it comes to you," observes Lorraine Hansberry, "the thing that makes you exceptional, if you are at all, is inevitably that which must also make you lonely" (1969, 148).

Just as migrating between Black and White families raised special issues for Black women domestic workers, moving among different and competing interpretive communities raises similar epistemological concerns for Black feminist thinkers. The dilemma facing Black women scholars, in particular, engaged in creating Black feminist thought illustrates difficulties that can accompany grappling with multiple interpretive communities. A knowledge claim that meets the criteria of adequacy for one group and thus is judged to be acceptable may not be translatable into the terms of a different group. Using the example of Black English, June Jordan illustrates the difficulty of moving among epistemologies:

> You cannot "translate" instances of Standard English preoccupied with abstraction or with nothing/nobody evidently alive into Black English. That would warp the language into uses antithetical to the guiding perspective of its community of users. Rather you must first change those Standard English sentences, themselves, into ideas consistent with the person-centered assumptions of Black English. (Jordan 1985, 130)

Although both worldviews share a common vocabulary, the ideas themselves defy direct translation.

Once Black women scholars face the notion that on certain dimensions of a Black women's standpoint, it may be fruitless to try to translate into other frameworks truths validated by Black feminist epistemology, then other choices emerge. Rather than trying to uncover universal knowledge claims that can withstand the translation from one epistemology to another (initially, at least), Black women intellectuals might find efforts to rearticulate a Black women's standpoint especially fruitful. Rearticulating a Black women's standpoint refashions the particular and reveals the more universal human dimensions of Black women's everyday lives. "I date all my work," notes Nikki Giovanni, "because I think poetry, or any writing, is but a reflection of the moment. The universal comes from the particular" (1988, 57). Lorraine Hansberry expresses a similar idea: "I believe that one of the most sound ideas in dramatic writing is that in order to create the universal, you must pay very great attention to the specific. Universality, I think, emerges from the truthful identity of what is" (1969, 128).

Toward Truth

The existence of Black feminist thought suggests another path to the universal truths that might accompany the "truthful identity of what is." In this volume I place Black women's subjectivity in the center of analysis and examine the interdependence of the everyday, taken-for-granted knowledge shared by African-American women as a group, the more specialized knowledge produced by Black women intellectuals, and the social conditions shaping both types of thought. This approach allows me to describe the creative tension linking how social conditions influenced a Black women's standpoint and how the power of the ideas themselves gave many African-American women the strength to shape those same social conditions. I approach Black feminist thought as situated in a context of domination and not as a system of ideas divorced from political and economic reality. Moreover, I present Black feminist thought as subjugated knowledge in that African-American women have long struggled to find alternative locations and epistemologies for validating our own self-definitions. In brief, I examined the situated, subjugated standpoint of African-American women in order to understand Black feminist thought as a partial perspective on domination.

Because U.S. Black women have access to the experiences that accrue to being both Black and female, an alternative epistemology used to rearticulate a Black women's standpoint should reflect the convergence of both sets of experiences. Race and gender may be analytically distinct, but in Black women's everyday lives, they work together. The search for the distinguishing features of an alternative epistemology used by African-American women reveals that some ideas that Africanist scholars identify as characteristically "Black" often bear remarkable resemblance to similar ideas claimed by feminist scholars as characteristically "female." This similarity suggests that the actual contours of intersecting oppressions can vary dramatically and yet generate some uniformity in the epistemologies used by subordinate groups. Just as U.S. Black women and African women encountered diverse patterns of intersecting oppressions yet generated similar agendas concerning what mattered in their feminisms, a similar process may be at work regarding the epistemologies of oppressed groups. Thus the significance of a Black feminist epistemology may lie in its ability to enrich our understanding of how subordinate groups create knowledge that fosters both their empowerment and social justice.

This approach to Black feminist thought allows African-American women to explore the epistemological implications of transversal politics. Eventually this approach may get us to a point at which, claims Elsa Barkley Brown, "all people can learn to center in another experience, validate it, and judge it by its own standards without need of comparison or need to adopt that framework as their own" (1989,

922). In such politics, "one has no need to 'decenter' anyone in order to center some-one else; one has only to constantly, appropriately, 'pivot the center'" (p. 922).

Rather than emphasizing how a Black women's standpoint and its accompanying epistemology differ from those of White women, Black men, and other collectivities, Black women's experiences serve as one specific social location for examining points of connection among multiple epistemologies. Viewing Black feminist epistemology in this way challenges additive analyses of oppression claiming that Black women have a more accurate view of oppression than do other groups. Such approaches sug-gest that oppression can be quantified and compared and that adding layers of oppression produces a potentially clearer standpoint (Spelman 1988). One implica-tion of some uses of standpoint theory is that the more subordinated the group, the purer the vision available to them. This is an outcome of the origins of standpoint approaches in Marxist social theory, itself reflecting the binary thinking of its Western origins. Ironically, by quantifying and ranking human oppressions, stand-point theorists invoke criteria for methodological adequacy that resemble those of positivism. Although it is tempting to claim that Black women are more oppressed than everyone else and therefore have the best standpoint from which to understand the mechanisms, processes, and effects of oppression, this is not the case.

Instead, those ideas that are validated as true by African-American women, African-American men, Latina lesbians, Asian-American women, Puerto Rican men, and other groups with distinctive standpoints, with each group using the epistemological approaches growing from its unique standpoint, become the most "objective" truths. Each group speaks from its own standpoint and shares its own partial, situated knowledge. But because each group perceives its own truth as partial, its knowledge is unfinished. Each group becomes better able to consider other groups' standpoints without relinquishing the uniqueness of its own standpoint or suppressing other groups' partial perspectives. "What is always needed in the appreciation of art, or life," maintains Alice Walker, "is the larger perspective. Connections made, or at least attempted, where none existed before, the straining to encompass in one's glance at the varied world the common thread, the unifying theme through immense diversity" (1983, 5). Partiality, and not universality, is the condition of being heard; individuals and groups forwarding knowledge claims with-out owning their position are deemed less credible than those who do.

Alternative knowledge claims in and of themselves are rarely threatening to conventional knowledge. Such claims are routinely ignored, discredited, or simply absorbed and marginalized in existing paradigms. Much more threatening is the challenge that alternative epistemologies offer to the basic process used by the powerful to legitimate knowledge claims that in turn justify their right to rule. If the epistemology used to validate knowledge comes into question, then all prior knowl-edge claims validated under the dominant model become suspect. Alternative episte-mologies challenge all certified knowledge and open up the question of whether what has been taken to be true can stand the test of alternative ways of validating truth. The existence of a self-defined Black women's standpoint using Black feminist epistemology calls into question the content of what currently passes as truth and simultaneously challenges the process of arriving at that truth.

248   *Feminist Theories*

NOTE

1   My use of the term *subjugated knowledge* differs somewhat from Michel Foucault's (1980a) definition. According to Foucault, subjugated knowledges are "those blocs of historical knowledge which were present but disguised," namely, "a whole set of knowledges that have been disqualified as inadequate to their task or insufficiently elaborated: naive knowledges, located low down on the hierarchy, beneath the required level of cognition or scientificity" (p. 82). I suggest that Black feminist thought is not a "native knowledge" but has been made to appear so by those controlling knowledge validation procedures. Moreover, Foucault argues that subjugated knowledge is "a particular, local, regional knowledge a differential knowledge incapable of unanimity and which owes its force only to the harshness with which it is opposed by everything surrounding it" (p. 82). The component of Black feminist thought that analyzes Black women's oppression partially fits this definition, but the long-standing, independent, African-derived influences within Black women's thought are omitted from Foucault's analysis.

REFERENCES

Alexander, M. Jacqui, and Chandra Talpade Mohanty, eds. 1997. *Feminist Genealogies, Colonial Legacies, Democratic Futures*. New York: Routledge.

Andersen, Margaret L., and Patricia Hill Collins, eds. 1998. *Race, Class, and Gender: An Anthology, Third Edition*. Belmont, CA: Wadsworth Press.

Brown, Elsa Barkley. 1989. "African-American Women's Quilting: A Framework for Conceptualizing and Teaching African-American Women's History" *Signs* 14 (4): 92–29.

——. 1994. "Negotiating and Transforming the Public Sphere: African American Political Life in the Transition from Slavery to Freedom." *Public Culture* 7(1): 107–46.

Childress, Alice. [1956] 1986. *Like One of the Family: Conversations from a Domestic's Life*. Boston: Beacon.

Collins, Patricia Hill. 1986. "Learning from the Outsider Within: The Sociological Significance of Black Feminist Thought." *Social Problems* 33 (6): 14–32.

——. 1998. *Fighting Words: Black Women and the Search for Justice*. Minneapolis: University of Minnesota Press.

Crenshaw Kimberle Williams. 1997. "Color Blindness, History, and the Law." In *The House That Race Built*, ed. Wahneema Lubiano, 280–88. New York: Pantheon.

Diop, Cheikh. 1974. *The African Origin of Civilization: Myth or Reality?* New York: L. Hill.

Giovanni, Nikki. 1988. *Sacred Cows . . . and Other Edibles*. New York: Quill/William Morrow.

Gutman, Herbert. 1976. *The Black Family in Slavery and Freedom, 1750–1925*. New York: Random House.

Gwaltney, John Langston. 1980. *Drylongso, A Self-Portrait of Black America*. New York: Vintage.

Hansberry, Lorraine. 1969. *Young, Gifted and Black*. New York: Signet.

Jordan, June. 1985. *On Call*. Boston: South End Press.

Lee, Valerie. 1996. *Granny Midwives and Black Women Writers: Double-Dutched Readings*. New York: Routledge.

Massey. Douglas S., and Nancy A. Denton. 1993. *American Apartheid: Segregation and the Making of the Underclass*. Cambridge, MA: Harvard University Press.

Mirza, Heidi Safia, ed. 1997. *Black British Feminism: A Reader*. New York: Routledge.

Paris, Peter J. 1995. *The Spirituality of African Peoples: The Search for a Common Moral Discourse*. Minneapolis: Fortress.

Smitherman, Geneva. 1977. *Talkin and Testifyin: The Language of Black America*. Boston: Houghton Mifflin.

Sobel, Mechal. 1979. *Trabelin' On: The Slave Journey to an Afro-Baptist Faith* Princeton: Princeton University Press.

Spelman, Elizabeth V. 1988. *Inessential Woman: Problems of Exclusion in Feminist Thought* Boston; Beacon.

Squires, Gregory D. 1994 *Capital and Communities in Black and White: The Intersection of Race, Class, and Uneven Development.* Albany State University of New York Press.

St. Jean, Yanick, and Joe R. Feagin. 1998. *Double Burden: Black Women and Everyday Racism.* Armonk, NY: M. E. Sharpe.

Sudarska, Niara. 1981. "Interpreting the African Heritage in Afro-American Family Organization." In *Black Families*, ed. Harriette Pipes McAdoo, 37–53. Beverly Hills, CA: Sage.

Takaki, Ronald. 1993. *A Different Mirror: A History of Multicultural America.* Boston: Little, Brown.

Walker, Alice. 1977. "Zora Neale Hurston: A Cautionary Tale and a Partisan View." Foreword to *Zora Neale Hurston: A Literary Biography,* by Robert Hemenway, xi–xviii Urbana: University of Illinois Press.

——. 1983. *In Search of Our Mothers Gardens.* New York: Harcourt Brace Jovanovich.

Webber, Thomas L. 1978. *Deep Like the Rivers.* New York: W.W. Norton.

——. 1983. *In Search of Our Mother's Gardens.* New York: Harcourt Brace Jovanovich.

Yuval-Davis, Nira. 1997. *Gender and Nation.* Thousand Oaks, CA: Sage.

13E Patricia Hill Collins from *Intersectionality's Definitional Dilemmas*

Original publication details: Patricia Hill Collins, 2015. "Intersectionality's Definitional Dilemmas." *Annual Review of Sociology* 41: 3–5, 14–15. Reproduced with permission of Annual Reviews, Inc.

Racial Formation Theory, Knowledge Projects, and Intersectionality

Intersectionality faces a particular definitional dilemma – it participates in the very power relations that it examines and, as a result, must pay special attention to the conditions that make its knowledge claims comprehensible. Because analyzing the relations between knowledge and power is the traditional bailiwick of the sociology of knowledge, this field provides important theoretical vocabulary for conceptualizing intersectionality as both reflecting and shaping the power relations that house it. A sociology of knowledge framework suggests that knowledge – including knowledge aimed at better understanding intersectionality – is socially constructed and transmitted, legitimated, and reproduced. Yet within this core tenet, scholars have placed various emphases on the types of knowledge deemed worthy of study, the conceptions of social structure that house and/or are shaped by knowledge, and the influence of knowledge itself in shaping power relations (Balibar 2007, Berger & Luckmann 1966, Foucault 1980, Mannheim 1954, Swidler & Arditi 1994).

Within a broader critical race theory landscape (Delgado & Stefancic 2013), racial formation theory shows special promise for addressing intersectionality's definitional dilemma [Omi & Winant 2014 (1994)]. Because it conceptualizes race as situated within the recursive relationship between social structures and cultural representations, racial formation theory conflates neither discourses about race (e.g., racial meanings, representations, and social identities) nor the power relations in which racial meanings are situated. Both are held separate yet interconnected. Historically constructed, ever-changing racial formations organize racialized groups, the specific patterns of racial inequality that link racialized populations, and social problems that ensue. For example, in the United States, the racial formation of color-conscious racism has relied on a deep-seated logic of segregation that was applied to all aspects of social structures and cultural representations. In contrast, contemporary color-blind racism constitutes a differently organized yet equally powerful racial formation that manages to replicate racial hierarchies, often without overt attention to race itself (Bonilla-Silva 2003, Brown et al. 2003). Despite being more visible in different historical periods or across cross-national settings – both South Africa's racial apartheid and Brazil's racial democracy established racial hierarchies that persist – color-conscious and color-blind racial formations do not displace one another. As structural forms of power, one or the other racial formation may predominate, yet typically they coexist.

Racial formations have distinctive configurations of racial projects for which interest groups advance various interpretations of racial inequality. Within racial formation theory, ideas matter, not simply as hegemonic ideologies produced by elites but also as tangible, multiple knowledge projects that are advanced by specific interpretive communities. Because groups aim to have their interpretations of racial inequality prevail, knowledge lies at the heart of racial projects.

The question is less whether race is real or whether racial projects exist, but rather what kinds of racial projects appear and disappear across specific racial formations and why. For example, African American intellectual production has a storied history of protesting both the social structural dimensions of racism and the cultural representations of people of African descent (Kelley 2002). Yet despite these efforts, the richness of these knowledge projects rarely make it into the legitimated canon of established fields. Similarly, the eugenics projects that advanced widely accepted scientific knowledge about race had significant impact on the public policies of the United States, Germany, and many nation-states. Eugenics arguments fell out of favor in the post-World War II era, suggesting that counterarguments claiming that race was socially constructed with no connections to biology had prevailed. Yet in a post-genomic age, the resurgence of race in science, law, and medicine points to the resiliency of biological understandings of race within contemporary racial projects of science itself, typically without racially discriminatory intent (Duster 2015). The word "eugenics" fell out of favor, but ideas about the centrality of biology, newly defined in determining various aspects of human social behavior, have been more difficult to uproot. Just as racial formations change in response to racial projects, racial projects change in relation to changing racial formations.

Racial formation theory offers one additional benefit for intersectionality. Through its analysis of racial projects, racial formation theory can account for change in ways that retain the agency of individual human actors and group-based action. In contrast to the sociology of knowledge's traditional emphasis on individual intellectuals as superior if not the sole producers of knowledge – whether Mannheim's intelligentsia or Gramsci's organic intellectuals – this theory makes room for multiple interpretive communities. Because understanding racial inequality remains central to racial formation theory, it provides intellectual and political space for subordinated social groups such as African Americans, Latinos, Asians, and indigenous peoples. Such groups find intellectual and political space within racial formation theory for the group-based knowledge of racial projects that oppose racial hierarchy and racial inequality (Collins 1998, pp. 201–28). Racial formation theory offers social actors guidance as to how their individual and collective actions matter in shaping racial inequality.

The strength of racial formation theory lies in how it links specific knowledge projects (racial projects) with historically constructed power relations (racial formations). Intersectionality can build on this foundation by moving beyond a mono-categorical focus on racial inequality to encompass multiple forms of inequality that are organized via a similar logic. As an initial step, this framework can be applied to other social formations and knowledge projects that reproduce inequality, for example, social formations of patriarchy, capitalism, heterosexism, and their characteristic knowledge projects. Yet intersectionality goes farther than this mono-system analysis, introducing a greater level of complexity into conceptualizing inequality. Whereas racial formation theory (ironically, itself a knowledge project) focuses on racism as a mono-categorical system of power, intersectionality examines social formations of multiple, complex social inequalities. In order to build on racial formation theory's promise, however, intersectionality would need to flesh out a more nuanced sociological understanding of how social structures and cultural representations interconnect. Knowledge projects are not free-floating phenomena; they are grounded in specific sociological processes experienced by actual people. Here a robust analysis of the new politics of community provides a way of grounding the more theoretical arguments in both racial formation theory and intersectionality (Collins 2010). Linking power with knowledge, the construct of community provides an important framework for understanding the interpretive communities that advance intersectionality's many knowledge projects.

Intersectionality can be conceptualized as an overarching knowledge project whose changing contours grow from and respond to social formations of complex social inequalities; within this overarching umbrella, intersectionality can also be profitably conceptualized as a constellation of knowledge projects that change in relation to one another in tandem with changes in the interpretive communities that advance them. The broader knowledge project provides a set of ideas that provide moments of definitional consensus. Overarching intersectional frameworks have been so successful because they remain broad and unspecified. They provide the illusion that the constellation of smaller knowledge projects can be uncritically categorized under intersectionality's big tent umbrella. Yet the sets of practitioners that lay claim to intersectionality via multiple cross-cutting and competitive intersectional knowledge projects reveal a lack of consensus about intersectionality's history, current organization, and future directions. Intersectionality's definitional dilemma occurs in this intellectual and political space.

In consideration of this framework, intersectional knowledge projects typically focus on three interdependent concerns. The first focal point makes intersectionality as a field of study the object of investigation. Examining the content and themes that characterize the field constitutes the main task. Why does this field exist? How is this field of study situated within prevailing power relations? How does this social location shape the kinds of themes and approaches that characterize intersectionality as a field of study?

The second focal point of intersectional knowledge projects examines intersectionality as an analytical strategy. These projects rely upon intersectional frameworks to produce new knowledge about the social world. Garnering the lion's share of attention within intersectionality as a field of study, this approach uses intersectional frameworks to investigate social phenomena, e.g., social institutions, practices, social problems, and the epistemological concerns of the field itself.

The third focal point emphasizes intersectionality as a form of critical praxis, especially its connections with social justice. This praxis perspective does not separate scholarship from practice, with scholarship providing theoretical frameworks that people are encouraged to apply to practice. Instead, both scholarship and practice are recursively linked, with practice being foundational to intersectional analysis.

[...]

Epistemological Challenges

Neither the new knowledge created within these areas of intersectional scholarship nor the research methodologies used to produce it stand outside power relations; both are deeply embedded in what they aim to study. Philosopher Kristie Dotson's (2013) analysis of epistemic oppression claims that knowledge is not politically neutral. Intersectionality would do well to consider how epistemic oppression might play out against and within its own parameters. When empirical work that claims to be using intersectionality fails to consider the epistemological assumptions of its own practice, such work can unwittingly uphold the same complex social inequalities that it aims to understand. Proceeding as though intersectionality, as much as any other theoretical framework, is already a social theory that can be used and critiqued within prevailing academic norms misreads this field.

In the same way that my earlier discussion of Black feminism and its shift to race/class/gender studies provided a context for the themes that characterized these projects, my selective rendition of how scholars use intersectionality as an analytical strategy constitutes a comparable preliminary entry point into similar epistemological terrain. The thematic emphases described above – (a) attending to social institutions such as work, (b) expanding systems of power beyond race, class, and gender, (c) applying an intersectional lens to social problems, (d) giving considerable attention to identity, and (e) casting a self-reflexive eye on intersectionality's epistemological and methodological issues – produce a loose set of guiding assumptions or guiding themes. Stated differently, based on a cursory survey of publications as data for analysis, these guiding assumptions may flesh out intersectionality's analytical sensibility discussed above. These guiding themes need not be present simultaneously, nor is each theme unique to intersectionality.

My reading of intersectional knowledge projects is that they embrace one, some combination, or all of the following provisional list of guiding assumptions:

- Race, class, gender, sexuality, age, ability, nation, ethnicity, and similar categories of analysis are best understood in relational terms rather than in isolation from one another.

- These mutually constructing categories underlie and shape intersecting systems of power; the power relations of racism and sexism, for example, are interrelated.
- Intersecting systems of power catalyze social formations of complex social inequalities that are organized via unequal material realities and distinctive social experiences for people who live within them.
- Because social formations of complex social inequalities are historically contingent and cross-culturally specific, unequal material realities and social experiences vary across time and space.
- Individuals and groups differentially placed within intersecting systems of power have different points of view on their own and others' experiences with complex social inequalities, typically advancing knowledge projects that reflect their social locations within power relations.
- The complex social inequalities fostered by intersecting systems of power are fundamentally unjust, shaping knowledge projects and/or political engagements that uphold or contest the status quo.

The current unevenness across how scholars use intersectionality as an analytical strategy reflects differing degrees of emphasis on specific guiding assumptions. Some themes are definitely more popular than others. For example, work and identity constitute popular topics, whereas sustained attention to the connections between complex social inequalities and social justice is less prominent. Overall, this provisional list of guiding assumptions is far from a working definition, but it does elucidate how intersectionality as an analytical strategy is unfolding.

But this all begs the underlying epistemological question of how these emerging patterns contribute to clarifying intersectionality's definitional dilemmas. One way to understand intersectionality as an analytical strategy is to place the earlier themes of community organizing, identity politics, coalitional politics, interlocking oppressions, and social justice in dialogue with the guiding assumptions of contemporary intersectional scholarship. Stuart Hall's construct of articulation may prove highly useful in examining the dynamic patterns of how scholars use intersectionality as an analytical strategy. Hall posits that a theory of articulation is "both a way of understanding how ideological elements come, under certain conditions, to cohere together within a discourse, and a way of asking how they do or do not become articulated, at specific conjunctures, to certain political struggles" (Grossberg 1996, pp. 141–42). Stated differently, how do and how might these two sets of ideas articulate to shape intersectionality's emerging canonical knowledge?

With hindsight, I see how this unanswered (and, some would say, unanswerable) question of how to articulate multiple points of view on intersectionality frames its definitional dilemmas. Yet the epistemological issues that affect any use of intersectionality as an analytical strategy may take a different form outside the scholarly requirements of the academy. When it comes to intersectionality as critical praxis, practitioners might use both sets of ideas differently.

REFERENCES

Balibar, E. 2007. *The Philosophy of Marx*. New York: Verso.

Berger, P.L., Luckmann. T. 1966. *The Social Construction of Reality: A Treatise in the Sociology of Knowledge*. New York: Anchor.

Bonilla-Silva, E. 2003. *Racism Without Racists: Color-Blind Racism and the Persistence of Racial Inequality in the United States*. Lanham, MD: Rowman & Littlefield.

Brown, M.I., Carnoy M, Currie E., Duster T., Oppenheimer D.B., et al. 2003. *Whitewashing Race: The Myth of a Color-Blind Society*. Berkeley: University of California Press.

Collins, P.H. 1998. *Fighting Words: Black Women and the Search for Justice*. Minneapolis: University of Minnesota Press.

Collins, P.H. 2010. The new politics of community. *American Sociologial Review* 75: 7–30.

Delgado, R, Stefancic, J., eds. 2013. *Critical Race Theory: The Cutting Edge*. Philadelphia: Temple University Press.

Dotson, K. 2013. Conceptualizing epistemic oppression. *Social Epistemology* 14: 1–23.

Duster, T. 2015. A post-genomic surprise: the molecular reinscription of race in science, law and medicine. *British Journal of Sociology*. 66: 1–27.

Foucault, M. 1980. *Power/Knowledge: Selected Interviews and Other Writings, 1972–1977*. New York: Pantheon.

Grossberg, L. 1996. On postmodernism and articulation: an interview with Stuart Hall. In *Critical Dialogues in Cultural Studies*, ed. D. Morley, K.-H. Chen, pp. 131–50. New York: Routledge.

Mannheim, K. 1954. *Ideology and Utopia: An Introduction to the Sociology of Knowledge*. New York: Harcourt, Brace &World.

Omi, M., Winant, H. 2014 (1994). *Racial Formation in the United States*. New York: Routledge.

Swidler, A., Arditi, J. 1994. The new sociology of knowledge. *Annual Review of Sociology* 20: 305–29.

13F R.W. Connell and James W. Messerschmidt from *Hegemonic Masculinity: Rethinking the Concept*

Original publication details: R.W. Connell and James W. Messerschmidt, 2005. "Hegemonic Masculinity: Rethinking the Concept." *Gender & Society* 19: 846–847. Reproduced with permission of Sage Publications, Inc.

The concept of hegemonic masculinity was first proposed in reports from a field study of social inequality in Australian high schools (Kessler et al. 1982); in a related conceptual discussion of the making of masculinities and the experience of men's bodies (Connell 1983); and in a debate over the role of men in Australian labor politics (Connell 1982). The high school project provided empirical evidence of multiple hierarchies – in gender as well as in class terms – interwoven with active projects of gender construction (Connell et al. 1982).

These beginnings were systematized in an article, "Towards a New Sociology of Masculinity" (Carrigan, Connell, and Lee 1985), which extensively critiqued the "male sex role" literature and proposed a model of multiple masculinities and power relations. In turn, this model was integrated into a systematic sociological theory of gender. The resulting six pages in *Gender and Power* (Connell 1987) on "hegemonic masculinity and emphasized femininity" became the most cited source for the concept of hegemonic masculinity.

[...]

The Gramscian term "hegemony" was current at the time in attempts to understand the stabilization of class relations (Connell 1977). In the context of dual systems theory (Eisenstein 1979), the idea was easily transferred to the parallel problem about gender relations. This risked a significant misunderstanding. Gramsci's writing focuses on the dynamics of structural change involving the mobilization and demobilization of whole classes. Without a very clear focus on this issue of historical change, the idea of hegemony would be reduced to a simple model of cultural control. And in a great deal of the debate about gender, large-scale historical change is not in focus. Here is one of the sources of later difficulties with the concept of hegemonic masculinity.

Even before the women's liberation movement, a literature in social psychology and sociology about the "male sex role" had recognized the social nature of masculinity and the possibilities of change in men's conduct (Hacker 1957). During the 1970s, there was an explosion of writing about "the male role," sharply criticizing role norms as the source of oppressive behavior by men (Brannon 1976). Critical role theory provided the main conceptual basis for the early antisexist men's movement. The weaknesses of sex role theory were, however, increasingly recognized (Kimmel 1987; Pleck 1981). They included the blurring of behavior and norm, the homogenizing effect of the role concept, and its difficulties in accounting for power.

Power and difference were, on the other hand, core concepts in the gay liberation movement, which developed a sophisticated analysis of the oppression of men as well as oppression by men (Altman 1972). Some theorists saw gay liberation as bound up with an assault on gender stereotypes (Mieli 1980). The idea of a hierarchy of masculinities grew directly out of homosexual men's experience with violence and prejudice from straight men. The concept of homophobia originated in the 1970s and was already being attributed to the conventional male role (Morin and Garfinkle 1978). Theorists developed increasingly sophisticated accounts of gay men's ambivalent relationships to patriarchy and conventional masculinity (Broker 1976; Plummer 1981).

An equally important source was empirical social research. A growing body of field studies was documenting local gender hierarchies and local cultures of masculinity in schools (Willis 1977), in male-dominated workplaces (Cockburn 1983), and in village communities (Herdt 1981; Hunt 1980). These studies added the ethnographic realism that the sex-role literature lacked, confirmed the plurality of masculinities and the complexities of gender construction for men, and gave evidence of the active struggle for dominance that is implicit in the Gramscian concept of hegemony.

[. . .]

Hegemonic masculinity was distinguished from other masculinities, especially subordinated masculinities. Hegemonic masculinity was not assumed to be normal in the statistical sense; only a minority of men might enact it. But it was certainly normative. It embodied the currently most honored way of being a man, it required all other men to position themselves in relation to it, and it ideologically legitimated the global subordination of women to men.

Men who received the benefits of patriarchy without enacting a strong version of masculine dominance could be regarded as showing a complicit masculinity. It was in relation to this group, and to compliance among heterosexual women, that the concept of hegemony was most powerful. Hegemony did not mean violence, although it could be supported by force; it meant ascendancy achieved through culture, institutions, and persuasion.

These concepts were abstract rather than descriptive, defined in terms of the logic of a patriarchal gender system. They assumed that gender relations were historical, so gender hierarchies were subject to change. Hegemonic masculinities therefore came into existence in specific circumstances and were open to historical change. More precisely, there could be a struggle for hegemony, and older forms of masculinity might be displaced by new ones. This was the element of optimism in an otherwise rather bleak theory. It was perhaps possible that a more humane, less oppressive, means of being a man might become hegemonic, as part of a process leading toward an abolition of gender hierarchies.

[...]

We would argue that social science and humanities research on masculinities has flourished during the past 20 years precisely because the underlying concept employed is not reified or essentialist. The notion that the concept of masculinity essentializes or homogenizes is quite difficult to reconcile with the tremendous multiplicity of social constructions that ethnographers and historians have documented with the aid of this concept (Connell 2003). Even further removed from essentialism is the fact that researchers have explored masculinities enacted by people with female bodies (Halberstam 1998; Messerschmidt 2004). Masculinity is not a fixed entity embedded in the body or personality traits of individuals. Masculinities are configurations of practice that are accomplished in social action and, therefore, can differ according to the gender relations in a particular social setting.

The idea that a recognition of multiple masculinities necessarily turns into a static typology is likewise not borne out by the development of research. A paradigmatic example is Gutmann's (1996) Mexican ethnography. . . . Gutmann is able to tease out different categories of masculinity – for example, the macho and the *mandilón* – while recognizing, and showing in detail, that these are not monadic identities but always are relational and constantly are crosscut by other divisions and projects. Warren's (1997) observations in a British elementary school provide another example. Different constructions of masculinity are found, which generate effects in classroom life, even though many boys do not fit exactly into the major categories; indeed, the boys demonstrate complex relations of attachment and rejection to those categories.

Although the idea that the concept of gender embeds heteronormativity is now a familiar criticism (Hawkesworth 1997), it is a contested criticism (Scott 1997). While it correctly identifies a problem in categorical models of gender, it is not a valid criticism of relational models of gender (e.g., Connell 2002; Walby 1997) nor of historical approaches where the construction of gender categories is the object of inquiry. In the development of the concept of hegemonic masculinity, divisions among men – especially the exclusion and subordination of homosexual men – were quite central issues (Carrigan, Connell, and Lee 1985). The policing of heterosexuality has been a major theme in discussions of hegemonic masculinity since then.

The idea that the concept of masculinity marginalizes or naturalizes the body (because it is supposed to rest on a sex-gender dichotomy) is perhaps the most startling of the claims in this critique. Startling, because the interplay between bodies and social processes has been one of the central themes of masculinity research from its beginning. One of the first and most influential research programs in the new paradigm was Messner's (1992) account of the masculinity of professional athletes, in which the use of "bodies as weapons" and the long-term damage to men's bodies were examined. The construction of masculinity in a context of disability (Gerschick and Miller 1994), the laboring bodies of working-class men (Donaldson 1991), men's health and illness (Sabo and Gordon 1995), and boys' interpersonal violence (Messerschmidt 2000) are among the themes in research showing how bodies are affected by social processes. Theoretical discussion has explored the relevance of the "new sociology of the body" to the construction of masculinity (e.g., Connell 1995, chap. 2).

Critiques of the concept of masculinity make better sense when they point to a tendency, in research as well as in popular literature, to dichotomize the experiences of men and women. As Brod (1994) accurately observes, there is a tendency in the men's studies field to presume "separate spheres," to proceed as if women were not a relevant part of the analysis, and therefore to analyze masculinities by looking only at men and relations among men. As Brod also argues, this is not inevitable. The cure lies in taking a consistently relational approach to gender – not in abandoning the concepts of gender or masculinity.

What Should Be Retained

The fundamental feature of the concept remains the combination of the plurality of masculinities and the hierarchy of masculinities. This basic idea has stood up well in 20 years of research experience. Multiple patterns of masculinity have been identified in many studies, in a variety of countries, and in different institutional and cultural settings. It is also a widespread research finding that certain masculinities are more socially central, or more associated with authority and social power, than others. The concept of hegemonic masculinity presumes the subordination of nonhegemonic masculinities, and this is a process that has now been documented in many settings, internationally.

Also well supported is the idea that the hierarchy of masculinities is a pattern of hegemony, not a pattern of simple domination based on force. Cultural consent, discursive centrality, institutionalization, and the marginalization or delegitimation of alternatives are widely documented features of socially dominant masculinities. Also well supported is the original idea that hegemonic masculinity need not be the commonest pattern in the everyday lives of boys and men. Rather, hegemony works in part through the production of exemplars of masculinity (e.g., professional sports stars), symbols that have authority despite the fact that most men and boys do not fully live up to them.

The original formulations laid some emphasis on the possibility of change in gender relations, on the idea that a dominant pattern of masculinity was open to challenge – from women's resistance to patriarchy, and from men as bearers of alter-native masculinities. Research has very fully confirmed the idea of the historical construction and reconstruction of hegemonic masculinities. Both at a local and a broad societal level, the situations in which masculinities were formed change over time. These changes call forth new strategies in gender relations (e.g., companionate marriage) and result in redefinitions of socially admired masculinity (e.g., the domestic partner rather than the Victorian patriarch).

[. . .]

What Should Be Rejected

Two features of early formulations about hegemonic masculinity have not stood up to criticism and should be discarded. The first is a too-simple model of the social relations surrounding hegemonic masculinities. The formulation in *Gender and Power* attempted to locate all masculinities (and all femininities) in terms of a single pattern of power, the "global dominance" of men over women (Connell 1987, 183). While this was useful at the time in preventing the idea of multiple masculinities from collapsing into an array of competing lifestyles, it is now clearly inadequate to our understanding of relations among groups of men and forms of masculinity and of women's relations with dominant masculinities. For instance, dominance in gen-der relations involves an interplay of costs and benefits, challenges to hegemonic masculinity arise from the "protest masculinities" of marginalized ethnic groups, and bourgeois women may appropriate aspects of hegemonic masculinity in con-structing corporate or professional careers. Clearly, better ways of understanding gender hierarchy are required.

[. . .]

Gender Hierarchy

Compared with original formulations of the concept, contemporary research has shown the complexity of the relationships among different constructions of mascu-linity. The recent research in discursive psychology indicates how different con-structions of masculinity at the local level may serve as tactical alternatives. Structured relations among masculinities exist in all local settings, motivation toward a specific hegemonic version varies by local context, and such local versions inevitably differ somewhat from each other. Demetriou's (2001) notion of dialectical pragmatism captures the reciprocal influence of masculinities on each other; hegem-onic masculine patterns may change by incorporating elements from the others.

Analyses of relations among masculinities now more clearly recognize the agency of subordinated and marginalized groups – often conditioned by their specific location (as discussed below). "Protest masculinity" (Poynting, Noble, and Tabar 2003) can be understood in this sense: a pattern of masculinity constructed in local working-class settings, sometimes among ethnically marginalized men, which embodies the claim to power typical of regional hegemonic masculinities in Western countries, but which lacks the economic resources and institutional authority that underpins the regional and global patterns.

Research has also documented the durability or survivability of nonhegemonic patterns of masculinity, which may represent well-crafted responses to race/ethnic marginalization, physical disability, class inequality, or stigmatized sexuality. Hegemony may be accomplished by the incorporation of such masculinities into a functioning gender order rather than by active oppression in the form of discredit or violence. In practice, both incorporation and oppression can occur together. This is, for instance, the contemporary position of gay masculinities in Western urban centers, where gay communities have a spectrum of experience ranging from homo-phobic violence and cultural denigration to toleration and even cultural celebration and political representation. Similar processes of incorporation and oppression may occur among girls and women who construct masculinities (Messerschmidt 2004).

The concept of hegemonic masculinity was originally formulated in tandem with a concept of hegemonic femininity – soon renamed "emphasized femininity" to acknowledge the asymmetrical position of masculinities and femininities in a patriarchal gender order. In the development of research on men and masculinities, this relationship has dropped out of focus. This is regrettable for more than one reason. Gender is always relational, and patterns of masculinity are socially defined in contradistinction from some model (whether real or imaginary) of femininity.

Perhaps more important, focusing only on the activities of men occludes the practices of women in the construction of gender among men. As is well shown by life-history research, women are central in many of the processes constructing masculinities – as mothers; as schoolmates; as girlfriends, sexual partners, and wives; as workers in the gender division of labor; and so forth. The concept of emphasized femininity focused on compliance to patriarchy, and this is still highly relevant in contemporary mass culture. Yet gender hierarchies are also affected by new configurations of women's identity and practice, especially among younger women – which are increasingly acknowledged by younger men. We consider that research on hegemonic masculinity now needs to give much closer attention to the practices of women and to the historical interplay of femininities and masculinities.

We suggest, therefore, that our understanding of hegemonic masculinity needs to incorporate a more holistic understanding of gender hierarchy, recognizing the agency of subordinated groups as much as the power of dominant groups and the mutual conditioning of gender dynamics and other social dynamics. We think this will tend, over time, to reduce the isolation of men's studies and will emphasize the relevance of gender dynamics to the problems – ranging from effects of globalization to issues of violence and peacemaking – being explored in other fields of social science.

REFERENCES

Altman, D. 1972. *Homosexual: Oppression and Liberation*. Sydney, Australia: Angus and Robertson.

Brannon, R. 1976. "The Male Sex Role: Our Culture's Blueprint of Manhood, and What It's Done for us Lately," in D.S. David and R. Brannon, eds. *The Forty-Nine Percent Majority: The Male Sex Role*. Reading, MA: Addington-Wesley.

Brod, H. 1994. "Some Thoughts on Some Histories of Some Masculinities: Jews and Other Others," in D.S. David and R. Brannon, eds. *Theorizing Masculinities*. Thousand Oaks, CA: Sage.

Broker, M. 1976. "'I May be a Queer, but at least I am a Man': Male Hegemony and Ascribed versus Achieved Gender," in D. Leonard Barker and S. Allen, eds. *Sexual Divisions and Society*. London: Tavistock.

Carrigan, T., R.W. Connell, and J. Lee. 1985. "Toward a New Sociology of Masculinity." *Theory and Society* 14(5): 551–604.

Cockburn, C. 1983. *Brothers: Male Dominance and Technological Change*. London: Pluto.

Connell, R.W. 1977. *Ruling Class, Ruling Culture*. Cambridge, UK: Cambridge University Press.

____. 1982. "Class, Patriarchy, and Sartre's Theory of Practice." *Theory and Society* 11: 305–20.

____. 1983. *Which Way Is Up? Essays on Sex, Class and Culture*. Sydney, Australia: Allen and Unwin.

____. 1987. *Gender and Power*. Sydney, Australia: Allen and Unwin.

____. 1995. *Masculinities*. Cambridge, UK: Polity Press.

____. 2002. *Gender*. Cambridge, UK: Polity Press.

____. 2003. "Masculinities, Change and Conflict in Global Society: Thinking about the Future of Men's Studies." *Journal of Men's Studies* 11(3): 249–66.

Connell, R.W., D.J. Ashenden, S. Kessler, and G.W. Dowsett. 1982. *Making the Difference: Schools, Families and Social Division*. Sydney, Australia: Allen and Unwin.

Demetriou, D.Z. 2001. "Connell's Concept of Hegemonic Masculinity: A Critique." *Theory and Society* 30(3): 337–61.

Donaldson, M. 1991. *Time of our Lives: Labor and Love in the Working Class*. Sydney, Australia: Allen and Unwin.

Eisenstein, Z.R. 1979. *Capitalist Patriarchy and the Case for Socialist Feminism*. New York: Monthly Review Press.

Gerschick, T.J., and A.S. Miller. 1994. "Gender Identities at the Crossroads of Masculinity and Physical Disability." *Masculinities* 2(1): 34–55.

Gutmann, M.C. 1996. *The Meanings of Macho: Being a Man in Mexico City*. Berkeley: University of California Press.

Hacker, H.M. 1957. "The New Burdens of Masculinity." *Marriage and Family Living* 19(3): 227–33.

Halberstam, J. 1998. *Female Masculinity*. Durham, NC: Duke University Press.

Hawkesworth, M. 1997. "Confounding Gender." *Signs: Journal of Women in Culture and Society* 22 (3).

Herdt, G.H. 1981. *Guardians of the Flutes: Idioms of Masculinity*. New York: McGraw-Hill.

Hunt, P. 1980. *Gender and Class Consciousness*. London: Macmillan

Kessler, S. J., D. J. Ashenden, R.W. Connell, and G.W. Dowsett. 1982. *Ockers and Disco-maniacs*. Sydney, Australia: Inner City Education Center.

Kimmel, M.S. 1987. "Rethinking 'Masculinity': New Directions in Research," in M. S. Kimmel, ed. *Changing Men: New Directions in Research on Men and Masculinity*. Newbury Park, CA: Sage.

Messerschmidt, J.W. 2000. *Nine Lives: Adolescent Masculinities, the Body, and Violence*. Boulder, CO: Westview.

____. 2004. *Flesh & Blood: Adolescent Gender Diversity and Violence*. Lanham, MD: Rowman & Littlefield.

Messner, M.A. 1992. *Power at Play: Sports and the Problem of Masculinity*. Boston: Beacon.

Mieli, M. 1980. *Homosexuality and Liberation: Elements of a Gay Critique*. Trans. D. Fernbach. London: Gay Men's Press.

Morin, S.F., and E.M. Garfinkle. 1978. "Male Homophobia." *Journal of Social Issues* 34(1): 29–47.

Pleck, J. 1981. *The Myth of Masculinity.* Cambridge, MA: MIT Press.

Plummer, K., ed. 1981. *The Making of the Modern Homosexual.* London: Macmillan.

Poynting, S., G. Noble, and P. Tabar. 2003. "'Intersections' of Masculinity and Ethnicity: A Study of Male Lebanese Immigrant Youth in Western Sydney." Unpublished manuscript, University of Western Sydney.

Sabo, D., and D.F. Gordon, eds. 1995. *Men's Health and Illness: Gender, Power and the Body.* Thousand Oaks, CA: Sage.

Scott, J.W. 1997. "Comment on Hawkesworth's 'confounding gender'." *Signs: Journal of Women in Culture and Society* 22(3): 697–702.

Walby, S. 1997. *Gender Transformations.* London: Routledge.

Warren, S. 1997. "Who do These Boys Think They Are? An Investigation into the Construction of Masculinities in a Primary Classroom. *International Journal of Inclusive Education* 1(2): 207–22.

Willis, P. 1977. *Learning to Labor: How* Working Class Kids get Working Class Jobs. Farnborough, UK: Saxon House.

CHAPTER FOURTEEN

POSTCOLONIAL THEORIES

CHAPTER MENU

Postcolonial theory refers in broad terms to the many perspectives articulated in making sense of the legacies of slavery and colonialism and of the relations of domination they institutionalized in social structures and in everyday culture. The first sociologist to draw attention to the economic, social, political and

Concise Reader in Sociological Theory: Theorists, Concepts, and Current Applications,
First Edition. Edited by Michele Dillon. Editorial material and organization
© 2021 John Wiley & Sons Ltd. Published 2021 by John Wiley & Sons Ltd.

cultural consequences of slavery was **W.E. Burghardt Du Bois** (1868–1963). Most notably, Du Bois, an American, argued (see excerpt *14a The Souls of Black Folk*) that slavery produced a double-consciousness among Black people such that, despite their emancipation from slavery in 1860, they must invariably see themselves through the eyes of white people. The continuation of systems of exploitation – in employment, in voting rights, in housing, in education, and in access to opportunities more generally – make it impossible for Blacks, Du Bois argued, to have legitimacy as an American *and* as a Black person; they live with a bifurcated identity, a warring of the (double) self, that requires them to suppress those elements of the self and of a collective history that if spoken challenges the ideology of America as a land of freedom, equality, and opportunity. The "color line," whether visible or more subtle, is a potent force that despite equality before the law, means that Black people are treated in many instances and across many spheres as second-class citizens, whose histories and cultural identities are deemed unworthy of recognition.

Just as slavery dehumanized Black people and assaulted the dignity of their person-hood and their human-social identity, colonialism in its various guises around the world imposed an Otherness on those that were subjugated by the dominant – and dominating – colonial powers (e.g. Great Britain, France, Belgium, Spain, Portugal). Colonialism is a multifaceted phenomenon that has variously impacted a broad swath of geographically dispersed regions and cultures; essentially, it is "the process by which a politically and/or militarily controlled population is not only stripped of its political and economic sovereignty, but systematically constructed as being inferior - in legal, social, cultural, and biological/racial terms" (Dillon 2020). The Palestinian-born literary scholar **Edward W. Said** (1935–2003) focuses on the construal of the Otherness of the Orient in the Western mind and in its literatures, political discourses, and other cultural representations (see excerpt *14b Orientalism*). As he elaborates, the Orientalization of the Orient by European and American writers is not only a sign of the economic, political, and cultural power of the West over Arab and other Eastern geographical regions and countries but also a statement of the (assumed) political and cultural superiority of the West. The colonized Other is invariably an inferior Other, and this is not merely a cultural representation but a political fact whose con-sequences endure long after the colonizer has departed from the geographical space of those whom it has dispossessed. Otherness creates a hierarchy of difference that the colonized struggle to erase even as they know/imagine, that as a postcolonial people in their politically independent postcolonial context, they cannot fully accom-plish this goal.

The phenomenology of experiencing Otherness day-in, day-out is evocatively conveyed by **Frantz Fanon** (1925–61), a writer and medical doctor who was born and lived in Martinique (a Caribbean island colonized and still controlled by France). We see in his account how, in line with Mead's construal of the self as always a thoroughly social self (based on dynamics of the "I–Me" interaction), he experiences his self and his everyday reality through how others see him, how they speak to him, and how they respond to him (see excerpt *14c Black Skin, White Masks*). The "fact of Blackness," as he conveys is indeed a social fact – that as Durkheim would elaborate, exerts an external, collective force on Fanon, exists in relation to other social forces (e.g. Whiteness), and heavily constrains what he can do and how others regard him. He is required, as he recounts (1967: 114–15), to behave not like a man, but like a *Black man*. His Blackness is always present, always looming for others, no matter the situation or the context. For Fanon, as for others whose racial identity is delegitimated by White power structures and the racism they create, this systemically imposes, and relentlessly so, a battered down self which functions to maintain the (imposed) superiority of the batterer. As Fanon elaborates, the fact of Blackness and the fact of "color prejudice" notwithstanding his qualifications and demonstrated competence as a medical doctor, meant that he "was hated, despised, detested, not by the neighbor across the street . . . but by an entire race" (1967: 118).

Stuart Hall (1932–2014), a Jamaican-born theorist who lived in England, approaches postcolonialism with a focus on cultural identity and pop cultural representations amid postcolonial struggles. He highlights the dynamic reappropriation by previously colonized racial and ethnic groups of multiple cultural resources from within their particular history, a history, he emphasizes, that encompasses highly specific precolonial, colonial, and postcolonial experiences attendant on any given group's particular positionality relative to other groups (including other subordinate ethnic/racial groups). Injecting a rich sense of agency into the formation of cultural identity, Hall argues for an understanding that recognizes that cultural identity is not just about *being* (cohering around an inherited shared, largely passive, collective culture), but also about *becoming* (see excerpt *14d Cultural Identity and Diaspora*). In this framing, any given particular group identity or social positionality has transformative potential within the specific sociohistorical context in which its past and present intersect and whose multiple resources (including shared narratives of colonial suppression as they or earlier generations experienced colonialism) can be reworked to forge a future grounded in a new identity that has greater emancipatory potential (notwithstanding the burdensome legacy of colonialism). The notion – and reality – of being Black *and* British in the contemporary UK exemplifies how identity as *becoming* works; it represents the everyday forging of an integrated identity, and one that both an immigrant family from India or Jamaica and a well-established white English family in an earlier time (e.g. the 1950s), might well have thought impossible. Thus in the UK, notwithstanding the persistence of multiple forms of racial inequality, there is discernible progress from a moment in which the empirically and culturally correct statement that "there ain't no Black in the Union Jack" (Gilroy 1987) has resonance to a moment when the winner of the *Great British Bake Off* in 2015 is Nadiya Hussein, an English-born, hijab-wearing Muslim woman whose Bangladeshi parents came to the UK in the 1970s. And her winning "classic British cake" was a lemon wedding cake which she decorated with jewels from her own wedding and a wide ribbon in the colors of the Union Jack (Dillon 2020). Attentiveness to the fact that cultural identity is not set in stone for all time by a particular racial or historical inheritance also allows for the differences of experience that invariably exist within any shared history to be brought to the fore. Also, it avoids the temptation to think stereotypically of all colonized peoples, or all people from a specific geographical region such as the Caribbean or from Africa, Asia, or Central or South America as being the same.

Raewyn Connell and colleagues apply a postcolonial lens to the production, dissemination and certification of knowledge, including sociology (see excerpt *14e Toward a Global Sociology of Knowledge*). They discuss how what is taken as meritorious research and knowledge across the globe is invariably anchored in North American and Western European universities and centers, thus perpetuating the pattern characteristic of colonization whereby the various ruling colonial powers drew on their own Western-trained knowledge workers (e.g. teachers, lawyers, accountants) and their knowledge practices to impose colonization as a matter of course in the institutional and organizational routines of daily life in the colonized locations. Thus as Connell and colleagues argue, this Northern bias in knowledge-production silences both the salience of the important local knowledge that is generated and the different, local-specific knowledge goals that are pressing in regions outside the global metropole. Connell (2007) thus calls for a Southern Theory which would seek to redress the Northern bias by featuring research and commentaries from scholars and others not only living in but educated in the Global South.

Somewhat ironically, given that scholars have paid so much attention in recent decades to the social construction and cultural dynamics of race and racial identities (and of cultural racism; see Gilroy 2000), scientific developments in the field of genetics have revived earlier historical interest in and assumptions about the biology of race. Genetic testing, though lauded for its illumination of the biological carriers of inheritable diseases, has also, unexpectedly, refocused attention on the measurement and genetic composition of a given racial category. An interesting turn here, however, is the use of genetic analysis as a tool in racial reconciliation projects. **Alondra Nelson**, whose impactful book *The Social Life of DNA: Race, Reparations and Reconciliation after the Genome* (2016), focused on the prevalence of DNA testing beyond medical purposes and the uses and implications of such analysis, elaborates (see excerpt *14f The Social Life of DNA*) on efforts by elite universities to make reparations for their past institutional practices colluding with slavery and otherwise perpetuating racial inequality. As she discusses, with a formally articulated commitment to the ethics of justice, universities such as Brown and Georgetown are deploying DNA testing in order to identify the descendants of slaves whose sale or labor benefited the university, and to make reparations to them through admission to and financial support for their university education. Such DNA identity-tracking processes also help to restore the lost social identity and community (that slavery ruptured) by helping descendants find one another and to collectively partake of their shared history.

REFERENCES

Connell, RW. 2007. *Southern Theory: The Global Dynamics of Knowledge in Social Science*. Sydney: Allen and Unwin.

Dillon, Michele. 2020. *Introduction to Sociological Theory: Concepts and their Applicability to the Twenty-First Century*. 3rd ed. Oxford: Wiley.

Fanon, Frantz. 1967. *Black Skin, White Masks*. Trans. Charles Lam Markmann. New York: Grove Press.

Gilroy, Paul. 1987. *"There Ain't No Black in the Union Jack": The Cultural Politics of Race and Nation*. London: Hutchinson.

Gilroy, Paul. 2000. *Against Race: Imagining Political Culture Beyond the Color Line*. Cambridge, MA: Harvard University Press.

Nelson, Alondra. 2016. *The Social Life of DNA: Race, Reparations and Reconciliation after the Genome*. New York: Random House.

14A W. E. Burghardt Du Bois from *The Souls of Black Folk*

Original publication details: W. E. Burghardt Du Bois, 1903/1969. *The Souls of Black Folk*, edited by Nathan Hare and Alvin F. Poussaint, pp. 43–50. New York: Signet. Public domain.

BETWEEN me and the other world there is ever an masked question: unasked by some through feelings of delicacy; by others through the difficulty of rightly framing it. All, nevertheless, flutter round it They approach me in a half-hesitant sort of way, eye me curiously or compassionately, and then, instead of saying directly, How does it feel to be a problem? they say, I know an excellent colored man in my town; or, I fought at Mechanicsville; or, Do not these Southern outrages make your blood boil? At these I smile, or am interested, or reduce the boiling to a simmer, as the occasion may require. To the real question, How does it feel to be a problem? I answer seldom a word.

And yet, being a problem is a strange experience, – peculiar even for one who has never been anything else, save perhaps in babyhood and in Europe. It is in the early days of rollicking boyhood that the revelation first bursts upon one, all in a day, as it were. I remember well when the shadow swept across me, I was a little thing, away up in the hills of New England, where the dark Housatonic winds between Hoosac and Taghkanic to the sea. In a wee wooden schoolhouse, something put it into the boys' and girls' heads to buy gorgeous visiting-cards – ten cents a package – and exchange. The exchange was merry, till one girl, a tall newcomer, refused my card, – refused it peremptorily, with a glance. Then it dawned upon me with a certain suddenness that I was different from the others; or like, mayhap, in heart and life and longing, but shut out from their world by a vast veil. I had thereafter no desire to tear down that veil, to creep through; I held all beyond it in common contempt, and lived above it in a region of blue sky and great wandering shadows. That sky was bluest when I could beat my mates at examination-time, or beat them at a foot-race, or even beat their stringy heads. Alas, with the years all this fine contempt began to fade; for the words I longed for, and all their dazzling opportunities, were theirs, not mine. But they should not keep these prizes, I said; some, all, I would wrest from them. Just how I would do it I could never decide: by reading law, by healing the sick, by telling the wonderful tales that swam in my head, – some way. With other black boys the strife was not so fiercely sunny: their youth shrunk into tasteless sycophancy, or into silent hatred of the pale world about them and mocking distrust of everything white; or wasted itself in a bitter cry, Why did God make me an outcast and a stranger in mine own house? The shades of the prison-house closed round about us all: walls strait and stubborn to the whitest, but relentlessly narrow, tall, and unscalable to sons of night who must plod darkly on in resignation, or beat unavailing palms against the stone, or steadily, half hopelessly, watch the streak of blue above.

After the Egyptian and Indian, the Greek and Roman, the Teuton, and Mongolian, the Negro is a sort of seventh son, born with a veil, and gifted with second-sight in this American world, – a world which yields him no true self-consciousness, but only lets him see himself through the revelation of the other world. It is a peculiar sensation, this double-consciousness, this sense of always looking at one's self through the eyes of others, of measuring one's soul by the tape of a world that looks on in amused contempt and pity. One ever feels his twoness, – an American, a Negro; two souls, two thoughts, two unreconciled striving; two warring ideals in one dark body, whose dogged strength alone keeps it from being torn asunder.

The history of the American Negro is the history of this strife, – this longing to attain self-conscious manhood, to merge his double self into a better and truer self. In this merging he wishes neither of the older selves to be lost. He would not Africanize America, for America has too much to teach the world and Africa. He would not bleach his Negro soul in a flood of white Americanism, for he knows that Negro blood has a message for the world. He simply wishes to make it possible for a man to be both a Negro and an American, without being cursed and spit upon by his fellows, without having the doors of Opportunity, closed roughly in his face.

This, then, is the end of his striving: to be a co-worker in the kingdom of culture, to escape both death and isolation, to husband and use his best powers and his latent genius. These powers of body and mind have in the past been strangely wasted, dispersed, or forgotten. The shadow of a mighty Negro past flits through the tale of Ethiopia the Shadowy, and of Egypt the Sphinx. Through history, the powers of single black men flash here and there like fallings stars, and die sometimes before the world has rightly gauged their brightness. Here in America, in the few days since Emancipation, the black man's turning hither and thither in hesitant and doubtful striving has often made his very strength to lose effectiveness, to seem like absence of power, like weakness. And yet it is not weakness, – it is the contradiction of double aims. The double-aimed struggle of the black artisan – on the one hand to escape white contempt for a nation of mere hewers of wood and drawers of water, and on the other hand to plough and nail and dig for a poverty-stricken horde – could only result in making him a poor craftsman, for he had but half a heart in either cause. By the poverty and ignorance of his people, the Negro minister or doctor was tempted toward quackery and demagogy; and by the criticism of the other world, toward ideals that made him ashamed of his lowly tasks. The would-be black *savant* was confronted by the paradox that the knowledge his people needed was a twice-told tale to his white neighbors, while the knowledge which would teach the white world was Greek to his own flesh and blood. The innate love of harmony and beauty that set the ruder souls of his people a-dancing and a-singing raised but confusion and doubt in the soul of the black artist; for the beauty revealed to him was the soul-beauty of a race which his larger audience despised, and he could not articulate the message of another people. This waste of double aims, this seeking to satisfy two unreconciled ideals, has wrought sad havoc with the courage and faith and deeds of ten thousand thousand people, – has sent them often wooing false gods and invoking false means of salvation, and at times has even seemed about to make them ashamed of themselves.

Away back in the days of bondage they thought to see in one divine event the end of all doubt and disappointment; few men ever worshipped Freedom with half such unquestioning faith as did the American Negro for two centuries. To him, so far as he thought and dreamed, slavery was indeed the sum of all villainies, the cause of all sorrow, the root of all prejudice; Emancipation was the key to a promised land of sweeter beauty than ever stretched before the eyes of wearied Israelites. In song and exhortation swelled one refrain – Liberty; in his tears and curses the God he implored had Freedom in his right hand. At last, it came, – suddenly, fearfully, like a dream. With one wild carnival of blood and passion came the message in his own plaintive cadences: –

"Shout, O children!
Shout, you're free!
For God has bought your liberty!"

Years have passed away since then, – ten, twenty, forty; forty years of national life, forty years of renewal and development, and yet the swarthy spectre sits in its accustomed seat at the Nation's feast. In vain do we cry to this our vastest social problem: –

"Take any shape but that, and my firm nerves
Shall never tremble!"

The Nation has not yet found peace from its sins; the freedman has not yet found in freedom his promised land. Whatever of good may have come in these years of change, the shadow of a deep disappointment rests upon the Negro people, – a disappointment all the more bitter because the unattained ideal was unbounded save by the simple ignorance of a lowly people.

The first decade was merely a prolongation of the vain search for freedom, the boon that seemed ever barely to elude their grasp, – like a tantalizing will-o'-the-wisp, maddening and misleading the headless host. The holocaust of war, the terrors of the Ku-Klux Klan, the lies of carpet-baggers, the disorganization of industry, and the contradictory advice of friends and foes, left the bewildered serf with no new watchword beyond the old cry for freedom. As the time flew, however, he began to grasp a new idea. The ideal of liberty demanded for its attainment powerful means, and these the Fifteenth Amendment gave him. The ballot, which before he had looked upon as a visible sign of freedom, be now regarded as the chief means of gaining and perfecting the liberty with which war had partially endowed him. And why not? Had not votes made war and emancipated millions? Had not votes enfranchised the freedmen? Was anything impossible to a power that had done all this? A million black men started with renewed zeal to vote themselves into the kingdom. So the decade flew away, the revolution of 1876 came, and left the half-free sef weary, wondering, but still inspired. Slowly but steadily, in the following years, a new vision began gradually to replace the dream of political power, – a powerful movement, the rise of another ideal to guide the unguided, another pillar of fire by night after a clouded day. It was the ideal of "book-learning"; the curiosity, born of compulsory ignorance, to know and test the power of the cabalistic letters of the white man, the longing to know. Here at last seemed to have been discovered the mountain path to Canaan; longer than the highway of Emancipation and law, steep and rugged, but straight, leading to heights high enough to overlook life.

Up the new path die advance guard toiled, slowly, heavily, doggedly; only those who have watched and guided the faltering feet, the misty minds, the dull understandings, of the dark pupils of these schools know how faithfully, how piteously, this people strove to learn. It was weary work. The cold statistician wrote down the inches of progress here and there, noted also where here and there a foot had slipped or some one had fallen. To the tired climbers, the horizon was ever dark, the mists were often cold, the Canaan was always dim and far away. If, however, the vistas disclosed as yet no goal, no resting-place, little but flattery and criticism, the journey at least gave leisure for reflection and self-examination; it changed the child of Emancipation to the youth with dawning self-consciousness, self-realization, self-respect. In those sombre forests of his striving his own soul rose before him, and he saw himself, – darkly as through a veil; and yet he saw in himself some faint revelation of his power, of his mission. He began to have a dim feeling that, to attain his place in the world, he must be himself, and not another. For the first time he sought to analyze the burden he bore upon his back, that dead-weight of social degradation partially masked behind a half-named Negro problem. He felt his poverty; without a cent, without a home, without land, tools, or savings, he had entered into competition with rich, landed, skilled neighbors. To be a poor man is hard, but to be a poor race in a land of dollars is the very bottom of hardships.

14B Edward W. Said from *Orientalism*

Original publication details: Edward W. Said, 1978. *Orientalism*, pp. 4–8. New York: Random House. © 1978 Edward W. Said. Reproduced with permission of Pantheon Books, an imprint of the Knopf Doubleday Publishing Group, a division of Penguin Random House LLC. All rights reserved.

I have begun with the assumption that the Orient is not an inert fact of nature. It is not merely *there*, just as the Occident itself is not just *there* either. We must take seriously Vico's great observation that men make their own history, that what they can know is what they have made, and extend it to geography: as both geographical and cultural entities – to say nothing of historical entities – such locales, regions, geographical sectors as "Orient" and "Occident" are man-made. Therefore as much as the West itself, the Orient is an idea that has a history and a tradition of thought, imagery, and vocabulary that have given it reality and presence in and for the West. The two geographical entities thus support and to an extent reflect each other.

Having said that, one must go on to state a number of reasonable qualifications. In the first place, it would be wrong to conclude that the Orient was *essentially* an idea, or a creation with no corresponding reality. When Disraeli said in his novel *Tancred* that the East was a career, he meant that to be interested in the East was something bright young Westerners would find to be an all-consuming passion; he should not be interpreted as saying that the East was *only* a career for Westerners. There were – and are – cultures and nations whose location is in the East, and their lives, histories, and customs have a brute reality obviously greater than anything that could be said about them in the West. About that fact this study of Orientalism has very little to contribute, except to acknowledge it tacitly. But the phenomenon of Orientalism as I study it here deals principally, not with a correspondence between Orientalism and Orient, but with the internal consistency of Orientalism and its ideas about the Orient (the East as career) despite or beyond any correspondence, or lack thereof, with a "real" Orient. My point is that Disraeli's statement about the East refers mainly to that created consistency, that regular constellation of ideas as the pre-eminent thing about the Orient, and not to its mere being, as Wallace Stevens's phrase has it.

A second qualification is that ideas, cultures, and histories cannot seriously be understood or studied without their force, or more precisely their configurations of power, also being studied. To believe that the Orient was created – or, as I call it, "Orientalized" – and to believe that such things happen simply as a necessity of the imagination, is to be disingenuous. The relationship between Occident and Orient is a relationship of power, of domination, of varying degrees of a complex hegemony, and is quite accurately indicated in the title of K. M. Panikkar's classic *Asia and Western Dominance*.[1] The Orient was Orientalized not only because it was discovered to be "Oriental" in all those ways considered commonplace by an average nineteenth-century European, but also because it *could be* – that is, submitted to being – *made* Oriental. There is very little consent to be found, for example, in the fact that Flaubert's encounter with an Egyptian courtesan produced a widely influential model of the Oriental woman; she never spoke of herself, she never represented her emotions, presence, or history. *He* spoke for and represented her. He was foreign, comparatively wealthy, male, and these were historical facts of domination that allowed him not only to possess Kuchuk Hanem physically but to speak for her and tell his readers in what way she was "typically Oriental." My argument is that Flaubert's situation of strength in relation to Kuchuk Hanem was not an isolated instance. It fairly stands for the pattern of relative strength between East and West, and the discourse about the Orient that it enabled.

This brings us to a third qualification. One ought never to assume that the structure of Orientalism is nothing more than a structure of lies or of myths which, were the truth about them to be told, would simply blow away. I myself believe that Orientalism is more particularly valuable as a sign of European-Atlantic power over the Orient than it is as a veridic discourse about the Orient (which is what, in its academic or scholarly form, it claims to be). Nevertheless, what we must respect and try to grasp is the sheer knitted-together strength of Orientalist discourse, its very close ties to the enabling socio-economic and political institutions, and its redoubtable durability. After all, any system of ideas that can remain unchanged as teachable wisdom (in academies, books, congresses, universities, foreign-service institutes) from the period of Ernest Renan in the late 1840s until the present in the United States must be something more formidable than a mere collection of lies. Orientalism, therefore, is not an airy European fantasy about the Orient, but a created body of theory and practice in which, for many generations, there has been a considerable material investment. Continued investment made Orientalism, as a system of knowledge about the Orient, an accepted grid for filtering through the Orient into Western consciousness, just as that same investment multiplied – indeed, made truly productive – the statements proliferating out from Orientalism into the general culture.

Gramsci has made the useful analytic distinction between civil and political society in which the former is made up of voluntary (or at least rational and noncoercive) affiliations like schools, families, and unions, the latter of state institutions (the army, the police, the central bureaucracy) whose role in the polity is direct domination. Culture, of course, is to be found operating within civil society, where the influence of ideas, of institutions, and of other persons works not through domination but by what Gramsci calls consent. In any society not totalitarian, then, certain cultural forms predominate over others, just as certain ideas are more influential than others; the form of this cultural leadership is what Gramsci has identified as *hegemony*, an indispensable concept for any understanding of cultural life in the industrial West. It is hegemony, or rather the result of cultural hegemony at work, that gives Orientalism the durability and the strength I have been speaking about so far. Orientalism is never far from what Denys Hay has called the idea of Europe,[2] a collective notion identifying "us" Europeans as against all "those" non-Europeans, and indeed it can be argued that the major component in European culture is precisely what made that culture hegemonic both in and outside Europe: the idea of European identity as a superior one in comparison with all the non-European peoples and cultures. There is in addition the hegemony of European ideas about the Orient, themselves reiterating European superiority over Oriental backwardness, usually overriding the possibility that a more independent, or more skeptical, thinker might have had different views on the matter.

In a quite constant way, Orientalism depends for its strategy on this flexible *positional* superiority, which puts the Westerner in a whole series of possible relationships with the Orient without ever losing him the relative upper hand. And why should it have been otherwise, especially during the period of extraordinary European ascendancy from the late Renaissance to the present? The scientist, the scholar, the missionary, the trader, or the soldier was in, or thought about, the Orient because he *could be there*, or could think about it, with very little resistance on the Orient's part. Under the general heading of knowledge of the Orient, and within the umbrella of Western hegemony over the Orient during the period from the end of the eighteenth century, there emerged a complex Orient suitable for study in the academy, for display in the museum, for reconstruction in the colonial office, for theoretical illustration in anthropological, biological, linguistic, racial, and historical theses about mankind and the universe, for instances of economic and sociological theories of development, revolution, cultural personality, national or religious character. Additionally, the imaginative examination of things Oriental was based more or less exclusively upon a sovereign Western consciousness out of whose unchallenged centrality an Oriental world emerged, first according to general ideas about who or what was an Oriental, then according to a detailed logic governed not simply by empirical reality but by a battery of desires, repressions, investments, and projections.

NOTES

1   Pannikar, K.M. 1959. *Asia and Western Dominance*. London: George Allen & Unwin.

2   Hay, Denys. 1968. *Europe: The Emergence of an Idea*, 2nd ed. Edinburgh: Edinburgh University Press.

14C Frantz Fanon from *Black Skin, White Masks*

Original publication details: Frantz Fanon, 1952/1967. *Black Skin, White Masks*, translated by Charles Lam Markmann, pp. 109–113. New York: Grove Press. Reproduced with permission of Grove / Atlantic, Inc.

The Fact of Blackness

I came into the world imbued with the will to find a meaning in things, my spirit filled with the desire to attain to the source of the world, and then I found that I was an object in the midst of other objects.

Sealed into that crushing objecthood, I turned beseechingly to others. Their attention was a liberation, running over my body suddenly abraded into nonbeing, endowing me once more with an agility that I had thought lost, and by taking me out of the world, restoring me to it. But just as I reached the other side, I stumbled, and the movements, the attitudes, the glances of the other fixed me there, in the sense in which a chemical solution is fixed by a dye. I was indignant; I demanded an explanation. Nothing happened. I burst apart. Now the fragments have been put together again by another self.

As long as the black man is among his own, he will have no occasion, except in minor internal conflicts, to experience his being through others. There is of course the moment of "being for others," of which Hegel speaks, but every ontology is made unattainable in a colonized and civilized society. It would seem that this fact has not been given sufficient attention by those who have discussed the question. In the *Weltanschauung* of a colonized people there is an impurity, a flaw that outlaws any ontological explanation. Someone may object that this is the case with every individual, but such an objection merely conceals a basic problem. Ontology – once it is finally admitted as leaving existence by the wayside – does not permit us to understand the being of the black man. For not only must the black man be black; he must be black in relation to the white man. Some critics will take it on themselves to remind us that this proposition has a converse. I say that this is false. The black man has no ontological resistance in the eyes of the white man. Overnight the Negro has been given two frames of reference within which he has had to place himself. His metaphysics, or, less pretentiously, his customs and the sources on which they were based, were wiped out because they were in conflict with a civilization that he did not know and that imposed itself on him.

The black man among his own in the twentieth century does not know at what moment his inferiority comes into being through the other. Of course I have talked about the black problem with friends, or, more rarely, with American Negroes. Together we protested, we asserted the equality of all men in the world. In the Antilles there was also that little gulf that exists among the almost-white, the mulatto, and the [Negro]. But I was satisfied with an intellectual understanding of these differences. It was not really dramatic. And then. . . .

And then the occasion arose when I had to meet the white man's eyes. An unfamiliar weight burdened me. The real world challenged my claims. In the white world the man of color encounters difficulties in the development of his bodily schema. Consciousness of the body is solely a negating activity. It is a third-person consciousness. The body is surrounded by an atmosphere of certain uncertainty. I know that if I want to smoke, I shall have to reach out my right arm and take the pack of cigarettes lying at the other end of the table. The matches, however, are in the drawer on the left, and I shall have to lean back slightly. And all these movements are made not out of habit but out of implicit knowledge. A slow composition of my *self* as a body in the middle of a spatial and temporal world – such seems to be the schema. It does not impose itself on me; it is, rather, a definitive structuring of the self and of the world – definitive because it creates a real dialectic between my body and the world.

For several years certain laboratories have been trying to produce a serum for "denegrification"; with all the earnestness in the world, laboratories have sterilized their test tubes, checked their scales, and embarked on researches that might make it possible for the miserable Negro to whiten himself and thus to throw off the burden of that corporeal malediction. Below the corporeal schema I had sketched a historico-racial schema. The elements that I used had been provided for me not by "residual sensations and perceptions primarily of a tactile, vestibular, kinesthetic, and visual character,"[1] but by the other, the white man, who had woven me out of a thousand details, anecdotes, stories. I thought that what I had in hand was to construct a physiological self, to balance space, to localize sensations, and here I was called on for more.

"Look, a Negro!" It was an external stimulus that flicked over me as I passed by. I made a tight smile.

"Look, a Negro!" It was true. It amused me.

"Look, a Negro!" The circle was drawing a bit tighter. I made no secret of my amusement.

"Mama, see the Negro! I'm frightened!" Frightened! Frightened! Now they were beginning to be afraid of me. I made up my mind to laugh myself to tears, but laughter had become impossible.

I could no longer laugh, because I already knew that there were legends, stories, history, and above all *historicity*, which I had learned about from Jaspers. Then, assailed at various points, the corporeal schema crumbled, its place taken by a racial epidermal schema. In the train it was no longer a question of being aware of my body in the third person but in a triple person. In the train I was given not one but two, three places. I had already stopped being amused. It was not that I was finding febrile coordinates in the world. I existed triply: I occupied space. I moved toward the other . . . and the evanescent other, hostile but not opaque, transparent, not there, disappeared. Nausea. . . .

I was responsible at the same time for my body, for my race, for my ancestors. I subjected myself to an objective examination, I discovered my blackness, my ethnic characteristics; and I was battered down by tom-toms, cannibalism, intellectual deficiency, fetishism, racial defects, slave-ships, and above all else, above all: "Sho' good eatin'."

On that day, completely dislocated, unable to be abroad with the other, the white man, who unmercifully imprisoned me, I took myself far off from my own presence, far indeed, and made myself an object. What else could it be for me but an amputation, an excision, a hemorrhage that spattered my whole body with black blood? But I did not want this revision, this thematization. All I wanted was to be a man among other men. I wanted to come lithe and young into a world that was ours and to help to build it together.

But I rejected all immunization of the emotions. I wanted to be a man, nothing but a man. Some identified me with ancestors of mine who had been enslaved or lynched: I decided to accept this. It was on the universal level of the intellect that I understood this inner kinship – I was the grandson of slaves in exactly the same way in which President Lebrun was the grandson of tax-paying, hard-working peasants. In the main, the panic soon vanished.

In America, Negroes are segregated. In South America, Negroes are whipped in the streets, and Negro strikers are cut down by machine-guns. In West Africa, the Negro is an animal. And there beside me, my neighbor in the university, who was born in Algeria, told me: "As long as the Arab is treated like a man, no solution is possible."

"Understand, my dear boy, color prejudice is something I find utterly foreign. . . . But of course, come in, sir, there is no color prejudice among us. . . . Quite, the Negro is a man like ourselves. . . . It is not because he is black that he is less intelligent than we are. . . . I had a Senegalese buddy in the army who was really clever. . . ."

Where am I to be classified? Or, if you prefer, tucked away?

"A Martinican, a native of 'our' old colonies."

Where shall I hide?

NOTE

1 Jean Lhermitte. 1939. *L'Image de notre corps*. Paris, Nouvelle Revue critique, p. 17.

14D Stuart Hall from *Cultural Identity and Diaspora*

Original publication details: Stuart Hall, 1990. "Cultural Identity and Diaspora," pp. 223, 224–228 in *Identity: Community, Culture, Difference*, edited by Jonathan Rutherford. London: Lawrence & Wishart. Reproduced with permission of Lawrence & Wishart via PLS Clear.

There are at least two different ways of thinking about 'cultural identity'. The first position defines 'cultural identity' in terms of one, shared culture, a sort of collective 'one true self', hiding inside the many other, more superficial or artificially imposed 'selves', which people with a shared history and ancestry hold in common. Within the terms of this definition, our cultural identities reflect the common historical experiences and shared cultural codes which provide us, as 'one people', with stable, unchanging and continuous frames of reference and meaning, beneath the shifting divisions and vicissitudes of our actual history. This 'oneness', underlying all the other, more superficial differences, is the truth, the essence, of 'Caribbeanness', of the black experience. It is this identity which a Caribbean or black diaspora must discover, excavate, bring to light and express through cinematic representation.

Such a conception of cultural identity played a critical role in all the post-colonial struggles which have so profoundly reshaped our world.

[...]

... images offer a way of imposing an imaginary coherence on the experience of dispersal and fragmentation, which is the history of all enforced diasporas. They do this by representing or 'figuring' Africa as the mother of these different civilisations. This Triangle is, after all, 'centred' in Africa. Africa is the name of the missing term, the great aporia, which lies at the centre of our cultural identity and gives it a meaning which, until recently, it lacked. No one who looks at these textural images now, in the light of the history of transportation, slavery and migration, can fail to understand how the rift of separation, the 'loss of identity', which has been integral to the Caribbean experience only begins to be healed when these forgotten connections are once more set in place. Such texts restore an imaginary fullness or plentitude, to set against the broken rubric of our past. They are resources of resistance and identity, with which to confront the fragmented and pathological ways in which that experience has been reconstructed within the dominant regimes of cinematic and visual representation of the West.

There is, however, a second, related but different view of cultural identity. This second position recognises that, as well as the many points of similarity, there are also critical points of deep and significant *difference* which constitute 'what we really are'; or rather – since history has intervened – 'what we have become'. We cannot speak for very long, with any exactness, about 'one experience, one identity', without acknowledging its other side – the ruptures and discontinuities which constitute, precisely, the Caribbean's 'uniqueness'. Cultural identity, in this second sense, is a matter of 'becoming' as well as of 'being'. It belongs to the future as much as to the past. It is not something which already exists, transcending place, time, history and culture. Cultural

identities come from somewhere, have histories. But, like everything which is historical, they undergo constant transformation. Far from being eternally fixed in some
essentialised past, they are subject to the continuous 'play' of history, culture and
power. Far from being grounded in a mere 'recovery' of the past, which is waiting to
be found, and which, when found, will secure our sense of ourselves into eternity,
identities are the names we give to the different ways we are positioned by, and position ourselves within, the narratives of the past.

It is only from this second position that we can properly understand the traumatic
character of 'the colonial experience'. The ways in which black people, black experiences, were positioned and subject-ed in the dominant regimes of representation were
the effects of a critical exercise of cultural power and normalisation. Not only, in Said's
'Orientalist' sense, were we constructed as different and other within the categories of
knowledge of the West by those regimes. They had the power to make us see and experience *ourselves* as 'Other'. Every regime of representation is a regime of power formed,
as Foucault reminds us, by the fatal couplet, 'power/knowledge'. But this kind of knowledge is internal, not external. It is one thing to position a subject or set of peoples as the
Other of a dominant discourse. It is quite another thing to subject them to that 'knowledge', not only as a matter of imposed will and domination, by the power of inner
compulsion and subjective con-formation to the norm. That is the lesson – the sombre
majesty – of Fanon's insight into the colonising experience in *Black Skin, White Masks*.

This inner expropriation of cultural identity cripples and deforms. If its silences are
not resisted, they produce, in Fanon's vivid phrase, 'individuals without an anchor,
without horizon, colourless, stateless, rootless – a race of angels'.[1] Nevertheless, this
idea of otherness as an inner compulsion changes our conception of 'cultural identity'.
In this perspective, cultural identity is not a fixed essence at all, lying unchanged outside history and culture. It is not some universal and transcendental spirit inside us
on which history has made no fundamental mark. It is not once-and-for-all. It is not
a fixed origin to which we can make some final and absolute Return. Of course, it is
not a mere phantasm either. It is *something* – not a mere trick of the imagination. It
has its histories – and histories have their real, material and symbolic effects. The past
continues to speak to us. But it no longer addresses us as a simple, factual 'past', since
our relation to it, like the child's relation to the mother, is always-already 'after the
break'. It is always constructed through memory, fantasy, narrative and myth. Cultural
identities are the points of identification, the unstable points of identification or
suture, which are made, within the discourses of history and culture. Not an essence
but a *positioning*. Hence, there is always a politics of identity, a politics of position,
which has no absolute guarantee in an unproblematic, transcendental 'law of origin'.

This second view of cultural identity is much less familiar, and more unsettling. If
identity does not proceed, in a straight, unbroken line, from some fixed origin, how
are we to understand its formation? We might think of black Caribbean identities as
'framed' by two axes or vectors, simultaneously operative: the vector of similarity
and continuity; and the vector of difference and rupture. Caribbean identities always
have to be thought of in terms of the dialogic relationship between these two axes.
The one gives us some grounding in, some continuity with, the past. The second

reminds us that what we share is precisely the experience of a profound discontinuity: the peoples dragged into slavery, transportation, colonisation, migration, came predominantly from Africa – and when that supply ended, it was temporarily refreshed by indentured labour from the Asian subcontinent. (This neglected fact explains why, when you visit Guyana or Trinidad, you see, symbolically inscribed in the faces of their peoples, the paradoxical 'truth' of Christopher Columbus's mistake: you *can* find 'Asia' by sailing west, if you know where to look!) In the history of the modern world, there are few more traumatic ruptures to match these enforced separations from Africa – already figured, in the European imaginary, as 'the Dark Continent'. But the slaves were also from different countries, tribal communities, villages, languages and gods. African religion, which has been so profoundly formative in Caribbean spiritual life, is precisely *different* from Christian monotheism in believing that God is so powerful that he can only be known through a proliferation of spiritual manifestations, present everywhere in the natural and social world. These gods live on, in an underground existence, in the hybridised religious universe of Haitian voodoo, pocomania, Native pentacostalism, Black baptism, Rastafarianism and the black Saints Latin American Catholicism. The paradox is that it was the uprooting of slavery and transportation and the insertion into the plantation economy (as well as the symbolic economy) of the Western world that 'unified' these peoples across their differences, in the same moment as it cut them off from direct access to their past.

Difference, therefore, persists – in and alongside continuity. To return to the Caribbean after any long absence is to experience again the shock of the 'doubleness' of similarity and difference. Visiting the French Caribbean for the first time, I also saw at once how different Martinique is from, say, Jamaica: and this is no mere difference of topography or climate. It is a profound difference of culture and history. And the difference *matters*. It positions Martiniquains and Jamaicans as *both* the same *and* different. Moreover, the boundaries of difference are continually repositioned in relation to different points of reference. Vis-a-vis the developed West, we are very much 'the same'. We belong to the marginal, the underdeveloped, the periphery, the 'Other'. We are at the outer edge, the 'rim', of the metropolitan world – always 'South' to someone else's *El Norte*.

At the same time, we do not stand in the same relation of the 'otherness' to the metropolitan centres. Each has negotiated its economic, political and cultural dependency differently. And this 'difference', whether we like it or not, is already inscribed in our cultural identities. In turn, it is this negotiation of identity which makes us, vis-a-vis other Latin American people, with a very similar history, different – Caribbeans, *les Antilliennes* ('islanders' to their mainland). And yet, vis-a-vis one another, Jamaican, Haitian, Cuban, Guadeloupean, Barbadian, etc . . .

NOTE

1   Frantz Fanon. 1963. *The Wretched of the Earth*. London: Grove Press, p. 176.

14E Raewyn Connell, Fran Collyer, João Maia, and Robert Morrell from *Toward a Global Sociology of Knowledge: Post-Colonial Realities and Intellectual Practices*

Original publication details: Raewyn Connell, Fran Collyer, João Maia, and Robert Morrell, 2017. "Toward a Global Sociology of Knowledge: Post-Colonial Realities and Intellectual Practices." *International Sociology* 32: 24, 25–26, 29–30, 31–32. Reproduced with permission of Sage Publications Ltd.

Colonization was undertaken by a workforce that from the start included knowledge workers: priests, clerks, engineers, map-makers, and soon enough lawyers, accountants, architects, teachers and researchers. Indigenous knowledge holders were sometimes killed, sometimes coopted. Increasing numbers of the colonized were drawn into knowledge work on new terms in the new colonial society, such as the *évolués* of Francophone Africa and the *babus* of British India. The terms on which this happened were contested, often bitterly, with the colonizers debating whether natives could become Christian priests, teachers and lawyers.

These issues reflect a crucial fact about knowledge, which became stark in the conditions of colonization. In the older sociology of knowledge, frameworks of knowledge were figured as emanating from a social class or a community in a generalized way: as a mental deposit from the interactions of everyday life, in Berger and Luckmann's model; as a consequence of underlying interests, in Lukács's and Mannheim's. But knowledge is not just an abstract social 'construct'. It is specifically a social *product,* generated by and embodied in particular forms of work.

[. . .]

A telling example [of the socio-historical specificity of knowledge] is provided by the citation practices of contemporary academics. It is required, in writing a journal article, to refer to 'the literature' – essentially, to treat one's new contribution as a modification of the knowledge obtained from the work of a designated selection of previous researchers. In principle, this allows a cumulation and expansion of knowledge, which we see in all three domains in our study. With cultural and organizational pressures, well known to university workers, it may also result in a conservative repetition of disciplinary norms.

In the course of their labour, knowledge workers locate their arguments in texts that arise within a specific and objectively definable historical and geo-socio-political space. This has strategic consequences at the aggregate, if not individual, level. Thus we find, empirically, workers in peripheral countries primarily citing the texts of authors from the global North, while workers in the North mostly cite each other, and mostly ignore the ideas and studies produced by workers in the global South (Collyer, 2014). The overall effect has been a structuring of knowledge production where Northern-produced knowledge is treated as the 'gold standard', while the possibilities for disciplinary diversity and innovation are constrained.

[. . .]

Southern Situations and Global Arenas

No society, whether formally colonized or not, is now outside the economic, political and cultural world created by European empire and the global neoliberal economy. Epistemologies of the South exist in complex but strong relations with the North, not in isolation nor in rupture. These relations are practical, significantly institutionalized, and massive. They are also ridden by tensions, and constantly in change.

The long shadow of colonial history falls across whole domains of knowledge. The struggle with HIV, for instance, was compromised in its early stages by official denial. In the United States, the virus was often figured as an alien import originating in Africa, spreading as a result of deviant lifestyles, and many lives were lost because prevention strategies were hampered by racism and homophobia. In a number of developing countries, AIDS was figured as a product of Western decadence, and international criticism of government inaction was rejected as Western racism. With the mass roll-out of antiretroviral therapy that moment has passed. But tensions around race and stigma, and the influence of missionary Christianity, still hamper social action to stop the epidemic.

The shadow of colonial history also falls inside knowledge institutions. Since the ending of apartheid in 1994 the role of South African universities has been in the spotlight. In some instances the state has pursued change using the authoritarian tools of new managerialism and the language of a racial imperative (Chetty and Merrett, 2014). In others, student activism has fuelled a national debate about knowledge construction and colonial legacies. In a recent, dramatic case the 'Rhodes Must Fall' movement at the University of Cape Town demanded the removal of a campus statue of the 19th-century imperialist leader Cecil Rhodes. It contributed to a wider national conflict around the racial profile of universities' staff, language of instruction and curriculum content. That in turn sparked a debate about decolonizing knowledge (Mbembe, 2015; Ramoupi, 2014; Worger, 2014), which continues at the time of writing.

As Mbembe argues in some detail – following Fanon – disengaging from a Eurocentric knowledge regime does not require substituting an Afrocentric one. It means developing new practices, especially new pedagogies and arrangements about popular access that democratize the knowledge institutions.

[. . .]

Brazil, South Africa and Australia are all post-colonial countries though not part of a 'third world'; indeed each is a regional hegemon in economic terms. They have very different demographies and class structures, and though in all three class is interwoven with racial hierarchy, the different dynamics of race and class reflect three different histories of colonization and post-colonial development. Crucially for our research, each has a state-funded research apparatus interwoven with a university system, though noticeably smaller than the systems in Europe or North America.

In all three, higher education curricula are mainly based on the Northern-centred economy of knowledge; though in South Africa there is stronger pressure to incorporate indigenous knowledge and perspectives. Universities are entirely Anglophone in Australia, mainly Anglophone in South Africa, and Lusophone in Brazil. The language difference creates very different possibilities for the circulation of knowledge, and the recruitment of knowledge workers, in an increasingly Anglophone global knowledge economy. The fact that most researchers in Brazil are civil servants working in state-funded universities must also be considered. This situation provides job security for certain knowledge workers but makes it difficult to attract scientists from other parts of the world.

Given these differences, multiplied across the continents (and the oceans: Hau'ofa, 2008), can we make any general claims about knowledge relations between global North and South? Not if these claims assume a fixed global relation of dominance and subordination. Nor if they assume homogeneity within such a category as North or South.

But there is no contradiction between recognizing deep diversity, and recognizing structures of centrality and inequality in a world economy of knowledge. The crucial requirement is to see the issue historically. The knowledge economy we now inhabit has been produced by the colonization of the world, and the tension-ridden working of imperialism and global neoliberalism. Struggle and transformation are endemic to that history and are still going on. The central analytic problem about 'society and knowledge', we argue, is to identify the world-scale dynamics of change in the economy of knowledge. The central political problem is to move those dynamics in a democratic direction.

These world-level problems are addressed, in different ways, in decolonial projects for knowledge (Santos, 2014); in attempts to build on past or emerging Southern theory (Comaroff and Comaroff, 2011; Connell, 2007); and in social movement debates on multiple perspectives, notably in feminism and indigenous politics (Bulbeck, 1998). This is not an easy terrain. For instance, it is important to recognize, even celebrate, epistemological plurality (Olivé et al., 2009). Yet in doing so we risk falling into a mosaic epistemology that fragments rather than connects knowledge and political practice.

The practice-based approach to knowledge described in this article will not solve all these difficulties. But we think it has a useful capacity to map and understand the interplay between different knowledge projects and the workforces that undertake them. For instance, it is clear that one important dynamic of change is the creation of new arenas of knowledge that, under the pressure of events, break down existing discipline boundaries within organized knowledge and also the institutional boundaries of knowledge institutions.

The HIV/AIDS epidemic is an important example of this, with the main biomedical research effort in the global North, the main burden of infection in the global South. The practical knowledge about effects, prevention and care therefore accumulates far from the virology research centres. The domain has been full of conflict, the South African dispute over antiretroviral therapy and indigenous knowledge being only one among many. In the last 15 years the AIDS domain has seen a gradual reassertion of dominance for a biomedical perspective, centred in North America and supported by transnational drug companies, which tends to replace community action with pharmaceuticals.

Movement in a democratic direction, then, is not ordained by history. If it occurs it will be through social and intellectual struggle, as well as political and economic shifts. The approach we have suggested helps identify necessary sites of struggle. One is the situation of the knowledge workforce, always partly casualized, currently subject to increasing pressure from neoliberal governments and managements. Another is the scientific communication system, currently being commodified and concentrated in the hands of a small group of corporations, but challenged by a popular open-access movement. A third is the formation of intellectual workers, in education systems increasingly privatized and homogenized on a world scale but also active sites of cultural contestation. A fourth is the production of knowledge in social movements such as environmentalism, challenging both the disinformation spread by the fossil fuel industry and the hierarchies of knowledge in mainstream science.

REFERENCES

Bulbeck, C. 1998. *Re-orienting Western Feminisms: Women's Diversity in a Postcolonial World.* Cambridge: Cambridge University Press.

Chetty, N. and Merrett, C. 2014 *The Struggle for the Soul of a South African University: The University of Kwazulu-Natal – Academic Freedom, Corporatisation and Transformation.* Self published. Pietermaritzburg.

Collyer, F. 2014. "Sociology, Sociologists and Core–Periphery Reflections." *Journal of Sociology* 50(3): 252–68.

Comaroff, J. and Comaroff, J.L. 2011. *Theory from the South: Or, How Euro-America is Evolving towards Africa.* Boulder, CO: Paradigm.

Connell, R. 2007. *Southern Theory: The Global Dynamics of Knowledge in Social Science.* Sydney: Allen and Unwin.

Hau'ofa, E. 2008. *We Are the Ocean.* Honolulu: University of Hawai'i Press.

Mbembe, A. 2015. "Decolonizing Knowledge and the Question of the Archive." Available at: https://africaisacountry.atavist.com/decolonizing-knowledge-and-the-question-of-the-archive (accessed 12 January 2016).

Olivé, L, Santos, B.S., De La Torre, C.S. et al. 2009. *Pluralismo Epistemológico.* La Paz: Muela del Diablo/Comuna/CLACSO/CIDES-UMSA.

Ramoupi, N.L.L. 2014. "African Research and Scholarship: 20 Years of Lost Opportunities to Transform Higher Education in South Africa." *Ufahamu: A Journal of African Studies* 38(1): 269–86.

Santos, B.S. 2014. *Epistemologies of the South: Justice against Epistemicide.* Boulder, CO: Paradigm Publishers

Worger, W.H. 2014. "The Tricameral Academy: Personal Reflections on Universities and History Departments in 'Post-Apartheid' South Africa." *Ufahamu: A Journal of African Studies* 38(1): 193–216.

14F Alondra Nelson from *The Social Life of DNA: Racial Reconciliation and Institutional Morality after the Genome*

Original publication details: Alondra Nelson, 2018. "The Social Life of DNA: Racial Reconciliation and Institutional Morality after the Genome. British Journal of Sociology 69: 523–525, 526, 528–529. Reproduced with permission of John Wiley & Sons Ltd.

Postgenomic

We can mark the start of the genomic era with the launch of the Human Genome Project (HGP) by the United States Department of Energy in 1990, during the administration of George H.W. Bush, or with the 2003 announcement of the successful completion of a full genome sequence and digital tools to analyse it, during the early months of the presidency of George W. Bush. *Postgenomic*, therefore, may be both an institutional and a chronological indicator, suggesting the where and the when of the genome and its afterlives (Richardson 2013). Postgenomic may mark a range of sociotechnical developments as well: Sarah S. Richardson and Hallam Stevens offer that the term captures 'new methods and approaches' in life sciences research, including the 'advent of whole-genome technologies as a shared platform for biological research across many fields,' (3) 'funding and investment' strategies premised on the anticipated efficacy of genomic analysis, and even an affect of humility, as techniques such as genome-wide association studies yield more questions and mysteries, than answers (3–5). Evelyn Fox Keller further suggests that the postgenomic is characterized by a conceptual shift from the gene to the genome as the predominant unit of analysis, with a concomitant reckoning that the genome is 'a dynamic and reactive system' and not merely a static structure (Keller 2015:10).

A dynamism of use follows this re-conceptualization of structure. While the HGP has yet to live up to its booster's loftiest biomedical promises, it has certainly succeeded in broadening 'the social life of DNA' (Nelson 2016). So much so that it can be said the postgenomic also concerns the move of genomics out of the formal biological sciences into a wider sociotechnical ecology. Thus, as Jenny Reardon puts it, the postgenomic era should prompt further examination of 'the uses, significance and value of the human genome sequence' (2013: 2). These include, for example, the panoply of 'interests and agendas of commercial pharmaceutical, biotechnology and direct-to-consumer genetics enterprises . . . [that] apply human genomic data and technologies to locate variation in the human genome that may be marketable as a biomarker for disease, forensics, ancestry or human enhancement' (Richardson 2017:208). Following from this, the postgenomic therefore also refers to the technical ability and the market desire to mine the minuscule veins of difference said to distinguish human groups.

The commercialization of genetics has launched possibilities for DNA that social theorists had not fully anticipated. Indeed, returning to Keller's insight about the transformation in our conceptual understanding of molecular biology, it is important to note that some early social science analysis assumed the gene as the unit of analysis, rather than the more cipher-like genome and, in so doing, left some of the pitfalls and the possibilities of the postgenomic era unexplored.

Keller describes the commercial uses of genetic science, and particularly as these products work to revive the 'genetics of race', as one of the more problematic features of the postgenomic era (Keller 2015:10). Yet, just as our notion of the gene has been transformed in the postgenomic era, so too must our understanding of what novel understandings of and uses for DNA mean for racial paradigms and politics. Long-standing ways of thinking about the relationship between race, genetics and heritability took up an appreciably new form in the last two decades in a process that Fullwiley (2007) calls the 'molecularization of race'

There remains distinct evidence that the advent of genetic genealogy testing is a worrisome 'backdoor to eugenics' (Duster 2007; Phelan, Link and Feldman 2004), new bottles for the old wine of racial essentialism. But this isn't all there is. Racism, then and now, has had many paradigms, including Jim Crow, laissez-faire (Bobo, Kluegel and Smith 1997), colour blind (Bonilla-Silva 2003; Brown et al. 2003), white nationalist (Daniels 1997), and digital (Daniels 2009). Race, too, is cross-cutting and experienced on 'multiple dimensions' (Roth 2016), including identity, self-classification, ascription, phenotype, and ancestry. Race and racism, then and now are also relational and site- or institutionally specific (Nelson 2016) – a 'dynamic and reactive' system, much like Keller's genome.

Reconciliation Projects

Bookended by two conservative US presidential administrations, the HGP emerged out of a colour-blind racial paradigm. Forgetting and masking are characteristic of this ideology. On the one hand, this paradigm frames racism as 'a remnant of the past' and, therefore, something to be forgotten; on the other hand, the colour-blind paradigm obscures structural discrimination –the deeply rooted institutional practices and long-term disaccumulation that sustains racial inequality' (Brown et al. 2003: 37). The commercialization of genomics activates and reinforces the pernicious dynamics of the genetics of race, privileging essentialist ways of knowing and being classified by Roth such as ascription and phenotype. At the same time, however, other, potentially benevolent 'dimensions' of race are also given voice through the practice of genetic genealogy, such as self-classification and ancestral identity. It is in this heterodox milieu a prevailing racial paradigm and racial multidimensionality, that the logic of using novel applications of genomics to recover, debate and reconcile accounts of the past takes shape.

At the intersection of postgenomics, the multiple dimensions of race, and colour-blind racism lie 'reconciliation projects'. Genetic analysis is today being applied in social endeavours in which DNA analysis is put to the use of repairing or reconciling the past. These are global social practices that take up genetic analyses in social, political and historical claims-making and may include reparations claims or campaigns to obtain apologies from the state for past atrocities. Reconciliation projects may be efforts to repair ruptures caused by fractious social and political struggles or efforts to (re)unite communities. They can be found in the courtroom, in the science laboratory, or within the practice of religious ceremonies, to name a few sites. Their aim is a desire to come to some mutual (if not consensual) understanding of the past with outcomes ranging the spectrum from unspecified endpoints to precise restitution. With the end uncertain, the endeavours themselves warrant our attention. Closure is not necessarily what is sought or can be accomplished, for as moral philosopher Susan Dwyer offers, 'reconciliation is *fundamentally a process* whose aim is to lessen the sting of a tension: to make sense of injuries, new beliefs, and attitudes in the overall narrative context of personal or national life' (Dwyer 1999:, emphasis added).

One of the appeals of genetic ancestry testing is its presumed ability to highlight the origins of not only root-seekers themselves, but also social heredities of the contemporary moment. African Americans may use genetic ancestry testing to enter into a new political relationship with the past, one that foregrounds the fact and impact of racial slavery and makes this past a proximate, usable and, indeed, a living history, rather than something distant and, therefore, immaterial to the present (as colour-blind racism would have it).

In my book, *The Social Life of DNA: Race, Reparations and Reconciliation after the Genome* (Nelson 2016), I follow several reconciliation projects involving persons of African descent, including a West African religious ceremony or 'sara' in which self-described 'DNA Sierra Leoneans' sought and performed a psychic and spiritual reckoning with their ancestors, who had been trafficked as chattel. I also trace the use of genetic genealogy testing as a tactic to obtain legal restitution for the unpaid labour of enslaved Africans on the part of their descendants by attempting to demonstrate a genealogical kinship (and therefore also a legal relationship). In recent years, a notable reconciliation project has emerged in the US in which genetic genealogy is being engaged in efforts concerning elite institutions' foundational dependence on the slave trade.
[. . .]

Slavery and Justice

In 2001, Ruth Simmons became the first African American and first woman leader of an Ivy League institution of higher education when she took the helm of Brown University as its eighteenth president. She took over leadership at a time when Brown was lagging behind its peers in both scholarly imminence and fiscal health.[1] After quickly putting herself to the work of improving the university's educational and fiscal profiles, Brown turned to its moral one. In 2003, she commissioned the Brown University Steering Committee on Slavery and Justice in order to investigate and address the institution's ties to the slave trade.
[. . .]

In devoting a committee to the study of slavery and *justice,* Simmons supplied a new ethical valence to institutions of higher education. She insisted that the liberal arts tradition could and should be harnessed to better understand even the most deeply entrenched forms of inequality. Simmons also suggested that edification included attention to issues of justice.

NOTE

1 FitzGerald, F. "Peculiar Institutions," *The New Yorker*, September 12, 2005. Available at https:// www.newyorker.com/magazine/2005/09/12/peculiar-institutions. Accessed February 26, 2018.

REFERENCES

Bobo, L., Kluegel, J.R., and Smith, R.A. 1997. 'Laissez Faire Racism: The Crystallization of a Kinder, Gentler, Antiblack Ideology', in S. Tuch, and J.K. Martin, eds. *Racial Attitudes in the 1990s: Continuity and Change*. Westport, CT: Praeger, 15–42.

Bonilla-Silva, E. 2003. *Racism Without Racists: Color-blind Racism and the Persistence of Racial Inequality in America*. Lanham, MD: Rowman & Littlefield.

Brown, M.K., Carnoy, M., Currie, E., Duster, T., Oppenheimer, D.B., Shultz, M.M., et al. 2003. *White-washing Race: The Myth of a Color-blind Society*. Berkeley, CA: University of California Press.

Daniels, J. 1997. *White Lies: Race, Class, Gender and Sexuality in White Supremacist Discourse*. New York, NY: Routledge.

Daniels, J. 2009. *Cyber Racism: White Supremacy Online and the New Attack on Civil Rights*. Lanham, MD: Rowman & Littlefield.

Duster, T. 1990. *Backdoor to Eugenics*. New York, NY: Routledge.

Dwyer, S. 1999. "Reconciliation for Realists." *Ethics and International Affairs* 13(1): 81–98.

Fullwiley, D. 2007 "The Molecularization of Race: Institutionalizing Racial Difference in Pharmacogenetics Practice." *Science as Culture* 16(1): 1–30.

Keller, E.F. 2015. ""The Postgenomic Genome," in S.S. Richardson and H. Stevens, eds. *Postgenomics: Perspectives on Biology after the Genome*. Durham, NC: Duke University Press, 9–31.

Nelson, A. 2016. *The Social Life of DNA: Race, Reparations and Reconciliation after the Genome*. Boston, MA: Beacon Press.

Phelan, J.C., Link, B., and Feldman, N.M. 2013. "The Genomic Revolution and Beliefs about Essential Racial Differences: A Backdoor to Eugenics?" *American Sociological Review* 78(2): 167–91.

Richardson, S. 2013. *Sex Itself: The Search for Male and Female in the Human Genome*. Chicago, IL: University of Chicago Press.

Richardson, S.S. and Stevens, H. eds. 2015. Postgenomics: *Perspectives on Biology after the Genome*. Durham, NC: Duke University Press.

Roth, W.D. 2016. "The Multiple Dimensions of Race." *Ethnic and Racial Studies* 39(8): 1310–38.

CHAPTER FIFTEEN

GLOBALIZATION AND THE REASSESSMENT OF MODERNITY

CHAPTER MENU

Not surprisingly, the multiple far-reaching changes associated with increased globalization over the last few decades have earned the attention of sociologists as we seek to assess the extent to which the core theoretical ideas articulated by earlier generations of theorists still offer analytical authority amid a rapidly changing empirical reality. As I have noted in prior sections, it is evident that the theorizing of the early founders of sociology and their successors not only still illuminate institutional and cultural processes in our contemporary globalized society but in some cases are in fact all the more pervasively applicable than when such ideas were first

Concise Reader in Sociological Theory: Theorists, Concepts, and Current Applications,
First Edition. Edited by Michele Dillon. Editorial material and organization
© 2021 John Wiley & Sons Ltd. Published 2021 by John Wiley & Sons Ltd.

articulated; the writings of Marx and of the Frankfurt School theorists stand out in this regard. Similarly, the theorizing of Durkheim on the functional interdependence across social actors – whether institutions or whole countries – and of Weber on bureaucratization and the differentiation of class, status and power endure in their applicability to global society. Globalization as a construct helps to capture the fact that our lives today are to a large extent governed by transnational actors, sites, and processes (see Sklair 2002). Transnational actors include transnational corporations (e.g. Coco-Cola, IBM, Google, Apple, Walmart/Asda) and transnational political and legal entities (e.g. the European Union [EU], the World Trade Organization [WTO]) and treaties (e.g. the Paris Accord on climate change). Transnational sites include Davos (Switzerland) where every year the world's leading financiers, corporate titans, political leaders and celebrities (e.g. Bono, George Clooney) convene for a week to network and discuss the state of the world. And global cities (e.g. New York, London, Shanghai, Hong Kong, Sao Paolo) are key sites in both the transnational flow and concentration of people, ideas, trade, culture, and power. As Saskia Sassen (2007: 73) discusses:

> The global economy needs to be produced, reproduced, serviced, and financed . . . [Its operational functions] have become so specialized that they can no longer be contained in the functions of corporate headquarters. Global cities are strategic sites for the production of these specialized functions to run and coordinate the global economy. Inevitably located in national territories, global cities are the organizational and institutional space for the major dynamics of denationalization. (Sassen 2007: 73)

Transnational processes range from the diversity of consumer goods, people and ideas found in, and that impact, almost any given local community (including the trans-national character of any specific Premier league football team), to the increasingly polarized character of trans-national economic inequality (Sklair 2002).

Amid all the globalizing economic, cultural and political trends and the impact of the exponential growth and acceleration of digital technology on everyday reality, an array of theorists are variously engaged in reassessing this moment of modernity. Some like Anthony Giddens (excerpt *15b*) call our era that of late modernity, and others such as David Harvey (1990), postmodernity. Essentially, scholars use these terms to signify that the character of today's society, our contemporary experience of modernity, is different to that of the post-World War II era – the post-industrial society energized by the rise of professional, service and information workers and the attendant growth in affluence and consumerism (see, for example, Hochschild 1983; Mills 1951; 1956) – and both in turn are different to the industrial capitalism and related changes (e.g. urbanization, expansion of public education, mass European immigration to the US) of the late nineteenth and early twentieth centuries.

Zygmunt Bauman (see excerpt *15a Liquid Modernity*) takes a pessimistic view of the impact of trans-national political processes and their alleged erasure of community and national solidarity. He argues that the financial policies promulgated by transnational entities such as the European Union (the EU) give priority to ensuring stability and growth in state and EU finances and are indifferent to how such rationalized, impersonal policies adversely impact the welfare of individuals and communities. In his assessment, the nation, the exemplar (following Weber's construal) of modern political and economic independence, and the core unit in anchoring and sustaining national solidarity, has lost its institutional power to defend its own and its people's material and symbolic interests in the face of trans-national behemoths; this post-national context, he argues, has rendered a nation's citizens as unprotected orphans.

Anthony Giddens highlights what he calls the disembeddedness of time and space that is the condition of late modernity (see excerpt *15b Modernity and Self-Identity*). He probes how technological advances disrupt the anchoring hold of time and space/place on individuals and communities. Disembeddedness is emancipatory in that we have much greater flexibility to conduct our lives and achieve our specific goals "electronically" (e.g. online courses, online shopping, online dating, online banking, etc.), and we have far more opportunities to communicate, connect, identify and form meaningful relationships with an amazing array of people in distant places – some like us in our social marginality or in our minority political views, and others not like us in any way at all – and to do so on a schedule that works for us. Yet, at the same time, this disembeddedness and flexibility, as well as the reams of information we can readily access about all kinds of things at any time, present the self with dilemmas of trust and mistrust that require our constant negotiation.

Ulrich Beck highlights the globalization of risk (see excerpt *15c Risk Society*), and importantly, our increased access to broad swaths of information about the multiple risks that variously threaten individuals (e.g. one's genetic propensity to be a carrier of a specific disease), local communities (water lead pollution) and society at large (e.g. climate change). He argues that while less affluent individuals, communities, and countries are frequently more exposed to an array of risks than their more affluent counterparts, nonetheless, many of today's risks – whether the negative impact of global warming or the disruption created by COVID-19 or cybersecurity violations – are not class-, group-, or country-specific, but are more encompassing of entire populations and geographic regions. In short, Beck underscores, risk is our shared fate as global citizens. And because of this, he and his colleague **Edgar Grande** argue (see excerpt *15d Varieties of Second Modernity*) that global society, notwithstanding the empirical variations across the world in how modernity has taken hold (the political and cultural differences, for example, between the US and Western Europe compared to China or South Korea) requires a new ethical stance. Cosmopolitization, Beck and Grande argue, requires a new attitude that recognizes that different societies and peoples can learn from one another. They thus push back against the established idea that the First World is invariably superior in all things to those whose histories and experiences have taken a different path. Cosmopolitization requires deep appreciation of the mutuality and interdependence of all countries and of respect for the validity of multiple histories and of multiple differences.

In a somewhat similar ethical vein, **Jurgen Habermas** (see excerpt *15e Notes on Post-Secular Society*) argues for recognition of the fact that while secularization (the relative decline of religious institutional authority and the tendency toward the privatization of religious belief and worship) is the settled empirical reality in western society, religion nonetheless has not disappeared and continues to have public relevance. Accordingly, he argues, secular actors (whether states/governments, institutions or individuals) have to adjust to the fact that religion still matters and, moreover, he maintains, moderate religious traditions have resources that can (and should) be used to help reorient the ethical direction of contemporary society as it attempts to deal with the problems of modernity (e.g. economic inequality, cultural exclusion of immigrants and refugees, environmental degradation). And in this ethical reorientation, Habermas argues, religious and secular actors have to treat each other with mutual respect and engage in conversation with each other rather than simply dismiss each other's respective standpoints. Beyond post-secularity, and whatever the issue, respect for the experiences of others is essential to building local and global community.

REFERENCES

Harvey, David. 1990. *The Condition of Postmodernity.* Oxford: Blackwell.

Hochschild, Arlie. 1983. *The Managed Heart: Commercialization of Feeling.* Berkeley: University of California Press.

Mills, C.W. 1951. *White Collar: The American Middle Classes.* New York: Oxford University Press.

Mills, C.W. 1956. *The Power Elite.* New York: Oxford University Press.

Sassen, Saskia. 2007. *A Sociology of Globalization.* New York: Norton.

Sklair, Leslie. 2002. *Globalization: Capitalism and Its Alternatives.* Oxford: Oxford University Press.

15A Zygmunt Bauman from *Liquid Modernity*

Original publication details: Zygmunt Bauman, 2000. *Liquid Modernity*, pp. 185–192. Cambridge, UK: Polity. Reproduced with permission of Polity Press Ltd.

After the Nation-state

In modern times, the nation was 'another face' of the state and the principal weapon in its bid for sovereignty over the territory and its population. A good deal of the nation's credibility and its attraction as the warrant of safety and durability has been derived from its intimate association with the state, and – through the state – with the actions aimed at laying the certainty and security of citizens on a durable and trustworthy, since collectively insured, foundation. Under the new conditions little can be gained by the nation from its close links with the state. The state may not expect much from the mobilizing potential of the nation which it needs less and less as the mass conscript armies held together by the feverishly beefed-up patriotic frenzy are replaced by the elitist and coldly professional high-tech units, while the wealth of the country is measured not so much by the quality, quantity and morale of its labour force, as by the country's attractiveness to coolly mercenary forces of global capital.

In a state that is no longer the secure bridge leading beyond the confinement of individual mortality, a call to sacrifice individual well-being, let alone individual life, for the preservation or the undying glory of the state sounds vacuous and increasingly bizarre, if not amusing. The centuries-long romance of nation with state is drawing to an end; not so much a divorce as a 'living together' arrangement is replacing the consecrated marital togetherness grounded in unconditional loyalty. Partners are now free to look elsewhere and enter other alliances; their partnership is no longer the binding pattern for proper and acceptable conduct. We may say that the nation, which used to offer the substitute for the absent community at the era of *Gesellschaft*, now drifts back to the left-behind *Gemeinschaft* in search of a pattern to emulate and to model itself after. The institutional scaffolding capable of holding the nation together is thinkable increasingly as a do-it-yourself job. It is the dreams of certainty and security, not their matter-of-fact and routinized provision, that should prompt the orphaned individuals to huddle under the nation's wings while chasing the stubbornly elusive safety.

Of salvaging the certainty-and-security services of the state there seem to be little hope. The freedom of state politics is relentlessly eroded by the new global powers armed with the awesome weapons of exterritoriality, speed of movement and evasion/escape ability; retribution for violating the new global brief is swift and merciless. Indeed, the refusal to play the game by the new global rules is the most mercilessly punishable crime, which the state powers, tied to the ground by their own territorially defined sovereignty, must beware of committing and avoid at all cost.

More often than not, the punishment is economic. Insubordinate governments, guilty of protectionist policies or generous public provisions for the 'economically redundant' sectors of their populations and of recoiling from leaving the country at the mercy of 'global financial markets' and 'global free trade', would be refused loans or denied reduction of their debts; local currencies would be made global lepers, speculated against and pressed to devalue; local stocks would fall head down on the global exchanges; the country would be cordoned off by economic sanctions and told to be treated by past and future trade partners as a global pariah; global investors would cut their anticipated losses, pack up their belongings and withdraw their assets, leaving local authorities to clean up the debris and bail out the victims out of their added misery.

Occasionally, though, the punishment would not be confined to the 'economic measures'. Particularly obstinate governments (but not too strong to resist for long) would be taught an exemplary lesson intended to warn and frighten their potential imitators. If the daily, routine demonstration of the global forces' superiority appeared insufficient to force the state to see reason and to cooperate with the new 'world order', the military might would be deployed: the superiority of speed over slowness, of the ability to escape over the need to engage, of exterritoriality over locality, all would be spectacularly manifested with the help, this time, of armed forces specialized in hit-and-run tactics and the strict separation of 'lives to be saved' and lives unworthy of saving.

Whether as an ethical act the way the war against Yugoslavia was conducted was right and proper is open to discussion. That war made sense, though, as the 'promotion of global economic order by other than political means'. The strategy selected by the attackers worked well as the spectacular display of the new global hierarchy and the new rules of the game which sustain it. If not for its thousands of quite real 'casualties' and a country cast into ruin and deprived of livelihood and self-regenerative ability for many years to come, one would be tempted to describe it as a *sui generis* 'symbolic war'; the war itself, its strategy and tactics was (consciously or subconsciously) a symbol of the emergent power relationship. The medium was indeed the message.

As a teacher of sociology, I kept repeating to my students, year in, year out, the standard version of the 'history of civilization' as marked by a gradual yet relentless rise of sedentariness and the eventual victory of the settled over the nomads; it went without further argument that the defeated nomads were, in their essence, the regressive and anti-civilizational force. Jim MacLoughlin has recently unpacked the meaning of that victory, sketching a brief history of the treatment accorded to the 'nomads' by the sedentary populations within the orbit of modern civilization.[1] Nomadism, he points out, was seen and treated as 'characteristics of "barbarous" and underdeveloped societies'. Nomads were defined as primitive, and, from Hugo Grotius on, there was a parallel drawn between 'primitive' and 'natural' (that is, uncouth, raw, pre-cultural, uncivilized): 'the development of laws, cultural progress and the enhancement of civilization were all intimately linked to the evolution and improvement of man–land relations over time and across space'. To make a long story short: progress was identified with the abandonment of nomadism in favour of the sedentary way of life. All that, to be sure, happened at the time of heavy modernity, when domination implied direct and tight engagement and meant territorial conquest, annexation and colonization. The founder and the main theorist of 'diffusionism' (a view of history once highly popular in the empires' capitals), Friedrich Ratzel, the preacher of the 'rights of the stronger' which he thought were ethically superior as much as inescapable in view of the rarity of civilizational genius and commonality of passive immitation, grasped precisely the mood of the time when he wrote at the threshold of the colonialist century that

> The struggle for existence means a struggle for space . . . A superior people, invading the territory of its weaker savage neighbours, robs them of their land, forces them back into corners too small for their support, and continues to encroach even upon their meagre possession, till the weaker finally loses the last remnants of its domain, is literally crowded off the earth . . . The superiority of such expansionists consists primarily in their greater ability to appropriate, thoroughly utilize and populate territory.

Clearly, no more. The game of domination in the era of liquid modernity is not played between the 'bigger' and the 'smaller', but between the quicker and the slower. Those who are able to accelerate beyond the catching power of their opponents rule. When velocity means domination, the 'appropriation, utilization and population of territory' becomes a handicap – a liability, not an asset. Taking over under one's own jurisdiction and even more the annexation of someone else's land imply

capital-intensive, cumbersome and unprofitable chores of administration and policing, responsibilities, commitments – and, above all, cast considerable constraint on
one's future freedom to move.

It is far from clear whether more hit-and-run-style wars will be undertaken, in
view of the fact that the first attempt ended up in immobilizing the victors – burdening
them with the cumbersome jobs of ground occupation, local engagements and managerial and administrative responsibilities quite out of tune with liquid modernity's
techniques of power. The might of the global elite rests on its ability to escape local
commitments, and globalization is meant precisely to avoid such necessities, to divide
tasks and functions in such a way as to burden local authorities, and them only, with
the role of guardians of law and (local) order.

Indeed, one can see many signals of the tide of 'second thoughts' swelling in the
camp of the victors: the strategy of the 'global police force' is subject once more to an
intense critical scrutiny. Among the functions which the global elite would rather
leave to the nation-states-turned-local-police-precincts a growing number of influential voices would include the efforts to solve gory neighbourly conflicts; the solution to such conflicts, we hear, should be also 'decongested' and 'decentralized',
reallocated down in the global hierarchy, human rights or no human rights, and
passed over 'where it belongs', to the local warlords and the weapons they command
thanks to the generosity or 'well understood economic interest' of global companies
and of governments intent on promoting globalization. For instance, Edward N.
Luttwak, Senior Fellow at the American Center for Strategic and International Studies
and for many years a reliable barometer of changing Pentagon moods, has appealed
in the July–August 1999 issue of *Foreign Affairs* (described by the *Guardian* as 'the
most influential periodical in print') to 'give war a chance'. Wars, according to Luttwak,
are not altogether bad, since they lead to peace. Peace, though, will come only 'when
all belligerents become exhausted or when one wins decisively'. The worst thing (and
NATO did just such a thing) is to stop them midway, before the shoot-out ends in
mutual exhaustion or the incapacitation of one of the warring parties. In such cases
conflicts are not resolved, but merely temporarily frozen, and the adversaries use the
time of truce to rearm, redeploy and rethink their tactics. So, for your own and their
sake, do not interfere 'in other people's wars'.

Luttwak's appeal may well fall on many willing and grateful ears. After all, as the
'promotion of globalization by other means' goes, abstaining from intervention and
allowing the war of attrition to reach its 'natural end' would have brought the same
benefits without the nuisance of direct engagement in 'other people's wars', and particularly in their awkward and unwieldy consequences. To placate the conscience
aroused by the imprudent decision to wage war under a humanitarian banner, Luttwak
points out the obvious inadequacy of military involvement as a means to an end: 'Even
a large-scale disinterested intervention can fail to achieve its ostensibly humanitarian
aim. One wonders whether the Kosovars would have been better off had NATO simply
done nothing.' It would probably have been better for the NATO forces to go on with
their daily drills and leave the locals to do what the locals had to do.

What caused the second thoughts and prompted the victors to regret the interfer-
ence (officially proclaimed a success) was their failure to escape the selfsame eventuality

which the hit-and-run campaign was meant to ward off: the need for invasion and for the occupation and administration of conquered territory. By the paratroopers' landing and settling in Kosovo the belligerents had been prevented from shooting themselves to death, but the task of keeping them at a safe distance from the shooting range brought the NATO forces 'from heaven to earth' and embroiled them with responsibility for the messy realities on the ground. Henry Kissinger, a sober and perceptive analyst and the grandmaster of politics understood (in a somewhat old-fashioned way) as the art of the possible, warned against another blunder of shouldering the responsibility for the recovery of the lands devastated by the bombers' war.[2] That plan, Kissinger points out, 'risks turning into an open-ended commitment toward ever deeper involvement, casting us in the role of gendarme of a region of passionate hatreds and where we have few strategic interests'. And 'involvement' is precisely what the wars aimed to 'promote globalization by other means' are meant to avoid! Civil administration, Kissinger adds, would inevitably entail conflicts, and it will fall on the administrators, as their costly and ethically dubious task, to resolve them by force.

Thus far, there are few, if any, signs that the occupying forces may acquit themselves in the conflict-resolution task any better than those whom they bombed out and replaced on account of their failure. In a sharp opposition to the fate of the refugees in whose name the bombing campaign was launched, the daily lives of returnees seldom get into the headlines, but the news which does occasionally reach the readers and listeners of the media is ominous. 'A wave of violence and continued reprisals against Serbs and the Roma minority in Kosovo threatens to undermine the province's precarious stability and leave it ethnically cleansed of Serbs only a month after NATO's troops took control'; reports Chris Bird from Pristina.[3] NATO forces on the ground seem lost and helpless in the face of raging ethnic hatreds, which looked so easy to ascribe to the malice aforethought of but one villain, and so to resolve, when watched from the TV cameras installed on ultrasonic bombers.

Jean Clair, alongside many other observers, expects the immediate outcome of the Balkan war to be a profound and durable destabilization of the whole area, and the implosion rather than maturation of young and vulnerable, or still unborn; democracies of the Macedonian, Albanian, Croatian or Bulgarian type.[4] (Daniel Vernet supplied his survey of the views expressed on that subject by high-class Balkan political and social scientists with the title 'The Balkans face a risk of agony without end'.[5]) But he also wonders how the political void opened by cutting the roots of the nation-states' viability will be filled. Global market forces, jubilant at the prospect of no longer being stemmed and obstructed, would probably step in, but they would not wish (or manage, if they wished) to deputize for the absent or disempowered political authorities. Nor would they necessarily be interested in the resurrection of a strong and confident nation-state in full command of its territory.

'Another Marshal plan' is the most commonly suggested answer to the present quandary. It is not just the generals who are notorious for constantly fighting the last victorious war. But one cannot pay one's way out of every predicament, however large the sums laid aside for the purpose. The Balkan predicament is starkly different from that of the rebuilding by nation-states after War World II of their sovereignty together with the livelihood of their citizens. What we are facing in the Balkans after the Kosovo war is not only the task of material reconstruction almost from scratch (the Jugoslavs' livelihood has been all but destroyed) but also the seething and festering interethnic chauvinisms which have emerged from the war reinforced. The inclusion of the Balkans in the network of global markets would not do much to assuage intolerance and hatred, since it will add to, rather than detract from that insecurity which was (and remains) the prime source of boiling tribal sentiments. There is, for instance, a real danger that the weakening of Serbian power to resist will serve as a standing invitation to its neighbours to engage in a new round of hostilities and ethnic cleansings.

Given the NATO politicians' unprepossessing and off-putting record of clumsy handling of the delicate and complex issues typical of the Balkan 'belt of mixed populations' (as Hannah Arendt perceptively called it), one can fear a further series of costly blunders. One would not be wide of the mark either when suspecting the imminence of a moment at which European leaders, having made sure that no new wave of refugees and asylum-seekers is threatening their affluent electorate, will lose their interest in the unmanageable lands as they already have so many times before – in Somali, Sudan, Rwanda, East Timor and Afghanistan. We may then be back at square one, after a detour strewn with corpses. Antonina Jelyazkova, the director of the International Institute for Minority Studies, expressed this well (as quoted by Vernet): 'One cannot solve the question of minorities with bombs. The blows let loose the devil on both sides.'[6] Taking the side of nationalistic vindications, NATO actions beefed up further the already frenzied nationalisms of the area and prepared the ground for the future repetitions of genocidal attempts. One of the most gruesome consequences is that the mutual accommodation and friendly coexistence of languages, cultures and religions of the area have been made less likely than ever before. Whatever the intentions, the outcomes go against the grain of what a truly ethical undertaking would have us expect.

The conclusion, preliminary as it is, is inauspicious. The attempts to mitigate the tribal aggression through the new 'global police actions' have thus far proved inconclusive at best, and more likely counterproductive. The overall effects of the relentless globalization have been sharply unbalanced: the injury of renewed tribal strife has come first, while the medicine needed to heal it is, at best, at the test (more likely the trial-and-error) stage. Globalization appears to be much more successful in adding new vigour to intercommunal enmity and strife than in promoting the peaceful coexistence of communities.

NOTES

1   See Jim MacLaughlin, 'Nation-building, social closure and anti-traveller racism in Ireland', *Sociology*, February 1999. pp. 129–51. Also for Friedrich Rabel quotation.

2   See Jean Clair, 'De Guernica à Belgrade', *Le Monde*, 21 May 1999, p. 16.

3   *Newsweek*, 21 June 1999.

4   See Chris Bird, 'Serbs flee Kosovo revenge attacks', *Guardian*, 17 July 1999.

5   See Daniel Vernet, 'Les Balkans face au risque d'une tourmente sans fin', *Le Monde*, 15 May, p. 18.

6   Vernet, 'Les Balkans face au risque d'une tourmente sans fin'.

15B Anthony Giddens from *Modernity and Self-Identity: Self and Society in the Late Modern Age*

Original publication details: Anthony Giddens, 1991. *Modernity and Self-Identity: Self and Society in the Late Modern Age*, pp. 71–75. Stanford: Stanford University Press. © 1991 Anthony Giddens. All rights reserved. Reproduced with permission of Stanford University Press (www.sup.org) and Polity Press Ltd.

Modernity produces certain distinct social forms, of which the most prominent is the nation-state. A banal observation, of course, until one remembers the established tendency of sociology to concentrate on 'society' as its designated subject-matter. The sociologist's 'society', applied to the period of modernity at any rate, is a nation-state, but this is usually a covert equation rather than an explicitly theorised one. As a sociopolitical entity the nation-state contrasts in a fundamental way with most types of traditional order. It develops only as part of a wider nation-state system (which today has become global in character), has very specific forms of territoriality and surveillance capabilities, and monopolises effective control over the means of violence.[1] In the literature of international relations, nation-states are often treated as 'actors' – as 'agents' rather than 'structures' – and there is a definite justification for this. For modern states are reflexively monitored systems which, even if they do not 'act' in the strict sense of the term, follow coordinated policies and plans on a geopolitical scale. As such, they are a prime example of a more general feature of modernity, the rise of the *organisation*. What distinguishes modern organisations is not so much their size, or their bureaucratic character, as the concentrated reflexive monitoring they both permit and entail. Who says modernity says not just organisations, but organisation – the regularised control of social relations across indefinite time-space distances.

Modern institutions are in various key respects *discontinuous* with the gamut of pre-modern cultures and ways of life. One of the most obvious characteristics separating the modern era from any other period preceding it is modernity's extreme dynamism. The modern world is a 'runaway world': not only is the *pace* of social change much faster than in any prior system, so also is its *scope*, and the *profoundness* with which it affects pre-existing social practices and modes of behaviour.[2]

What explains the peculiarly dynamic character of modern social life? Three main elements, or sets of elements, are involved – and each of them is basic to the arguments deployed in this book. The first is what I call the *separation of time and space*. All cultures, of course, have possessed modes of time-reckoning of one form or another, as well as ways of situating themselves spatially. There is no society in which individuals do not have a sense of future, present and past. Every culture has some form of standardised spatial markers which designate a special awareness of place. In pre-modern settings, however, time and space were connected *through* the situatedness of place.

Larger pre-modern cultures developed more formal methods for the calculation of time and the ordering of space – such as calendars and (by modern standards) crude maps. Indeed, these were the prerequisites for the 'distancing' across time and space which the emergence of more extensive forms of social system presupposed. But in pre-modern eras, for the bulk of the population, and for most of the ordinary activities of day-to-day life, time and space remained essentially linked through place. 'When' markers were connected not just to the 'where' of social conduct, but to the substance of that conduct itself.

The separation of time from space involved above all the development of an 'empty' dimension of time, the main lever which also pulled space away from place. The invention and diffusion of the mechanical clock is usually seen – rightly – as the prime expression of this process, but it is important not to interpret this phenomenon in too superficial a way. The widespread use of mechanical timing devices facilitated, but also presumed, deeply structured changes in the tissue of everyday life – changes which could not only be local, but were inevitably universalising. A world that has a universal dating system, and globally standardised time zones, as ours does today, is socially and experientially different from all pre-modern eras. The global map, in which there is no privileging of place (a universal projection), is the correlate symbol to the clock in the 'emptying' of space. It is not just a mode of portraying 'what has always been there' – the geography of the earth – but is constitutive of quite basic transformations in social relations.

The emptying out of time and space is in no sense a unilinear development, but proceeds dialectically. Many forms of 'lived time' are possible in social settings structured through the separation of time and space. Moreover, the severance of time from space does not mean that these henceforth become mutually alien aspects of human social organisation. On the contrary: it provides the very basis for their recombination in ways that coordinate social activities without necessary reference to the particularities of place. The organisations, and organisation, so characteristic of modernity are inconceivable without the reintegration of separated time and space. Modern social organisation presumes the precise coordination of the actions of many human beings physically absent from one another; the 'when' of these actions is directly connected to the 'where', but not, as in pre-modern epochs, via the mediation of place.

We can all sense how fundamental the separation of time from space is for the massive dynamism that modernity introduces into human social affairs. The phenomenon universalises that 'use of history to make history' so intrinsic to the processes which drive modern social life away from the hold of tradition. Such historicity becomes global in form with the creation of a standardised 'past' and a universally applicable 'future': a date such as the 'year 2000' becomes a recognisable marker for the whole of humanity.

The process of the emptying of time and space is crucial for the second major influence on modernity's dynamism, the *disembedding* of social institutions. I choose the metaphor of disembedding in deliberate opposition to the concept of 'differentiation' sometimes adopted by sociologists as a means of contrasting pre-modern with modern social systems. Differentiation carries the imagery of the progressive separation of functions, such that modes of activity organised in a diffuse fashion in pre-modern societies become more specialised and precise with the advent of modernity. No doubt this idea has some validity, but it fails to capture an essential element of the nature and impact of modern institutions – the 'lifting out' of social relations from local contexts and their rearticulation across indefinite tracts of time-space. This 'lifting out' is exactly what I mean by disembedding, which is the key to the tremendous acceleration in time-space distanciation which modernity introduces.

Disembedding mechanisms are of two types, which I term 'symbolic tokens' and 'expert systems'. Taken together, I refer to these as *abstract systems*. Symbolic tokens are media of exchange which have standard value, and thus are interchangeable across a plurality of contexts. The prime example, and the most pervasively important, is money. Although the larger forms of pre-modern social system have all developed monetary exchange of one form or another, money economy becomes vastly more sophisticated and abstract with the emergence and maturation of modernity. Money brackets time (because it is a means of credit) and space (since standardised value allows transactions between a multiplicity of individuals who never physically meet one another). Expert systems bracket time and space through deploying modes of technical knowledge which have validity independent of the practitioners and clients who make use of them. Such systems penetrate virtually all aspects of social life in conditions of modernity – in respect of the food we eat, the medicines we take, the buildings we inhabit, the forms of transport we use and a multiplicity of other phenomena. Expert systems are not confined to areas of technological expertise. They extend to social relations themselves and to the intimacies of the self. The doctor, counsellor and therapist are as central to the expert systems of modernity as the scientist, technician or engineer.

Both types of expert system depend in an essential way on *trust*, a notion which, as has been indicated, plays a primary role in this book. Trust is different from the form of confidence which Georg Simmel called the 'weak inductive knowledge' involved in formal transactions.[3] Some decisions in life are based on inductive inferences from past trends, or from past experience believed in some way to be dependable for the present. This kind of confidence may be an element in trust, but it is not sufficient in itself to define a trust relation. Trust presumes a leap to commitment, a quality of 'faith' which is irreducible. It is specifically related to absence in time and space, as well as to ignorance. We have no need to trust someone who is constantly in view and whose activities can be directly monitored. Thus, for example, jobs which are monotonous or unpleasant, and poorly paid, in which the motivation to perform the work conscientiously is weak, are usually 'low-trust' positions. 'High-trust' posts are those carried out largely outside the presence of management or supervisory staff.[4] Similarly, there is no requirement of trust when a technical system is more or less completely known to a particular individual. In respect of expert systems, trust brackets the limited technical knowledge which most people possess about coded information which routinely affects their lives.

Trust, of varying sorts and levels, underlies a host of day-to-day decisions that all of us take in the course of orienting our activities. But trusting is not by any means always the result of consciously taken decisions: more often, it is a generalised attitude of mind that underlies those decisions, something which has its roots in the connection between trust and personality development. We *can* make the decision to trust, a phenomenon which is common because of the third underlying element of modernity. . .: its intrinsic reflexivity. But the faith which trust implies also tends to resist such calculative decision-making.

Attitudes of trust, in relation to specific situations, persons or systems, and on a more generalised level, are directly connected to the psychological *security* of individuals and groups. Trust and security, risk and danger: these exist in various historically unique conjunctions in conditions of modernity. The disembedding mechanisms, for example, purchase wide arenas of relative security in daily social activity. People living in the industrialised countries, and to some extent elsewhere today, are generally protected from some of the hazards routinely faced in pre-modern times – such as those emanating from inclement nature. On the other hand, new risks and dangers are created through the disembedding mechanisms themselves, and these may be local or global. Foodstuffs purchased with artificial ingredients may have toxic characteristics absent from more traditional foods; environmental hazards might threaten the ecosystems of the earth as a whole.

Modernity is essentially a post-traditional order. The transformation of time and space, coupled with the disembedding mechanisms, propel social life away from the hold of pre-established precepts or practices. This is the context of the thoroughgoing *reflexivity* which is the third major influence on the dynamism of modern institutions. The reflexivity of modernity has to be distinguished from the reflexive monitoring of action intrinsic to all human activity. Modernity's reflexivity refers to the susceptibility of most aspects of social activity, and material relations with nature, to chronic revision in the light of new information or knowledge. Such information or knowledge is not incidental to modern institutions, but constitutive of them – a complicated phenomenon, because many possibilities of reflection about reflexivity exist in modern social conditions. . . [T]he social sciences play a basic role in the reflexivity of modernity: they do not simply 'accumulate knowledge' in the way in which the natural sciences may do.

In respect both of social and natural scientific knowledge, the reflexivity of modernity turns out to confound the expectations of Enlightenment thought – although it is the very product of that thought. The original progenitors of modern science and philosophy believed themselves to be preparing the way for securely founded knowledge of the social and natural worlds: the claims of reason were due to overcome the dogmas of tradition, offering a sense of certitude in place of the arbitrary character of habit and custom. But the reflexivity of modernity actually undermines the certainty of knowledge, even in the core domains of natural science. Science depends, not on the inductive accumulation of proofs, but on the methodological principle of doubt. No matter how cherished, and apparently well established, a given scientific tenet

---

The dynamism of modernity

Separation of time and space: the condition for the articulation of social relations across wide spans of time-space, up to and including global systems.

Disembedding mechanisms: consist of symbolic tokens and expert systems (these together = abstract systems). Disembedding mechanisms separate interaction from the particularities of locales.

Institutional reflexivity: the regularised use of knowledge about circumstances of social life as a constitutive element in its organisation and transformation.

might be, it is open to revision – or might have to be discarded altogether – in the light of new ideas or findings. The integral relation between modernity and radical doubt is an issue which, once exposed to view, is not only disturbing to philosophers but is *existentially troubling* for ordinary individuals.

NOTES

1   Giddens, Anthony. 1985. *The Nation-State and Violence*. Cambridge: Polity.
2   See Giddens, 1985. *Consequences of Modernity*. Cambridge: Polity.
3   Simmel, Georg. 1978. *The Philosophy of Money*. London: Routledge, p.179.

4   Fox, Alan. 1974. *Beyond Contract*. London: Faber. For one of the few generalised discussions of trust in systems, see Susan P. Schapiro, 1987, "The Social Control of Impersonal Trust." *American Journal of Sociology*, 93.

15C Ulrich Beck from *Risk Society: Towards a New Modernity*

Original publication details: Ulrich Beck, 1992. *Risk Society: Towards a New Modernity*, translated by Mark Ritter, pp. 19–20, 21–24, 39–40. London: Sage. Reproduced with permission of Sage Publications Ltd.

On the Logic of Wealth Distribution and Risk Distribution

In advanced modernity the social production of *wealth* is systematically accompanied by the social production of *risks*. Accordingly, the problems and conflicts relating to distribution in a society of scarcity overlap with the problems and conflicts that arise from the production, definition and distribution of techno-scientifically produced risks.

This change from the logic of wealth distribution in a society of scarcity to the logic of risk distribution in late modernity is connected historically to (at least) two conditions. First, it occurs – as is recognizable today – where and to the extent that *genuine material need* can be objectively reduced and socially isolated through the development of human and technological productivity, as well as through legal and welfare-state protections and regulations. Second, this categorical change is likewise dependent upon the fact that in the course of the exponentially growing productive forces in the modernization process, hazards and potential threats have been unleashed to an extent previously unknown.[1]

To the extent that these conditions occur, one historical type of thinking and acting is relativized or overridden by another. The concepts of 'industrial' or 'class society', in the broadest sense of Marx or Weber, revolved around the issue of how socially produced wealth could be distributed in a socially unequal and *also* 'legitimate' way. This overlaps with the new *paradigm of risk society* which is based on the solution of a similar and yet quite different problem. How can the risks and hazards systematically produced as part of modernization be prevented, minimized, dramatized, or channeled? Where they do finally see the light of day in the shape of 'latent side effects', how can they be limited and distributed away so that they neither hamper the modernization process nor exceed the limits of that which is 'tolerable' – ecologically, medically, psychologically and socially?

We are therefore concerned no longer exclusively with making nature useful, or with releasing mankind from traditional constraints, but also and essentially with problems resulting from techno-economic development itself. Modernization is becoming *reflexive*; it is becoming its own theme. Questions of the development and employment of technologies (in the realms of nature, society and the personality) are being eclipsed by questions of the political and economic 'management' of the risks of actually or potentially utilized technologies – discovering, administering, acknowledging, avoiding or concealing such hazards with respect to specially defined horizons of relevance. The promise of security grows with the risks and destruction and must be reaffirmed over and over again to an alert and critical public through cosmetic or real interventions in the techno-economic development.

[. . .]

In the past, the hazards could be traced back to an *under*supply of hygienic technology. Today they have their basis in industrial overproduction. The risks and hazards of today thus differ in an essential way from the superficially similar ones in the Middle Ages through the global nature of their threat (people, animals and plants) and through their *modern* causes. They are risks *of modernization*. They are a *wholesale product* of industrialization, and are systematically intensified as it becomes global.

The concept of risk is directly bound to the concept of reflexive modernization. *Risk* may be defined as a *systematic way of dealing with hazards and insecurities induced and introduced by modernization itself*. Risks, as opposed to older dangers, are consequences which relate to the threatening force of modernization and to its globalization of doubt. They are *politically reflexive*.

Risks, in this meaning of the word, are certainly as old as that development itself. The immiseration of large parts of the population – the 'poverty risk' – kept the nineteenth century holding its breath. 'Threats to skills' and 'health risks' have long been a theme of automation processes and the related social conflicts, protections (and research). It did take some time and struggle to establish social welfare state norms and minimize or limit these kinds of risk politically. Nevertheless, the ecological and high-tech risks that have upset the public for some years now, which will be the focus of what follows, have a new quality. In the afflictions they produce they are no longer tied to their place of origin – the industrial plant. By their nature they endanger *all* forms of life on this planet. The normative bases of their calculation – the concept of accident and insurance, medical precautions, and so on – do not fit the basic dimensions of these modern threats. Atomic plants, for example, are not privately insured or insurable. Atomic accidents are accidents no more (in the limited sense of the word 'accident'). They outlast generations. The affected even include those not yet alive at the time or in the place where the accident occurred but born years later and long distances away.

This means that the calculation of risk as it has been established so far by science and legal institutions *collapses*. Dealing with these consequences of modern productive and destructive forces in the normal terms of risk is a false but nevertheless very effective way of legitimizing them. Risk scientists normally do so as if there is not the gap of a century between the local accidents of the nineteenth century and the often creeping, catastrophic potentials at the end of the twentieth century. Indeed, if you distinguish between calculable and non-calculable threats, under the surface of risk calculation new kinds of *industrialized, decision-produced incalculabilities and threats* are spreading within the globalization of high-risk industries, whether for warfare or welfare purposes. Max Weber's concept of 'rationalization' no longer grasps this late modern reality, produced by successful rationalization. *Along with the growing capacity of technical options [Zweckrationalität] grows the incalculability of their consequences.* Compared to these global consequences, the hazards of primary industrialization indeed belonged to a different age. The dangers of highly developed nuclear and chemical productive forces abolish the foundations and categories according to which we have thought and acted to this point, such as space and time, work and leisure time, factory and nation state, indeed even the borders between continents. To put it differently, in the risk society the unknown and unintended consequences come to be a dominant force in history and society.[2]

The social architecture and political dynamics of such potentials for self-endangerment in civilization will occupy the center of these discussions. The argument can be set out in five theses:

1 Risks such as those produced in the late modernity differ essentially from wealth. By risks I mean above all radioactivity, which completely evades human perceptive abilities, but also toxins and pollutants in the air, the water and foodstuffs, together with the accompanying short- and long-term effects on plants, animals and people. They induce systematic and often *irreversible* harm, generally remain *invisible*, are based on *causal interpretations*, and thus initially only exist in terms of the (scientific or anti-scientific) *knowledge* about them. They can thus be changed, magnified, dramatized or minimized within knowledge, and to that extent they are particularly *open to social definition and construction*. Hence the mass media and the scientific and legal professions in charge of defining risks become key social and political positions.

2 Some people are more affected than others by the distribution and growth of risks, that is, *social risk positions* spring up. In some of their dimensions these follow the inequalities of class and strata positions, but they bring a fundamentally different distributional logic into play. Risks of modernization sooner or later also strike those who produce or profit from them. They contain a *boomerang effect*, which breaks up the pattern of class and national society. Ecological disaster and atomic fallout ignore the borders of nations. Even the rich and powerful are not safe from them. These are hazards not only to health, but also to legitimation, property and profit. *Connected* to the recognition of modernization risks are *ecological devaluations and expropriations*, which frequently and systematically enter into contradiction to the profit and property interests which advance the process of industrialization. Simultaneously, risks produce *new international inequalities*, firstly between the Third World and the industrial states, secondly among the industrial states

themselves. They undermine the order of national jurisdictions. In view of the universality and supra-nationality of the circulation of pollutants, the life of a blade of grass in the Bavarian Forest ultimately comes to depend on the making and keeping of international agreements. Risk society in this sense is a world risk society.

3   Nevertheless, the diffusion and commercialization of risks do not break with the logic of capitalist development completely, but instead they raise the latter to a new stage. There are always losers but also winners in risk definitions. The space between them varies in relation to different issues and power differentials. Modernization risks from the winners' points of view are *big business*. They are the insatiable demands long sought by economists. Hunger can be sated, needs can be satisfied, but *civilization* risks are a *bottomless barrel of demands*, unsatisfiable, infinite, self-producible. One could say along with Luhmann that with the advent of risks, the economy becomes 'self-referential', independent of the surrounding satisfaction of human needs. But that means: with the economic exploitation of the risks it sets free, industrial society produces the hazards and the political potential of the risk society.

4   One can *possess* wealth, but one can only be *afflicted* by risks; they are, so to speak, *ascribed* by civilization. [Bluntly, one might say: in class and stratification positions being determines consciousness, while in risk positions *consciousness determines being*.] Knowledge gains a new political significance. Accordingly the political potential of the risk society must be elaborated and analyzed in a sociological theory of the origin and diffusion of *knowledge about risks*.

5   Socially recognized risks, as appears clearly in the discussions of forest destruction, contain a peculiar political explosive: what *was* until now *considered unpolitical becomes political – the elimination of the causes in the industrialization process itself*. Suddenly the public and politics extend their rule into the private sphere of plant management – into product planning and technical equipment. What is at stake in the public dispute over the definition of risks is revealed here in an exemplary fashion: not just secondary health problems for nature and mankind, but the *social, economic and political consequences of these side effects* – collapsing markets, devaluation of capital, bureaucratic checks on plant decisions, the opening of new markets, mammoth costs, legal proceedings and loss of face. In smaller or larger increments – a smog alarm, a toxic spill, etc. – what thus emerges in risk society is the *political potential of catastrophes*. Averting and managing these can include a *reorganization of power and authority*. Risk society is a *catastrophic* society. In it the exceptional condition threatens to become the norm.

[...]

Risk Positions are not Class Positions

With the globalization of risks a social dynamic is set in motion, which can no longer be composed of and understood in class categories. Ownership implies non-ownership and thus a social relationship of tension and conflict, in which reciprocal social identities can continually evolve and solidify – 'them up there us down here'.

The situation is quite different for risk positions. Anyone affected by them is badly off, but deprives the others, the non-affected, of nothing. Expressed in an analogy: the 'class' of the 'affected' does not confront a 'class' that is not affected. It confronts at most a 'class' of not-yet-affected people. The escalating scarcity of health will drive even those still well off today (in health and well-being) into the ranks of the 'soup kitchens' provided by insurance companies tomorrow, and the day after tomorrow into the pariah community of the invalid and the wounded.

The perplexity of authorities in the face of toxic accidents and toxic waste scandals, and the avalanche of legal, jurisdictional and compensation issues that is triggered each time, all speak a clear language. To wit, freedom from risk can turn overnight into irreversible affliction. The conflicts that arise around modernization risks occur around *systematic causes* that coincide with the motor of progress and profit. They relate to the scale and expansion of hazards and the ensuing demands for compensation and/or a fundamental change of course. In those conflicts what is at stake is the issue of whether we can continue the exploitation of nature (including our own), and thus, whether our concepts of 'progress', 'prosperity', 'economic growth', or 'scientific rationality' are still correct. In this sense, the conflicts that erupt here take on the character of *doctrinal struggles* within *civilization* over the proper road for modernity. In many respects, these resemble the doctrinal struggles of the Middle Ages more than the class conflicts of the nineteenth and early twentieth centuries.

NOTES

1 *Modernization* means surges of technological rationalization and changes in work and organization, but beyond that it includes much more: the change in societal characteristics and normal biographies, changes of lifestyle and forms of love, change in the structures of power and influence, in the forms of political repression and participation, in views of reality and in norms of knowledge. In social science's understanding of modernity, the plough, the steam locomotive and the microchip arc visible indicators of a much deeper process, which comprises and reshapes the entire social structure. Ultimately the *sources of certainty* on which life feeds are changed (Etzioni 1968; Kosellcck 1977; Lepsius 1977; Eisenstadt 1979). In the last year (after the third edition of this book in Germany) there has been a new wave of modernization theory. Now the discussion centers on the possible post-modern problematization of modernity (Berger 1986; Bauman 1989; Alexander and Sztompka 1990).

2 For more sophisticated distinctions between risk in industrial society and risk in risk society see Beck (1988) and (1992).

REFERENCES

Jeffrey Alexander and Piotr Sztompka, eds. 1990. *Rethinking Progress*. Boston.

Zygmunt Bauman, 1989. *Modernity and the Holocaust*. Cambridge.

Ulrich Beck. 1988. *Counter-Poisons*. Cambridge.

Ulrich Beck. 1992. "From Industrial Society to Risk Society." *Theory, Culture and Society* 9(1): 97–123.

J. Berger, ed. 1986. Die Moderne – Kontinuitaten und Zasuren. Special issue 4 of *Soziale Welt*.

S. N. Eisenstadt. 1979. *Tradition, Wandel and Modernitat*. Frankfurt.

Amitai Etzioni. 1968. *The Active Society*. New York.

R. Koselleck, ed. 1977. *Studien uber den Beginn der modernen Welt*. Stuttgart.

R. Lepsius 1977. "Soziologische Theoreme uber die Sozialstruktur der 'Moderne' und der 'Modernisieurung'," in R. Koselleck, ed. *Studien uber den Beginn der modernen Welt*. Stuttgart.

15D Ulrich Beck and Edgar Grande from *Varieties of Second Modernity: The Cosmopolitan Turn in Social and Political Theory and Research*

Original publication details: Ulrich Beck and Edgar Grande, 2010. "Varieties of Second Modernity: The Cosmopolitan Turn in Social and Political Theory Research." *British Journal of Sociology* 61(3): 413, 417–419. Reproduced with permission of John Wiley & Sons Ltd.

The point of a 'cosmopolitan turn' in social theory is to open it up to the possibility of a variety of different and autonomous interlinked modernities ('plurality of modernities'), on the one hand; and to new, global imperatives, pressures and constraints, on the other hand. These new 'cosmopolitan imperatives'[1] are not universal given, but accumulate (historically) at the beginning of the twenty-first century and create new conflict structures, conflict dynamics and new processes of community building.

[...]

The starting point of our analysis here is with the two dimensions of the concept of cosmopolitanism. In the first, the vertical dimension, cosmopolitanism refers to individual or collective responsibilities towards mankind. In this context, the theory of reflexive modernization argues that modern societies – Western and non-Western alike – are confronted with qualitatively new problems, which create 'cosmopolitan imperatives'. These cosmopolitan imperatives arise because of global risks: nuclear risks, ecological risks, technological risks, economic risks created by insufficiently regulated financial markets, etc. These new global risks have at least two consequences: firstly, they mix the 'native' with the 'foreign' and create an everyday global awareness; and secondly therefore, they create chains of interlocking political decisions and outcomes among states and their citizens, which alter the nature and dynamics of territorially defined governance systems. These risks link the global North and the global South in ways that were unknown hitherto. However, the result of global interconnectedness is not a normative cosmopolitanism of a world without borders. Instead, these risks produce new cosmopolitan responsibilities, cosmopolitan imperatives, which no one can escape. What emerges, is the universal possibility of 'risk communities' which spring up, establish themselves and become aware of their cosmopolitan composition – 'imagined cosmopolitical communities' which come into existence in the awareness that dangers or risks can no longer be socially delimited in space or time. In the light of these cosmopolitan imperatives a reformulated theory of reflexive modernization must argue that nowadays we all live in a Second, Cosmopolitan Modernity – regardless of whether we have experienced First Modernity or not.

In its second dimension, cosmopolitanism is a theory of diversity, more precisely, of a specific way of interpreting and coping with diversity (Delanty 2009; Tyfield and Urry 2009). To speak of a cosmopolitan modernity in this context means broadening our horizon to include a variety of western and non-western modernities. The conceptual challenge for a theory of cosmopolitan modernization is to identify the patterns of variation, their origin and their consequences. In short, the idea of cosmopolitan modernity must be developed out of the variety of modernities, out of the inner wealth of variants of modernity. Cosmopolitan modernization, however, must not be equated with the concept of pluralization. It not only highlights the existence of a variety of different types of modern society, it also emphasizes the dynamic intermingling and interaction between societies. In this regard it takes up key concepts of the literature on post-colonialism, such as 'entanglement' (Randeria 2004), and on globalization, such as 'interconnectedness' (Held et al. 1999), and it takes them further by introducing the concept of 'dialogical imagination' or the 'internalization of the other': the global other is in our midst. Cosmopolitization relates and connects individuals, groups and societies in new ways, thereby changing the very position and function of the 'self' and the 'other'. Such an 'internalization of the other' can be the product of two entirely different processes. On the one hand, it can be the result of an active, deliberate and reflexive opening of individuals, groups and societies to other ideas, preferences, rules and cultural practices; on the other hand, however, it can also be the outcome of passive and unintended processes enforcing the internalization of otherness. Hence, cosmopolitization is not, by definition, a symmetrical and autonomous process; it may well be the product of asymmetries, dependencies, power and force, and it may also create new asymmetries and dependencies within and between societies.

In integrating these two dimensions of cosmopolitization, it becomes apparent that a cosmopolitan modernity differs significantly from a Kantian world of 'perpetual peace'. It is characterized, rather, by structural contradictions resulting from two conflicting processes, which create what we call a *'cosmopolitan dialectic'*. On the one hand, there is a centripetal, unifying process, the formation of a 'world risk society' (Beck 1999, 2009). At the same time, the Second Modernity is subject to powerful, centrifugal, diversifying processes resulting from the co-existence, and probably even the hegemonic competition between different types and visions of modernity; and from resistances to economic, political and cultural globalization within societies (cf. Kriesi et al. 2008): The more the world is brought together by global risks (climate change, nuclear threats, financial crisis), the more it is also torn apart by global risks. How do these contradictory tendencies accommodate each other?

This can be condensed into the argument that the coming 'world society' of the Second Modernity is characterized by new forms of 'systemic competition' between ways and visions of modernity and new types of cosmopolitical conflict and violence. Global entanglement and interconnectedness are not only the preconditions for the establishment of new 'cosmopolitan communities of fate'; they are at the same time the sources of the emergence of powerful counter-movements. In order to adequately observe and fully understand these processes and dynamics, sociological theory must, however, give up its 'nationalist' perspective and its universalistic assumptions.

NOTE

1   For example, human rights regime (see Levy 2010; Levy and Sznaider 2010) or in relation to global risks "cooperate or fail!"

REFERENCES

Beck, U. 1999. *World Risk Society*. Cambridge, UK/ Malden, MA: Polity Press.

Beck, U. 2009. *World at Risk*. Cambridge, UK/ Malden, MA: Polity Press.

Delanty, G. 2009. *The Cosmopolitan Imagination: The Renewal of Critical Social Theory*. Cambridge, UK/New York: Cambridge University Press.

Held, D., McGrew, A., Goldblatt, D., and Perraton, J. 1999. Global Transformations: Politics, Economics and Culture. Cambridge, UK/Stanford, CA: Polity Press/Stanford University Press.

Kriesi, H., Grande, E., Lachat, R., Dolezal, M., Bornschier, S, and Frey, T. 2008. *West European Politics in the Age of Globalization*. Cambridge, UK/New York: Cambridge University Press.

Levy, D. 2010. "Recursive Cosmopolitanization: Argentina and the Global Human Rights Regime." *British Journal of Sociology* 61(3): 580–97.

Levy, D. and Sznaider, N. 2010. *Human Rights and Memory*. University Park, PA: Penn State University Press.

Randeira, S. 2004. "Verwobene Moderne. Zivilgesellschaft, Kastenbildung und nichtstaatliches Familienrecht im (post)kolonialen Indien," in S. Randeira, M. Fuchs, and A. Linkenbach, eds. *Konfigurationen der Moderne. Diskurse zu Indien (Soziale Welt:Sonderband 15)*, Baden-Baden: Nomos Verlagsgesellschaft.

Tyfield, D. and Urry, J. 2009. "Cosmopolitan China? Lessons from International Collaboration in Low-Carbon Innovation." *British Journal of Sociology* 60(4): 793–812.

15E Jürgen Habermas from *Notes on Post-Secular Society*

Original publication details: Jürgen Habermas, 2008. "Notes on Post-Secular Society," *New Perspectives Quarterly* 25: 3–5, 6, 7, 11–12. Reproduced with permission of John Wiley & Sons Ltd.

The Descriptive Account of a "Post-Secular Society" – and the Normative Issue of How Citizens of Such a Society Should Understand Themselves

I cannot discuss in detail the controversy among sociologists concerning the supposed sonderweg of the secularized societies of Europe in the midst of a religiously mobilized world society. My impression is that the data collected globally still provide surprisingly robust support for the defenders of the secularization thesis. In my view the weakness of the theory of secularization is due rather to rash inferences that betray an imprecise use of the concepts of "secularization" and "modernization." What is true is that in the course of the differentiation of functional social systems, churches and religious communities increasingly confined themselves to their core function of pastoral care and had to renounce their competencies in other areas of society. At the same time, the practice of faith also withdrew into more a personal or subjective domain. There is a correlation between the functional specification of the religious system and the individualization of religious practice.

However, as Jose Casanova correctly points out, the loss of function and the trend toward individualization do not necessarily imply that religion loses influence and relevance either in the political arena and the culture of a society or in the personal conduct of life. Quite apart from their numerical weight, religious communities can obviously still claim a "seat" in the life of societies that are largely secularized. Today, public consciousness in Europe can be described in terms of a "post-secular society" to the extent that at present it still has to "adjust itself to the continued existence of religious communities in an increasingly secularized environment." The revised reading of the secularization hypothesis relates less to its substance and more to the predictions concerning the future role of "religion." The description of modern societies as "post-secular" refers to a change in consciousness that I attribute primarily to three phenomena.

First, the broad perception of those global conflicts that are often presented as hinging on religious strife changes public consciousness. The majority of European citizens do not even need the presence of intrusive fundamentalist movements and the fear of terrorism, defined in religious terms, to make them aware of their own relativity within the global horizon. This undermines the secularistic belief in the foreseeable disappearance of religion and robs the secular understanding of the world of any triumphal zest. The awareness of living in a secular society is no longer bound up with the certainty that cultural and social modernization can advance only at the cost of the public influence and personal relevance of religion.

Second, religion is gaining influence not only worldwide but also within national public spheres. I am thinking here of the fact that churches and religious organizations are increasingly assuming the role of "communities of interpretation" in the public arena of secular societies. They can attain influence on public opinion and will formation by making relevant contributions to key issues, irrespective of whether their arguments are convincing or objectionable. Our pluralist societies constitute a responsive sounding board for such interventions because they are increasingly split on value conflicts requiring political regulation. Be it the dispute over the legalization of abortion or voluntary euthanasia, on the bioethical issues of reproductive medicine, questions of animal protection or climate change – on these and similar questions the divisive premises are so opaque that it is by no means settled from the outset which party can draw on the more convincing moral intuitions.

Pushing the issue closer home, let me remind you that the visibility and vibrancy of foreign religious communities also spur the attention to the familiar churches and congregations. The Muslims next door force the Christian citizens to face up to the practice of a rival faith. And they also give the secular citizens a keener consciousness of the phenomenon of the public presence of religion.

The third stimulus for a change of consciousness among the population is the immigration of "guest-workers" and refugees, specifically from countries with traditional cultural backgrounds. Since the 16th century, Europe has had to contend with confessional schisms within its own culture and society. In the wake of the present immigration, the more blatant dissonances between different religions link up with the challenge of a pluralism of ways of life typical of immigrant societies. This extends beyond the challenge of a pluralism of denominations. In societies like ours which are still caught in the painful process of transformation into postcolonial immigrant societies, the issue of tolerant coexistence between different religious communities is made harder by the difficult problem of how to integrate immigrant cultures socially. While coping with the pressure of globalized labor markets, social integration must succeed even under the humiliating conditions of growing social inequality. But that is a different story.

I have thus far taken the position of a sociological observer in trying to answer the question of why we can term secularized societies "post-secular." In these societies, religion maintains a public influence and relevance, while the secularistic certainty that religion will disappear worldwide in the course of modernization is losing ground. If we henceforth adopt the perspective of participants, however, we face a quite different, namely normative question. How should we see ourselves as members of a post-secular society and what must we reciprocally expect from one another in order to ensure that in firmly entrenched nation states, social relations remain civil despite the growth of a plurality of cultures and religious worldviews?

[. . .]

This constitutional state is only able to guarantee its citizens equal freedom of religion under the proviso that they no longer barricade themselves within their religious communities and seal themselves off from one another. All subcultures, whether religious or not, are expected to free their individual members from their embrace so that these citizens can mutually recognize one another in civil society as members of one and the same political community. As democratic citizens they give themselves laws which grant them the right, as private citizens, to preserve their identity in the context of their own particular culture and worldview. This new relationship of democratic government, civil society and subcultural self-maintenance is the key to correctly understanding the two motives that today struggle with each other although they are meant to be mutually complementary. For the universalist project of the political Enlightenment by no means contradicts the particularist sensibilities of a correctly conceived multiculturalism.

[. . .]

"Tolerance" is, of course, not only a question of enacting and applying laws; it must be practiced in everyday life. Tolerance means that believers of one faith, of a different faith and non-believers must mutually concede to one another the right to those convictions, practices and ways of living that they themselves reject. This concession must be supported by a shared basis of mutual recognition from which repugnant dissonances can be overcome. This recognition should not be confused with an appreciation of an alien culture and way of living, or of rejected convictions and practices. We need tolerance only vis-a-vis worldviews that we consider wrong and vis-a-vis habits that we do not like. Therefore, the basis of recognition is not the esteem for this or that characteristic or achievement, but the awareness of the fact that the other is a member of an inclusive community of citizens with equal rights, in which each individual is accountable to the others for his political contributions.

Now that is easier said than done. The equal inclusion of all citizens in civil society requires not only a political culture that preserves liberal attitudes from being confused with indifference; inclusion can only be achieved if certain material conditions are met. These include full integration and compensatory education in kindergartens, schools and universities, and equal opportunities in access to the labor market. However, in the present context what is most important to me is the image of an inclusive civil society in which equal citizenship and cultural difference complement each other in the right way.

For example, as long as a considerable portion of German citizens of Turkish origin and of Muslim faith have stronger political ties to their old homeland than their new one, those corrective votes will be lacking in the public sphere and at the ballot boxes which are necessary to expand the range of values of the dominant political culture. Without the inclusion of minorities in civil society, the two complementary processes will not be able to develop hand in hand, namely, the opening of the political community to a difference-sensitive inclusion of foreign minority cultures, on the one hand, and, on the other, the reciprocal opening of these subcultures to a state which encourages its individual members participate in the political life at large.

Certainly, the domain of a state, which controls the means of legitimate coercion, should not be opened to the strife between various religious communities, otherwise the government could become the executive arm of a religious majority that imposes its will on the opposition. In a constitutional state, all norms that can be legally implemented must be formulated and publicly justified in a language that all the citizens understand. Yet the state's neutrality does not preclude the permissibility of religious utterances within the political public sphere, as long as the institutionalized decision-making process at the parliamentary, court, governmental and administrative levels remains clearly separated from the informal flows of political communication and opinion formation among the broader public of citizens. The "separation of church and state" calls for a filter between these two spheres – a filter through which only "translated," i.e., secular, contributions may pass from the confused din of voices in the public sphere into the formal agendas of state institutions.

Two reasons speak in favor of such liberal practice. First, the persons who are neither willing nor able to divide their moral convictions and their vocabulary into profane and religious strands must be permitted to take part in political will formation even if they use religious language. Second, the democratic state must not pre-emptively reduce the polyphonic complexity of the diverse public voices, because it cannot know whether it is not otherwise cutting society off from scarce resources for the generation of meanings and the shaping of identities. Particularly with regard to vulnerable social relations, religious traditions possess the power to convincingly articulate moral sensitivities and solidaristic intuitions. What puts pressure on secularism, then, is the expectation that secular citizens in civil society and the political public sphere must be able to meet their religious fellow citizens as equals.

INDEX